UNDERSTANDING TRANSFERENCE

2ND EDITION

UNDERSTANDING TRANSFERENCE

THE CORE CONFLICTUAL RELATIONSHIP THEME METHOD

LESTER LUBORSKY

PAUL CRITS-CHRISTOPH

AMERICAN PSYCHOLOGICAL ASSOCIATION

WASHINGTON, DC

Published by
American Psychological Association
750 First Street, NE
Washington, DC 20002

Copies may be ordered from
APA Order Department
P.O. Box 92984
Washington, DC 20090-2984

In the UK and Europe, copies may be ordered from
American Psychological Association
3 Henrietta Street
Covent Garden, London
WC2E 8LU England

Typeset in Goudy by EPS Group Inc., Easton, MD

Printer: Data Reproductions Corporation, Auburn Hills, MI
Jacket Designer: Minker Design, Bethesda, MD
Technical/production editor: Edward B. Meidenbauer

Library of Congress Cataloging-in-Publication Data
Luborsky, Lester, 1920–
     Understanding transference : the core conflictual relationship theme method /
by Lester Luborsky and Paul Crits-Christoph. — [Rev. and expanded]
          p.   cm.
     Includes bibliographical references (p.   ) and index.
     ISBN 1-55798-453-0 (acid-free paper)
     1. Transference (Psychology)   2. Psychoanalysis—Case studies.
  I. Crits-Christoph, Paul, 1954–   II. Title.
  RC489.T73L83   1997
  616.89'17—dc21   97-26192
                                                                              CIP

British Library Cataloguing-in-Publication Data
A CIP record is available from the British Library

Printed in the United States of America
Second edition, first printing

CONTENTS

FOREWORD

Are you a psychotherapist of any stripe, practicing or in training? Are you a clinical researcher? Are you a patient in psychotherapy? If so, this book will illuminate and guide.

Sigmund Freud believed that psychotherapy was not effective merely because of the rapport between doctor and patient, although he acknowledged that rapport was vital. He asserted that cure took place through the analysis of transference, a mysterious process in which the ancient conflicts of the patient were played out on the current stage of psychotherapy. The leading role was, of course, played by the patient, but the other leads—mother, father, siblings, lovers, teachers—were played by the therapist. The reenactment of the early relationships in the current relationship with the therapist, and the insight gained into them, constituted cure through analysis of transference. A wealth of clinical evidence has accumulated to support this idea.

Cognitive and behavioral therapists believe something very different about the relationship between patient and therapist. The relationship is important, and a good one may be necessary for cure to take place, but it is secondary. Cure is brought about primarily by these techniques: systematic desensitization, challenging automatic thoughts, undoing depressogenic assumptions, assertiveness training, and the like. Furthermore, these techniques can be scientifically studied and refined. An equally impressive body of clinical and experimental evidence has accumulated to support this opposing view.

Understanding Transference is a bridge between these two seemingly irreconcilable perspectives. Lester Luborsky, Paul Crits-Christoph, and their colleagues and students have taken the notion of transference, objectified it, and shown us how and why it works. These lessons apply to both worlds of therapy. Luborsky's thinking shows the way toward reunification.

Most scientists take phenomena that are in the light and shed further light on them. Other scientists (brave souls) take phenomena that are in the dark and bring them into the penumbra. I number Freud and most of his followers among them. Still others, perhaps those from whom we learn the most, take what is in the penumbra and bring it into the light. Lester Luborsky has, through his long and productive career, always been an example of this last kind of scientist. *Understanding Transference* is a sterling example of his work.

The authors of this clear and wise book, which is now revised and expanded, take the up-until-now mysterious notion of transference (and the notions of "insight" and "self-understanding," as well) and show us what it really is. They propose and confirm a reliable measure of transference, the Core Conflictual Relationship Theme (CCRT), which can be objectively tested.

After validating the basic concept and its measure, they show how the CCRT stands at the heart of psychotherapy. The major contribution of this book is to demonstrate that this reliable measure, the CCRT, correlates meaningfully with other theoretically related phenomena. Among these attributes of the CCRT are (a) its pervasiveness across relationships, (b) its similarity for the relation to the therapist and the relations to other people, (c) its appearance in different modes of expression—in fact, it appears in both dreams and waking narratives, (d) its usefulness to the therapist as a guide to beneficial interpretations, and so on. These kinds of correlates are part of the set of observations that Freud made when he put forward the transference concept. The research in this book implies that the clinical-level psychoanalytic observations are well worth following up through empirical studies.

What awaits the reader, then, is a powerful act of demystification. A crucial idea, transference, that has dwelt in the penumbra since Freud, now emerges into the light.

With this book, a science of transference is finally ongoing.

Martin E. P. Seligman
Professor of Psychology
    and former Director of Clinical Training,
University of Pennsylvania, Philadelphia

FOREWORD

Few theoretical issues in psychoanalysis have been as constantly and passionately argued as the status of our discipline as a science. For Freud the status was self-evident, and he labored unceasingly over his lifetime to create and maintain a unitary theoretical structure for psychoanalysis in a natural science mold. However, he never encouraged the empirical research through which science normally tests and expands its hypotheses and accrues new knowledge. Instead, he relied on his clinical case study method to accumulate the observational base that would then generate the causal explanatory network of the metapsychology (the general theory) that he was so painstakingly elaborating.

Nonetheless, it was only in the so-called classical, or mainstream, ego psychology development in America that this legacy of a unified theoretical structure within a natural science framework endured. The whole metapsychological edifice in the first post-World War II decades was brought to its position of almost unquestioned hegemony, at least within American psychoanalysis, in the ego psychology associated with the names of Hartmann, Kris, Loewenstein, Rapaport, and a host of others. In Europe, Latin America, and the rest of the world, it was quite otherwise from the start. What we have come to call our psychoanalytic theoretical diversity, or pluralism, began even during Freud's lifetime with the emergence of Kleinian analysis, ideas developed out of Melanie Klein's initial work with children. These ideas evolved into an alternative metapsychology and an alternative theory of technique that soon claimed as many adherents as did Freud's structural theory and its ego psychology, if not more. Then, in an almost bewildering development, came the British object relations school, coalescing out of the innovative thinking and creative theorizing of a galaxy of original minds—Fairbairn, Winnicott, Guntrip, Balint, Bowlby, and others—followed by the far-reaching Bionian extensions of Kleinian thinking. From France, and in a distinctively French voice, came

Lacan's linguistic conceptualization of the nature of the psychoanalytic enterprise. This in turn was part of the larger fabric of a Franco-German hermeneutic accounting of psychoanalysis, sparkplugged by Habermas and abetted by Ricoeur. It was an effort, embedded in the critical theory of the Frankfurt school, to turn psychoanalysis entirely away from what were declared to be misguided positivist, natural science directions, unfortunate carryovers of Freud's 19th-century natural science roots in Helmholtz school physiology.

Two main trends have become clear in this steady progression of ramifying theorizing in psychoanalysis. One is the increasing theoretical diversification within the overall psychoanalytic corpus. The other is the progressive erosion of the (natural) science commitment as the identifying and determining hallmark of the discipline. Both these trends have by now become well established in the United States. Even early in the period of almost monolithic supremacy of the ego psychological metapsychology paradigm, dissident perspectives arose. They included the Sullivanian interpersonal school and the Horneyan culturalist movement, but they were pushed to the margins of organized psychoanalysis or extruded altogether. Subsequent decades brought first a small enclave of Kleinian thinking to the United States, followed in more recent years by the explosive emergence of Kohut's self psychology as a completely alternate metapsychology (and theory of technique). Kohut fashioned a psychology primarily of deficit and its repair, rather than central conflict and its resolution. In the same years, a U.S. object relations stream crystallized, coalescing out of the work of Jacobson, Mahler, and Kernberg and building on its British progenitors as well.

Even within the once almost monolithic domain of ego psychology in the United States, varieties of divergent and revisionist theoretical positions have emerged, albeit with contrapuntal, passionate defenses by its continuing adherents. This is what I have called the Great Metapsychology Debate in our field. Certainly in today's post-ego psychology world, the United States has staunch and persuasive advocates (Gill, Schafer, G. Klein, Spence, and others) of all the varieties of hermeneutic, phenomenological, exclusively subjectivistic, or linguistically based conceptualizations of the field. Together, these advocates challenge our traditional and customary conception of our discipline as a reasonably uniform entity—and that entity properly a science.

Where does the history explored leave our century-old discipline today? Certainly, for those of us who have commitments to the empirical enterprise as the route to the organization and advance of knowledge in disciplines putatively rooted in science, it is by now abundantly clear that today psychoanalysis worldwide consists of multiple and divergent theories of mental functioning, psychic development, pathogenesis, treatment, and cure. Many of these theories claim in varying degrees a natural science framework, whereas some repudiate such a heritage altogether. My own firm conviction is that, in their present stage of conceptual development with regard to the logic of theory construction, our psychoanalytic general theories, our metapsychologies—and here I interpolate a reminder of Freud's metaphoric commentary, our *witch* metapsychology—our widely different theoretical frameworks that mark our psychoanalytic pluralism, are to a major extent primarily still metaphoric. They are merely large-scale explanatory metaphors, or symbolisms, that we employ to give a needed sense of coherence and closure to our psychoanalytic understandings and therefore to our interventions. To me, they are still only the metaphors we live by, our pluralistic psychoanalytic articles of faith. In our current developmental stage, as general theory, or metapsychology, none of them is formulated in ways amenable to empirical study and scientific process, even though they seem to be cast within a natural science explanatory language (the ego psychology paradigm) or, oppositely, into an avowedly hermeneutic—and anti-natural science—system of language.

And yet we do have—and must have—a psychoanalytic common ground that enables us all to be recognizably psychoanalysts doing reasonably comparable clinical work with reasonably comparable patients around the world, whatever our theoretical allegiance or our regional, cultural, or linguistic perspective. This common ground I find not in our overarching high-level general theories, or metapsychologies, for all the reasons adduced. Rather, the unifying element of psychoanalysis lies in our contrasting low-level, experience-near, and common, *clinical* theory, the level of theory of transference and countertransference, of resistance and defense, of anxiety and conflict and compromise, of self and object representation. It is at this level that the empirical referents—the clinical phenomena of our consulting rooms—link by means of discernible and traceable canons of inference to these *clinical* theoretical constructs. Furthermore, it is at this level that these clinical constructs can be put to the kind of empirical study and test that will determine the extent to which, in psychoanalysis, we are indeed fashioning a body of science that in turn can guide our clinical therapeutic work ever more precisely.

It is at this point and at this level that Lester Luborsky and Paul Crits-Christoph, and their collaborators and students, have pitched their investigative activity over many years of hard work. They have fastened on the centrality of the clinically derived conception of the idiosyncratically evolved core neurotic conflict that powers the guiding unconscious fantasies and their manifestations, lifelong in character and in symptom, and that emerges in the therapy of our patients as the major transference paradigm. They have endeavored to operationalize this conception to render it amenable to the usual varieties of scientific study and testing. What has gradually evolved, and is continually being refined and clarified, is their operationalized conception, the Core Conflictual Relationship Theme

(CCRT). They have developed a strategy for reliably recognizing the CCRT through the study of the interpersonal narratives recounted in analytic therapy, which they call relationship episodes (REs). This transition from the unguided use of the transference concept—that is, in the clinical formulations of the psychoanalytic therapist—to an operational measure, the CCRT, based on stepwise, systematic, guided formulation methods, is key in their work. The possibilities for achieving reliability in clinical judgment and then pushing on to explore conceptual validity, empirical usefulness, scientific hypothesis testing, and solidly established new knowledge accrual in psychoanalytic investigation are all dependent on this concept.

This is the ambitious agenda and it is, to me, squarely in the proper domain. Scientific advance can and must be made, in our discipline, within the common ground of our experience-near clinical theory constructions, if indeed scientific advance is to be made at all. It is, of course, up to readers to decide for themselves how well Luborsky and Crits-Christoph succeed in rendering a meaningful study of the transference concept, in enlarging the possibilities for increasing useful knowledge about it, and in garnering investigative rewards from the continuing lines of research that they outline—as well as how much all this advances our field scientifically. What those of us interested in the ultimate fate of psychoanalysis as a science can certainly fully agree on is that this is precisely the kind of research that is necessary to be able to answer these questions properly and fairly. For this, our discipline owes these authors and their devoted labor of love, so lucidly chronicled in this newly revised edition of the book, a collective vote of great gratitude.

Robert S. Wallerstein
Professor of Psychiatry,
University of California at San Francisco

PREFACE

This second edition of *Understanding Transference* has much in it that is new, along with the essentially unchanged CCRT method. All of the chapters have been revised and updated, and six are entirely new to the book. Some of the chapters had their origins in coauthored journal articles, but they too have been reedited. Taken all together, this new book gives the most complete guidance to users of the CCRT method, adds to the readers' knowledge of discoveries about the patients' central relationship patterns, and points to the clinical applications of the CCRT method.

The revised book's contents can be best summed up by listing each chapter's special contribution. Part I has eight chapters surveying the idea for the CCRT, its history, its source in the narratives spontaneously told in psychotherapy sessions (chapter 1), its precise scoring rules (chapter 2), and its standard categories (chapter 3). The scoring of the positive and negative qualities of CCRT patterns is defined and examined (chapter 4); detailed illustrations are given of the CCRT scoring of narratives that can speed up the learning of the scoring procedures (chapter 5); and the essence of the largest collection of results of independent scoring of 9 samples of patients is presented (chapter 6). We also offer another method for obtaining narratives: a versatile, easily used alternative source of narratives told on request, the Relationship Anecdotes Paradigms interview (chapter 7). This major section ends with explanations for why each of the CCRT procedures was chosen (chapter 8).

The book then takes the reader further into the facets of validity of the CCRT: In Part II it tells of our discoveries during 10 explorations to find the meaning of the CCRT measure. These chapters report the most typical types of narratives (chapter 9), the pervasiveness and generality of the CCRT within sessions and across the treatment (chapter 10), the degree of parallel of the CCRT for the therapist versus the CCRT for other people (chapter 11), and a newly expanded study of the parallel of the CCRT within narratives as compared with the CCRT within dreams (chapter 12). The chapters then deal with three aspects of the patient's and the therapist's "accuracy" in using the CCRT: (a) the accuracy of the therapist's interpretations (chapter 13), (b) the accuracy of self-understanding (chapter 14), and (c) another kind of accuracy, the degree of parallel between the patient's and the clinician's perspective on the CCRT (chapter 15). Finally, two new explorations with the CCRT reveal its considerable consistency across time, (a) from age 3 to age 5 (chapter 16) and (b) from before psychotherapy to during psychotherapy (chapter 17). This section ends with an extension beyond the CCRT: a reliable method for moving beyond the assessment of the conflicts in the usual CCRT to evaluating the degree of mastery of the conflicts shown in the narratives (chapter 18).

The book turns in Part III to the even more clinical applications of the CCRT method, with a chapter on the everyday uses of the CCRT in practice (chapter 19), and a new exploration and the most complete set of descriptions of the continually lengthening stream of alternative central relationship pattern measures (chapter 20).

The book ends with an integrative wind up, the two broad summary chapters of Part IV. The first is on the convergences of the many CCRT findings with Freud's 23 observations about the transference pattern (chapter 21), and the last chapter is an even more reflective summary: a status report on the book's contributions, a takeoff into the stratosphere of super-clinical theories that account for the existence and maintenance of a CCRT in everybody, along with a set of prescriptions for the continued healthy growth of the CCRT measure (chapter 22).

ACKNOWLEDGMENTS

With thanks to these sources of financial support:

The first seed money to nourish the germination of the CCRT idea that sprouted in 1974 providently came from the Luborsky Biopsychosocial Foundation. The earliest substantial sustenance for the CCRT method was a 2-year grant from the Fund for Psychoanalytic Research of the American Psychoanalytic Association (1 January 1984 to 31 December 1985). The long-term continuance of the research on the CCRT method was sustained by a 3-year National Institute for Mental Health (NIMH) grant (ROlMH39673) to me, which was then renewed for another 3 years (1 December 1987 to 30 November 1990), and by another grant (ROlMH40472) to Paul Crits-Christoph. Over the expanse of time from 1968 to the present, my program of research has been supported in part by USPHS NIMH Research Scientist Award MH407010 and National Institute on Drug Abuse Research Scientist Award DA00168. Paul Crits-Christoph's research, which has provided much help to our collaboration, has been supported in part by USPHS NIMH Career Development Award MH00756 and Coordinating Center Grant U18-DA07090.

With thanks to these supportive people and places:

I thank the Menninger Foundation for providing the fertile locale for my 13 years of satisfying work (1947–1959), with the last 6 as part of the Menninger Foundation Psychotherapy Research Project with Robert Wallerstein as director. The years at "Menninger's" helped me develop sophistication about central relationship patterns, especially through the central relationships with such stars in the field as David Rapaport, Karl Menninger, George Klein, Robert Wallerstein, Robert Holt, Philip Holzman, Herbert Schlesinger, Donald Spence, Otto Kernberg, Margaret Brenman-Gibson, Howard Shevrin, Merton Gill, Gardner Murphy, Lois B. Murphy, and Hartvig Dahl. After the Meninger period, Robert Rosenthal of Harvard University has been a crucially generative guide.

The earliest collaborating group in Philadelphia (1978–1979) that rallied around to try the CCRT scoring method on psychotherapy transcripts included Frederic J. Levine, Richard Kluft, Thomas Wolman, and myself.

For several years, stimulation of ideas and support for myself and Paul Crits-Christoph came from participation in the Open Laboratory on Conscious and Unconscious Processes (sponsored by the John D. and Catherine T. MacArthur Foundation), whose director, Mardi Horowitz, shares basic interests with us in relationship schemas.

The Ulm (Germany) University Department of Psychotherapy and Psychosomatics, with Horst Kächele (current chairman) and Helmut Thomä (past chairman), has continued for almost 2 decades to keep up an exchange of ideas through seminars that led to the first published guide to the CCRT (Luborsky & Kächele, 1988). From the Ulm group came Dorothee Dengler to help apply the CCRT to narratives told by 3-year-olds, with data generously lent by the University of Denver's Helen Buchsbaum and Robert Emde. From the Ulm group Robert Eckert also worked with us for two periods of several months each and was the mainstay of the CCRT study of depression. The Breuninger Foundation of West Germany helped to finance the early Ulm exchanges, for which I am much indebted. Horst Kächele and his Ulm group have continued to be outstandingly productive with CCRT research. The culmination of their collaboration came in 1995, with the 10th anniversary of their Ulm CCRT group: They staged a beautiful and illuminating conference and celebration, with CCRT articles presented by researchers from the far corners of the globe, including Australia, Japan, and Russia.

Continual backing has come from colleagues within our own Department of Psychiatry at the University of Pennsylvania, led by its chairman, Peter Whybrow, who has effectively encouraged and supported us in our research. Special among the steadfast friends and colleagues in the department who have helped on a variety of projects over many years have been A. Thomas McLellan, George Woody, and Charles O'Brien; the many joint papers with them reflect the productivity of our collaboration and include various "firsts" in method development. Our colleague Jacques Barber in our University of Pennsylvania Center for Psychotherapy Research did a detailed editorial and evaluative review of the first edition and served as an able participant in many of its research studies.

A 2-decade-long collaboration with Martin E. P. Seligman of the Department of Psychology has generated advances in our powers for explaining narratives. Hartvig Dahl of Downstate Medical Center has been generous with research exchanges and with case materials, in particular for the dream study described in chapter 12, this volume. Herbert Schlesinger, head of clinical psychology at the New School for Social Research until recently, has helped with clinical and research ideas and assisted with making transcripts of sessions containing dreams.

Among the people who took part in applying the CCRT in recent studies were these significant long-term players in the advancement of CCRT research: Jim Mellon, Scott Friedman, Paul van Ravenswaay, Anita V. Hole, Anna Rose Childress, Amy Demorest, Karen Stewart, Jeffrey Faude, Laura Dahl, and David Mark. Jim Mellon of the East–West University in Hawaii worked full time for about 4 years as a highly reliable CCRT judge and data overseer. For at least 5 years, Carol Popp of Emory University directed and organized studies of dreams for chapter 12. Robert Waldinger of the Massachusetts Mental Health Center and the Judge Baker Foundation in Boston has developed precise CCRT scoring systems and recently provided a thoughtful, helpful critique of the entire manuscript based on his deep understanding of the CCRT. In the management of the computer's prodigious output of chapters, Joyce Bell has been marvelously speedy, reliable, and knowledgeable. The constant efficient research assistance of Suzanne Johnson lightened the load of the arduous tasks of many different aspects of writing the revision of the book and doing the research. John Cacciola did an expert job as evaluator and diagnostician of the patients in some samples. For the past year, Jill Levine has ably overseen many of the revisions; recently she has been succeeded by the equally capable Elizabeth Krause. For the past 2 years, David Seligman has been the organizational overseer of the research and its presentations; he was helped by Amanda Horn and, more recently, by Joanna Liebman, Jessica Kline, Alicia Starkman, Avi Benus, Julie Kilman, Abraham Cotto, and Niharika Desai who have lightened the load of the CCRT-related studies. In 1995–1996 Monica Bishop served as an editorial coordinator participating in the completion of the editorial process. Gregory Halpern was resident guru on permissions and oversaw the last checking of the final corrections of all chapters.

Ellen Luborsky has been an ingenious general advisor about style and order of presentation and consultant on developmental theory. Lise Luborsky has provided expert legal opinion. Miranda Outman has been helpful with editorial improvements. Peter Luborsky and Catherine Goubault Luborsky have been there to consult with when translations were needed. Paul Gerin of Lyon, France, and James Bond and Howard Shevrin of the University of Michigan have a special place in the field of CCRT research because they were early outside-of-Philadelphia contributors.

My wife, Ruth Samson Luborsky, as always, has been a supremely supportive, expressive, and versatile facilitator of the prospering of this book, both in its exposition and in its scope.

The American Psychological Association has been a superb publisher. My special thanks to my old friend Gary VandenBos, its executive director, and to his helpful director of APA Books, Julia Frank-McNeil, as well as to his gifted advisor and acquisitions editor, Peggy Schlegel. Andrea Phillippi, as development editor, generated a sophisticated, detailed (20 plus pages) evaluation of the entire manuscript; it gave a big boost to the quality of the exposition. The contribution that concluded the book's production was carried out by Ed Meidenbauer, the technical/production editor.

Because some of the multiauthored chapters had been previously published or presented, their authors were again included, in order to recognize their past contribution. Yet in the present edition, I was primarily responsible for changes from and additions to the original versions that rounded out and updated each chapter and made each chapter consistent with the rest of the book in style and content.

Lester Luborsky

PROJECT PARTICIPANTS

Jacques P. Barber, PhD, *University of Pennsylvania*
Helen Buchsbaum, PhD, *University of Colorado, Denver*
John Cacciola, PhD, *Philadelphia VA Hospital and University of Pennsylvania*
Andrew Cooper, PhD, *Philadelphia, PA*
Amy Demorest, PhD, *Amherst College*
Dorothee Dengler, MD, *University of Ulm, Germany*
Louis Diguer, PhD, *Laval University, Canada*
Robert Emde, MD, *University of Colorado, Denver*
Robert Eckert, MD, *Nürnberg, Germany*
Jeffrey Faude, PhD, *University of Pennsylvania*
Deborah Fried, MD, *Yale University*
Scott Friedman, PhD, *Georgia Institute of Technology*
Brin F. S. Grenyer, PhD, *University of Wollongong, Australia*
Anita V. Hole, PhD, *Philadelphia VA Hospital*
Suzanne Johnson, BA, *Temple University*
Horst Kächele, MD, *University of Ulm, Germany*
Jill Levine, BA, *Boston University*
Ellen Luborsky, PhD, *Riverdale Mental Health Center, New York*
Jim Mellon, AB, *University of Hawaii at Hilo*
Margaret Morris, BA, *University of New Mexico*
Carol Popp, MD, PhD, *Emory University*
Norman Schaffer, PhD, *Interpsych Associates, King of Prussia, PA*
Pamela Schaffler, AB, *Harvard School of Public Health*
Kelly Schmidt, BA, *George Washington University*
David Seligman, BA, *Boston University*
Paul van Ravenswaay, MD, *Philadelphia, PA*
Robert Waldinger, MD, *Massachusetts Mental Health Center and Judge Baker Children's Center, Boston*

I

THE BASICS OF THE CCRT METHOD AND ITS SCORING

1

THE EARLY LIFE OF THE IDEA FOR THE CORE CONFLICTUAL RELATIONSHIP THEME METHOD

LESTER LUBORSKY

A new measure of personality, the Core Conflictual Relationship Theme (CCRT) method, is what this book is about. The CCRT is the central relationship pattern, script, or schema that each person follows in conducting relationships. It is derived from the consistencies across the narratives people tell about their relationships.

The measure came into being quietly, for at the time it was conceived there was not much sense of what it would become. At first it was just an offshoot of another measure, the therapeutic alliance (Luborsky, 1976). But once the relationship pattern in the alliance measure had been shaped, its use led to the natural next question: How does the relationship pattern in the alliance fit into the broader central pattern of relationships? If, for example, a patient is ready to feel helped by the therapist and shows other signs of a positive alliance, such an alliance might be part of a general pattern: the patient's readiness to feel helped by other people as well as by the therapist. This broadened perspective led to the first glimpse of the scope of the idea that would become the CCRT method.

A closer look at the new measure followed my playing around with

3

systems for inferring a general pattern of relationships from the transcripts of a set of psychotherapy sessions. In this exercise I tried to trace the bases for my own inferences about a general relationship pattern as they emerged while reading transcripts of sessions. My first self-observation was that I was making most inferences while I was most closely attending to *the patient's narratives of interactions with the therapist and with other people*. Then, as I continued to read the narratives, I became aware that I was particularly attentive to *their most recurrent interactions*. After that I came to realize that I was paying most attention to three facets of these interactions: *what the patient wanted from the other people, how the other people reacted*, and *how the patient reacted to their reactions*. After trying these and other facets, I came back to these three as the most routinely evident and serviceable for inferring the general relationship pattern.

After a couple of years of practice in identifying these categories and then of my colleagues' trying to do the same, it became clear that the Core Conflictual Relationship Theme method was ready to be born and to begin an independent life. I first showed it off at the Downstate Medical Center meeting on Communicative Structures and Psychic Structures on Saturday, January 17, 1976, at 2 in the afternoon (Luborsky, 1977b); it showed clear signs of fitting its name and already contained all of the essential qualities of the measure described in chapter 2, this volume. It looked like this:

The CCRT looked much like it belonged in the family of Freud's (1912/1958a) concept of the transference template. Yet it had the special gift of being endowed with a reliable system for guiding inferences about each person's recurrent central relationship pattern. It behaved much as many experienced psychodynamic clinicians do in making their usual inferences in formulating transference patterns, but it relied on formalized explicit principles of inference making. Like the inferences of clinical judges, the inferences that are aided by the CCRT rely on the three facets of narratives about interactions with other people: the types of wishes, needs, and intentions concerning the other person; responses from the other person; and responses of the self. The final step in coming to the CCRT measure is the combination of the most pervasive of each type of these components found across the sample of narratives.

The fashioning of the CCRT is a resounding success story; it has transformed a useful clinical concept into an even more useful clinical–quantitative measure (Luborsky, in press). Over the past 50 years, I was doing what clinicians typically do in the course of each session: shaping a formulation of the patient's central relationship patterns so that I could derive interpretations that fit the formulation. Now, with the use of the CCRT method, I had the support of a reliable guided system to help with this routinely necessary task.

THE LINEAGE OF THE CENTRAL RELATIONSHIP PATTERN CONCEPT

Naturally, after having looked after its inception, gestation, and growth, all the way along up to its young maturity, I began to be more and more curious about the concept's lineage, and so I dug up more of its background and placed what I unearthed of its relatives into the following five generic categories.

From the Psychoanalysts

I reread Freud's ur-accounts of transference, especially his 1912 "Dynamics of Transference." I expected some congruence between the observations that led Freud to his concept of a transference relationship template and the CCRT results, but the high degree of congruence was striking. The parallels are marshaled in detail in chapter 21, this volume, and Paul Crits-Christoph and I have tested some of them, with results given in other chapters. Freud's transference template appeared, with each study, to be a good candidate for a cognate concept of the central relationship pattern.

Several analysts since Freud have rediscovered concepts like the central relationship pattern or the transference template. A similar concept was posited by Blos (1941), who used the term *residual trauma*. French and Wheeler (1963) suggested the related idea of a single "nuclear conflict" in each patient.

Arlow (1961, 1969a, 1969b), writing in 1961 about the recurrence of a single, overwhelmingly pervasive theme, said that "fantasies are grouped around certain basic instinctual wishes and such a group is composed of different versions or different editions of attempts to resolve the intrapsychic conflict over these wishes" (p. 377). In one of his articles (1969a), he developed the idea further:

> The organization of these fantasies takes shape early in life and persists in this form with only minor variations throughout life. To borrow an analogy from literature, one could say the plot line of the fantasy remains the same although the characters and the situations may vary. (p. 47)

His last sentence states vividly the observation that has emerged from research with the Core Conflictual Relationship Theme method. Arlow, in his discussion of my Downstate Medical Center findings (Luborsky, 1977b), viewed the Core Conflictual Relationship Theme as an offshoot of a more basic substrate composed of unconscious fantasies. Actually, both may be the product of highly ingrained patterns or scripts or schemas of relationships. The heart of both the unconscious fantasies and the Core Conflictual Relationship Theme of the narratives may be fruitfully conceived of as related expressions of the pervasive central relationship patterns that are expressed when wishes are activated toward other people and even to the self.

Several other analysts, on the basis of follow-up sessions, have examined recurrent conflictual relationship patterns that persist long after treatment has been terminated, even after very successful treatments. For example, Pfeffer (1963) wrote, "In analysis repetition is not eliminated but the content and substance of what is repeatable is changed" (p. 241). Similarly, Schlessinger and Robbins (1975) described a patient's follow-up that illustrates the preservation of conflictual themes after the analysis but with the difference that "the significant outcome of the analysis is the development of a self-analytic function" (p. 781). Time trends in transference within analyses have been reported by Graff and Luborsky (1977), who compared two relatively more successful analyses with two relatively less successful analyses by means of daily postsession therapist ratings of amount of transference and resistance. Transference was even more evident in the later than in the earlier stages of the more successful analyses, suggesting that the earlier concept of a reduction in the amount of transference in a successful analysis (Ekstein, 1956) should be reformulated.

From the Personality Researchers

Henry Murray (1938), the preeminent personologist, proposed a Thematic Apperception Test (TAT) scoring principle that reflects a rediscovery of a version of Freud's (1912/1958a) concept of the transference template. It is in a little-known footnote, at the end of a chapter in Murray's *Explorations in Personality* (the passage was pointed out to me by Robert R. Holt, personal communication, 1978). Murray referred to the "principle of unification which raises certain interests to the apex of the hierarchy of aims" (p. 396). But Murray never fully presented this idea of a central relationship pattern; in his footnote he deferred to the need to conserve space. His concept would have advanced research in the same domain as the transference pattern and the CCRT if it had been followed up. Later in the same book, in the introduction to one of the case histories, Murray

(1938) further explained his "unity-thema" and the central relationship pattern concept evident in it:

> Experience was to teach us that . . . it was possible to find in most individuals an underlying reaction system, termed by us *unity-thema*, which was the key to his unique nature . . . because if one assumed the activity of this unity-thema many superficially unintelligible actions and expressions became, as it were, psychologically inevitable. A *unity-thema* is a compound of interrelated—collaborating or conflicting—dominant needs that are linked to [the] press[es] to which the individual was exposed on one or more particular occasions, gratifying or traumatic, in early childhood. The thema may stand for a primary infantile experience or a subsequent reaction formation to that experience. But, whatever its nature and genesis, it repeats itself in many forms during later life.
>
> As soon as we realized the force of the unity-thema, its importance in the interpretation of each session began to dawn upon us. For if every response is the objectification of an aspect of a particular personality and the most fundamental and characteristic determinant of a personality is its unity-thema, then many responses cannot be fully understood except in terms of their relation to the unity-thema. (pp. 604–605)

Another method that has had a long career in academic psychology, Kelly's Role Construct Repertory (1955), may well tap a similar phenomenon, although I do not include it as a central relationship pattern measure because it is not based on the patient's expressions in interviews. Rather, it uses a concept formation method: The participants sort people into different categories, for example, a teacher they liked, a teacher they disliked, their spouse, their father, and so on. They then sort these people according to ways they are alike and different. The method identifies the main constructs each person uses for significant other people. Kelly believed that his measure, as applied for each person, was highly stable over time.

Yet another concept, the theoretically based "nuclear script" (Tomkins, 1979), is similar to the clinically based central relationship pattern concepts (and as such is summarized in chapter 20, this volume). The concept is related to Tomkins' "nuclear scene," which reappears in memories with variations over a person's life, as exemplified by Carlson (1981). A script is composed of the person's rules for understanding and dealing with a set of scenes. A nuclear script involves the interpretation of present situations in terms of their similarity to childhood nuclear scenes. A scene is a basic element in the theory; it is an organized unit that includes persons, places, actions, and feelings.

From the Developmental and the Object Relations Researchers

The CCRT research has much in common with the work of the object relations theorists, particularly those who have relied on attachment theory, such as Bowlby (1973). A series of studies by Sroufe and Waters (1977) and Sroufe (1983) on children's relationship patterns has advanced the study of attachment patterns. An adult form of the attachment interview (George, Kaplan, & Main, 1985) has facilitated this type of research, particularly with Main and Goldwyn's (1985) classification system. Their interview consists of questions about relationships with parents and requires recounting of memories of childhood. The relationships revealed were rated on such qualities as "rejection by parent" and "loved versus unloved in childhood."

A systematic clinical assessment method for relationship patterns, Mayman's Early Memories Test (1968), has some basic similarities to the CCRT approach in that the patient is asked to give actual memories, not stories or fantasies as in the Thematic Apperception Test. Mayman's method differs from the CCRT method in that only early memories are asked for and the method of scoring is clinical but not quantitative (Mayman & Faris, 1960).

Some of the basic concepts of the CCRT method are like those of commonsense social psychology as presented by Heider (1958). According to Heider, an intrapsychic analysis helps the analyst understand interpersonal relations. It is congruent with Heider's view that people have a need to form concepts of their relationship environment. The narratives that are used as the basis for the CCRT contain the person's view of the expected or actual responses of other people, under the category of "response from other." People are seen as having wishes and as trying to cause changes in their relationships with others.

The extended family of central relationship pattern concepts also includes the "core organizing principle" of Meichenbaum and Gilmore (1984) and the "problematic reaction in the description of events" of Rice and Greenberg (1984). Many other such concepts are comprehensively reviewed by Singer (1985) and Singer and Salovey (1991).

In general, it seems fair to conclude that—with only a few exceptions, such as Kelly's (1955) Role Construct Repertory method, Tomkins's (1979) script theory, and attachment theory and research (George et al., 1985)—academic psychology has neglected to develop operational measures of the central relationship pattern. Academic psychologists have generally missed even seeing the expressions of the concept because they lack a method for measuring and an appreciation of the value of the concept, although recently their level of appreciation may be on the rise (Thorne, 1989). Dynamic psychotherapists are able to recognize and to use such a concept in the form of the transference pattern, because they are willing to rely on the results of their clinical method of observation and they believe the concept is essential for their therapeutic techniques.

From the Early Attempts to Develop a Transference Measure

The needed transition from the traditional unguided reliance on a clinical method of inferring the transference concept to an operational measure of it has been my recurrent preoccupation. Luborsky and Schimek (1964), for example, considered making a measure of "transference resolution" but thought it to be virtually impossible because of the difficulty of measuring the transference: "No one has yet gone far into the measurement . . . of this concept" (p. 96). Now, looking back, I can make better sense of a series of abortive attempts to achieve a reliable central relationship pattern measure. These attempts are worth a review here because they are not just a matter for the record; they attest to the difficulty of the task yet offer some leads worth following through on. They are listed here in the order of the timing of their attempt.

Systematic Clinical Formulation of the Transference Paradigms

The first attempt goes back to my 1953–1959 participation in the Menninger Foundation Psychotherapy Research Project (Kernberg et al., 1972; Wallerstein, 1986). In that first experience, as the head of the team assigned to the task of evaluating the patients at the termination of psychotherapy, I contributed to the construction and first use of a form that required an assessment of the transference pattern (Wallerstein, Robbins, Sargent, & Luborsky, 1956). The form was filled out initially, at termination, and at follow-up. The form called for a statement of the essence of the "transference paradigms" and within that of "the kinds of interpersonal expectations of the patient that will be recreated in the therapeutic situation. . . . What are the earlier models on which these are based?" (p. 249). "What are the . . . impulses that are being defended against and simultaneously seeking gratification?" (p. 244). The research team was given the task of assembling information about the patient's relationships and extracting from them a transference formulation following its own estimate of the conventional definition of transference. Today, it still would be a useful comparison to see how these relatively unguided conventional transference pattern formulations compare with CCRT formulations.

Agreement on the Conventional Unguided Transference Formulations

Before the advent of the CCRT measure, only a few researchers had tried to judge the reliability of measures of this concept on the basis of the psychotherapy sessions themselves. One of the earliest of such research attempts was made by Seitz (1966) and his research group at the Chicago

Psychoanalytic Institute, who spent several years trying to decide whether a concept of this sort could be reliably inferred by clinicians. His conclusion was that it could not. But his conclusion was based on the use of the usual unguided judgment system: His judges were free to respond on any inference level and with any language, so that it was hard to evaluate agreement or disagreement. Because he did not have a method that would permit a decision either for or against its reliability, his verdict that the concept could not be judged reliably remained on shaky ground.

Rating the Amount of Transference

Another episode in the off-and-on search for an objective relationship pattern measure was played out by the Analytic Research Group of the Institute of the Pennsylvania Hospital. The group's aim was to develop a measure of transference. However, because this aim presented us with a formidable task, we settled on a limited version of the goal: to judge the *amount*, rather than the *content*, of transference and related variables. In our project we studied thirty 5-minute segments from one psychoanalytic patient (Luborsky, Graff, Pulver, & Curtis, 1973). The agreement between judges was only modest ($r = .26$) when the amount of overall transference in a segment was rated. But the agreement was higher when the assessment was for "transference likely" ($r = .46$, $p < .01$), when the judgment was based on the amount of transference expressed in relation to each person referred to in the segment. A similarly aimed study (Strupp, Chassan, & Ewing, 1966) also found only slight agreement among independent judges in their ratings of amount of transference in entire sessions.

Formulation of the Patient's Main Communication in a Session as a Focus for Interpretations

In an earlier attempt that allowed some progress with the measurement of the content of the transference (Auerbach & Luborsky, 1968), I constructed a two-phase measure. In the first phase, the judge formulated the patient's main communication across the session; in the second phase, the judge estimated the degree to which the therapist responded adequately in each interpretation to this main communication. The study was done on samples of sessions in which the therapist was judged to have responded adequately versus inadequately to the patient's communications. Three judges achieved moderate agreement ($r = .68$) in their global ratings of the adequacy of the therapist's main responses to the patient. Because the concept of the patient's main communication requires of the clinical judge a formulation that has a kinship to the main relationship pattern, the experience with this measure is included here as part of the history of attempts to develop an objective measure of the central relationship pattern.

Formulation and Rating of the Symptom-Context Theme

One other early attempt appeared in retrospect to have been formative in moving toward an objective measure. The idea of a core conflictual relationship theme was evident in my System-Context Theme research (Luborsky, 1967; Luborsky & Auerbach, 1969). In that research a particular theme was found for each patient within the psychotherapy session and also just before recurrent symptoms appeared. This theme is recurrent within each patient but different from patient to patient. In the 1967 paper I noted the similarity of this symptom-onset theme to the themes evident in the patient's dreams and to the other themes in the same session. The parallel of the CCRT based on therapy narratives with the CCRT based on dreams has been carried further in the research reported in chapter 12, this volume. The study of the commonality between the Symptom-Context Theme and the CCRT was carried forward in a paper in which we examined the phobic symptoms of a patient by the symptom-context approach and found considerable parallel with the CCRT (Luborsky, Mellon, & Crits-Christoph, 1985b). A similar commonality with the CCRT was observed with another symptom, momentary forgetting (Luborsky, 1988b, 1988c). A core content within each patient's context for forgetting was found to be similar to a component of the patient's CCRT for 3 of the 4 patients examined, and somewhat similar for the 4th as well. These parallels were further established in my book on the symptom-context method (Luborsky, 1996).

In summary, all of these early starts toward fashioning a transference measure formed part of the preparatory stages that led to the successful construction of the CCRT. These starts toward creating the new CCRT measure came from a goal-directed tinkering process much like the one followed by the discoverer of the Epstein–Barr (E-B) virus, Anthony Epstein, who explained his research style when he was interviewed about how his new knowledge came about (Wolpert & Richard, 1988):

> Interviewer: What do you think your skill is as a scientist? You're not a theoretician?
> Epstein: No, not at all, I don't understand any of that. I think just sort of messing about is the answer. You've got to keep messing about at the bench. You see how to change this just a little bit, you see how to change that a bit, and you want to tinker with something and find a slightly different and new way of doing it. (p. 165)

CONCLUSION

- From the experiences in constructing the CCRT, I have come to a new stage in understanding central relationship pattern measures. Now I can more fully state the inclusion criteria for this class of measures:

1. The measure must be based on extraction of a pattern from a sample of self–other narratives about relationship interactions. Each one is part of either (a) a narrative about such interactions or (b) a direct observation of an enactment within transcripts of audio or video recordings.

2. The pattern extracted should be of a central relationship pattern, with *central* defined as the most pervasive across the self–other interactions.

3. The process of extraction of the pattern must be based in part on clinical–quantitative judgment, not only on responses to a questionnaire filled out by the patient or on unguided clinical judgment.

4. The measure must be at least partly capable of reliable application.

These decisions about criteria are more specifically described in chapter 8, this volume, as they apply to the CCRT measure and in chapter 20 for the many alternative measures of the central relationship pattern that have been appearing since the launching of the CCRT. There may be other criteria that could apply, but they are too abstract or too inferential, such as that the measure also serve an integrating function. There are other measures that come close to fitting our criteria, such as Gottschalk and Gleser's (1969) content codes for free association samples, but the other measures are not included here because they describe specific aspects of the content of the patient's utterances rather than of a broad central relationship pattern. Additional criteria need to be examined empirically, as I have begun to do in chapter 21, this volume.

- Freud's transference concept, as judged by clinicians each in their own way, has been relied on routinely since the turn of the century as a guide to making interpretations by clinicians who do dynamic psychotherapies as well as by many other therapists. The concept has not, however, been as well represented in personality theory and research as it deserves to be because of the earlier lack of reliable methods of measurement. After nearly a century of clinical use of Freud's transference concept of a central relationship pattern, the field now has a defined and measured version of this pattern: the CCRT. It is a method that should advance the field, for it can be used with confidence about its measurement capacities.

■ The lineage of the CCRT measure has been traced back to (a) the concept of the transference and (b) the early precursors of the eventual CCRT, such as Kelly's role construct method (1955) and the early memories method of Mayman and Faris (1960). The CCRT captures a pattern that is much like the transference template. As I recounted at the beginning of this chapter, at the outset of examining the concept I had merely looked for a reliable measure of the central relationship pattern. But the discoveries that gradually accumulated suggested that what is measured by the CCRT has much in common with what is covered by the transference concept. Many of the many users of the transference concept have been realizing that the idea of the CCRT as a measure of the central relationship pattern is not a violation of the transference concept but, in fact, fosters its understanding and its use in practice.

2

A GUIDE TO THE CCRT METHOD

LESTER LUBORSKY

The CCRT is derived from narratives about relationship episodes that patients typically tell or sometimes even enact during their psychotherapy sessions. Two major evaluation phases for these narratives are required by the CCRT method: Phase A is for locating and identifying the relationship episodes, and Phase B is for extracting the CCRT from the set of narratives. In addition to explaining how to proceed through Phase A and Phase B, this chapter also lists six optional steps for CCRT scoring, each serving special scoring needs. The chapter ends with explanations for crucial supplementary issues: reliability of tailor-made categories, the judge's need for minimal information about the patient, the necessary sample size of relationship episodes for deriving the CCRT, the use in the CCRT of dreams and fantasies, and the best procedures for training CCRT judges. All of these scoring issues are essential for the *research* use of the CCRT method that are described in this chapter. Note that the *clinical* uses of the CCRT method require special guidelines, and these are explained in chapter 19.

PHASE A: LOCATING RELATIONSHIP EPISODES

This section helps to locate narratives about relationship episodes in the transcripts of psychotherapy sessions. It includes the definition of a relationship episode, a classification of its varieties, and an explanation of how to select passably complete ones.

Definition of a Relationship Episode

A *relationship episode* (RE) is a part of a session that is a relatively discrete episode of explicit narration about relationships with others or with the self. Although the entire session has some characteristics of a narrative (Schafer, 1983), the focus is limited here to the most explicit narratives about relationships.

In each relationship episode, a main other person with whom the patient is interacting is identified. Usually this main other person is easy to identify. Sometimes the patient talks about other people as well, but this is not a problem as long as one person is identifiable as the main other person. If another of the other persons in an episode is talked about sufficiently, a separate, additional relationship episode may be scorable (see "Completeness of Relationship Episodes," following).

The demarcation of the length of the relationship episode is facilitated by the fortunate fact that as a narrative it tends to have a beginning, a middle, and an end. The intent to begin a story is often signaled by conventional stereotypical markers, such as the beginning of a narrative about another person, a relatively long pause, signs of a transition to a new topic, or even a direct introductory statement. Often the narrative is told to explain a self-observation or an observation about another person with whom the patient is interacting. Such introductory observations, like the following two, simplify the task of the judge in recognizing the beginning point:

> Patient: (*pause*) Anyway, I remember another incident . . .
> or
> Patient: I want to tell you something that happened . . .

A narrative is sometimes told as an example of a characteristic of the patient or of the kind of event that happens to the patient. Therefore, words such as *like* or *for example* are used as part of the preface to the narrative, which suggests that the patient is providing an illustration or analogic representation of types or relationships. These explanatory introductions should be included with the narrative, as in this preliminary to a relationship episode:

> Patient: I've been bothered . . . with people telling me what to do or trying to give me directions, like, just, well, for example, I've been registering for school all week and . . .

The length of each relationship episode in a session transcript is marked off by a continuous line along the left margin, extending from the beginning (together with the prefatory comments) to the end of the relationship episode. The number of the relationship episode and the name of the main person with whom the patient is interacting are noted at the start of the line. The relationship episodes remain in their actual serial order within the session's transcript. In that way the judge can read the entire session and know the context in which the patient told the relationship episode.

Transcripts are faster to evaluate than tape recordings. Transcripts also have the advantage of easy access to rereading that helps the judge to remember the details of the relationship episodes. On the other hand, recordings convey additional information through the voice. Our net conclusion is that transcripts are adequate and preferable for purposes of extracting the CCRT, but a combination of transcript and tape would be optimal.

Types of Other Persons in Relationship Episodes

The relationship episodes used for the CCRT method are about relationships with people, including the therapist, and relationships with the self. Most often these relationships with people are with the parents, spouse, friends, and bosses. Relationships with inanimate objects in narratives are excluded only because they are rare. The following paragraphs identify the main types of persons in the narratives.

RE: Specific Other People

Relationship episodes that involve specific other people are by far the most frequent type. The main specific other person is usually readily identifiable, but at times a patient may narrate an incident that involves several people or a group of people (for example, the patient's family, classmates, or friends) without indicating a specific person. In these infrequent cases it is acceptable to designate the "other person" as a group of people, such as "family" or "friends."

RE: Therapist

The therapist is one kind of other person who needs to be considered as a separate category. Although the entire session can be considered an interaction with the therapist, some parts of a session are especially identifiable as either of these two kinds of relationship episodes manifestly about the therapist:

RE: Therapist (narrative). The patient recounts an episode about past or current interactions with the therapist. Because this subtype of relationship episode is a narrative, it is like the usual RE.

RE: Therapist (enactment). The patient engages during the session in a delimited behavioral episode of conflictual interaction with the therapist. These relatively infrequent episodes form a special class of relationship episodes because they are actual *enactments of interactions* (as further described by McLaughlin, 1987), rather than the more usual *narratives about interactions*. In these enactments the patient may initiate the episode by asking a challenging question to which the therapist may respond non-therapeutically, as happened in this episode from Mr. T. Dodge's[1] session:

> Patient: Would you please mail the bill to my father?
> Therapist: No, it is meant for you.
> Patient: I would only have to mail it on again to my father.
> Therapist: No, it is not possible. Your father is not the patient.
> Patient: It is unfair to make me do that.

In this enactment both the patient and the therapist play a part: The patient makes his wishes known to the therapist; the therapist does not go along with the patient's wishes; and the patient feels unfairly treated and the therapist does not deal with the meaning of the exchange.

RE: Self

The few relationship episodes that qualify as "RE: Self" are narratives about the patient's interactions with the patient's own self. In contrast, most of the patient's references to self tend to be self-descriptions and therefore do not qualify as developed relationship episodes about the self.

Characteristic of "RE: Self" narratives is a patient's recollection of a specific interaction with the self that included feeling or thoughts about the self that involved confronting herself. For example, Ms. Sheila Garrett provided a relationship episode about herself that qualified:

> Patient: Even the other day I heard a song. I started crying. Then I thought to myself, my God, Katie, you were so happy at first when you broke up with Dave. You felt like it was a rebirth. Why now are you crying or why is he popping back into your dreams again? I wanted to be over him.

In another example, Ms. Carol Kraft provided a relationship episode about herself that also qualified:

---

[1]All names of patients are fictitious.

Patient: I'm just very, very independent, very much a loner. Like I don't like people to hem me in at all and back me into a corner, and once I remember I backed myself into a corner and it happened in this way. . .

Current Versus Past Relationship Episodes

Relationship episodes can cover any time span from the very earliest memories to the present, as exemplified systematically by Thorne (1995a). The judge should estimate the approximate age of the patient at the time of the event in the narrative and, if possible, should estimate the date of the event. "Current" is defined as within the session or in the last few days (REc); "recent" is in the last 3 years (REr); all else is past (REp). (The time of events in the episode may make a difference in the CCRT: Perhaps a higher proportion of early events produces a more pervasive CCRT across the narratives.)

Completeness of Relationship Episodes

A patient in psychotherapy is usually told nothing specific about what to say but to "say whatever comes to mind" or "whatever you want to speak about." As a result, what is available are the narratives the patient has chosen to tell, in the way the patient has chosen to tell them. Thus, it is to be expected that narratives about relationship episodes will vary widely in completeness.

The RE judges have the task of deciding which relationship episodes are complete enough and which are too sketchy and incomplete to use for judgments about the CCRT. It is useful for RE judges to rate each relationship episode on its degree of completeness on a scale of 1 to 5, from *least* to *most detailed*. The usual cutoff for inclusion is a mean of judges' ratings of 2.5 or more. The following five principles concerning completeness of narratives can aid the evaluation:

1. An important aspect of the narrative's completeness is the specific detailing of the patient's interaction with the other person. A relatively complete relationship episode would be likely to contain an account of an interaction in which the narrator includes the exchange of the patient and therapist, the events that occurred, the wishes, the responses from the other person and of the self, and the outcome of the event. Accounts of specific events are probably more informative than general accounts combining several incidents, although the latter may be acceptable as relationship episodes.

2. The very incomplete relationship episodes—less than 2.5 on the 5-point scale—should be excluded because their CCRT components are difficult to identify. Such exclusion is justified as long as the decision about

TABLE 1
Completeness Ratings of Hypothetical Relationship Episodes

Rating	Essence of the Relationship Episode
1.0	I met Joe and we talked. (No CCRT components)
1.5	I met Joe and we talked and he said little. (A fairly vague response from other)
2.0	I met Joe, we talked and he said little. He's an old friend from school who I like. (More vague components, a hint of a wish and a response of self)
2.5	I met Joe, we talked, he said little. He's an old friend from school who I like. I was disappointed he said so little about the event we went through together. (Enough information to score a wish, response from other, and response of self)
3.0	(Beyond the 2.5 level, the completeness ratings are based on how much the patient elaborates on the story and how detailed the information for each of the components is.)
3.5	
4.0	I met Joe, we talked, he said little. He's an old friend from school who I like. I was disappointed he said so little about the event we went through together.
	I was kind of trying to relive those days and get back the feeling of that event we shared, but Joe seemed distracted. I suggested we meet for lunch next week and he agreed. (All three components are more detailed and more explicit)
4.5	(Like the 4.0 description above, but with even more detail)
5.0	(Like the 4.5 description above, but with even more detail)

whether to use a relationship episode is based primarily on its degree of detail. In addition, there is no indication that exclusion of incomplete relationship episodes distorts the eventual CCRT, and the supply of detailed relationship episodes is usually adequate anyway. The percentage of REs excluded tends to be small—no more than 20–30% and usually much less.

3. The demarcation of the beginning or the end of an episode may be unclear. Because this is not a serious deficiency, such episodes can be used.

4. At times a continuation of an episode occurs later in the session. If the later addition is clearly part of the same episode, it should be used and labeled "continued from RE No. ____ on page ____." The relationship episode with its continuations is to be scored as one unit.

5. Some episodes can be understood as subepisodes of larger narratives, but unless they are discrete, they are not to be considered as separate episodes.

Table 1, showing graded examples, will assist the RE judge in the rating of completeness.

Two RE judges rated this example of a marginally complete relationship episode from Mr. Ben Nevin on the 5-point completeness scale, with 1 being the low end; one judge rated it 1.5, the other 2.0:

> Patient: . . . and uh you know, the same thing with the drawing course I'd like to get into. Fool around with something like that. It's uh, the course, I guess—the teacher, I hear is pretty good. Like he doesn't really care about your uh, technical ability to render, so much as he cares about getting you to see, y'know, to be aware of, uh, space. Architectural space and perspective, and things like that. And I'm uh, kind of excited over, over getting y'know, getting into something like that. . . .

To include even such a skimpy relationship episode as this one would do no harm, but its inclusion is hardly worthwhile because the description of the interaction with the teacher is so incomplete. But even that brief description suggests a possible basis for the patient's attraction to the teacher: The patient might anticipate that a relationship with this encouraging teacher would minimize the chances that his central relationship problem—being incapable of asserting himself against domination—would be activated.

The directions for locating relationship episodes and judging their completeness were examined in a sample of sessions for which two RE judges independently selected the relationship episodes on the basis of the ratings of completeness: Agreement was good for the selection of the relationship episodes as well as for their demarcation (detailed in chapter 7).

Assignment of Scoring Judges

It is best to have two independent sets of judges, one for locating the relationship episodes and the other for scoring the CCRT, although this separation is not essential. The relationship episodes should be demarcated and rated for completeness before the CCRT judges begin their job. Having two sets of judges eases the time-consuming job of the CCRT judge: Although the task of the RE judge takes only a little longer than the time needed to read the transcript, the task for the CCRT judge varies from 1 hour to 2½ hours per session depending on the number of relationship episodes to be scored.

PHASE B: SCORING THE CCRT

To guard against confusion about the details of scoring, I begin with a simplified diagram of the essence of the method for extracting the CCRT from the narratives about relationship episodes (see Figure 1). The diagram shows that a judge usually inspects in succession 10 narratives about rela-

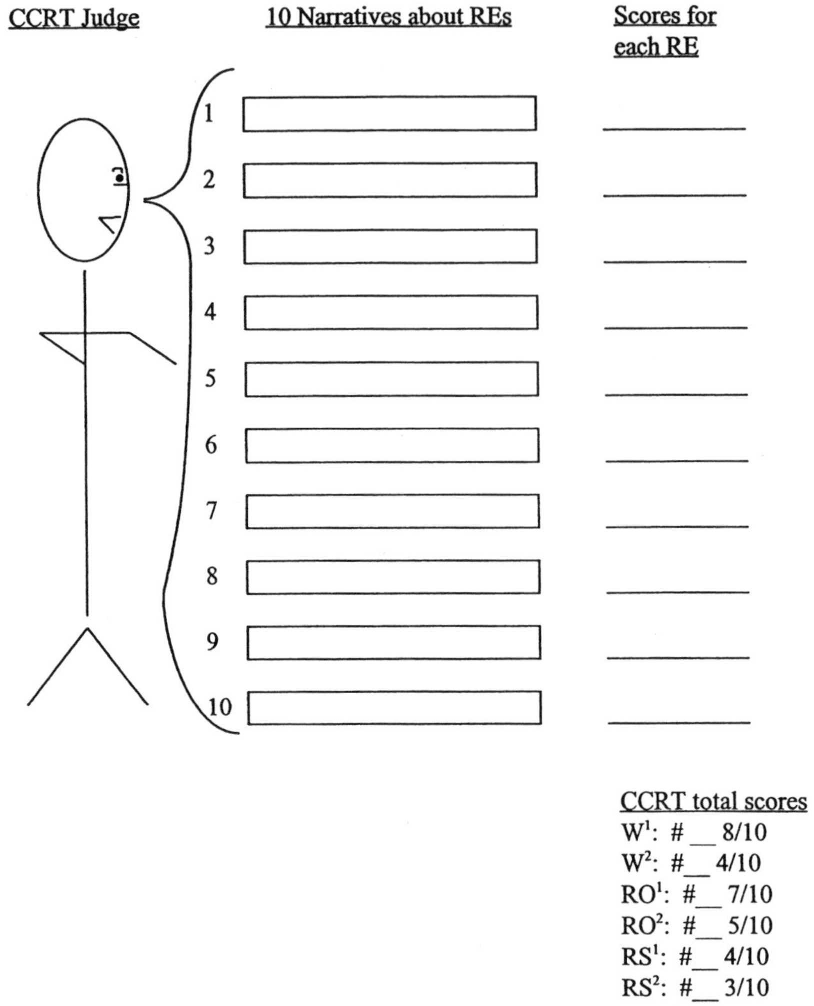

CCRT Judge   **10 Narratives about REs**   **Scores for each RE**

1

2

3

4

5

6

7

8

9

10

CCRT total scores
W^1: # ___ 8/10
W^2: # ___ 4/10
RO^1: # ___ 7/10
RO^2: # ___ 5/10
RS^1: # ___ 4/10
RS^2: # ___ 3/10

Figure 1. Diagram of the essentials of the CCRT method applied to 10 REs from psychotherapy sessions. W^1 = Wish, Standard Category # ___ with highest frequency, W^2 = Standard Category # ___ with second highest frequency, etc. Frequency is expressed as a proportion of the 10 narratives that contain the component.

tionship episodes and scores all the scorable thought units in each for wishes, responses from others, and responses of self. The frequency of each is totaled, and the highest frequencies constitute the CCRT; that is the essence of the CCRT method in brief.

Two repeated pairs of essential steps for discerning the CCRT are summarized in this section: Step 1 calls for the judge to identify types of components to be scored in each relationship episode, and Step 2 requires the judge to summarize them. Then, in Step 1' the judge re-identifies types of components and in Step 2' resummarizes them. More explanation is given in later sections, and examples are given in chapter 5, this volume.

Step 1: Identifying the Types of CCRT Components

Locating and Underlining Parts of the Relationship Episode to Be Scored

After the length of each relationship episode has been marked off by a vertical line on the left margin of the transcript, the CCRT judge reads, rereads, and scores the relationship episodes on the transcript of the session. While reading, the judge underlines (or marks off with slash marks) the parts of the text of each relationship episode that will be the basis for inferences about CCRT components. Each underlined part is a single thought unit as defined by Benjamin (1986b) and as illustrated in the case examples in chapter 5, this volume. Usually each thought unit is given a score for a single component; occasionally two components are scored from a single thought unit.

Identifying Types of Components

Three components are to be identified in each relationship episode: (a) the wishes, needs, or intentions: W; (b) the responses from others: RO; and (c) the responses of the self: RS. The categories scored for each *type* of component are to be written on the left margin of the transcript along-side each underlined thought unit, as illustrated in chapter 5. This annotation must be done legibly and in sufficient detail because it will be relied on by researchers to make their tallies of scores. To make the linkage clear, the judge should draw an arrow linking the underlined thought unit in the text with the scores from the wishes, responses from other, and responses of self components derived from them, as shown in Figure 2.

Preparing the Transcript for Scoring

A further variant simplifies the job of scoring: The *first* CCRT judge (a) marks the thought units and (b) adds a notation of the type of component to be scored at the start of each thought unit; the subsequent CCRT judges use the same scorable thought units and components. This type of preparation of the transcript eases the job of the CCRT judges and, even more important, simplifies the computation of reliability, because all

Scores: **Thought Unit in the Text:**
NRO: Critical of me ————————→ "He was criticizing me and
NRS: Anger ————————————→   I sort of felt annoyed by it"

Figure 2. Examples of linking of the score with the thought unit in the text.

CCRT judges score the same thought units in terms of the same components.

A more time-consuming method is to arrange for a prescoring judge to prepare the transcript for the CCRT judges by (a) identifying the initial thought units and (b) adding a notation above the beginning of each scorable thought unit of the type of component to be scored.

Keeping Within the Range of Levels of Inference From Literal to Moderately Abstract

The judge infers the wishes or responses within a range between two levels of inference: the level of virtually direct expression by the patient, in which the judge stays close to the literal wording used by the patient in the transcript, and the level of moderate inference from what the patient says. Guidance for staying within this range is given later in this chapter, although some of the criteria remain inherently unspecifiable. The responses from other and responses of self are also divided into positive and negative categories (as defined later in this chapter and in chapter 4).

Step 2: Counting the Types of Components and Formulating the CCRT

The judge counts the scores noted in the left margin of the transcript for the occurrences of particular types of components to see which have the highest frequency across the relationship episodes. Now, to make a preliminary CCRT formulation, the judge reviews the scores, one type of component at a time across relationship episodes, to find the theme or themes that apply to the most relationship episodes. The most frequent of each type of component constitutes the preliminary CCRT formulation. This step usually requires more labor for formulation of the wish than for the generally more concrete response from other and response of self.

Only occasionally does the most common theme across the relationship episodes obligingly leap into view. Usually, the process requires time and patience for review and re-review of the wishes across relationship episodes until a general formulation at the most fitting level of inference is recognized. The key to finding thematic consistencies across the episodes is the rereading of the episodes and, especially, the re-inspecting of the types of components across episodes. Earlier episodes become more understandable to the judge after the later ones are studied, and newly recognized redundant themes within and across episodes rearrange themselves from time to time in saltatory accretions of eurekas.

It does not matter if some episodes remain opaque or do not fit with the others, because the main aim of the CCRT method is to locate the themes that repeat themselves the most. The most recurrent components of the episodes point to where the main conflicts lie; the inclusion of the word *conflictual* in the CCRT label rests on this assumption.

It is important to keep the general formulation only as abstract as is necessary to fit the most relationship episodes. This step, with its necessity for keeping within a moderate level of inference, especially requires the wet, gray software, the cortex of a human judge—a tool not likely to be supplanted by the dry, any-color hardware or any-style software of the computer.

Step 1': Re-Identifying the Types of CCRT Components to Make a Final Formulation

The Step 1 phase can be improved by a review to be sure all of the components that make up the general formulation have been considered and scored in the relationship episodes. In light of the preliminary formulation, the judge may now see a particular component with new insight.

It is of research value to preserve the notations of Step 1 scoring separately from the notations of Step 1' scoring. Therefore, the judge writes the additions and alterations resulting from Step 1' in capital letters in the left margin of the transcript. Again, judges should draw arrows between the scored components on the left margin and the text from which they are derived.

Step 2': Recounting and Reformulating the CCRT on the Basis of Step 1'

Step 2' is a repeat of Step 2. The judge lists each type of component on the CCRT summary sheet in order of frequency across episodes. This *is* the CCRT: the most frequent wish, followed by the most frequent response from other, followed by the most frequent response of self. The judge should group similar types of components (for example, the response "hostile" with "angry" or "afraid" with "anxious") as one type of component and add the frequency of each to yield a single sum. *If the same type of component occurs more than once within a relationship episode, the frequency of that type of component is still limited to only 1 for that relationship episode.* As is further explained in chapter 8, this volume, the rationale for this is that the measure of the CCRT rests on pervasiveness of each type of component *across* narratives, not *within* narratives.

Step 3: Choosing and Rating the Standard Categories for the CCRT

What is described in Steps 1, 2 and 1', 2' is the tailor-made system first presented by Luborsky (1977b). A major asset of tailor-made categories is their supreme ability to capture the individuality of each patient. The tailor-made system works well but has two major limitations for research: (a) the need for equivalent categories across subjects for large groups of subjects and (b) the need for the calculation of standard reliability and validity coefficients. For example, the standard categories are a way to cope with a situation where one CCRT judge may have said the patient "wishes to be close," and another judge may have said the patient "wishes not to be cut off from contact." Are these two wish statements the same, similar, or different?

Options Among Standard Category Lists

The procedure for standard CCRT categories avoids such ambiguities by requiring that all judges apply the same categories to the narratives so that comparison between judges is simplified. The recommended practice for scoring combines the assets of tailor-made and the assets of standard categories: First, one presents the tailor-made inference, and then one translates it into standard categories. I have relied on the three lists of standard categories that are introduced here but are described in greater detail in chapter 3, this volume.

Edition 1: Standard categories. This set of standard categories (Luborsky, 1986b) was based on a list of the most frequently used categories within a normative sample of 16 cases. This list was used in a number of studies, including those by Luborsky, Mellon, and Crits-Christoph (1985a); Luborsky, Crits-Christoph, and Alexander (1990); and Crits-Christoph, Cooper, and Luborsky (1988), and it continues to be used by some researchers, although less often. Some of these standard categories are much like those in the Thematic Apperception Test (TAT), with scoring categories from Murray (1938) and Aron (1949). The similar categories were not deliberately selected; some of the similarity derives from the fact that the these categories are evident in both the narratives used for the CCRT and the stories used for the TAT.

Edition 2: Expanded standard categories. This list of standard categories (Crits-Christoph & Demorest, 1988) represents a large expansion of the earlier categories reported by Luborsky (1986b). The added categories drew on major category sets, such as Murray's (1938) "need" and "press" categories. The set in the current Edition 2 has 35 wishes, 30 responses from other, and 30 responses of self. Edition 2 has been used in several studies, including those by Crits-Christoph and Demorest (1991); Eckert, Luborsky, Barber, and Crits-Christoph (1990); Luborsky, Luborsky, et al. (1995).

Edition 3: Reduction of Edition 2 to eight clusters. Naturally, the large number of categories in Edition 2 has much redundancy; this was demonstrated by a cluster method that reduced the number to eight clusters for each component (see chapter 3).

Related Lists of Standard Categories

Several of these lists are included in the alternative central relationship pattern measures described in chapter 20. One of these frequently used lists is known as the Structural Analysis of Social Behavior (Benjamin, 1974); an adaptation of it was developed for the CCRT by Crits-Christoph, Demorest, Muenz, and Baranackie (1994). Future improved standard category lists may emerge from an expanded assessment of the personality domain and from increased normative data.

Applications of Standard Categories

The standard categories can be applied to a session in either of two ways: (a) by using tailor-made categories followed by a translation into standard categories or (b) by using standard categories directly from the text without the tailor-made categories. It is the first method that is most highly recommended.

After the tailor-made categories are inferred from the text, each one is translated into the standard categories, as was typically done in most studies. This system benefits from the virtues of a combination of the tailor-made and standard categories, that is, from categories that specifically fit the case as well as from categories that are standard across cases. The translation from the tailor-made to the standard can be done by the original scorer or it can be done by a different judge. One of the following two systems differing in completeness must be chosen:

System 1

The one best-fitting category (or a best-fitting category followed by a next best) is chosen from the approximately 30 in each of the three lists of types of components. In making choices from Edition 2, review the list of standard categories from time to time to be sure that all of them have been considered. This procedure of choosing just one (or two) of the categories has the virtue of a rapid ranking system, but it misses considerable information. Some of this loss is inadvertent; it comes from the inherent difficulty of attending to and then choosing one (or two) of the categories in a long list.

System 2

All 30 or so categories of each component in Edition 2 are rated for each of the scorable thought units in a relationship episode: Because of the limits of System 1, System 2, which involves rating all categories on the following scale (see Figure 3), can be used with the three convenient forms in Appendix B, this chapter. On each form, at the top of each column is a space to write the thought unit that is to be rated on all categories.

For the sake of completeness, one also notes on the listed ratings the

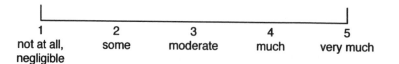

Figure 3. A graphic scale for rating each category in the list of components.

best-fitting (by a circle around the rating) and the next-best-fitting (by a square around the rating) categories. This combination of the rating system with the ranking system is desirable because it provides considerable information. This system becomes even more convenient when the number of standard categories is reduced by cluster analysis (as illustrated in chapter 3, this volume).

On the summary sheet for each type of component, the judge should list in parentheses the relationship episodes that contained that component. For example, for Mr. Ben Nevin's second most frequent wish, the summary score sheet would read: "Wish: to not go along with wishes of others (RE 3, 4, 7)."

Detailed Guides for Scoring the Components: Wishes, Responses From Other, and Responses of Self

The CCRT judge usually starts scoring after identifying the relationship episodes and the scorable thought units within them. The CCRT judge (or a prescoring judge) identifies by underlining or slash marks every instance on the transcript in which a patient reiterates a wish, response from other, or response of self, either by repeating a phrase verbatim or by attempting to describe it in different terms, but each different type of response *counts only once for that relationship episode* on the summary sheet. In the following excerpt, from a relationship episode of Mr. Uri Irion, the patient describes in several ways his feelings of being relieved and unburdened. The judge would count the type of response of self as "relief of pressure" only once on the summary sheet.

> Patient: I remember it felt like someone had been on my shoulders, like I was carryin' them around in a swimming pool or somethin' for 10 minutes . . . then they got off my shoulders. You feel as though you just float. I felt as though somethin' had been taken off my brain.

The response from other and response of self categories tend to be easier to score than the wish category because they are more directly expressed. They tend to be consequences of a wish, although not every response is recognizably linked up with a wish. Even though many of the linkages of the components with each other are evident, it is sufficient for the judge to note all wishes and responses without having to connect them as a sequence.

Wishes

The usual two levels of inference need to be distinguished for the wishes, in particular, but also for responses from other and responses of self: (a) those that are explicit or almost explicit: W, and (b) those that are not explicit but moderately inferable: (W).

Explicit level of inference: W. An explicit wish is often directly stated as a wish by words such as "I wish," "I want," "I hunger for," "I need," and so on.

Moderate level inference: (W). Parentheses around the component indicate a moderate level of inference. These often are recognizable when the judge reviews and makes inferences across different relationship episodes from the same patient. Instances of (W) are essential to the CCRT method because they are more likely than instances of W to be evident within many of the relationship episodes. In contrast, the Ws tend to be more specific and limited to each relationship episode. (This explication for using the moderate level of inference emerged from a personal communication with James Bond, 1986.) The judge should list as many Ws and (W)s as are applicable; it is useful for the judge to consider both an explicit level score and a moderate level score for each of the to-be-scored thought units. There is no reason for the judge to worry about getting too many scores; in the CCRT method only the most recurrent scores get into the CCRT anyway. Also, as with any component, if no wish is moderately clearly inferable in a relationship episode, no wish score is given.

The wish formulation in the tailor-made system should be no more abstract than necessary. An example of an applicable but sometimes overly abstract wish statement was "I wish to be independent." A review of the relationship episodes showed that a more fitting word than *independent* was *assertive.*

Table 2, derived from sessions of Mr. Ben Nevin, illustrates the levels of inference in scoring W versus (W) on the basis of the text examples in the right column.

Responses From Other

A response from other should be scored only with respect to the main other person (as listed in the left margin at the beginning of the relationship episode).

Responses of Self

Responses of self should also include the patient's symptoms when these are evident in the relationship episode. The consistent inclusion of the symptom as response of self each time it appears in a narrative permits an understanding of the symptom's CCRT context (as discussed by Luborsky, 1996).

TABLE 2
Level of Inference in Scoring Wishes

	Scoring of W and (W)	Text Example of Wish
RE 1	W: to assert self against being put down by putting the other guy down	"... in the end of the fantasies, the position was reversed and I was stepping on *him* like that ..."
RE 4	W: not to get sexually involved with the woman	"I really don't want to get involved with her sexually ..."
	(W): to assert myself by not going along with the woman[a]	"I really don't want to get involved ..."
	(W): to get sexually involved[b]	"I really don't want to get involved ..."
	W: to have people around	"I'm sort of hungry to have people around ..."

[a]Note that this formulation of the inference gains specificity by its inclusion of the response from other.
[b]This one is even more inferential because it involves the denial of the wish.

Positive and Negative Responses

Each type of response from other and response of self is also scored as mainly positive (P) or mainly negative (N); usually a further subdivision is made at the extremes as PP or NN, as explained in chapter 4.

A *negative* response is defined as one in which, *to the patient,* interference with satisfaction of the wishes has occurred or is expected to occur. A *positive* response is one in which there is noninterference or expectation of noninterference with the satisfaction of wishes or a sense of mastery in being able to deal with the wishes.

> Patient: When I went to see my advisor yesterday ... and told her that, um, that I uh decided not to go back full-time and she asked me why ... and I explained to her ... I really was waiting for her to say to me ... "Well, why? I really thought you ought to go on" and "Why don't you get finished" and stuff like that that ... and she didn't say it at all. She said, "Well, it's your decision and you're probably better off doing that." I guess I was a little disappointed.

In this episode, Ms. Nan Iolanta wishes and expects her advisor to try to talk her out of her decision not to go back to school full-time, but the advisor supports her capacity to make the decision, leaving the patient feeling disappointed. Although *the judge* may perceive the advisor's response to be a positive one, *the patient* perceives the response as one that interferes with the satisfaction of her wish. Thus, the response from other would be scored "negative." The response of self of disappointment would also be scored "negative."

Because all responses in a relationship episode should be scored, even if they are not clearly associated with a wish, at times it is hard to determine whether a response should be labeled positive or negative. In these instances the judge should choose a score and add a question mark.

RO and RO-Expected

Only when the other person in a relationship episode actually performs an action or responds in some way does the judge score an RO. For example, "He did hang up on me," is scored "RO: Rejection." But if the patient has only an expectation or fantasy that the other will respond in a particular way, the incident is scored as in this example: "I didn't call him because I expected he'd hang up on me. RO-expected: Rejection."

OPTIONAL STEPS

Step 4: Distinguishing Between Expressed and Not Expressed Responses of Self

This step and all that follow are optional to the scoring procedure. The distinction of *expressed* (expr) versus *not expressed* (not expr) may be a valuable one, especially in studying the CCRT as a measure of change. For example, "that irritated me" is not an expressed response if the patient makes it clear that he did not express his irritation to the other person. Expression of irritation in later sessions *might* be considered a positive change for this patient.

Step 5: Judging the Intensity of Theme Components

Intensity refers to the degree to which the speaker expresses and experiences affect. A scale from 1 to 5 can be used for rating each type of component, in which 1 is *little or none* and 5 is *very much* (included when all standard categories are to be rated, the rating forms in Appendix A are used when *all* standard categories are rated for each thought unit). However, further research is necessary to specify what is gained by the addition of intensity ratings, for it may emerge, that intensity of a type of component

TABLE 3
Intensity Ratings

Intensity Ratings	Text Example
RS (4)	"That irritated me."
RO (3)	"He tries to dominate the conversation."
W (3)	"I wish to assert myself."

is largely redundant with frequency of appearance, which is the basis for the CCRT scoring. Table 3 lists three intensity ratings for Mr. Ben Nevin.

Step 6: Recording the Sequence of the Appearance of Each Component

A record of the sequence of the wish, response from other, and response of self within each relationship episode can provide further insight into each patient's typical relationship interaction sequences (as suggested by Ellen Berman, personal communication, 1979). The sequences may even be longer and more complex than just W → RO → RS. A frequent longer sequence is W → RO → RS → W. While reading the relationship episodes, the judge can note the sequence of the appearance of each component by numbering them consecutively on the transcript and then indicating the sequence numbers along with the CCRT scores. My experience with this step indicates that interactional sequences are highly stereotyped (see chapter 9, this volume).

A newly discovered facet of the sequence of components was constructed by Mitchell (1995) called the Coherence of the Relationship Theme. It measures the degree to which the patient describes himself and others as in interaction. The main measure is the "link percentage," which is the percentage of CCRT components that are linked together. A higher percentage of links was found to be associated with the patients' degree of relatedness to others and based on the severity of the diagnosis. For example, "I didn't want to be close to her (mother)" is a linked response of self. It is a link of the wish with the response of self. "She was rejecting me" is a linked response from other.

Step 7: Estimating the Patient's Moment-to-Moment Experience of the Components of the CCRT in the Relationship With the Therapist

The types of components of the CCRT vary in the degree to which they are experienced in the relationship with the therapist; these variations can be useful for the therapist to note. One system is called the Patient's Experience of the Relationship With the Therapist (Gill & Hoffman, 1982b), described in chapter 20, this volume. Unlike other central relationship pattern measures, this measure aims to identify *when* in the course of the session the experience of and awareness of the experience of the relationship with the therapist are clearest, so that the therapist can consider interpreting them. According to the psychoanalytic theory of psychotherapeutic change (Luborsky, 1984), patients who improve in the course of psychoanalytic therapy should develop improved access to awareness of their experiences in relationships, especially the one with the therapist. This thesis can be examined by having judges score the degree to which the patient experiences each type of relationship component and when in the session the experience is most evident. (For a sample, see notations in the Appendix A, step 7. Although the notations and definitions are mine, their basis is the system by Gill & Hoffman, 1982b.) For example, for Mr. Edward Howard (chapter 9, this volume) the wish "to be close" is the most frequent wish. The judge scores the category "Jet" which means the judges infer that the patient experiences the wish because the patient appears to be aware of the wish in relation to the therapist, although he does not directly express it. Scoring categories are then applied to the response from other and response of self components.

Step 8: Randomizing Relationship Episodes Before Scoring

The relationship episodes are usually scored in the order and in the context in which they are given because they are more meaningful that way. But for some research purposes it may be of value to randomize them to see what is conveyed by each relationship episode by itself (see Crits-Christoph & Demorest, 1991; Crits-Christoph, Demorest, Muenz, & Baranackie, 1994). Eventually, a research-based comparison of the naturalistic clinical versus randomized conditions will be made.

Step 9: Additional Quantitative Specification of the CCRT

The specification includes two elements: (a) the exact pervasiveness score across narratives and (b) the range of scores. An example from chapter 5, Table 3, conveys this point exactly. The usual CCRT presentation includes only the most frequent types of components. This proposed additional specification would include the following from the CCRT:

Wish (five types of wishes scored); Category 13, to be helped, 3/5; Category 18, to oppose others, 2/5.

Negative responses from other (types were scored); Category 4, were rejecting, 3/5; Category 14, are helpful, 3/5.

Negative response of self (six types scored); Category 21, feel angry, 2/5; Category 22, feel depressed, 2/5.

SUPPLEMENTARY ISSUES

Estimating Reliability of Tailor-Made Categories

Agreement Judges

The job of agreement judges is to rate the degree of agreement of pairs of CCRT judges with each other. This is the most common reliability method for tailor-made categories, but it has inherent problems of subjectivity. Each agreement judge reviews the scoring of the CCRT judges and merely classifies on a clinical basis the degree to which CCRT judges' scores on each of the categories are in clear agreement, questionable agreement, questionable disagreement, or clear disagreement. The agreement judges generally report that this job can be done with a sense of confidence.

Paired Comparisons

A more controlled reliability system for tailor-made categories is based on the paired-comparisons method: Each scored formulation by each judge is paired with the scoring of the other judges on the same case as well as on other cases; the pairs are then judged for similarity. This procedure is described as the method of mismatched cases (Levine & Luborsky, 1981; Luborsky, Mellon, van Ravenswaay, et al., 1985). The method gives information on the level of agreement in the similarity of the tailor-made pairs of categories for the same-case pairs versus the similarity for the mismatched pairs. The method as diagrammed in chapter 11, this volume, is most suitable for dealing with tailor-made categories because the tailor-made system is not designed for conventional reliability methods. We have demonstrated by this method that judges agree with each other significantly more when the formulation by each judge is compared with the formulation of the other judges on the same case than when the pair includes formulations from other (mismatched) cases.

The Need of the CCRT Judge for Uniform Background Information About the Patient

The judges should have some uniform minimal information about the patient beyond what may be inferable from the transcript of the session. At least the age and sex of the patient should be given; the adequate reliabilities reported in chapter 6, this volume, were achieved by judges who had only these two extra-session items of information. In addition, the judge should be given an explanation of the relationship to the patient of certain named people; for example, "John" is the boyfriend, "Sarah" is the sister, and so on. It may also be desirable for the relationship episodes to be judged within the full transcript so that the CCRT judge can understand the context in which they are told.

It would be of interest to compare the therapist's scoring of the therapist's own cases with the scoring of these cases by other judges. The other judges probably would be at a disadvantage because, as Spence (1983b) would say, they are not "privileged"; the therapist is "privileged" through knowing much more about the patient.

The Best Sample Size of Relationship Episodes for Deriving the CCRT

It is important to have an adequate sample of relationship episodes to obtain a CCRT that is representative of the treatment or of the treatment phases. It is usually sufficient to sample at least two early and two late sessions to locate 10, or close to 10, relationship episodes in the early sessions and 10, or close to 10, relationship episodes in the late sessions. In the inaugural CCRT study (Luborsky, 1977a), the relationship episodes were selected from four 20-minute segments from each session (two early and two late). Within each of these segments of each session, 4 to 6 relationship episodes were usually found, but occasionally there were as many as 10. The fact that there was considerable consistency in content from the early CCRT to the late CCRT implies that even fewer than 10 relationship episodes can be enough to discern the CCRT. More research is needed to determine how many relationship episodes in how many sessions need to be sampled as an adequate basis for the CCRT.

When a single session's relationship episodes are scored, as in some examples given in chapter 5, this volume, the CCRT should be referred to as a "session CCRT" rather than a "treatment CCRT." A treatment CCRT is based on assembling the relationship episode scores from a sample of more than one session. A session CCRT is a special version of the CCRT and may differ some or very much from the treatment CCRT.

The Use of Dreams and Fantasies

Whether to include dreams and fantasies as relationship episodes, in addition to the usual narratives, has not yet been fully decided. However, if they are included, there will be relatively few of them in each treatment and they will be lost among the larger number of relationship episodes told as accounts of patient's actual interactions with other people. The best resolution for now is to score dreams and fantasies but not include them in the CCRT, then note how they compare with the usual relationship-episode-based CCRT. A comparative study along these lines is reported in chapter 12, this volume.

Training Procedures for Learning to Score the CCRT

For high agreement of judges to be achieved, it is necessary that judges be well trained in the use of the method. This training sequence is recommended:

1. Judges should have had some clinical training and should be interested in learning the CCRT. Despite the preference to use as judges experienced clinicians who have a psychodynamic orientation, a few graduate students, including nonclinical students, have also performed well as judges; clearly the task does not require that the judge be trained in or committed to a particular school of psychotherapy.

2. It is recommended that each judge study the CCRT instructions in this chapter and the scored examples in chapter 5. A good first step in training is to score the examples in chapter 5, this volume, after first covering the score on the left side of each page.

3. The experience of scoring several practice cases is helpful for improving skill. The practice cases are scored one by one, with feedback on the trainee's performance after each one by the person in charge of training. The feedback is based on the trainee's agreement with other judges who have scored the same cases as well as the adherence of the judge to the procedures outlined in this chapter. The sequence of cases provided to the trainee is graded to begin with easier cases. This kind of training followed by feedback on three cases usually is required to bring the judge up to an adequate level of agreement with trained judges. (The present series of practice cases includes Mr. G. Heyman, Mr. Ben Nevin, Mr. O. Disims, and Ms. G. Diane.) In fact, Bond, Hansell, and Shevrin (1987) found evidence for increased agreement among judges after greater experience in the task. More about the special procedures for clinical use of the CCRT is given in chapter 18.

CONCLUSION

- The scoring instructions presented so far in this chapter provide a foundation for becoming proficient in the CCRT method. But to become even more proficient requires building one's skill by reviewing the basic steps for scoring outlined in Appendix A, this chapter, by applying the lists of standard categories given in Appendix B, also this chapter, and by practicing with the examples presented in chapter 5. After scoring three or four cases, the average judge becomes reasonably competent; however, even the competent judge may have to consult this basic chapter again and again as scoring problems appear.

APPENDIX A

Summary of Basic Steps for Scoring the CCRT

PHASE A: LOCATING RELATIONSHIP EPISODES

Locate the relationship episodes (REs) in the session (if these have not already been located for you by an independent RE judge).

Notations for the Relationship Episodes
RE = relationship episode
RE_C = current RE (within the session or the last few days)
RE_{C3} = within past 3 years
RE_p = past RE (Note patient's age at the time of the event and the date of the event. Approximate this information when it is not available and note when it is estimated age by parentheses.)

PHASE B: EXTRACTING THE CCRT

Step 1

1. Underline (or use slash marks) each scorable thought unit in the relationship episodes (if this has not already been done for you by an independent judge).

2. Tailor-made scoring. Write the scores you give for each underlined scorable thought unit in the left margin of the page. Connect by an arrow the underlined unit with your inference in the margin. Remember to consider scoring each of the underlined thought units at *two* levels of inference: (a) the less inferential level, that is, close to the manifest level, and (b) the more inferential, that is, at a moderate level of inference; these scores are enclosed in parentheses.

Step 2

Copy all scores from the transcript onto the score sheets, count them, and formulate the CCRT.

Step 1'

Review the scores to see whether anything was missed or needs revision. Additions and revisions are to be written in capital letters.

Step 2'

Recount the main types of components on the score sheet summary and reformulate the CCRT. (Be sure to note alongside each type of component the relationship episode number in which each is present.)

Step 3

Standard category scoring:

Top two choices: For each underlined thought unit, choose the best-fitting standard category and then the next-best-fitting one. Write their numbers in parentheses after the tailor-made category.

Rate all: An even more complete method to use for the standard categories in Edition 2 and 3 is first to rate *all* of them for each underlining and then choose the two best-fitting ones. (Remember to include only the ratings for each *different* type of component in *each* relationship episode; Steps 1' and 2' need not be done for scoring by standard categories.)

Step 4

Differentiate between expressed and not expressed response of self.

Step 5 (optional)

Consider the intensity: Give a rating of 1 to 5 (1 = *least*, 5 = *most*) of the intensity of each type of theme component (W, RO, RS).

Step 6 (optional)

Note the sequence of components: (1), (2), (3), etc. = the position of each W, RO, and RS in each relationship episode.

Step 7 (optional)

Consider awareness of one's experience (see Gill & Hoffman, 1982b) with a rating of 1 to 5 (1 = *little or none*, 5 = *very much*).

et = directly expressed awareness by the patient of an experience in the relationship with the therapist in the session

Jet = inference by the judge of awareness of an experience in the relationship with the therapist

eto = directly expressed awareness of the parallel between the relationship with the therapist and other relationships

Step 8 (optional)

Randomization of REs before scoring

Step 9 (optional)

Quantitative specification of the CCRT

NOTATIONS FOR THE CCRT COMPONENTS

Steps 1–2 and 1'–2'

Wishes

W = wish, need, or intention, as directly or almost directly stated by the patient

(W) = wish, need, or intention as inferred by the judge when moderate inference is used

Responses From Other

RO = actual response from other

RO-expected = response expected from other

    N = negative (e.g., NRO = negative response from other, from the patient's perspective; use NN for very negative)

    P = positive (e.g., PRO = positive response from other, from the patient's perspective; use PP for very positive)

Responses of the Self

RS = response of the self

    N = negative (e.g., NRS = negative response of self, NN = very negative)

    P = positive (e.g., PRS = positive response of self, PP = very positive)

    expr = an expressed response of self (e.g., NRSexpr = negative response of self that is expressed to other person)

    not expr = not expressed response of self (e.g., NRS not expr = negative response of self that is not expressed to other person)

WISHES

Rate intensity of <u>all</u> standard
categories for each thought unit

1	2	3	4	5
slight	somewhat	moderate	much	very much

Date: _____ (Write in each to-be-scored

Rated by: _____ thought <u>unit and its RE #</u>

(continue on extra pages)

Edition 3 (clusters)	Edition 2											
1. to assert self & be independent	21. to have self-control											
	28. to be my own person											
	34. to assert myself											
	23. to be independent											
2. to oppose, hurt & control others	18. to oppose others											
	16. to hurt others											
	19. to have control of others											
3. to be controlled, hurt, & not responsible	15. to be hurt											
	20. to be controlled by others											
	29. to be <u>not</u> respon/obligated											
	13. to be helped											
	27. to be like others											
4. to be distant & avoid conflicts	17. to avoid conflicts											
	14. to not be hurt											
	10. to be distant from others											
5. to be close & accepting	4. to accept others											
	5. to respect others											
	9. to be open											
	6. to have trust											
	8. to be opened up to											
	11. to be close to others											
6. to be loved & understood	33. to be loved											
	3. to be respected											
	1. to be understood											
	2. to be accepted											
	7. to be liked											
7. to feel good & comfortable	30. to have stability											
	31. to feel comfortable											
	32. to feel happy											
	24. to feel good about self											
8. to achieve & help others	22. to achieve											
	25. to better myself											
	12. to help others											
	26. to be good											
	35. to compete with someone for another's affection											

RESPONSES FROM OTHER
Rate intensity of <u>all</u> standard
categories for each thought unit

1	2	3	4	5
slight	somewhat	moderate	much	very much

Date: _____
Rated by: _____

(Write in each to-be-scored
thought <u>unit and its RE#</u>)
(continue on extra pages)

Edition 3 (clusters)	Edition 2													
1. strong	24. strong													
	23. independent													
	29. happy													
2. controlling	26. strict													
	20. controlling													
3. upset	16. hurt													
	22. dependent													
	28. anxious													
	27. angry													
	19. out of control													
4. bad	8. not trustworthy													
	25. bad													
5. rejecting & opposing	7. don't trust me													
	6. don't respect me													
	2. are not understanding													
	4. rejecting													
	10. dislike me													
	12. distant					.								
	14. unhelpful													
	17. oppose me													
	15. hurt me													
6. helpful	13. are helpful													
	18. cooperative													
7. likes me	30. loves me													
	5. respects me													
	9. likes me													
	21. gives me independence													
8. understanding	11. open													
	1. understanding													
	3. accepting													

RESPONSES OF SELF
Rate intensity of <u>all</u> standard
categories for each thought unit

1	2	3	4	5
slight	somewhat	moderate	much	very much

Date: _____
Rated by: _____

(Write in each to-be-scored
thought <u>unit and its RE#</u>
(continue on extra pages)

Edition 3 (clusters)	Edition 2												
1. helpful	7. am open												
	1. understand												
	9. am helpful												
2. unreceptive	2. don't understand												
	8. am not open												
	6. dislike others												
3. respected & accepted	28. feel comfortable												
	29. feel happy												
	30. feel loved												
	4. feel respected												
	3. feel accepted												
	5. like others												
4. oppose & hurt others	11. oppose others												
	10. hurt others												
5. self-controlled & self-confident	14. self-controlled												
	15. independent												
	18. self-confident												
	12. controlling												
6. helpless	13. out of control												
	17. helpless												
	19. uncertain												
	16. dependent												
7. disappointed & depressed	21. angry												
	20. disappointed												
	22. depressed												
	23. unloved												
	24. jealous												
8. anxious & ashamed	27. anxious												
	26. ashamed												
	25. guilty												
	31. somatic symptoms												

3

A GUIDE TO THE CCRT STANDARD CATEGORIES AND THEIR CLASSIFICATION

JACQUES P. BARBER, PAUL CRITS-CHRISTOPH,
AND LESTER LUBORSKY

The CCRT scoring system uses well-constructed sets of standard categories. These categories describe the types of components of the CCRT for use in both psychotherapeutic and research settings. The tailor-made system tends to be more appropriate for clinical work or for case studies because it allows the therapist to derive a psychodynamic formulation that closely fits each patient. The standard category systems are usually more appropriate for research because they allow the researcher to compare reliably and easily different judges' selections of categories. Several procedures are recommended in chapter 2, this volume, to guide users of these lists of standard categories, but the most versatile procedure is for the judge to record the tailor-made categories and then to translate each of them into Edition 2 of the standard categories, which is described in this chapter. Such a combination of methods gives the richest information for both research and clinical purposes.

To facilitate construction of standard categories, we assembled lists of standard categories: Editions 1 and 2 (see Exhibit 1 and Table 1, this chap-

EXHIBIT 1
A Standard List of Scoring Categories: Edition 1 Based on the CCRT in a Normative Group ($n = 16$)

Wishes, Needs, Intentions

("I wish, need, or intend in relation to the other person . . .")

A. To assert myself
   A1. To assert my independence and autonomy
   A2. To dominate; to impose my will or control on others
   A3. To overcome other's domination; to be free of obligations imposed by others; to not be put down
   A4. To win in competition with another; to be better than the other person
   A5. To win the affection or attention of another over someone else (triangle or oedipal situation)
B. To submit
   B1. To submit; to give in; to be passive
C. To make contact with others; to be close and intimate with others
   C1. To make contact with others; to be close; to be friends
   C2. To receive affection; to not be deprived of continued affection
   C3. To be receptive (to open up) to others
   C4. To please the other person; to avoid hurting the other person
D. To get sexual gratification
   D1. To get sexual gratification
E. To receive acceptance
   E1. To receive acceptance; to be respected, recognized, approved, vindicated, reassured; to maintain one's self-esteem (to avoid disapproval, and so on)
   E2. To be fairly treated (to not be unfairly treated)
F. To get help and care from others
   F1. To get help, care, protection, and guidance from others
G. To achieve and be competent
   G1. To achieve, be competent, be successful
H. To hurt the other person
   H1. To hurt the other person; to get back at the other person; to express anger, hostility, or resentment to the other person
I. To exert control over myself
   I1. To exert control over myself

Responses From Others ("The other person becomes . . .")

Negative

1. Dominating, controlling, interfering, intimidating, intruding
2. Unfair, exploiting, taking advantage
3. Resentful, angry, irritated, hostile, violently aggressive
4. Critical, disapproving
5. Insensitive, inconsiderate (does not consider my feelings)
6. Unhelpful, uncooperative, noncompliant (does not gratify my wishes)
7. Distant, withdrawn
8. Unaffectionate
9. Does not understand

Positive

1. Supportive, reassuring
2. Treats fairly, respectfully

4. Accepting, approving
5. Concerned, interested
6. Helpful, cooperative, compliant

7. Close, expressive
8. Affectionate
9. Understanding

EXHIBIT 1 (*Continued*)

Responses From Others ("The other person becomes ...")

Negative	Positive
10. Dependent	
11. Hurt	
	12. Honest, open

Responses of Self ("I become ...")

Negative

1. Passive, submissive, dominated, compliant, deferential, controlled ("I give in to the power of other")
2. Dependent
3. Helpless, less confident, ineffectual ("I do not know how to do things")
4. Hopeless ("I give up; I feel nothing can be done")
5. Obligated
6. Rejected, unaccepted, disappointed
7. Uninvolved with people, lonely, detached, distant, quiet, nonresponsive, untalkative ("I pull away from people")
8a. Angry, resentful, hating
8b. Violently angry
9. Frustrated
10. Depressed
11. Anxious, tense, upset
12. Frightened, afraid
13. Guilty, self-blaming
14. Embarrassed
15. Jealous
16. Confused, indecisive, ambivalent

Positive

1. Assertive, express self assertively, gain control

3. Gain self-esteem, feel affirmed

7. Feel close to others

8a. Not angry

10. Happy

Note. Only the numbered categories, not the headings, are scored. Parentheses after a category contain a statement summarizing the essence of the category.

ter, and the three rating forms that make up Appendix B of chapter 2). In this chapter we present an account of the development of the Edition 2 classification of CCRT standard categories and the subsequent cluster analysis of these categories to derive Edition 3.

DEVELOPMENT OF THE STANDARD CATEGORIES

Our effort to create standard categories originated in the typical difficulties we experienced in using tailor-made assessments and trying to compare them. These standard categories provide the judges with a common language that has enabled us to compare patients' CCRTs quantitatively as well as to compare judges' performance in deriving the CCRT. To mea-

TABLE 1
Standard CCRT Categories: Edition 2

Category	Standard Category Components
WISHES, NEEDS, INTENTIONS	
1. TO BE UNDERSTOOD	To be comprehended; to be empathized with; to be seen accurately
2. TO BE ACCEPTED	To be approved of; to not be judged; to be affirmed
3. TO BE RESPECTED	To be valued; to be treated fairly; to be important to others
4. TO ACCEPT OTHERS	To be receptive to others
5. TO RESPECT OTHERS	To value others
6. TO HAVE TRUST	Others to be honest; others to be genuine
7. TO BE LIKED	Others to be interested in me
8. TO BE OPENED UP TO	To be responded to; to be talked to
9. TO BE OPEN	To express myself; to communicate
10. TO BE DISTANT FROM OTHERS	To not express myself/my feelings; to be left alone
11. TO BE CLOSE TO OTHERS	To be included; not to be left alone; to be friends
12. TO HELP OTHERS	To nurture others; to give to others
13. TO BE HELPED	To be nurtured; to be given support; to be given something valuable; to be protected
14. TO NOT BE HURT	To avoid pain and aggravation; to avoid rejection; to protect/defend myself
15. TO BE HURT	To be punished; to be treated badly; to be injured
16. TO HURT OTHERS	To get revenge; to reject others; to express anger at others
17. TO AVOID CONFLICT	To compromise; not to anger others; to get along; to be flexible
18. TO OPPOSE OTHERS	To resist domination; to compete against others
19. TO HAVE CONTROL OVER OTHERS	To dominate; to have power; to have things my own way
20. TO BE CONTROLLED BY OTHERS	To be submissive; to be dependent; to be passive; to be given direction
21. TO HAVE SELF-CONTROL	To be consistent; to be rational
22. TO ACHIEVE	To be competent; to achieve; to win
23. TO BE INDEPENDENT	To be self-sufficient; to be self-reliant; to be autonomous
24. TO FEEL GOOD ABOUT MYSELF	To be self-confident; to accept myself; to have a sense of well-being
25. TO BETTER MYSELF	To improve; to get well
26. TO BE GOOD	To do the right thing; to be perfect; to be correct
27. TO BE LIKE OTHER	To identify with other; to be similar to other; to model after other
28. TO BE MY OWN PERSON	Not to conform; to be unique

TABLE 1   (*Continued*)

Category	Standard Category Components
WISHES, NEEDS, INTENTIONS	
29. TO NOT BE RESPONSIBLE OR OBLIGATED	To be free; to not be constrained
30. TO BE STABLE	To be secure; to have structure
31. TO FEEL COMFORTABLE	To relax; to not feel bad
32. TO FEEL HAPPY	To have fun; to enjoy; to feel good
33. TO BE LOVED	To be romantically involved
34. TO ASSERT MYSELF	To compel recognition of one's rights
35. TO COMPETE WITH SOMEONE FOR ANOTHER PERSON'S AFFECTION	
RESPONSES FROM OTHERS	
1. ARE UNDERSTANDING	Are empathic; are sympathetic; see me accurately
2. ARE NOT UNDERSTANDING	Are not empathic; are unsympathetic; are inconsiderate
3. ARE ACCEPTING	Are not rejecting; approve of me; include me
4. ARE REJECTING	Are disapproving; are critical
5. RESPECT ME	Treat me fairly; value me; admire me
6. DON'T RESPECT ME	Don't treat me fairly; don't value me; don't admire me
7. DON'T TRUST ME	Don't believe me; are suspicious of me
8. ARE NOT TRUSTWORTHY	Betray me; are deceitful; are dishonest
9. LIKE ME	Are interested in me
10. DISLIKE ME	Are not interested in me
11. ARE OPEN	Are expressive; are disclosing; are available
12. ARE DISTANT	Are unresponsive; are unavailable
13. ARE HELPFUL	Are supportive; give to me; explain
14. ARE UNHELPFUL	Are not comforting; are not reassuring; are not supportive
15. HURT ME	Are violent; treat me badly; are punishing
16. ARE HURT	Are pained; are injured; are wounded
17. OPPOSE ME	Are competitive; deny/block my wishes; go against me
18. ARE COOPERATIVE	Are aggreeable
19. ARE OUT OF CONTROL	Are unreliable; are not dependable; are irresponsible
20. ARE CONTROLLING	Are dominating; are intimidating; are aggressive; take charge
21. GIVE ME INDEPENDENCE	Give me autonomy; encourage self-direction
22. ARE DEPENDENT	Are influenced by me; are submissive
23. ARE INDEPENDENT	Are self-directed; are not conforming; are autonomous
24. ARE STRONG	Are superior; are responsible; are important

Table continues

TABLE 1 *(Continued)*

Category	Standard Category Components
RESPONSES FROM OTHERS	
25. ARE BAD	Are wrong; are guilty; are at fault
26. ARE STRICT	Are rigid; are stern; are severe
27. ARE ANGRY	Are irritable; are resentful; are frustrated
28. ARE ANXIOUS	Are scared; are worried; are nervous
29. ARE HAPPY	Are fun; are glad; enjoy
30. LOVES ME	Is romantically interested in me
RESPONSES OF SELF	
1. UNDERSTAND	Comprehend; realize; see accurately
2. DON'T UNDERSTAND	Am confused; am surprised; have poor self-understanding
3. FEEL ACCEPTED	Feel approved of
4. FEEL RESPECTED	Feel valued; feel admired
5. LIKE OTHERS	Am friendly
6. DISLIKE OTHERS	Hate others
7. AM OPEN	Express myself
8. AM NOT OPEN	Am inhibited; am not expressive; am distant
9. AM HELPFUL	Am supportive; try to please others; am giving
10. HURT OTHERS	Am violent; act hostile
11. OPPOSE OTHERS	Am competitive; refuse/deny others; conflict with others
12. AM CONTROLLING	Am dominating; am influential; manipulate others; am assertive; am aggressive
13. AM OUT OF CONTROL	Am irresponsible; am impulsive; am unreliable
14. AM SELF-CONTROLLED	Am responsible
15. AM INDEPENDENT	Make my own decisions; am self-directed; am autonomous
16. AM DEPENDENT	Am submissive; am passive
17. AM HELPLESS	Am incompetent; am inadequate
18. FEEL SELF-CONFIDENT	Am or feel successful; feel proud; feel self-assured
19. AM UNCERTAIN	Feel torn; am ambivalent; feel conflicted
20. FEEL DISAPPOINTED	Am not satisfied; feel displeased; feel unfulfilled
21. FEEL ANGRY	Feel resentful; feel irritated; feel frustrated
22. FEEL DEPRESSED	Feel hopeless; feel sad; feel bad
23. FEEL UNLOVED	Feel alone; feel rejected
24. FEEL JEALOUS	Feel envious
25. FEEL GUILTY	Blame myself; feel wrong; feel at fault
26. FEEL ASHAMED	Am embarrassed; feel abashed
27. FEEL ANXIOUS	Feel scared; feel worried; feel nervous
28. FEEL COMFORTABLE	Feel safe; am or feel satisfied; feel secure

TABLE 1 (*Continued*)

Category	Standard Category Components
RESPONSES OF SELF	
29. FEEL HAPPY	Feel excited; feel good; feel joy; feel elated
30. FEEL LOVED	
31. SOMATIC SYMPTOMS	Headache; rash; pain

Note. The category label is in capital letters; the lower-case labels are variants of the capitalized label.

sure the agreement between two raters on a specific CCRT formulation, we had to make sure that they used a common language, because one cannot assess traditional agreement (for example, kappa or intraclass correlation) from idiographic narrative descriptions. In the past, we resolved this problem by presenting matched and mismatched pairs of CCRTs to judges and asking them to rate the similarity of these CCRTs (e.g., Levine & Luborsky, 1981). Now such a uniform language is achieved through the creation of standard categories.

Edition 1 of the standard categories (Exhibit 1) was abstracted from the judges' CCRT ratings of the 16 participants available at that time. These patients were mainly diagnosed with depressive or anxiety disorders and were considered representative of patients who were referred for psychotherapy. The categories chosen were the most frequent in this sample of narratives. Edition 1 was used by Luborsky, Mellon, et al. (1985a); Luborsky, Crits-Christoph, and Alexander (1990); and Crits-Christoph, Cooper, and Luborsky (1988).

Six main organizational principles were followed in constructing Edition 1: (a) The categories are the ones that most frequently fit the 16 cases scored by the CCRT method; (b) the categories are readily discriminable from each other, that is, nonoverlapping; (c) the subsidiary adjectives used within each category are fairly synonymous with each other and with the category label; (d) the categories are organized logically, psychologically, and conveniently from the point of view of ease of application by the judge; (e) the order of the categories is similar within each of the three types of components (for wishes, responses from other, and responses of self); this organizational principle is aimed at easing the judges' task in finding a particular category; and (f) the words selected for each category are the same in each of the three components lists, whenever reasonable, for example, W: to reject other's *domination*; RO: *dominates*; RS: feels *dominated*.

Later, Edition 2 was created to provide judges with a more representative collection of categories than was available in Edition 1. To prepare this new edition, Crits-Christoph and Demorest (1988) reviewed the relevant literature, such as Murray's (1938) list of needs. From these categories, they created a list of 34 wishes (to which a 35th has been added), 30 responses from others, and 30 responses of self. They then included up to five, but usually three, exemplifying subcategories for each one of these standard categories (see Table 1).

Through using standard categories, we could begin comparing patients in a more reliable manner, and we could assess changes in the CCRT during treatment without needing another special judge to assess the degree of similarity between the pretreatment and posttreatment CCRTs. It was clear to us, however, that the list of standard categories had some overlapping categories. For example, one judge would categorize a patient as having the wish "to be accepted," whereas another would specify the wish as "to be respected," and still another would identify the wish as "to be loved." To deal with such overlap, we went on to examine the underlying structure of our list of standard categories by a cluster analysis of similarity judgments of the standard categories.

PROCEDURE FOR A CLUSTER-BASED CLASSIFICATION

Another goal of the present study was to reduce the list of the standard categories of Edition 2 to a more practical size. Thirty-five wishes, 30 responses from others, and 30 responses of self were hard for our judges to use conveniently and reliably. To create a fairly comprehensive but still manageable list of categories to guide the judges, each of the standard categories within each CCRT component was paired with all other standard categories. All of these pairs to be compared were written in questionnaire form. Somatic symptoms (such as response of self No. 31) were not included in this questionnaire. A 35th wish was added to the list to represent an "oedipal wish," defined as the wish to compete with somebody to get another person's affection. There were 595 pairs of comparisons for the wishes and 435 each for the responses from other and responses of self.

Nine judges were asked to rate the degree of similarity of each pair of standard categories on a scale from 1 (*not similar at all*) to 7 (*extremely similar*). To avoid tedium, the judges could spread the work over more than one sitting.

RESULTS

For each CCRT component, an intraclass correlation was computed to assess the judges' reliability. Pooled-judge intraclass coefficients for the nine judges were .80 for the wishes, .90 for the responses from other, and .86 for the responses of self. Because the reliability of these judgments was acceptable, we averaged the judges' scores.

For each CCRT component, the average similarity scores were submitted to the SPSS/PC + (1986) cluster analysis procedure using the Ward method. This method is designed to optimize the minimum variance within each cluster.

Inspection of the tree of interrelated groupings ("dendograms") obtained from the cluster analyses led us to retain eight clusters for the wishes, eight for the responses from other, and eight for the responses of self. The clusters for each CCRT component—clustered standard categories—are listed in Table 2.

DISCUSSION

This study has achieved an encompassing level of description along with a convenient brevity by the cluster analyses for each of the three components of the standard categories. We recommend these clusters primarily for research use, especially in studies involving groups, whereas we recommend the standard categories both for clinical and research use.

Wishes

The clusters of wishes consist of the wish to be independent and have individuality (Cluster 1); the wish to hurt and control others (Cluster 2); its counterpart, the wish to be controlled and hurt (Cluster 3); the wish to withdraw (Cluster 4); the wish to be close (Cluster 5); the wish to be loved and understood (Cluster 6); the wish to feel good (Cluster 7); and the wish to achieve (Cluster 8).

The clusters are not entirely nonoverlapping, however, as we wished they would be. Clusters 1 and 2 are close in their meaning because both represent different aspects of expressing and maintaining independence. Clusters 5 and 6 also have a similar meaning to each other; both entail a wish for closeness. Thus, we are still left with two pairs of clusters that might lead to ambiguities with regard to the classification of a person's specific wishes.

Our eight clusters of wishes seem to represent a fairly complete list of human motivations as they appear in accounts of interpersonal encounters. Yet certain wishes and needs are not in these clusters, probably because for the majority in our society needs for survival, such as for food and shelter, are not a frequent source of interpersonal problems or of problems leading patients into psychotherapy. Higher level motivations such as self-fulfillment (e.g., Maslow, 1970) to not make up a moderate level of inference category and therefore do not appear in our list. The wish for mastery is probably included under Cluster 8, the wish to achieve; our judges did not usually use the word *mastery*, although they used *to achieve* to explain

TABLE 2
CCRT Clustered Standard Categories: Edition 3

Clusters	Standard Category Components
WISHES, NEEDS, INTENTIONS	
1. TO ASSERT SELF AND BE INDEPENDENT	To have self-control; to be my own person; to assert myself; to be independent
2. TO OPPOSE, HURT, AND CONTROL OTHERS	To oppose others; hurt others; have control over others
3. TO BE CONTROLLED, HURT, AND NOT RESPONSIBLE	To be hurt, controlled by others; not to be responsible or obligated; to be helped; to be like others
4. TO BE DISTANT AND AVOID CONFLICTS	To avoid conficts; to not be hurt; to be distant from others
5. TO BE CLOSE AND ACCEPTING	To accept others, respect others; to be open; to have trust; to be opened up to; to be close to others
6. TO BE LOVED AND UNDERSTOOD	To be loved, respected, understood, accepted, liked
7. TO FEEL GOOD AND COMFORTABLE	To have stability; to feel comfortable; to feel happy; to feel good about myself
8. TO ACHIEVE AND HELP OTHERS	To achieve; to better myself; to help others; to be good
RESPONSES FROM OTHER	
1. STRONG	Strong, independent, happy
2. CONTROLLING	Strict, controlling
3. UPSET	Hurt, dependent, anxious, angry, out of control
4. BAD	Not trustworthy, bad
5. REJECTING AND OPPOSING	Don't trust me; don't respect me; are not understanding; rejecting; dislike me; are distant; unhelpful; oppose me; hurt me
6. HELPFUL	Are helpful, cooperative
7. LIKES ME	Loves me; respects me; likes me; gives me independence
8. UNDERSTANDING	Open, understanding, accepting
RESPONSES OF SELF	
1. HELPFUL	Am open; understand; am helpful
2. UNRECEPTIVE	Don't understand; am not open; dislike others
3. RESPECTED AND ACCEPTED	Feel comfortable, happy, loved, respected, accepted; like others
4. OPPOSE AND HURT OTHERS	Oppose others; hurt others
5. SELF-CONTROLLED AND SELF-CONFIDENT	Self-controlled, independent; self-confident, controlling
6. HELPLESS	Out of control, helpless, uncertain, dependent
7. DISAPPOINTED AND DEPRESSED	Angry, disappointed, depressed, unloved, jealous
8. ANXIOUS AND ASHAMED	Anxious, ashamed, guilty

some narratives. It is likely that the wish for mastery represents a higher level of inference and abstraction than is generally used by judges. An even higher level of abstraction is not evident in the list and not recommended; reliability is low for such categories, as exemplified by self-realization, Eros, libido, masochism, and so on.

In their study of the scaling of interpersonal problems, Horowitz and Vitkus (1986) asked participants to sort a long list of interpersonal problems into categories of problems that seemed to be semantically similar. Following a hierarchical clustering procedure, they found clusters describing issues about "intimacy, assertiveness, aggression, compliance, dependency, independence and socializing" (p. 448). Although Horowitz and Vitkus used a list of interpersonal problems as their database, the results of their cluster analysis are similar to the ones we obtained by using a database of wishes and desires. A moderate-to-high level of similarity is also found between the subscales of the Inventory of Interpersonal Problems (Horowitz, Rosenberg, Baer, Ureno, & Villasensor, 1988) and our clusters. Clearly, there is an intricate relationship between what people view as problems and what they want for themselves. For an event to be described as a problem, it must hinder the fulfillment of some wish, need, or intention. The similarities between our clusters and the subscales of the Inventory of Interpersonal Problems increase our confidence in the validity of the results of our cluster analysis, as well as in the comprehensiveness of the final list of clustered categories found in this study.

Responses From Others

The clusters of responses from others also seem to describe a fairly exhaustive range of interpersonal responses. People are viewed as or expected to be strong and independent (Cluster 1), controlling (Cluster 2), upset (Cluster 3), bad (Cluster 4), rejecting (Cluster 5), helpful (Cluster 6), liking others (Cluster 7), and understanding (Cluster 8).

Responses of Self

The clusters of the responses of self also describe a fairly wide range of personal reactions. Participants feel open and helpful (Cluster 1), unreceptive to others (Cluster 2), respected (Cluster 3), in opposition to others (Cluster 4), self-controlled and confident (Cluster 5), helpless (Cluster 6), disappointed (Cluster 7), and anxious or ashamed (Cluster 8).

CONCLUSIONS

- This latest set of standard categories is therefore recommended. Compared with tailor-made categories, Luborsky,

Barber, and Schaffler (1989) showed that the use of standard categories and clustered standard categories yielded a greater agreement among three CCRT judges when scoring relationship episodes obtained from a specimen case at intake, termination, and follow-up evaluation.

- The process of developing a classification of categories is one of progressive refinement. The present cluster study is another step in the direction of creating a comprehensive, nonredundant list of standard categories. It represents what we have already achieved, but we are continually refining the classification. We certainly share with the readers the wish that a more finished set were available, although it is to be expected that we cannot have a final and definitive list describing the various aspects of interpersonal behavior encompassed in the CCRT. Nevertheless, we continue to work toward improved lists, and we have several studies in progress dealing with this important issue.

- A note of caution about cluster analysis is in order, however. One major problem, besides the choice of which clustering method to use for a specific data set, is that the researcher must make a decision about the optimal number of clusters to describe a set of categories (for a review of these problems and others, see Aldenderfer & Blashfield, 1984). Naturally, such decision making may be biased by the theories of the investigator.

- For the classification of standard categories, there are methods other than cluster analysis. One of them is the reliance on theories of personality. Perry's (1993) classification of wishes and fears is one of these; he followed the eight stages of development proposed by Erikson (1959). In Perry's classification scheme, wishes such as "to communicate one's needs, to be protected, or to survive" are included under Erikson's first stage, "basic trust versus mistrust." Fears associated with this first stage are, for example, fears of physical harm, being alone, being dependent on others, and so on. Others have relied on a different theoretical direction based on Benjamin's (1974) Structural Analysis of Social Behavior (SASB) as an organizational principle. Two of these groups are Demorest and Crits-Christoph (1989) and Schacht, Binder, and Strupp (1984). These theory-based methods have an important contribution to make alongside the cluster methods.

4

POSITIVE VERSUS NEGATIVE CCRT PATTERNS

BRIN F. S. GRENYER AND LESTER LUBORSKY

A traditional distinction in transference patterns is between a positive transference and a negative transference. Freud (1901–1905/1953a; 1912/1958a) made that distinction, or one like it, almost from the beginning of his use of the transference concept. The routine use by clinicians of positive versus negative transference over so many years suggests that it is a useful distinction and even that it probably can be made reliably.

The general aims of this chapter are to define the positive and negative patterns of the CCRT and their reliability and validity. The specific aims are to look into the following: (a) the reliability of scoring the positive and negative dimensions; (b) the results of other studies of scoring positive and negative narratives in patients, in nonpatients, and in children; (c) the changes in positive and negative patterns over the course of psycho-

The research in this chapter was supported in part by grants from the Australian Research Council to Brin Grenyer, with further support from other sources to Lester Luborsky by grants listed in the acknowledgments section of this book. An earlier version was given at the Society for Psychotherapy Research Annual Meeting, Amelia Island, Florida, June 1996, and to the International CCRT Workshop in Ulm, Germany, in May 1995. For assistance with data collection, we thank Mary Carse, Richard Rushton, Nadia Solowij, and Kelly Schmidt.

therapy; and (d) the relation of positive and negative patterns to the outcomes of psychotherapy.

From the beginning of the CCRT method Luborsky (1977b) also distinguished between positive and negative CCRTs (as discussed in chapter 2, this volume). At the start, all CCRTs were labeled as mainly positive (+) or mainly negative (−). *Positive* means that the patient's narrative describes noninterference or an expectation of noninterference with the satisfaction of wishes or a sense of mastery about being able to deal with the wishes. *Negative* means that the patient describes interference with the satisfaction of wishes that has occurred or is expected to occur. In CCRT terms, the positive pattern is based on relationship narratives containing a wish, such as "I wish to be loved," followed by a response from other, such as "the other is affectionate," followed by a response of self, such as "I feel close." This would be a positive CCRT because the wish to be loved is satisfied. An example of a negative pattern is the following: wish: I wish to be loved; response from other: but the other person rejects me; response of self: I become frustrated. This example is a negative pattern because the wish is unsatisfied and the person feels frustrated about being rejected.

RELIABILITY OF SCORING THE POSITIVE AND NEGATIVE DIMENSIONS OF THE CCRT

The Two-Category System

The original two-category distinction in scoring consisted of the scores positive (P) and negative (N) (Luborsky, 1977b). The agreement between two judges using this distinction is high: 95% for both the responses from others and the responses of self (see chapter 9, this volume). In terms of correlations, in chapter 12 we report that the reliability in scoring the negative dimension of the response from other was .67 ($p <$ .0001) and in scoring the negative dimension of the response of self was .79 ($p < .0001$).

A neutral or middle category between positive and negative was not used for both theoretical and empirical reasons. A theoretical position stated by Freud (1912/1958a) is that transference responses must be either positive or negative; for wishes, only gratification or frustration is possible. Research results that are probably related appear to be consistent with this position: Brief exposures of pictures to participants were experienced as emotionally tinged with either positive or negative quality and not neutral quality, and these perceptions appeared seemingly automatic and instantaneous (Bargh, Chaiken, Govender, & Felicia, 1992).

A New Four-Category Positive and Negative Scale

This section on reliability is based on a scale expanded from the two-category positive versus negative system to a four-category scale in which each response from other (RO) and response of self (RS) is rated using one of the following four categories: NN = strong negative, N = moderate negative, P = moderate positive, and PP = strong positive. For research purposes, these categories correspond to scores of -2, -1 and $+1$, $+2$, respectively. Although positive and negative scores are applied only to the RO and RS components, it is important in scoring for these to be evaluated in relation to the expressed or implied wishes. This is because the RO or RS is only positive or negative depending on the success in relation to gratifying a wish.

We investigated the reliability of this new four-category scoring method by having two independent judges rate the degree of positivity or negativity for the RS and RO components across a sample of 20 patients from the Penn Psychotherapy Project. Five of the cases came from the original 10 that were classified as most improved; 5 cases came from the original 10 that were classified as least improved; and 10 cases came from the original 21 in the middle group (see Luborsky, Crits-Christoph, Mintz, & Auerbach, 1988, for a fuller description of the sample). In this way we ensured that we had a sample that covered the full range of positive and negative CCRT scoring possibilities. Transcripts from both early in therapy (Sessions 3 and 5) and late in therapy (at 90% of treatment completion) formed the database. From these sessions 386 relationship episodes (generally 10 early in therapy and 10 late) were extracted, and the CCRT was scored. Prior to the rating task, an independent judge (BG) located all scorable CCRT components to ensure that judges each scored the same thought units. The two judges were both doctoral-level psychoanalytic researchers.

Of the 20 patients, 1 was married, 2 were divorced, and the rest (85%) were single. The average age was 23 (range 18–35); there were 10 females and 10 males; and none had children. Educationally they were diverse; 3 had only finished high school, 7 were in college, 3 had completed college, 5 were engaged in getting higher degrees, and another 2 had completed a postgraduate degree. All were engaged in psychodynamic psychotherapy, with a mean duration of 48 weeks (range 27–102 weeks). There were 19 therapists, with a mean age of 35 (range 26–47). All therapists were married, 12 had children, all were psychiatrists, and 13 were psychiatric residents at the time.

We looked at the reliability of the judges' scoring of the four categories of positive and negative in two ways. First, we examined the reliability, taking as the unit of analysis the relationship episode (RE). Over 386 REs, the interrater reliability using Pearson's correlation coefficient was moderate to high. For the RO dimension, $r = .64$, $p < .0001$, and for the RS dimension, $r = .72$, $p < .0001$. Second, we looked at instances of perfect agreement of scoring. For the RO, 278 of the 386 scored REs were scored identically between judges (72%), and for the RS, 274 were scored identically (71%). We then looked at the interjudge reliability taking subjects ($N = 20$) as the unit of analysis rather than REs ($N = 386$). We calculated average positive and negative scores for each subject for each judge. The interrater reliability for the RO component was $r = .77$, $p < .001$, and for the RS, $r = .93$, $p < .001$.

PROPORTION OF POSITIVE AND NEGATIVE NARRATIVES IN CHILDREN, ADULT PATIENTS, AND NORMAL CONTROLS

A few studies have compared the distinction of positive versus negative narratives across different samples. These findings have been discussed in detail in chapter 16, this volume, but we provide a brief overview here. Narratives were obtained from 18 children who were interviewed at 3 and 5 years of age using a guided and prompted story-completion task about a doll family (Buchsbaum & Emde, 1990). The children's narratives were scored with the CCRT, and the percentages of positive and negative components were computed. At age 3, 69% of the ROs were positive, and at age 5, 71% were positive. For the RS component, 63% were positive at age 3, and 77% were positive at age 5. Thus most of the doll family narratives told by the young children contained positive responses from other people and positive responses from the self.

These findings with children are in strong contrast with those typically found in adult patients in psychotherapy. For example, in the Penn Depression Study ($N = 30$), only 21% of combined RO and RS components were positive. Similarly, among patients with major depression seen on an outpatient basis at Penn ($N = 20$) only 19% of combined RO and RS components were positive (Eckert, Luborsky, Barber, & Crits-Christoph, 1990). These results are highly similar to those found in patient reports of dreams versus waking narratives told during psychotherapy (chapter 12, this volume). It was found that in both dreams and waking narratives told late in therapy, the percentages of negative components ranged from 67% to 76% for RO components and from 65% to 80% for RS. It is interesting that the response of self in waking narratives was significantly more negative than in dreams, which might suggest the influence of striving toward wish fulfillment in dreams.

For further contrast, two studies provided data on normal nonpatient adult controls. In Ulm, Germany, 36 normal young women (mainly medical students), mean age 23.8 years (range 20–30), were asked to provide narratives about their relationships, and the resulting narratives were CCRT scored (Dahlbender et al., 1992). Thirty-seven percent of RO and 43% of RS components were positive. In another German study of normal adults (N = 30), 35% of RS components were positive (Cierpka et al., 1992).

In summary, children's narratives appear to be far more positive in both RO and RS components than those of normal adults, and narratives of psychotherapy patients are even more negative. The different conditions under which the sets of narratives were collected may partly explain the results. With the children, actual interactions were not prompted; rather, the children completed a fictitious doll family story. Some of their answers, therefore, may be heavily infused with wish fulfillment fantasies. Also, the narratives collected from the patients were told in the context of psychotherapy, where presumably patients focus on their most troublesome problems through the telling of negative and problematic relationship narratives. Contextual factors within psychotherapy also may have an influence on the magnitude of the positive versus negative dimensions in psychotherapy. For example, as shown in chapter 9, this volume, relationship episodes told about the therapist by the patient were found to be less negative than relationship episodes told about others: For the RO and RS components, 55.8% and 61.5%, respectively, were negative for the therapist relationship episodes, compared with 81.5% and 88.5%, respectively, for other relationship episodes. This suggests either that patients had difficulty telling negative relationship episodes about the therapist in the presence of the therapist or that their relationship with the therapist was in fact less negative. In spite of these possible confounds, it remains plausible that there are genuine developmental differences in the emotional quality of relationship narratives from childhood through adulthood, with adults being "sadder yet wiser" in appraisal of both others' motives and their own.

CHANGES IN POSITIVE AND NEGATIVE DIMENSIONS OVER THE COURSE OF PSYCHOTHERAPY

We were interested in the distribution of positive and negative scores for the RO and RS dimensions using the expanded scoring method. Given the high interjudge agreement, we pooled the data from the two judges. Overall, for the RO there were 10% NN (very negative), 64% N (negative), 24% P (positive), and 2% PP (very positive) scores. For the RS, there were 12% NN, 58% N, 24% P, and 6% PP scores. These results are similar to the distributions of positive and negative components found in other psychotherapy samples, as reviewed previously. In general, it seems that the bulk of CCRT narratives told by patients in psychotherapy are negative; that is, wishes and needs are often unsatisfied.

To investigate changes in the proportion of positive and negative components over the course of psychotherapy, we calculated percentages

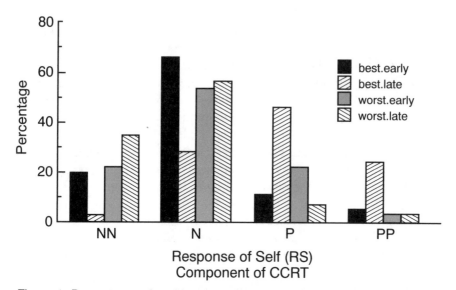

Figure 1. Percentages of positive versus negative scores for the response of self (RS) component of the CCRT for five highly improved patients (best) and five least improved patients (worst) measured early in psychotherapy (early) and late in psychotherapy (late). NN = strong negative; N = negative; P = positive; PP = strong positive.

of each component early and late in therapy. We further differentiated the data into the five most improved and the five least improved patients (based on the criteria in the Penn Psychotherapy Study of Luborsky, Crits-Christoph, et al., 1988). This was done to illustrate graphically some of the patterns of change in the percentages of the positive and negative dimensions. The results for the RS dimension appear in Figure 1 and for the RO dimension in Figure 2.

For the RS dimension it can be seen that for the five most improved patients (*best*, in Figure 1) there are large reductions in the number of negative (N and NN) components (about a 35% reduction for N) and a parallel increase in the number of positive (P and PP) components from early in therapy to late in therapy (a 35% increase for P). This is indicative of an increase in the satisfaction of wishes and needs. For the five least improved patients (*worst*, in Figure 1), the pattern is in the reverse direction: There are increases in the N component late in therapy and parallel reductions in the P component. For the least improved patients, there appear to be increases in the perception of others as blocking the gratification of wishes and overall their perception of others is very negative throughout therapy. As the CCRT judges observed, these patients seemed to be getting worse; their relationship narratives were more conflictual and negative toward the end of therapy compared with their initial level.

The pattern for the RO dimension (Figure 2) is similar to that of the RS dimension, but the changes are less striking. The most improved pa-

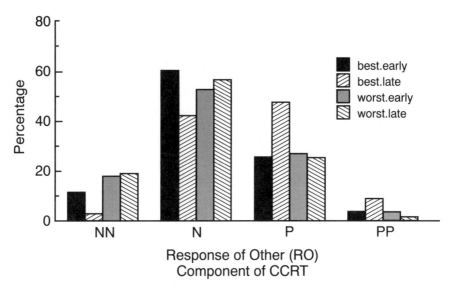

Figure 2. Percentages of positive versus negative scores for the response of other (RO) component of the CCRT for five highly improved patients (best) and five least improved patients (worst) measured early in psychotherapy (early) and late in psychotherapy (late). NN = strong negative; N = negative; P = positive; PP = strong positive.

tients again reduced their negativity and increased their positivity within relationship conflicts, and for the least improved patients, the reverse trend occurred, although only slightly. Overall, the response of other dimension did not change as much over the course of psychotherapy for either the most improved or the least improved patients.

RELATIONSHIP TO PSYCHOTHERAPY OUTCOMES

The final aim of this chapter is to investigate the relationship of the positive–negative dimension to two psychotherapy outcome measures, the Health–Sickness Rating Scale (HSRS) and the Mastery Scale. The HSRS is a commonly used outcome measure in which a 100-point scale of degrees of mental health–sickness is rated by a trained observer on the basis of data collected from a clinical interview. The Mastery Scale is a 6-point content analysis scale measuring degrees of self-control and self-understanding scored from relationship narratives told by patients in psychotherapy (Grenyer, 1994). It has high reliability and validity, and changes in self-understanding and self-control have been associated with good psychotherapy outcome as assessed by the patient, the therapist, and independent judges (see chapter 18, this volume). Table 1 presents the results of the analyses.

The RO component showed little relationship to the outcome vari-

TABLE 1
Pearson Correlations Between Positive and Negative CCRT Response
of Other (RO) and Response of Self (RS) Scores with the Health–
Sickness Rating Scale (HSRS) and Mastery Scale

Scale	RO.early	RO.late	RS.early	RS.late	RO.change	RS.change
Mastery.early	.67*	−.15	.68*	.15	−.47*	−.00
Mastery.late	.26	.35	.24	.82*	.30	.57*
HSRS.intake	.18	.45*	−.12	.38	.29	.39
HSRS.termination	.03	.47*	−.19	.64*	.47*	.46*
Mastery.change	.09	.31	.12	.70*	.38	.51*
HSRS.change	−.20	.19	.02	.49*	.32	.16

Note. Scores are for early in therapy (early), late in therapy (late), and residual change over therapy (change) (*N* = 20).
*p < .05.

ables. The RO early in therapy was related to mastery early in therapy, and changes in the RO over therapy were related to the termination score on the HSRS. In contrast, the RS component appears to be related in an important way to clinical changes. We found significant concordance between the RS components and the Mastery Scale scores both early and late in therapy. The RS late-in-therapy measure appeared to be a particularly good index of psychological health. There was a strong relationship between RS late and residual change in Mastery Scale scores (r = .70, p < .05) and residual change in the HSRS score (r = .49, p < .05). There was also a strong concordance between the RS late scores and the late-in-therapy Mastery Scale scores (r = .82, p < .05) and the HSRS termination scores (r = .64, p < .05). In addition, residual change in the RS component was significantly related to late Mastery Scale scores, termination HSRS scores, and residual change in Mastery Scale scores (r = .51, p < .05).

CONCLUSION

This study was the first to investigate the reliability and validity of the expanded scale method of scoring the positive and negative dimension of the CCRT. Some impressive results appear but they require replication with a larger sample. These are the clearest of the findings:

- Judges are able to agree very well on the scoring of the positive and negative dimensions. This seems to be due in part to the simplicity and clarity of the basic CCRT method of scoring these dimensions.
- Adult patients in therapy have very negative relationship narratives, particularly when compared with adults and with children who were not in therapy.
- The change in positive and negative dimensions from early

to late in psychotherapy typically is small, yet the change that does occur appears to be clinically meaningful.

- These findings about changes during therapy, however, relate primarily to the changes in the response of self dimension of the CCRT, which shifts in clinically meaningful ways (see Table 1). It appears from the data we have so far that the response of other dimension is only indirectly related to clinical changes. In fact we found far fewer changes overall from early to late in therapy in the percentage of positive and negative components in the response of other as compared with the response of self dimension (see Figures 1 and 2). We explain this in the following way: Psychotherapy does not eliminate all intrapsychic conflicts, so that most of the same CCRT patterns found early in therapy remain late in therapy. In other terms, the transference template is pervasive and resistant to change. This is consistent with the conclusion that what changes in psychotherapy is a person's mastery of his or her problems in the form of greater self-understanding and self-control (see chapter 22, this volume).

5

ILLUSTRATIONS OF THE CCRT SCORING GUIDE

LESTER LUBORSKY AND SCOTT FRIEDMAN

This chapter offers scored narratives to serve as guides to CCRT scoring procedures. These illustrations, which we draw on throughout the book, can be used by readers as practice cases for learning the CCRT procedures. The scoring is given for three patients' CCRTs, each engaged in a different type of dynamic therapy: Ms. Sandy Smyth in a short-term, time-limited psychodynamic psychotherapy, Mr. Edward Howard in a moderate-length psychodynamic psychotherapy, and Ms. Cathy Cunningham in a long-term psychoanalysis.

For each of the three patients, the chapter consists of (a) a clinician's brief sketch of the patient's state before and after the treatment, (b) a sample of the relationship episodes in the sessions early and late in the therapy, and (c) a sample of the CCRT scoring. The sample of scoring includes for each case, first for early and then for late sessions, the tailor-made score sheet, the tailor-made summary, and the standard category summary. Of all this, *the most useful materials for learning the CCRT method are the scored text of the relationship episodes and the summary of the scoring of the standard categories.* These procedures are especially suited for research uses; the clinical uses are discussed in chapter 19, this volume.

MS. SMYTH: SHORT-TERM PSYCHODYNAMIC
PSYCHOTHERAPY

The example from Ms. Smyth's sessions illustrates the application of the CCRT to a 16-session time-limited psychotherapy. The mode of treatment was supportive–expressive psychotherapy as guided by the recommendations of a manual for the treatment of major depression (Luborsky, Mark, Hole, Popp, Goldsmith, & Cacciola, 1995), which is a specific version of the general manual for supportive–expressive therapy (Luborsky, 1984).

Clinical Evaluation

Initial

At the time of the evaluation, Ms. Smyth was a 32-year-old single woman. The pretreatment diagnostic evaluation arrived at a *DSM-IV* diagnosis of alcohol dependence (303.90), sustained full remission; major depressive disorder, recurrent, moderate severity (296.32); and dysthymic disorder (300.4). She did not meet Axis II personality disorder criteria. The patient was a recovering alcoholic who had been abstinent for 3 years. She came for treatment for depression (with a high initial Beck Depression Inventory score of 25) after having flunked out of a job training program. The therapy began inauspiciously when she showed up half an hour late and said she was unable to schedule a next appointment. The therapist's reaction was one of anger, which the therapist did not express; however, she used her perception of her own experience to recognize the feeling that the patient was setting up in her. When the patient said she was afraid of "sabotaging" herself, the therapist did say she thought the patient was correct to be concerned.

Termination

Ms. Smyth continued to have difficulty in keeping appointments. Nevertheless, she benefited remarkably well and surprised the therapist by how well she did: At termination her Beck Depression Inventory score was 6. The therapist concluded in her termination evaluation, "I would not have thought someone with such severe depression and who already was making full use of self-help therapeutic groups [such as Alcoholics Anonymous] could have resolved her depression without the use of psychopharmacotherapy."

In the termination interview, Ms. Smyth stated that she was generally feeling "good" and that "everything's a lot better." She had been seeing a man for 5 months (since shortly after she began therapy) with whom she was pleased. She had also set up a stable living arrangement with a female roommate and was working regularly in a clerical job she was not pleased with. She still complained of premenstrual symptoms—tension and a headachy feeling. Recently her period had been late; she was concerned about being pregnant and believed she might have had a miscarriage. She generally seemed in far less turmoil and was less pessimistic and much more confident and hopeful. She gave the impression that she could take care of herself, in comparison with the time of the initial evaluation when she had a desperate, disorganized quality.

Six-Month Follow-up

Ms. Smyth continued *not* to feel depressed to any significant extent. Her Beck Depression Inventory score was 9. She has continued working full-time, although still at the same kind of work. Ms. Smyth has found out she is pregnant by the man she is involved with. She plans to be married, but the man is waffling on commitment. The patient is angry, anxious, and worried about the situation but feels she can handle whatever happens and will have the baby. At first news of her pregnancy, she developed a probable generalized anxiety disorder and missed some work. She and her boyfriend entered weekly couples therapy at that time and they continue in it. She has also maintained involvement with AA. She continued to live with the roommate and maintained contact with her family and a few close friends. Although this has been a difficult time because of her pregnancy and the ambivalent boyfriend, she expressed a resolve that she will get by, whatever it takes. Even with these stressors, although she was initially frantic for a short while, she is now basically okay and is not taking any medications for depression or anxiety.

CCRT Data and Results

In scoring each session the judge first reads the transcript, then scores the relationship episodes by placing notations in the left margin of the transcript (as an option, the scorer may also transfer the scores for each relationship episode to the CCRT score sheet; see Table 1), and then summarizes these on the CCRT summary sheet (see Tables 2 and 3). This juxtaposition of an unguided clinical sketch, next to a systematically guided clinical–quantitative description achieved by the CCRT, makes clearer what is contributed by the CCRT to the formulation of the central relationship pattern (Exhibit 1).

To illustrate the CCRT method, a set of relationship episodes from Sessions 3 and 5 are reproduced in a subsequent section, together with their scoring in the left margin. Only five scored relationship episodes are presented, to keep the example brief. For further simplification, the scoring written in the left margin is only by one experienced CCRT judge.

To specify precisely what is scored, the text is divided into single thought units (marked off by slashes); the marking of thought units can

EXHIBIT 1
SYMBOLS FOR CCRT SCORING TO BE APPLIED TO THE RELATIONSHIP EPISODES

//	Slashes mark the beginning and end of a thought unit.
W, RO, or RS P or N	Wish, response from other, or response of self, positive or negative (P or N) when appropriate, are to be scored in the left margin at the beginning of the thought unit.
---	Interrupted or broken-off speech.
xxx	Inaudible word.
xxx--	Inaudible text longer than one word.
. . .	Section of text omitted.
(20, 17)	Numbers in parentheses refer to the standard category numbers (see chapter 3, this volume). The first number indicates the best-fitting category; the second is for the next-best-fitting category. A line under a number means the episode is an exact fit to a category on the list; a question mark means a questionable fit. (Note that some thought units are not scored because they do not fit any scorable category or they have already been given a score of the same type.)

be done rapidly, as described by Benjamin (1986b). Those parts of relationship episodes that are to be scored are connected with the scores by an arrow.

Ms. Smyth's CCRT data and results include (a) the scored relationship episodes, (b) the score sheet for each relationship episode by tailormade categories (Exhibit 1), (c) the summary for all relationship episodes by tailor-made categories (Table 2), and (d) the summary for all relationship episodes by the standard category system (Table 3).

The main CCRT for the five relationship episodes that can be read from the tailor-made CCRT score sheet summary in Table 1 follows. The number in parentheses after each component is the number of relationship episodes out of the five scored in which the component is found:

> Wish: I want to end nonsupportive relationships (3) and to have support and caring (3).
> Response from other: But the other person—others include her exemployers, her brother, her boyfriend, and her father—is rejecting (4) and unsupportive (2).
> Response of self: I then feel angry (3) and feel bad (depressed) (2).

The CCRT from the standard category system using only the bestfitting standard category (Table 3) is similar to the one from the tailormade system:

> Wish: I want to oppose others (2) (to end nonsupportive relationships) and to be helped (3) (nurtured, supported, and given things I need).

Response from other: But the the person is rejecting (3), unhelpful (3), and not trustworthy (2).
Response of self: I then feel angry (2) and depressed (2) and ashamed (2).

It is noteworthy that by both the tailor-made and the standard category systems there are also a few positive responses from the other person, such as "others are helpful" (2). These may imply that there is for this patient, apparent in the early phase of treatment, a potential for positive relationships.

Ms. Smyth: CCRT Scoring of Relationship Episodes

Session 3

RE 2: *Ex-employers*, Completeness Rating 4.0

Scoring	Text
✔[1]NRO: Rejecting (4, 14)	//RO And then the other job, was, ah, they didn't even give
NRO: Rejecting (4, 14)	me a chance.//RO I was supposed to work on this computer and the computer wasn't hooked up and they said, well you don't
✔NRO: Give no help (14, 19?)	have to work on it.//RO We're replacing you with somebody
NRO: Rejecting (4, 14)	else.//RO So I was replaced with
✔NRS: Anger (21, 20?)	somebody else.//RS It really
✔NRS: Have no job, nothing (20?, 17)	pissed me off//RS [pause] 'cause I gave up another job to get this job and I ended up with nothing at all, no unemploy-
NRS: Horrible state (20?, 17?)	ment, no nothing.//RS It's hor-
✔W: I want job (help) (13?, 3?)	rible.//W I call 'em every
NRO: Rejecting (4, 14)	day,//RO but they always say we don't have anything.// It's just
✔NRS: Helpless (17, 19)	terrible.//RS Because I don't
✔NRS: Discouraged (22, 23?)	know what I'm going to do.//RS [pause] It's really discourag-
NRO: Rejecting (4, 15)	ing.//RO It's so hard to get out and—get the door slammed in my face constantly. [pause]//

---

[1]Checks mean that the items were used in the tallies in the summaries of the standard category.

RE 3: *Brother and His Wife*, Completeness Rating 4.5

✔W: To get out of bad rel. (13, 23) _____ //,^{W} Anyway, I want to move out of Bob and Jane's (brother and sister-in-law) house as soon as

✔NRO: Rejecting (4, 6?) _____ possible.//^{RO} Treated like a

✔NRS: Feel bad about self (26?, 17?) _____ second-rate citizen there.//,^{RS} It's not very good for my self-esteem.// Like they're both addicts and they have the per-

✔W: To be in good rel. (3, 2) _____ sonality of addicts.//,^{W} [pause] I guess . . . I, I much rather be around sober people.//. . . Yeah. The old tapes start running//

✔NRS: Feel bad (22?, 20?) _____ and it's just real bad.//,^{RS} I mean I start thinking negatively as soon as I'm around them, 'cause

✔NRO: Dishonest (8, 15) _____ they're both negative.//,^{RO} They're

NRO: Putting her down (8, 4) _____ dishonest.//,^{RO} They're acting like they're doing me a big favor, but I'm paying half the rent there, for their apartment,// and I have this tiny little room, no closet, and their junk's in the room, and uh I have to work

✔NRS: Anger (21, 6) _____ around their lives.//,^{RS} [pause] So, I ah just can't stand them.

RE 4: *Boyfriend*, Completeness Rating 5.0

✔(W): To stop bad rel. (18, 23) _____ //,^{W} Yeah, I've, and I've stopped

✔NRO: Rejecting (4, 14) _____ speaking to that married guy//,^{RO} 'cause he got to be a real ass-

✔PRS: Assertive about stopping _____ hole.//,^{RS} I mean I'm not taking

rejecting rel. (12, 11?) any shit from anybody this

✔NRO: Stopped talking to me (12?, 14) _ year—for the rest of my life//,^{RO} and, uh, he just sort of stopped

NRO: Didn't contact me (12, 4) _____ talking to me and, uh,//,^{RO} he didn't contact me, //he didn't even—where was I going to move to this week?// He didn't

✔NRS: Anger (21, 6) _____ contact me//,^{RS} so screw him,//,^{RS}

✔PRS: I stop contact with him (15, 23) I'm not going to contact him,

NRS: Anger (21, 6) _____ not at all, either . . . //,^{RS} it just

✔PRS: Reject other (6, 21) _____ makes me mad.//,^{RS} I really don't want anything at all to do

↙(W): Not to be lonely again (11, 14)

↙NRS: Lonely, crying (23?, 22?)

W: Not to feel isolated (11, 14?)

NRS: Isolated (23, 20)

NRS: Anger (21, 6)

↙PRO: Other friends gave support
(13, 3)

↙NRO: Gave no support (14, 4)

NRO: Gave no support (4, 14)

with him.//$_W$ Never again will I//$_{RS}$—Christmas Eve I spent alone in church crying my eyes out 'cause it was an intensely lonely feeling.//$_W$ and I said no way am I ever gonna feel that bad again. No way.//$_{RS}$ I'm isolated from my friends and family because of this guy I wanted—this married guy.// It's just a conflict between honesty and dishonesty.//$_{RS}$ . . . I just, ah, he pissed me off.//$_{RO}$ All my other friends gave me all kinds of moral support, even some financial support for this horrible dilemma I'm in right now.//$_{RO}$ He didn't do shit. . . .//$_{RO}$ He didn't buy me a Christmas present or a card or a birthday. . . .//

Session 5

RE 5: Father, Completeness Rating 3.0

↙NRO: Asshole (25?, 4?)

↙NRO: Rejecting, nonsupportive
(14, 4)

NRO: Rejecting, nonsupportive,
nonloving (14, 4)

NRO: Noncaring (14, 4)

//$_{RO}$ I mean he's acting just like an asshole.//I mean, to him I think my grandmother was always a pain in the ass.//$_{RO}$ That's how he treated his children too.// That's why he's just a total asshole. A couple of years ago she was sick and she had a sister that lived out in California.//$_{RO}$ He wanted to ship her out there so he wouldn't have to deal with her and all./ It was horrible.// And that's what—and soon after that when I found out how he treated his mother, I realized how he [sniff] he felt about me, and the rest of my sisters.//$_{RO}$ Like he didn't give a shit.// And I xxx my alcoholic father

✔PRS: Awareness of his nature (1?, 6?)

✔W: To be given to (13, 8?)

NRO: Nonsupportive (14?, 4?)

✔NRS: Shame about her asking for money (26, 25)

✔W: To end nonsupportive relationship (23, 18)

✔PRS: See his true nature (1?, 6?)

✔NRO: He is an asshole, although he denies it (8?, 2?)

after that.//RS It was just a matter of a couple of weeks. [pause] You know, I saw what he's really like// went to xxx to see him at Christmas time, New Year's//W and I went hoping to get money,//RO [Laughing quietly] xxx I didn't get any.... [laughing] And I needed it at the time.//RS I felt sort of like a whore but I needed money.//W ... [pause] I just want him out of my life.// He's just xxx. At one time xxx and denied that he was a bastard and an asshole//RS but then I saw right through his face what he really is.// I didn't want to know that I had a father that was a big asshole.//RO I found out that he was.// Just devastated me. [pause]// You know—definitely a dysfunctional family.//

RE 6: *Boss*, Completeness Rating 2.5

✔PRO: Nice people (13?, 9?)

✔PRS: Feel lucky (29?, 28?)

✔PRO: Spends time with me (3?, 9?)
PRS: It was nice (29, 28?)

P: //RO But these people I work for are very, very nice// xxx [pause]//RS Yeah, I feel lucky to have a boss like my boss.// xxx- Yeah I mean I went . . .
T: . . .
P: //and I was down in town with her xxx her husband and me.// Went to see a trade show this week//RO and he drove and we were out together.//RS It was nice.//xxx . . . There's a lot of them.
T: They included you with them?
P: Yeah.
T: And you just started working there?

PRO: Supports her (<u>13</u>, 9?)	P: Yeah.//^{RO} She followed me last week. My first week on the job when the car broke down, to make sure my car started.// She followed me down there
PRO: Helps even at a sacrifice (13, 11?)	xxx to my house//^{RO} which is like an hour out of her way.// T: Ha!
PRO: Concern (13, 3?)	P: //^{RO} And she was concerned about, like, you know, about
✔(W): Wish for concern and caring (<u>13</u>, 11)	me,//^(W) how I was feeling about my grandmother dying.// She
✔PRO: Nice lady (11?, 1?)	let me leave early.//[pause]//^{RO}
PRS: Feel blessed (29?, 28?)	Very nice lady.//^{RS} I feel blessed [pause] I don't know [pause] see I've had some bad experiences which ah [whispering] xxx . . . [long, inaudible]. Yeah, that will be fun. I've never been to Memphis.

MR. EDWARD HOWARD: PSYCHOANALYTIC PSYCHOTHERAPY

Clinical Evaluation

Initial

Mr. Howard was a 20-year-old man, born and raised in the same area in which he now was attending college. He had completed part of his third year of college when he came for psychotherapy to a practitioner in his hometown with complaints about these problems: anxiety, guilt, sporadic pain in the penis, difficulty in dealing with a new girlfriend, and resentment of his parents. In growing up he never felt close to his father but was very close to his mother; he felt the need to comfort and take care of her. In his relationships he recurrently felt he could not achieve the closeness and responsiveness from others that he needed.

He was expected to have a good outcome with the help of psychotherapy. He seemed to relate well to doctors; he was warm and open. He appeared to be well motivated and able to learn. Also, his conflicts were seen as perhaps no more than an exacerbation of normal adolescent conflicts, chiefly intense guilt over sex.

On the other hand, his thoughts about wanting to be like an exalted spiritual leader were somewhat confused: "I'd like to have what he had, with-

TABLE 1
CCRT Score Sheet for Each Relationship Episode, Tailor-Made System

Patient: *Ms. Sandy Smyth*   Date: *1/26/89*

Sessions *3 and 5*   Judge: *LL*

Number of REs: *5*

RE No. Person:	Wish, Need, Intention	Response From Others	Response of Self
RE 2 Ex-employers	To have job (help)	Rejecting	
		Not helpful	Angry
			Have nothing, no job
			Feel horrible; FEEL BAD[a]
			Feel helpless
			Discouraged
RE 3 Brother and wife	To get out of a nonsupportive relationship and be in a good one	Rejecting	I feel bad about myself
		Put me down	Angry
		Dishonest	
RE 4 Boyfriend	To end nonsupportive relationship	Rejecting	
	To not be lonely or hurt	Broke contact with me	Angry
		Not helpful/ supportive	I break contact with him
		PRO Others are supportive	Lonely, isolated
			Sad
			PRS: Assertive about ending relationship, rejects other Won't be lonely

TABLE 1 (*Continued*)

Patient: Ms. Sandy Smyth   Date: 1/26/89

Sessions 3 and 5   Judge: LL

Number of REs: 5

RE No. Person:	Wish, Need, Intention	Response From Others	Response of Self
RE 5 Father	To get money	Rejecting	Aware of his nature
	To end nonsupportive relationship	Nonsupportive	Ashamed of asking for money
		Nonloving	
		Noncaring	
		Dishonest	
		Asshole	
		Denies that he's an asshole	
RE 6 Boss	To have concern and caring	PROs:	PRSs:
		Nice	Feel lucky
		Spends time with me	It was nice
		Supportive	Feel blessed
		Helpful, even at a sacrifice	
		Concerned	
		Giving	

ᵃAdditions from Step 1 are put in captial letters, as noted in chapter 2. Capital letters indicate the name of the standard category.

out the preliminary steps." By "what he had," he may have meant the leader's spiritual power. This statement may simply be an expression of the patient's desire to be a great person, or it may reflect significant disturbance.

iw-1.1It was not clear whether there was prognostic significance in the fact that his guilt over sex took the form of a conversion symptom—pain in his penis—rather than simply the experience of guilt. The initial evaluation suggested only that later failure to improve would indicate either more significant disturbance, or that his underlying guilt was too strong, particularly his guilt-inducing attachment to his mother, or that both of these were true.

TABLE 2
CCRT Score Sheet, Tailor-Made System: Summary Across All Relationship Episodes

Patient: Ms. Smyth *Date: 1/26/89*

Sessions 3 and 5 *Judge: LL*

Number of REs: 5

Wish, Need, Intention (RE No.)	Response From Others (RE No.)	Response of Self (RE No.)
	Negative	*Negative*
W1: To end nonsupportive relationship (3, 4, 5)	Rejecting (2, 3, 4, 5)	Angry (2, 3, 4)
W1: To have support and caring (2, 5, 6)	Are not helpful or supportive (2, 4, 5)	Feel bad (2, 3)
W2: To not be lonely (4)	Dishonest (3, 5)	Feel helpless (2)
W3: To have job (2)	Puts me down (3)	Feel discouraged (2)
W3: To get money (5)	Won't contact me (4)	Have nothing, no job (2)
	Nonloving (5)	Lonely, isolated (4)
	Noncaring (5)	I break contact (4)
	Asshole (5)	Sad (4)
	Denies he's an asshole (5)	Aware of other's nature (5)
		Ashamed (5)
	Positive	*Positive*
	Others are supportive (4, 6)	Assertive (about ending nonsupportive relations) (4)
	Nice (6)	Feel lucky (6)
	Spends time with me (6)	It was nice (6)
	Helpful, even at a sacrifice (6)	Feel blessed (6)
	Concerned (6)	
	Giving (6)	

Termination (After About 90 Sessions)

The initial 2 months of treatment revealed that Mr. Howard had difficulties in knowing how to be assertive, be less passive, establish an identity, become separate from his family, and relate better to his peers, especially women. Although there was no evidence of an active thought

TABLE 3
CCRT Summary: Standard Categories

Patient: Ms. Smyth

Sessions 3 and 5   *Judge: LL*

Number of REs: 5 (In RE number 2, 3, 4, 5, 6)

Edition 2 Category Number	*RE No.*	*Frequency Across REs (first choices only)*
Wishes		
13: TO BE HELPED	2, 5, 6	3
18: TO OPPOSE OTHERS	3, 4	2
3: TO BE RESPECTED	3	1
11: TO BE CLOSE TO OTHERS	4	1
23: TO BE INDEPENDENT	5	1
Negative responses from others		
4: ARE REJECTING	2, 3, 4	3
14: ARE UNHELPFUL	2, 4, 5	3
8: ARE NOT TRUSTWORTHY	3, 5	2
12: ARE DISTANT	4	1
25: ARE BAD	5	1
Positive responses from others		
13: ARE HELPFUL	4, 6	2
3: ARE ACCEPTING	6	1
11: ARE OPEN	6	1
Negative responses of self		
21: FEEL ANGRY	2, 3, 4	3
22: FEEL DEPRESSED	2, 3	2
26: FEEL ASHAMED	3, 5	2
17: AM HELPLESS	2	1
20: FEEL DISAPPOINTED	2	1
23: FEEL UNLOVED	4	1
Positive responses of self		
1: UNDERSTAND	5	1
6: DISLIKE OTHERS	4	1
12: AM CONTROLLING	4	1
15: AM INDEPENDENT	4	1
29: FEEL HAPPY	6	1

disorder, before therapy the patient described "panicky feelings" about not being able to keep himself "in control" and the sense that he was so weak that he would need to be a spiritual leader in order to obtain any of his desires. This was part of the concern about the possibility of psychotic deterioration.

After his return from a holiday visit with his parents, the patient appeared to be remarkably more stable. He had not used the medication that was offered because he felt that it was not necessary. During the spring he examined his fear of closeness in relationships; he also continued a relationship with a freshman and experienced his first sexual intercourse with her. Through his relationship with his new girlfriend and with his therapist, he began to reexperience many of his oedipal conflicts.

During the summer he began more actively to examine his ambivalence in relationships. He experienced increased anxiety and described events that suggested ideas of reference. However, when he visited his parents during the summer, he found himself able to respond in a much more satisfactory and assertive fashion than previously and felt encouraged by that.

In the fall the patient returned to school; he and his girlfriend made arrangements to live together. As the anticipated problems developed, the patient began to be able to evaluate the transference relationship in the triangle created between him, his girlfriend, and his therapist. He seemed to understand more clearly the mechanism of his "need to be better" and found himself better able to maintain relationships.

He responded to the therapist's departure and the impending separation with a reawakening of his earlier feelings of needing to be all-powerful in order to survive and to satisfy his desires. But by the time of the final appointment, the patient had become better able to understand much of his current difficulty in terms of his transference and in the light of the way he had learned to respond to his situation at home during his earlier years. He entertained (ambivalently) the idea of marriage to his current girlfriend and made plans for his education and training.

CCRT Data and Results

The presentation of illustrations of the data and results for Mr. Howard include in this sequence:

Early: The relationship episodes from Session 3, the score sheets for each relationship episode by tailor-made categories (see Table 4), the summary score sheet for all relationship episodes by tailor-made categories (see Table 5), and the summary score sheet for all relationship episodes by standard categories (see Table 6).

Late: The same types of data are presented for the late period of treatment, including four relationship episodes (plus three dreams) selected from Sessions 82 and 83 and the score sheets (see Tables 7, 8, and 9).

Early CCRT: The CCRT for the six relationship episodes early in treatment in the illustration here is from Table 5 (session 3) based on the tailor-made system (The number that follows each component is the frequency of the component among the six rlationship episodes): I want to be close and receive affection (3) (and not experience the loss of relationships [2]). But the other person rejects my wish (3). I respond by feeling resentment (2) and self-blame (2). A similar pattern appears in Table 6 using more exact standard categories.

Late: The CCRT for the four relationship episodes late in treatment

TABLE 4
CCRT Score Sheet for Each Relationship Episode, Tailor-Made System

Patient: Mr. Howard   *Date: 1/26/89*

Session 3   *Judge: LL*

RE No. Person:	Wish, Need, Intention	Response From Others	Response of Self
RE 1 Mother	To get sexual information	Disagrees with my view	Frustration
	To get close to Mother	*PRO (past)* Explains	Shame/SELF-BLAME[a]
		Rejects	
RE 2 Mother	To be physically close	Disagrees with my view	
		PRO (past) Closeness	
		Rejection	
		Chooses other instead of me	
RE 3 Therapist		No rapport	Unresponsive, distant
	To be close, to have rapport		Headache
			Tense
			Lack of response
RE 4 Mother	To be close, have affection	Blames	*PRS (past)* Closeness, affection
			Felt alone
RE 5 Girlfriend	To not suffer loss of relationship	Cuts off relationship	Resentment
		Rejects	Fear of wish for attachment
			Self blame/SHAME
RE 6 Mother	To not be cut off from girlfriend	Hurts me	Resentment
		Assumes I love my mother like a girl	

[a]Additions from Step 1' are in capital letters.

TABLE 5
CCRT Score Sheet, Tailor-Made System: Summary Across All Relationship Episodes

Patient: Mr. Howard   Date: 1/26/89

Session 3   Judge: LL

Number of REs: 6 (In RE number 1, 2, 3, 4, 5, 6)

Wish, Need, Intention (RE No.)	Response from Others (RE No.) Negative	Response of Self (RE No.) Negative
To be close, have affection (1, 2, 4)	Rejects (1, 2, 5)	Resentment (5, 6)
To not lose relationship, be cut off (5, 6)	Disagrees with my view (1, 2)	Self-blame/shame (1, 5)
To get sexual information (1)	Chooses other instead of me (2)	Frustration (1)
	No rapport (3)	Unresponsive, distant (3)
	Blames (4)	Headache, tense (3)
	Cuts off relationship (5)	Lack of support, help (3)
	Hurts me (6)	Feel alone (4)
	Assumes I love mother like a girl (6)	Fear of wish for attachment (5)
	Positive	*Positive*
	(past) Explains things to me (1)	(past) Closeness, affection (4)
	(past) Closeness (2)	

(Tables 7, 8, 9) was the following: I want to be close (3) and to share with them (2). But the other person is stronger (4) and shows behavior that justifies distrust and does not give what I want. I am self-critical (2) and distrustful of others (2). Note that most of the pattern is recognizably similar late in treatment to what it was early in treatment. However, the patient shows greater signs of recognition of his own pattern, for example, in RE 3: "I realize I distrust everybody." The scores from the dreams are not counted with the RE scores, but we see that some of their CCRT components overlap with the most frequent components from the relationship episodes. (The overlap of CCRTs for dreams and narratives is shown more systematically in chapter 12, this volume.)

TABLE 6
CCRT Summary: Standard Categories

Patient: Mr. Howard

Session 3　　　　　　　　　　　　　　　　　　　　　　　　*Judge: LL*

Number of REs: 6 (In RE number 1, 2, 3, 4, 5, 6)

Edition 2 Category Number:	RE No.	Frequency Across REs (first choices only)
Wishes		
11: TO BE CLOSE TO OTHERS	1, 2, 4, 5, 6	5
8: TO BE OPENED UP TO	1	1
Negative responses from others		
4: ARE REJECTING	1, 2, 4, 5	4
8: ARE NOT TRUSTWORTHY	1, 2	2
2: ARE NOT UNDERSTANDING	6	1
12: ARE DISTANT	3	1
15: HURT ME	6	1
Positive responses from others		
11: ARE OPEN	1, 2	2
Negative responses of self		
21: FEEL ANGRY	1, 5, 6	3
8: AM NOT OPEN	3	1
19: AM UNCERTAIN	5	1
23: FEEL UNLOVED	4	1
25: FEEL GUILTY	5	1
26: FEEL ASHAMED	1	1
27: FEEL ANXIOUS	3	1
31: SOMATIC SYMPTOMS	3	1
Positive responses of self		
30: FEEL LOVED	4	1

Mr. Howard: CCRT Scoring of Relationship Episodes (Condensed)

　　Session 3

RE 1: Mother

✔NRO: Disagrees with his view (8, 14)

✔W: To get sexual information (8?, 11?)

✔(W): To get close to M. (11?, 8)

✔PRO: (past) Explains (11, 13)

✔NRO: Rejects (4, 12)

✔NRS: Frustration (21, 20?)

NRS: Shame (26, 25)

//This might have been a dream.//ᴿᴼ Mother says it didn't happen.//ᵂ,⁽ᵂ⁾ Up until we moved, when I had questions about sex,//ᴿᴼ mother would explain.// When we moved to ___, one day I asked and //ᴿᴼ she said, sorry we can't talk about that. You're getting to that age.//ᴿˢ Bothered me 'cause my young sister, age 9 or 10, laughed.//

TABLE 7
CCRT Score Sheet for Each Relationship Episode, Tailor-Made System

Patient: Mr. Howard   Date: 1/26/89

Sessions 82 and 83   Judge: LL

RE No. Person:	Wish, Need, Intention	Response From Others	Response of Self
RE 1 Therapist	To be close	T forces me to give up girlfriend	I must give up girlfriend
			Resentment
Dream A Trainers	To be with you, on your side; TO BE CLOSE	Stronger	Not good enough, rejected
		Rejects	
RE 2 Friend	To trust, to share	Could screw me (expected)	Am open, trusting
	To be close		
Dream B Store	To be fed	Too much ice cream	Overfed
			Sick
			Repelled
Dream C Store Owner	To buy something; TO SPEND MONEY	Shamed by ladies	
	To expose self sexually to woman	Pursued by man	
RE 3 Therapist	To have a trusting relationship; TO SHARE	Shows behavior that justifies distrust	Distrust
			Self-blame
RE 4 Father	To get money	Does not give money	Distrust

RE 2: Mother

✔NRO: Disagrees with his view (8, 14)____ //ᴿᴼAnother incident mother
✔PRO: (past) Closeness (11?, 13?)____ said never happened.//ᴿᴼ,⁽ᵂ⁾
✔(W): To be physically close (11, 8?)‾ We, brother and I before sister
was born . . . when it was really
cold, would sleep with par-
✔NRO: Rejection, choose someone____ ents.//ᴿᴼ Parents took my
else (4, 12) brother in bed with them and
they wouldn't take me.

TABLE 8
CCRT Score Sheet for Each Relationship Episode, Tailor-Made System: Summary Across All Relationship Episodes

Patient: Mr. Howard　　　　　　　　　　　　　*Date: 1/26/89*

Sessions 82 and 83　　　　　　　　　　　　　*Judge: LL*

Number of REs: 4

Number of Dreams: 3 (In RE number 1, 2, 3, 4)

Wish, Need, Intention (RE No.)	Response from Others (RE No.)	Response of Self (RE No.)
	Negative	*Negative*
To be close (1, 2, A)	Stronger, more powerful (1, A,[a] 2, C)	Distrust (3, 4)
To get things (B, C, 4)	Shows behavior that justifies distrust (3)	Self-critical and self-blame (3, A)
To trust, to share (2, 3)	Does not give me what I want (4)	I must give up what I want (1)
To expose self sexually to woman	Too much/excessive (B)	Overfed (B)(C)
	Shames me (C)	Sick (B)
	Rejects me (A)	Repelled (B)
		Resentment (1)
		Positive
		Am open, trusting (2)

[a]Capital letters refer to the dreams.

RE 3: Therapist

　　　　　　　　　　　　　　　　T: What's happening now?

✔NRS: Unresponsive, distant (<u>8</u>,16)　　P: //^{RS} I feel generally unre-

✔NRS: Headache(<u>31</u>?)　　　　　　　sponsive.//^{RS} I'm getting a head-

✔NRS: Tense (<u>27</u>, 19?)　　　　　　　ache,//^{RS} tense,//^{RS} thinking all

NRS: Lack of response on his part　　week about relating all this stuff

　(<u>8</u>, 16?)　　　　　　　　　　　to what I was 10 years ago [sigh]

　　　　　　　　　　　　　　　　and not getting any—I mean,

　　　　　　　　　　　　　　　　nothing comes out//. . . like

　　　　　　　　　　　　　　　　groups of guys who have embar-

✔NRO: No rapport (<u>12</u>, 14?)　　　　rassing moments of silence.//^{RO}

　　　　　　　　　　　　　　　　It proves no perfect rapport

NRS: Lack of response on his part　　exists.//^{RS} I feel blank.

　(<u>8</u>, 16?)

TABLE 9
CCRT Summary: Standard Categories

Patient: Mr. Howard

Sessions 82 and 83   *Judge: LL*

Number of REs: 7 (In RE number 1, A, 2, B, C, 3, 4)

Edition 2 Category Number:	RE No.	Frequency Across REs (first choices only)
Wishes		
13: TO BE HELPED	B,[a] C, 4	3
6: TO HAVE TRUST	2, 3	2
11: TO BE CLOSE TO OTHERS	1, A	2
33: TO BE LOVED	C	1
Negative responses from others		
4: ARE REJECTING	A, C	2
8: ARE NOT TRUSTWORTHY	2, 3	2
14: ARE UNHELPFUL	4	1
15: HURT ME	C	1
24: ARE INDEPENDENT	1	1
Positive responses from others		
24: ARE INDEPENDENT	A	1
Negative responses of self		
6: DISLIKE OTHERS	3	1
17: AM HELPLESS	A	1
20: FEEL DISAPPOINTED	4	1
21: FEEL ANGRY	1	1
25: FEEL GUILTY	3	1
31: SOMATIC SYMPTOMS	B	1
Positive responses of self		
7: AM OPEN	2	1

[a]Capital letters refer to the dreams.

RE 4: *Mother*

✔(W): To be close, have affection (11, 7)

✔PRS: (past) Closeness, affection (30, 5)

✔NRO: Blames (4, 27)

✔NRS: Felt alone (23, 20?)

//(W),RS Before I went to school, I always used to kiss my mother.// I'm not sure it was a big thing, but it was a big thing when it stopped.//RO She made a big thing about how I didn't want to kiss her anymore.//RS I was suddenly out in the cold again.

RE 5: Girlfriend

✔NRS: Resentment (<u>21</u>, 20?)

✔(W): To not suffer loss of rel. (11?, 33?)

✔NRO: Cuts off rel. (4, 14?)

✔NRS: Fear of wish for attachment (19?, 27?)

NRO: Rejects (4?, 15)

✔NRS: Blames self (<u>25</u>, 17?)

//^{RS} I'm beginning to feel a lot of resentment to E [girlfriend].//$^{(W)}$ I went with her for a couple of years.//^{RO} It's just been severed.//^{RS} I'm fearful of seeing her and feeling something for her.//^{RO} She just doesn't give a damn.//^{RS} Bothers me I used to be so screwed up about her.//

RE 6: Mother

✔NRS: Resentment (<u>21</u>, 11?)

✔(W): To not be cut off from girlfriend (<u>11</u>, 14?)

✔NRO: Hurts P. (<u>15</u>, 4)

✔NRO: Assumes P. loves girl like his mother—hurtful idea (2, 15)

//^{RS} One thing that started my resentment against my parents.//$^{(W)}$ I told her about E [girlfriend] that everything was cut off.// I said E's not writing and it upset me.//^{RO} She said, "Well, I'm sure about you and you aren't sure about her."// That really cut me up//^{RO} because of the rel . . . relationship she . . . she . . . a . . . assumes between us is like between E and me.//

Mr. Howard: CCRT Scoring of Relationship Episodes (Condensed) Sessions 82 and 83

RE 1: Therapist (Session 82)

✔(W): To be close (<u>11</u>, 17?)

✔NRS: Resentment (<u>21</u>, ?)

✔NRO: Forces me to give up girlfriend STRONGER, MORE POWERFUL (24, 17?)

//$^{(W)}$ Things going well but I feel I have to give up my girlfriend.//^{RS} I resent you//^{RO} because I have to give up things to get close to you.//

Dream A: Trainers[1]

✔(W): To be close to trainer (therapist?) (11?, 27?)

✔PRO: Stronger (<u>24</u>, ?)

✔NRO: Rejects (<u>4</u>, 17?)

✔NRS: Not good enough; SELF-CRITICAL (17, 20)

//$^{(W)}$ War. I enlisted as soldier on our side.//^{RO} The trainers of the soldiers had superior strength.//^{RO} You [therapist] will smile.//^{RS} I only got into the entertainment troops.//

---

[1]Dreams are included here to illustrate their consistency with relationship episodes (see chapter 12, this volume).

RE 2: Boyfriend

✔W: To trust, to share (6, 8)_____ //^{W} In preschool, I wanted to

✔PRS: Am open, trusting (7, 5?)_____ trust someone.//^{RS} I confided in

✔NRO [expected]: Could screw me ____ [boyfriend]//^{RO} but he could
   (8, 15) screw me.

Dream B: Store (Session 83)

✔(W): To be fed (<u>13</u>, 11)_____ //$^{(W)}$ I was going into the candy
   store with other kids.// The

✔NRS: Sick (31, 26?)_____ place is floating in ice cream.//^{RS}
   I got sick and repelled by it.

Dream C: Store Owner

✔(W): To buy something (<u>13</u>?, ?)_____ //$^{(W)}$ I was going into a store.//$^{(W)}$

✔(W): To expose self (<u>33</u>?, ?) I was naked.//^{RO} Two young

✔NRO: Shamed by ladies (<u>4</u>, 17) ladies said, "Tsk, tsk."//^{RO} I had

✔NRO: Pursued by man (<u>15</u>, 20?) to escape from the proprietor.//

RE 3: Therapist

✔(W): To have trusting relationship_____ //$^{(W),RS}$ I felt bad because of dis-
   (6, 3) trusting our relationship.//^{RO} I

✔NRS: Self-blame (<u>25</u>, 26) saw an article that makes me

✔NRO: Untrustworthy (<u>8</u>, 17?) distrust you.//^{RS} I realize that I

✔NRS: Distrust (6?, 19?) distrust everybody.//

RE 4: Father

✔W: To get money (13?, 8?)_____ //^{W} I wrote to Father for

✔NRO: Does not give me (14, 4)_____ money.//^{RO} It is not all right

✔NRS: Distrust (20?, ?)_____ with him to send me it.//^{RS} I
   lose trust.//

MS. CATHY CUNNINGHAM: PSYCHOANALYSIS

The clinical sketches for Ms. Cunningham before and after psychoanalysis draw largely on the material by Weiss, Sampson, and the Mount
Zion Psychotherapy Research Group (1986); the CCRT analyses draw on
our own examination of the sessions.

Clinical Evaluation

Initial

Ms. Cunningham was an attractive 30-year-old social worker in a
Catholic agency. She had been married for 4 years to a successful busi-

nessman. Her main symptom was sexual inhibition. She did not enjoy sex; she did not have orgasms and held back from having intercourse. Her inability to relax and enjoy herself affected other aspects of her life as well. The second symptom was her self-criticalness. The third was her passivity; she was afraid of "simply being a nonentity" and wished to be able to be assertive.

Her father was a successful businessman, and her mother was a house-wife. The patient was the second of four children. She had an older sister, a younger sister, and a younger brother. The father tyrannized the mother with his occasional fits of temper, and the mother took his abuse passively. The parents displayed little affection toward each other and appeared to be joyless and puritanical.

In the following episode, which occurred when the patient was 6, the parents showed their usual style of relating to her. The patient's sister had hit her in the stomach. She had gone weeping and complaining to her mother. When she could not get her mother's attention, she became frus-trated and hit her mother in the stomach. Her mother made no attempt to defend herself. She doubled over in pain, wept, and went to her room. When the father heard what the daughter had done, he became enraged; he beat her and threw her into a closet. The girl was horrified at the father's loss of control, and she believed for a short time her father had wanted to kill her. Not long after, she became enraged at her younger brother and wanted to kill him.

It is of interest to note the formulations about central relationship conflicts in the early sessions that were done independently and with dif-ferent emphases (from each other and from ours) by two research groups (Weiss et al., 1986):

By a clinical group. Ms. Cunningham's difficulties came after the birth of her brother when she was 6. She felt her parents, especially her father, valued her brother more than her. She assumed this was because the younger brother had a penis and she did not. Therefore, her primary unconscious wish was shown in envy of men and by aggressively withholding admiration and sexual response or criticizing and attacking them.

By a Mt. Zion research group. Ms. Cunningham's problems came not from unconscious envy but from unconscious guilt. She saw her parents as fragile and vulnerable. She believed the parents would be damaged if she held ideas or values different from theirs or disagreed with them or led an independent life that was less burdened and less joyless than theirs. She unconsciously felt superior to them. She protected herself from hurting them by making herself weak and helpless. (Evidence from the Mt. Zion research group's central relation pattern measure, the plan diagnosis sketched in chapter 17, this volume, favored this formulation.)

Termination (After About 1,300 Sessions)

The initial symptoms were markedly improved by the end of treatment. In fact, they had gradually improved throughout the period of treatment.

CCRT Data and Results

We present here a sample of the relationship episodes (condensed) for Ms. Cunningham for an early session (Session 5) and for a late session (Session 1,028). Session results are provided to illustrate the degree of agreement between independent judges that can be achieved for the re-

TABLE 10
CCRT Score Sheet for Each Relationship Episode, Tailor-Made System

Patient: Ms. Cunningham			Date: 1/26/89
Session 5			Judge: LL
RE No. Person	Wish, Need, Intention	Response From Others	Response of Self
RE 1 Asst.	To have the assistant to myself; TAKE WHAT I WANT[a]	Prefers the other person	Annoyed
RE 3 Husband	To get approval and direction; WANT REASSURANCE	Doesn't give what I want	Angry
			Funny mood
RE 4 Boys	To get students to obey; to dominate; be in control	Stay together, go against my wish	Undercontrol
		DOESN'T GIVE WHAT I WANT	Annoyed
			Upset
RE 5 Therapist	Want reassurance	Not reassuring	
RE 7 Professor	To assert my impulse to admire the man		Undercontrol
	TO HAVE SELF-CONTROL		Embarrassed
	To have what man has		

[a]Additions from Step 1' are in capital letters.

lationship episodes for Session 5 by tailor-made scores (see Tables 10 & 11); Table 12 does the same by standard categories. The two judges show moderate agreement, especially for the most frequent wishes, responses from others, and responses of self. As we explained in chapter 2, this volume, the tailor-made system is harder to cope with for showing reliability, even though the tailor-made categories more specifically fit the particular patient.

We used the scored case illustration with five relationship episodes from Session 5; one can see in the tailor-made CCRT summary score sheet (Table 11) that the CCRT is as follows: I wish to be in control (2). I also wish for reassurance (2). But the other person doesn't give what I want (2). I respond to becoming angry (3) and I show poor control of myself (undercontrol) (2). Table 12 by the more exact standard categories is similar. (This formulation is not the same as either of the two groups' formulations given by Weiss et al., 1986; however, it is more congruent with the Mt. Zion research group's because of its emphasis on conflicts about her wish to become more independent.)

TABLE 11
CCRT Score Sheet, Tailor-Made System: Summary Across All
Relationship Episodes

Patient: Ms. Cunningham   *Date: 1/26/89*

Session 5   *Judge: LL*

Number of REs: 5 (In RE number 1, 3, 4, 5, 7)

Wish, Need, Intention (RE No.)	Response from Other (RE No.)	Response of Self (RE No.)
	Negative	*Negative*
To be in control of self and others (4, 7)	Doesn't give what I want (3, 4)	Angry, annoyed (1, 3, 4)
To take what I want (1)	Prefers the other person (1)	Undercontrol (4, 7)
Want reassurance (3, 5)	Not reassuring (5)	
To assert my impulse to admire the man (7)		Embarrassed (7)
To have what man has (7)		Funny mood (3)
		Upset (4)

TABLE 12
CCRT Summary: Standard Categories

Patient: Ms. Cunningham

Session 5   *Judge: LL*

Number of REs: 5 (In RE number 1, 3, 4, 5, 7)

Edition 2 Category Number:	*RE No.*	*Frequency Across REs* (first choices only)
Wishes		
2: TO BE ACCEPTED	3, 5	2
19: TO HAVE CONTROL OVER OTHERS	4, 7	2
27: TO BE LIKE OTHERS	7	1
35: TO COMPETE WITH SOMEONE FOR ANOTHER PERSON'S AFFECTION	1	1
Negative responses from others		
2: ARE NOT UNDERSTANDING	3	1
6: DON'T RESPECT ME	1	1
14: ARE UNHELPFUL	5	1
25: ARE BAD	4	1
Negative responses of self		
21: FEEL ANGRY	1, 3, 4	3
13: AM OUT OF CONTROL	4, 7	2
17: AM HELPLESS	3	1
19: AM UNCERTAIN	4	1
26: FEEL ASHAMED	7	1

For the late session (1,028) with six relationship episodes, the CCRT is similar but somewhat changed (see Table 13 & 14): I wish to dominate the other person and get my way (3) and to control myself (2). I also which to be close and feel loving. The other person becomes angered. I am inclined to withdraw. The more exact standard category summary (Table 15) is especially similar in the wish to control (dominate) others.

In the late session there is a somewhat greater inclination to be close and feel loving (as is also pointed out by Weiss et al., 1986). Otherwise the wishes show considerable consistency from the early to the late session, even in this very long therapy (a finding that is confirmed by the studies of pervasiveness discussed in chapter 9, this volume). However, Ms. Cunningham is more able to achieve a positive response from others; her anger is less pervasive; and her undercontrol is less evident.

TABLE 13
CCRT Score Sheet for Each Relationship Episode, Tailor-Made System

Patient: Ms. Cunningham			Date: 12/26/89
Session 1,028			Judge: LL

RE No. Person	Wish, Need, Intention	Response From Others	Response of Self
RE 1	To rectify not getting bill		
	INCREASE CONTROL		
RE 2 Self	To lose weight		Feel fat and ugly
	To make myself be in control of weight		
RE 3 Asst.	To make the other more confident	Loving feeling (PRO) Depressed (NRO)	
	To be assertively thera- peutic like T.		Drawing back
	To be close		
RE 4	To make the other angry	Wants to make love	
	To dominate the other	Angry	Feel loving (PRS)
RE 5 Self	To arrange things so I can cook what I want most		Feel better (PRS)
			Feel tense
	To establish control over self		
RE 6	To insist on getting my way and have a baby by T.		
	To have father		
	To have my way		

Ms. Cunningham: CCRT Scoring of Relationship Episodes (Condensed)

Session 5

RE 1: *Assistant*
✔NRS: Annoyed (21, 6) _____ //^{RS} I am annoyed by her.//^{W} I
✔W: Want her for myself (35, 19) don't want to share her//^{RO}
✔NRO: Might prefer other (6?, 4?) because she might prefer the
other supervisor to me.//

TABLE 14
CCRT Score Sheet, Tailor-Made System: Summary Across All Relationship Episodes

Patient: Ms. Cunningham		Date: 1/26/89
Session 1,028		Judge: LL
Number of REs: 6		

Wish, Need, Intention (RE No.)	Response From Others (RE No.)	Response of Self (RE No.)
	Negative	Negative
To dominate the other; get my way (1, 4, 6)	Angry (4) Depressed (1)	Withdrawal (3)
To control myself and others (2, 5)		
To be close/feel loving (3)		Feel tense (5)
To rectify not getting bill (1)		Feel fat and ugly (2)
To lose weight (2)		
To make other more confident (3)		
To be assertively therapeutic like T. (3)		
To make other angry (4)		
To arrange things so I can cook what I want most (5)		
To have father (6)		
To have baby by T. (6)		
	Positive	Positive
	Loving feeling (3)	
	Wants to make love (4)	Feel loving (4)
		Feel better (5)

RE 3: *Husband*

✔NRS: Funny mood (17?, 19?) _____ //^RS I got home in a funny mood about what I'd done with the
✔W: Wanted approval (2, 20) _____ boys (in RE 4).//^W I wanted his
✔NRO: No approval (2, 6?) _____ approval or direction.//^RO he
✔NRS: Anger (21, 20?) _____ didn't//^RS so I got furious.

TABLE 15
CCRT Summary: Standard Categories

Patient: Ms. Cunningham

Session 1028   *Judge: LL*

Number of REs: 6 (In RE number 1, 2, 3, 4, 5, 6)

Edition 2 Category Number	RE No.	Frequency Across REs (first choices only)[a]
Wishes		
19: TO HAVE CONTROL OVER OTHERS	1, 4, 6	3
21: TO HAVE SELF-CONTROL	2, 5	2
12: TO HELP OTHERS	3	1
16: TO HURT OTHERS	4	1
23: TO BE INDEPENDENT	1	1
25: TO BETTER MYSELF	5	1
Negative responses from others		
28: ARE ANXIOUS	3	1
Positive responses from others		
30: LOVES ME	3, 4	2
Negative responses of self		
8: AM NOT OPEN	3	1
26: FEEL ASHAMED	2	1
27: FEEL ANXIOUS	5	1
Positive responses of self		
5: LIKE OTHERS	4	1
29: FEEL HAPPY	5	1

[a]In this tabulation, only the first choice of a standard category is listed.

RE 4: Boys and parents

✔NRS: Upset (19, 13)   //^{RS} I was upset.//^{RO} Two boys in
✔NRO: Not pay attention to her   the group stick together rather
  (25?, 17)   than mix.//$^{(W)}$ I'm trying to sep-
✔(W): To get control of them (19, 22?) arate them.//^{RS} I'm annoyed.//^{RS}
✔NRS: Annoyed (<u>21</u>, 20?)   I spoke to one parent — I
✔NRS: Under control (<u>13</u>, 17) hadn't intended to — but then
                          I couldn't stop.// I tried to con-
                          trol myself.//

RE 5: Therapist

                          T: You didn't express wanting
                          reassurance here yesterday.
✔W: To get reassurance (2, 13)   P: //^{W,RO} I won't get reassurance
✔NRO: Won't be given (<u>14</u>, 6)   here.//^{W} I want to be reassured
W: Wish for reassurance (2, 13)   you're listening.//

RE 7: Professor
✔(W): To admire what man has
   (27?, 22?)
(W): Wish to have what the man has
   (27?, 19?)
✔(W): TO HAVE SELF-CONTROL
   (<u>19</u>, 34)
✔NRS: Embarrassed (<u>26</u>, 25)
✔NRS: Undercontrol (<u>13</u>, 17)

//I noticed his tie was nubby, coarse-woven.//$^{(W)}$ I reached out and held it and said "this is a wonderful texture."//$^{(W),RS}$ I was horrified that I had done this.

Ms. Cunningham: CCRT Scoring of Relationship Episodes (Condensed)

   Session 1,208

RE 1: Therapist
✔W: To rectify not getting bill
   (23?, 26?)
✔(W): INCREASED CONTROL
   (19?, 21?)

//$^{W,(W)}$ I was thinking I should mention it first thing. I don't recall getting a bill last month.//

RE 2: Self
✔(W): To lose weight (21, 25?)
✔NRS: Feel fat and ugly (26, 13?)

//$^{(W)}$ I must have put weight on near the end of last week.//^{RS} I really felt fat and ugly today.//

RE 3: Assistant
✔NRO: Depressed (28?, ?)

//^{RO}She was depressed.// It can't work out with the guy she's dating// and she can't close it off.//$^{W,(W)}$ I was saying things to make her feel more confident// and she said "Oh, you've helped me so much"//^{RO} and "I love you."//^{RS} I could feel myself withdraw.

✔W: To make her more confident
   (12, 7?)
(W): To be therapeutic like T (12, 22?)
✔PRO: Loves me (30?, 9)
✔NRS: Withdraw (<u>8</u>, 19)

RE 4: Husband
✔PRO: Wish to make love (30, 11?)
✔W: Make him angry (<u>16</u>, 18)
✔(W): Dominate, have control over
   other (19, 28?)
✔PRS: Feel loving (5?, 29?)

//^{RO} It's like when husband wanted to make love//^{W} I would first have to get him angry at me//^{RS} then I would feel loving.//

RE 5: Self

✔PRS: Feel better (29?, 15?)_____

✔W: To cook what I like (25?, 29?)_____
✔NRS: Feel tense (27, 19?)_____
✔(W): To establish control over_____
    self (<u>21</u>, 22)

//I was putting recipes in order.//.^{RS} This time my response was different.// Before I went through whatever order the pile of recipes was in.//.^{W} Now it's ones I've done, favorites.//.^{RS} I feel tense.//.$^{(W)}$ Will I be able to throw away what I won't use?//

RE 6: Therapist

✔(W): To have my way (19, 34?)_____

W: To have my wish from father (19?)_____
(W): To have my wish from therapist
    (19?, ?)

T: You want to be pregnant and you want your father's child or my child and nothing else will do.
P: $^{(W)}$ I just discussed something like that with the assistant about "one element that's missing" with husband.//.$^{W,(W)}$ I'm holding on to my wish with father.//

CONCLUSIONS

- This chapter provided illustrations to accompany the guide to scoring in chapter 2; these should help in learning the CCRT method.
- Early and late CCRTs were scored for three cases in three kinds of psychotherapies: brief time-limited psychotherapy, middle-range open-ended psychoanalytic psychotherapy, and long-term psychoanalysis. The CCRT method was suitable and equally applicable to each of these different therapies.
- Within each therapy, the early versus late comparisons showed consistency of the CCRT, even over the long time period of the psychoanalysis, as well as some changes related to the patient's improvement. These trends are discussed in more detail in later chapters.

6

THE RELIABILITY OF THE CCRT MEASURE: RESULTS FROM EIGHT SAMPLES

LESTER LUBORSKY AND LOUIS DIGUER

It is time for an updated summary of reliability studies of the Core Conflictual Relationship Theme method. It is essential that the many CCRT researchers and educators know the degree to which the judges can agree. Since the first edition of this book (Luborsky & Crits-Christoph, 1990), 150 ongoing studies and 55 published articles have been included in the *partial* list in the *CCRT Newsletter* (Luborsky, Kächele, & Dahl-bender, 1997). The eight samples for which usable and available reliability studies are reported in terms of weighted kappas are reviewed here in terms of the level of agreement of judges on the selection of the narratives and the agreement of independent judges on the CCRT scoring.

The research reported in this chapter was partially supported by Research Scientist Award (NIDA) DA 00168-23A and NIDA Grant 5418 DA 07085 (to Lester Luborsky), by NIMH Clinical Research Center Grant P50 MH45178 and Coordinating Center Grant U18-DA 07090 (to Paul Crits-Christoph), and by Quebec FCAR Research Grant 95-NC-1277 (to Louis Diguer). We thank Robert DeRubeis and Carol Popp for helpful reviews of this chapter.

AGREEMENT ON THE SELECTION OF RELATIONSHIP EPISODES FROM SESSIONS

The RE judge's first task before scoring the CCRT is to locate the relationship episodes that patients commonly tell during psychotherapy sessions and to identify the main other person within each episode. These judges also rate each relationship episode for completeness on a 1-to-5 scale. Only relationship episodes with a mean rating by two judges of at least 2.5 are used for CCRT scoring. Ten relationship episodes for each patient are the usual basis for scoring the CCRT, and these 10 are usually all the relationship episodes in the two early sessions: Sessions 3 and 5. If 10 relationship episodes are not found in the two sessions, a third session is used; usually it is Session 4 or 6.

Reliabilities are assessed on three basic types of agreement for each narration about each relationship episode: (a) the completeness of each episode on a 1-to-5 scale, (b) the choice of the main other person in each episode, and (c) the location of the episode in the session by noting its beginning and end point. The results for these three aspects are reported here briefly but in more detail by Crits-Christoph, Luborsky, Dahl, Popp, Mellon, and Mark (1988) and Crits-Christoph, Luborsky, Popp, Mellon, and Mark (1990) on the basis of a sample of 111 relationship episodes scored by two judges.

Completeness of Each Relationship Episode

The agreement of the judges on completeness was satisfactory: The pooled-judge agreement in intraclass correlation was .68 ($p < .001$); the per-judge intraclass correlation was .51. However, when faced with episodes of very low completeness, such as a brief reference to another person, the judges tended not to give a score. Thus, there was a significant restriction of range for these completeness ratings.

Selection of the Main Other Person in Each RE

The choice of the main other person with whom the patient was interacting in the RE was made with considerable agreement. This study involved relationship episodes of acceptable completeness with a mean judge's rating of 2.5 or better on the 5-point scale. Of 80 episodes, 97% had the same other person identified by both judges, although for 8% of these cases the judges used different labels but were referring to the same other person. In only 3% of the cases was a different other person identified by the two judges, usually when several other persons were equally alluded to in the relationship episode.

Location of the Relationship Episode

The third type of agreement on the location of the relationship episode in the transcript was also moderately good. The complete relationship episode averaged 47.3 lines of text. The two RE-selection judges differed by an average of only 4.8 lines at the beginning of an episode but 7.9 lines at the end of an episode; it was apparently harder to agree about the end point of an episode than about the beginning of an episode. For the beginnings of episodes, the judges were within 7 lines of each other 85% of the time; for the end of relationship episodes, the judges were within 7 lines 70% of the time. Bond et al. (1987) reported similar findings using a somewhat different method.

AGREEMENT ON THE CCRT

To begin at the beginning of the stream of agreement studies, we first note three preliminary studies; then, in the body of this chapter, we describe the eight usable samples of patients in which we could compute kappas for the agreement of the CCRT judges. Most of these studies relied on training procedures for the CCRT judges that are described at the end of chapter 2, this volume.

The Earliest Study of CCRT Reliability

The inaugural study of the CCRT (Luborsky, 1976, 1977b) showed moderate interjudge agreement, but because it was done with only a few patients, the results are not given here.

Agreement on the CCRT for Matched Versus Mismatched Cases

A subsequent agreement study (Levine & Luborsky, 1981) was also based on a small sample: 16 graduate psychology student judges who individually scored the CCRT for one patient. The scoring of each of these judges was compared with the composite scoring of four research judges; agreement was good, with an average correlation of .88. In addition, agreement was demonstrated by the ingenious method of "mismatched cases," that is, a comparison between cases in which the components to be compared were drawn from the *same case* (showing high agreement) compared with a comparison in which the components were purposely drawn from a *mismatched case* (showing low agreement).

Agreement on the CCRT for One Patient

Another carefully done study of reliability (Guitar-Amsterdamer, Stahli, Schneider, & Berger, 1988) used only one patient with a sample of relationship episodes from four sessions. The method is a variation on Levine and Luborsky's (1981) study. The main result of interest for a review of reliability is that the weighted kappas for agreement judges in this study were not as good as they were in the study by Levine and Luborsky (1981) even though the procedures have much in common in terms of method.

From this point onward, we review the main studies constituting nine samples, eight of which contained kappas, that are summarized in Table 1 as Samples B through I.

Sample A: Agreement on the CCRT by Three Independent Judges for 8 Patients

This study (Luborsky, Crits-Christoph, & Mellon, 1986), although also based on a small sample (8 patients), used standard reliability method. Two well-trained judges compared the similarity of CCRT formulations of three CCRT judges in terms of whether their formulations were basically similar or basically different. The agreement between these two judges was high (96%): The three CCRT judges arrived at similar formulations across the 8 cases. Specifically, on the wish component, the three CCRT judges had similar formulations 75% of the time (6 out of the 8 cases); two of the three judges had similar formulations 100% of the time. For the negative responses from other, in 63% of the cases the three judges arrived at similar formulations, whereas two of the three judges arrived at similar formulations 88% of the time. For the negative responses of self, the three judges came to similar formulations 38% of the time, whereas two of the three reached similar formulations 88% of the time.

Sample B: The First Large-Scale Study of Interjudge Agreement on the CCRT

For examining the reliability of the application of CCRT scoring to 35 cases, two psychodynamically oriented clinicians served as CCRT judges (Crits-Christoph, Luborsky, et al., 1988). Only those narratives (relationship episodes) were included that reached or surpassed the minimum acceptable completeness rating of 2.5 by the mean rating of the RE-selection judges. We consider this preselection of the relationship episodes to be a reasonable hurdle; we were interested in applying the CCRT only to narratives that were at least moderately complete because the themes might be more easily scored in more complete narratives.

The agreement procedure on the standard CCRT categories relied on the independent CCRT judges and on Cohen's weighted kappa (Cohen, 1968). The kappa is defined simply as the proportion of agreement after chance agreement is removed. According to Cohen (1968), it is often necessary to weight the agreement to make it more precise. The rationale is that certain disagreements are less important than others and should be given a value somewhere between 1 (perfect agreement) and 0 (perfect disagreement). In scoring matches between judges, the highest weight (1.0) was given for full agreement, that is, when both CCRT judges listed the same wish, response from other, or response of self as the most frequent across the 10 relationship episodes; a lower weight of .66 was given when the highest frequency of a component of one CCRT judge matched the second highest frequency of the same component of the other CCRT judge; an even lower weight of .33 was given when the match was with the second highest frequency of each CCRT judge.

Landis and Koch (1970) provided useful standards on ranges for evaluating the degree of agreement using kappa: 0 to .39 = poor; .4 to .74 = fair to good; .75 to 1.00 = excellent. Our results show a range of agreement from fair to good in terms of weighted kappa: The wish and negative response of self components were .61, and the negative response from other component was .70 ($n = 35$, $p < .001$).

Samples C and D: A Comparison of the CCRT in Dreams Versus Narratives

We reported on a sample including 13 adult patients in psychoanalysis (Popp, Luborsky, & Crits-Christoph, 1990; Popp et al., 1996). For each patient we studied an average of 14.5 narratives from early and late phases of therapy and an average of 13.0 dreams from early and late phases.

To compare the two pairs of judges' agreements on the CCRT standard category clusters, we used the following system: We noted for each pair of judges (the pair for dreams and the pair for narratives) the most frequent first choice and the most frequent second choice wish, response from other, and response of self. To determine the closeness of a match between judges, we gave the following weights: a weight of 1.0 when the match was based on agreement between the first-choice CCRT component of Judge 1 and the first-choice CCRT component of Judge 2, a weight of .66 when the first-choice CCRT component of Judge 1 matched the second-choice CCRT component of Judge 2, and a weight of .33 when the match was based on agreement between the second-choice CCRT components of the two judges.

The results, seen in Table 1, showed weighted kappas for dreams ranging from .58 to .83. These weighted kappas showed fair-to-excellent agreement, according to the convention established by Landis and Koch (1970) noted earlier. Table 1 also shows that the kappas for the wishes in

TABLE 1
Summary of Eight Samples for Reliabilities of CCRT Components

Sample	Type of Sample	Type of Relationship Episodes	Reliability	
			Kappa, Weighted	%
A. Luborsky et al. (1986)	8 adult patients	Therapy sessions		W: 100%[a] RO: 88% RS: 88%
B. Crits-Christoph, Luborsky, et al. (1988)	35 adult patients	Therapy sessions	W: kw = .61 RO: kw = .70 RS: kw = .61	
C. Popp et al. (1996)	13 adult patients	Therapy sessions	W: kw = .67 RO: kw = .74 RS: kw = .75	
D. Popp et al. (1996)		Dreams	W: kw = .58 RO: kw = .70 RS: kw = .83	
E. Barber et al. (1995)	19 adult patients	Therapy sessions	W: kw = .81 RO: kw = .64 RS: kw = .73	W: 94% RO: 100% RS: 88%
F. Barber et al. (1995)		RAPs	W: kw = .68 RO: kw = .60 RS: kw = .65	W: 84% RO: 100% RS: 89%

Study	Sample	Type of material	Results
G. Luborsky, Luborsky, et al. (1995)	18 normal children at age 3 and 5	Stories[b]	W: 70% RO: 100% RS: 90%
H. Waldinger (1997a)	40 young adults (20 normals and 20 patients)	Peer relationship narratives[c]	W: kw = .33 RO: kw = .69 RS: kw = .60 W: kw = .37[d] RO: kw = .69 RS: kw = .76
I. Lefebvre et al. (1996)	50 adult patients	RAPs	W: kw = .71[e] RO: kw = .71 RS: kw = .71
		Averaged results:	W: kw = .60 RO: kw = .68 RS: kw = .71
			% agreement W: 87% RO: 97% RS: 89%

Note. W = wish; RO = response from other; RS = response of self. % = percentage of agreement; kw = weighted Cohen's kappa; RAP = Relationship Anecdote Paradigm.

[a]Agreement of two judges.
[b]Narratives that appear to combine accounts of imaginary events with real events.
[c]Examples of relationship events, taken from peer relationship interviews, not from formal RAP interviews.
[d]Averaged weighted kappas for four judges.
[e]Averaged weighted kappas for three judges.

both narratives and dreams were somewhat less than the kappas for response from other and response of self. These kappas also suggested a new observation: that the level of agreement of two judges in scoring the CCRT is about as good for the dreams as it is for the narratives (dreams average kappa = .70; narratives average kappa = .72).

Samples E and F: A Comparison of the CCRT for Session Narratives Versus Relationship Anecdote Paradigm Narratives

The comparison in another study (Barber, Luborsky, Crits-Christoph, & Diguer, 1995) was between two forms of narratives: those that appear spontaneously in psychotherapy sessions and those that appear in the Relationship Anecdote Paradigm (RAP) interview (Luborsky, 1990b) after a request to tell narratives about relationships with others. We therefore carried out two separate reliability studies, one for the session narratives and one for the RAP narratives.

Reliability of the CCRT From Psychotherapy Sessions (Sample E)

The CCRTs were rated by two independent judges for 19 patients. The percentage of agreement between the two judges on the clustered standard categories was 94% for wishes, 100% for responses from other and 88% for responses of self. The corresponding weighted kappas were .81, .64, and .73. It is notable and may be meaningful that the percentages of agreement and weighted kappas for the therapy sessions were higher than for the RAPs.

Reliability of the CCRT from RAP Narratives (Sample F)

The narratives in the 19 patients' RAP interviews were rated by two other independent judges. The percentage of agreement between the two judges on the clustered standard categories was 84% for wishes, 100% for responses from others (ROs), and 89% for responses of self (RSs). The corresponding weighted kappas were .68, .60, and .65. Weighted kappas were used to allow for different degrees of agreement: A weight of 1.0 was used if exact agreement was found on the most frequent clustered standard categories, a weight of .66 was used if the components were second highest for one set versus highest frequency for the other set, and a weight of .33 was given for agreement between two sets that were both next to the highest in frequency. The kappas were in the fair-to-good range according to Landis and Koch (1970). The percentage of agreement is also given (Table 1) to demonstrate that it would be difficult to find much higher kappas, especially in the ROs. Part of the basis for the high percentage of agreement, but only fair kappas, is the narrow range of the CCRT components for these patients.

Sample G: A Comparison of the CCRTs of Children From Age 3 to Age 5

Each of the 18 children in another study (Luborsky, Luborsky, et al., 1995) told 10 videotaped stories at age 3 and again at age 5. The experimenter started each story by offering, as an initial stimulus, a story-stem about a puppet family in which an upsetting event occurred, such as the loss of the key to the family car. The experimenter then conducted an inquiry to stimulate the telling of a story about what would happen next after the event in the story-stem.

Percentage of Agreement Between Two Judges

We used the narratives from 10 of the 3-year-olds that had been rated by the two judges. The judges completely agreed with each other on the wishes of 7 of the 10 children, on the responses from other of 10 of the 10 children, and on the responses of self of 9 of the 10 children. Agreement was defined as a match between the two judges in identifying the same cluster of each child with the highest average sum of standard categories.

Weighted Kappa Agreement

The weighted kappa was based on the assignment of 1.0 to instances in which the first choice was a match; partial matches were assigned a .5. The weighted kappas for each CCRT component were wishes, .33; responses from other, .69; responses of self .60. The lower kappa for the wishes may have reflected the very low variability of wish clusters.

Sample H: A Comparison of Adolescents at Age 14 and at Age 18 on the Basis of RAP Narratives

In a recent study (Waldinger, 1997a), the CCRT was applied to the Early Adult Close Peer Relationship Interview given to 40 persons at age 24 (20 male, 20 female). Twenty participants had had psychiatric care, and 20 had never had this experience. This semistructured interview, developed by Shultz, Hauser, and Allen (1990), asks participants to describe in depth their two closest relationships, one a platonic and one a romantic relationship. Transcripts of these interviews were coded for relationship episodes, and the CCRT was extracted from them by four independent judges. The averaged weighted kappas across the four judges showed evidence for the good reliability of the CCRT. W: kw (weighted Cohen's kappa) = .37; RO: kw = .69; RS: kw = .76.

Sample I: The Core Conflictual Relationship Themes of Borderline Personality Disorder

The aims of another study (Lefebvre, Diguer, Morissette, Rousseau, & Normandin, 1996) were to examine (a) whether the CCRT can be reliably applied to transcripts of patients with borderline personality disorder and (b) whether the CCRTs from this sample differ from those of patients with other disorders.

Twenty patients (6 female, 14 male) were included in the study. All presented with either an adjustment disorder or a mood or anxiety disorder using *DSM-III-R* criteria. Six of them met five *DSM-III-R* borderline personality disorder criteria and four met four criteria; the other 10 patients had no Axis II diagnosis. All patients were evaluated by three psychologists and three graduate students using the SCID for Axis I and the SCID II for Axis II (American Psychiatric Association, 1990). The patients were asked to tell 10 narratives involving incidents or events about themselves in relation to another person, following the RAP interview method (Luborsky, 1990b). Weighted Cohen's kappas showed high reliability among the three judges, who scored the transcripts independently: W: kw = .72; RO: kw = .61; RS: kw = .76. The results show that CCRT can indeed be reliably applied to narratives of patients with borderline personality disorder.

An additional study (Zander et al., 1995) is noted just because it is a reliability study of the CCRT. However, it is not included among the samples reviewed here because it has some variations in procedure that may explain why its level of reliability in applying the CCRT scoring categories is lower than in the other studies. The study is also difficult to summarize because only *ranges* of kappa were presented but not means or medians. It reported two blocks of data. In Study 1 the video-presentation kappas ranged from .44 to .58, whereas in the transcript presentation the kappas ranged from .38 to .47. In the second study the video presentations ranged from .14 to .52 and the transcript presentation from .35 to .48. One factor that may have contributed to the lower reliabilities is the high number of RAP narratives that the authors found were "not accepted for coding." For this to happen in a RAP interview implies that the RAP interviewer did not instruct the participants sufficiently on how to present reasonably complete narratives; if this had been done, the participants would have complied and told complete narratives most of the time, as is typically the case with RAP narratives. It also seems that the authors did not compute the usual weighted kappas. The net contribution of Zander et al. (1995) is the demonstration that (a) their video scoring and transcript scoring gave somewhat similar reliabilities and (b) not all CCRT reliability studies demonstrate the usual level of reliability in terms of kappas that is found in the more typically conducted studies reported in this chapter.

CONCLUSIONS

- Completeness of relationship episodes, the basic unit of analysis, can be reliably judged, as previously shown (Crits-Christoph, Luborsky, et al., 1988). Likewise, the main other person and the location of the relationship episode are both reliably judged.

- The findings on reliability of scoring the CCRT by the percentage agreement method show high agreement, although this method is not as precise as the weighted kappa method. For four samples, the means were W: 87%; RO: 97%; RS: 89%.

- The main findings on reliability of scoring the CCRT by weighted kappas, as summarized in Table 1, based on eight samples in six main studies, showed the mean level of reliability across the eight samples is "good," according to the categories proposed by Landis and Koch (1970), and not markedly different from sample to sample or even from component to component: W: kw = .60; RO: kw = .68; RS: kw = .71. Because of the consistency of the level of reliability across the eight samples with weighted kappas shown in Table 1, we expect future studies to show the same high level of reliability.

- An explanatory factor that may be significant, although it has not been tested, is that the wish component has a slightly lower mean weighted kappa than the response from other or response of self. This is especially evident for the wish component in the children's stories, which turns out to be atypically unreliable with a weighted kappa of .33 (*all* other samples have weighted kappas for wishes of .58 or higher). It may have been hard for judges to infer the wishes in children's stories.

- This analysis of reliability gives results only in terms of the agreement for each of the three types of components; we are working on studies that also give the level of agreement for each of the 94 standard categories in Edition 2 (34 wishes, 30 responses from others, 30 responses of self).

- We hope also that in future reliability studies some of the other factors influencing the CCRT's reliability will become better known. Among these may be the scoring skill of the judges.

7

THE RELATIONSHIP ANECDOTES PARADIGM (RAP) INTERVIEW AS A VERSATILE SOURCE OF NARRATIVES

LESTER LUBORSKY

The idea for an interview-style "RAP session" for eliciting narratives grew out of my restiveness with the initial format of the CCRT method, which was based only on the narratives spontaneously told in psychotherapy. What if the person was not in psychotherapy, or what if the psychotherapy sessions were not available? These "what-ifs" led me to construct a Relationship Anecdotes Paradigms (RAP) interview that could be applied to almost any sample of people and could serve to elicit narratives to use as data for the same variety of purposes as the narratives drawn from psychotherapy (Luborsky, 1990b). In fact, versions of the original unpublished Relationship Anecdotes Paradigms interview guide (Luborsky, 1978b) have been widely circulated among researchers for over 19 years.

The primary purpose of this chapter is to give a more complete and time-tested guide to the administration of the RAP interview. Other purposes are to examine what is known about characteristics of the narratives elicited by the RAP interview and to review research applications of the RAP, especially as a data source for the CCRT measure.

ADMINISTRATION OF THE RAP INTERVIEW

In the RAP interview the narrator tells about actual events in relationships with other people. Each narrative is an account of a specific interaction with a specific other person. The narrator is free to tell a narrative about any relationship episode, present or past, and is encouraged to describe the episode concretely and to include a sample of conversation with the other person: what the narrator said, what the other person said, and what happened at the end of the interaction.

Instructions

The interviewer gives the following instructions:

Please tell me some incidents or events, each involving yourself in relation to another person. Each one should be a *specific* incident. Some should be current and some old incidents. For each one tell (1) when it occurred, (2) who was the other person it was with, (3) some of what the other person said or did and what you said or did, (4) what happened at the end, and (5) when the event in the narrative happened. The other person might be anyone—your father, mother, brothers and sisters, or other relatives, friends or people you work with. It just has to be about a specific event that was personally important or a problem to you in some way. Tell at least ten of these incidents. Spend about three but no more than five minutes in telling each one. I will let you know when you come near to the end of five minutes. This is a way to tell about your relationships. Make yourself comfortable and engage in this RAP session as you would with someone who you want to get to know you.

The total expected time for each patient's telling of 10 episodes, is between 30 and 50 minutes. The interview is tape-recorded, beginning with the patient's name (or initials). The interviewer adds the date, name of the therapist (or initials) if the patient has a therapist, and the interviewer's name.

In the usual form of the RAP procedure, the patient is free to tell any incidents about any people. It is desirable that there be some variety among the people chosen. It is also useful if all the narratives are not from one time period; some should be from the present and some from the past. Each narrative should be about a specific incident, not a generalized amalgam of several incidents.

For special purposes, the form of the RAP procedure can be varied. The interviewee may be requested to provide narratives about specific types of other people, such as narratives about the spouse for patients in marital therapy. Each member of a couple may be asked to tell narratives about the other (with scoring suggested by concepts such as those from Bernal

& Baker, 1979). In an "object relations" RAP, the instructions include a request for four narratives about each of the main people in the participant's early life. In Mayman's (1968) version, only early memories are asked for. Another format for scoring concentrates on aspects of the structure of the narrative (Wilson, Passik, Morral, Turner, & Kuras, 1994).

Finally, the set of narratives can be drawn from those told as part of interviews done for a variety of other purposes, for example, interviews done as part of anthropological fieldwork or as part of a psychiatric evaluation. After such narratives have been located in the text of the interview, they can be scored as if the set were elicited by a RAP interview (as illustrated in the study of adolescents by Waldinger, 1997a).

Improving Rapport and Dealing With Special Contingencies

The patient should be sufficiently comfortable to tell a set of narratives about incidents that, from the patient's point of view, are reasonably accurate accounts of actual events that the patient has experienced. Once patients are comfortable with the RAP interviewer, they usually can perform the task without much difficulty. The interviewer may find it useful to increase rapport by explaining the confidentiality of the interview and its value in understanding the patient's relationships. These are some ways to deal with special contingencies in a RAP interview.

- To help patients who have difficulty being detailed or whose episodes are too brief: "Could you tell more about that incident?"
- To help patients who have difficulty finding any relationship anecdotes to tell: "Just tell about any incident, event, or interaction with anyone, either an old or a recent incident. Tell any that you happen to remember now."
- To help patients who find the words given in the instructions, to "describe events that were important to you," a hindrance to finding any events, the interviewer should deemphasize these words by saying, "Just give any incidents or events as you think of them."
- To help patients who find it hard to remember any conversation in relationship episodes: "It is not necessary to put in exact conversation; just say the general idea of it" or "just put in what you remember."

After all instructions have been given to the narrator, the interviewer should see that the narrator provides reasonably complete narratives. The best time to provide further guidance is at the end of the first narrative, saying, "That first one is fine; go on in the same way with the other narratives" or if further direction is needed, "go ahead with the other narra-

TABLE 1
Descriptive Characteristics of RAP Narratives in an Outpatient
Psychiatric Clinic Sample ($N = 24$)

Time	Mean	SD
Average time per narrative (min)	2.4	0.7
Total time per interview (min)	26.3	7.9

Content	Percentage	N of narratives
Other person		
Parents	21	15
Love relationships	18	14
Siblings	9	8
Other people	52	21
Number of different people represented	81	18
When episode occurred		
Adulthood, recent (past week)	31	26
Adulthood, past	53	23
Adolescence (10–18 years)	8	11
Childhood (less than 10 years)	8	14
Dominant emotion in narratives		
Positive	19	21
Negative	73	22
Mixed or neutral	8	7

tives; but please remember to _____" (fill in with whatever needs fine-tuning).

CHARACTERISTICS OF RAP NARRATIVES

When participants follow the instructions for the RAP, what kinds of narratives do they tell? The characteristics of narratives presented here are the first systematically recorded. They are based on 24 patients in psychotherapy at the outpatient psychiatric clinic (OPD) of the Department of Psychiatry of the University of Pennsylvania. This OPD sample is like other samples drawn from the OPD as described by Luborsky, Crits-Christoph, et al. (1988). The most frequent *DSM-IV* diagnoses in the present sample, in order of frequency from most to least, were typical nonpsychotic diagnoses: depression, anxiety, adjustment disorder, and personality disorders.

The areas covered in this description of characteristics of RAP narratives (see Table 1) include the time taken per narrative, the main type of other person the participant interacts with in the narrative, the number of others in the narrative, the stage of life from which the narrative is drawn, and the dominant emotion in the narrative.

The mean time taken to tell the narratives was 2 1/2-minutes. For the telling of 10 narratives, the mean time per interview was 26 minutes, with a mean time per narrative of about 2 1/2 minutes. These data show that, although the instructions allow a maximum of 5 minutes, for this sample the interviews consumed only about half of that per tape-recorded narrative.

The main type of other persons in the narrative was greatest for "other people." Each type of other person was classified into one of four categories, which occurred with the following frequencies: parents (21%), love relationship (18%), siblings (9%), other people (52%). Clearly, the largest category was "other people."

"Different other people" were most represented in the narrative. For this sample, on the average 81% of the relationship episodes of each narrator were about different other people. For example, if eight different other people were featured in 10 episodes of a narrator, the percentage would be 80.

The "current" time in the teller's life was when most of the action in the narrative took place. Four time periods were analyzed: recent adulthood (past week, 31%), past adulthood (53%), adolescence (10–18 years of age, 8%), and childhood (less than 10 years of age, 8%). Therefore, most often the time of the action of the narrative is either within the era of the participant's life that is current (past week) or in the recent past (past adulthood).

The negative dominant emotion of the relationship episode was very high. The scoring of the dominant emotion of each relationship episode was based on a rating of these categories: positive, negative, and mixed or neutral. Most of the relationship episodes (73%) had a negative dominant emotion. Similar percentages for negative emotions have been found in other patient samples, described in chapters 4 and 17.

USES OF RAP NARRATIVES

RAP Narratives as Data for the CCRT Measure

RAP interviews provide a supply of narratives that are more accessible but similar to those from the psychotherapy sessions. The scoring system applied to each type of narrative is the same as given in chapter 2, this volume. Our experience with each type of narrative leads us to expect that the CCRTs from the sessions versus from the RAP interview are likely to be much the same. Only one study so far gives quantitative support to this impression (Barber et al., 1995); in a sample of depressed patients given the RAP before therapy started, the CCRTs scored from the early sessions were not significantly different from the RAP results. The two independent judges were in agreement concerning the CCRT components 77% of the time for the wishes and responses of self and 100% of the time for the responses of other.

A brief example is provided in this chapter's appendix, taken from the Penn Psychotherapy Study, of a CCRT from Mr. Edward Howard based on a RAP interview at a follow-up session 8 years after the end of psychotherapy. This example not only illustrates the CCRT scoring of RAP narratives (see Table 2) but also allows comparison with the RE-based narratives from Session 3 of the psychotherapy (see chapter 4, this volume). The appendix includes only the first three relationship episodes as scored by only one of three judges who scored the 10 relationship episodes elicited in the RAP session. Another independent judge summarized the three judges' scores in the summary table (see Table 2). Several findings can be read from the summary table. Wish A shows considerable agreement among the three independent judges. Eight or 9 out of the 10 relationship episodes were scored by the three judges as containing the general version of Wish A. Wish A1 is one subcategory of Wish A that was found less frequently. For the response from others, the frequency of the negative responses ("rejects, criticizes me") was from 2 to 4 out of the 10 for the three judges.

For the responses of self, the highest frequency negative type was "frustrated, angry." The entire CCRT, on the basis of the usual principle of the highest frequency type of components, is "I wish to be close with, liked by, and cared about by the other person, but the other person rejects or criticizes me and I become frustrated and angry."

The reader may have a sense of having read this example before. In fact, the reader is partly right: The CCRT in this example from the RAP is much like the CCRT from Session 3 and Sessions 82 and 83 of Mr. Howard. What tends to change most in improved patients, such as this one, is that some of the responses from others and responses of self shift from negative to positive. Thus, it appears not only that the CCRT is consistent across time, but also that, even after an 8-year interval, there remains a congruence between the CCRT from the RAP narratives and the CCRT from psychotherapy sessions.

The CCRT has shown adequate reliability in terms of agreement between judges when scored from the narratives told during psychotherapy (see chapter 7, this volume); reliability studies using RAP narratives, such as those of Mr. Howard, tend to show similar themes and similar levels of reliability to those from psychotherapy (Barber et al., 1995; van Ravenswaay, Luborsky, & Childress, 1983).

Other Uses of the RAP Interview Procedure

The four uses reviewed here constitute only a small sample of a widening field of applications.

TABLE 2
CCRT Score Sheet Summary (Number of Relationship Episodes Containing Each Component)

Patient: Mr. Edward Howard, No. 44

Session: RAP

Number of REs: 10

Wish, Need, Intention	Judge			Negative Response From Other	Judge			Negative Response of Self	Judge		
	V	C	M		V	C	M		V	C	M
A. To be close with, liked by, and cared about by others	8	9	8	1. Rejects, criticized me	4	2	4	1. Frustrated, angry	3	2	4
A1. To be accepted, to receive approval	3	2	4	2. Angry	1	1	1	2. Confused	1	1	2
								3. Afraid of rejection	1	1	2
A2. To be close, connected	1	5	1	3. Indecisive, changes mind	2	0	2	4. Inhibits desire to be close	1	1	1
A3. To be cared for, emotionally supported	2	1	2	4. Feels silly, embarrassed	0	0	1				
				5. Needs support	0	0	1	5. Doesn't express anger	1	1	1
A4. To have more satisfying relationships with me	1	1	1								

As a Database for Studies of Explanatory Style

The RAP interview contains descriptions of events and often also gives explanations of the causes of the events. Such explanations are scorable in terms of a concept called "explanatory style" (Seligman et al., 1984). The explanatory style that is measured in this way can be thought of as part of an inference pattern about causes of the events. The explanations for good and bad events are scored on three dimensions: internal–external ("it is me" versus "it is not me"), stable–unstable ("it will always be me" versus "it will not always be me"), global–specific ("it will affect all aspects of my life" versus "it will affect just this aspect"). These explanatory styles have been shown to be associated with the development of depressive symptoms (Peterson & Seligman, 1984).

The explanatory style measure that has been applied to the RAP interview data is a procedure called the Content Analysis of Verbatim Explanations (CAVE) technique (Peterson & Seligman, 1984). Reliabilities of coding for each of the three dimensions are high: .93, .89, and .90 (Cronbach's alpha; four judges pooled for the internal, stable, and global ratings, respectively; Peterson, Bettes, & Seligman, 1985). In a study of a patient in psychotherapy who had precipitous mood swings, it was found that spontaneously given causal explanations about spontaneously reported negative events predicted the appearance of a mood swing (Luborsky, 1996, chap. 5; Peterson, Luborsky, & Seligman, 1983). For this patient the combined dimensions of internal, stable, and global explanations for bad events preceded shifts toward increased depression, whereas the combined dimensions of external, unstable, and specific explanations preceded shifts toward decreased depression.

As a Source of Data for Developmental Studies of Central Relationship Patterns

A special kind of interview developed by Buchsbaum and Emde (1990) has been applied to a sample of young children at age 3 and again at age 5 (Luborsky, Luborsky, et al., 1995). In their stories a combination of fantasy constructions and recounting of real events appears. To make the telling of stories about events easier for these very young children, family figure dolls and initial story-stems about conflictual situations are used.

In another developmental study, a RAP-type set of memories was also obtained from 23-year-olds retested as part of the Berkeley Longitudinal Study (Jack Block, personal communication, 1989). They were used to assess the developmental correlates of the central relationship pattern of the stories stemming from the participant's different age periods (Thorne, 1989, 1995a, 1995b; Thorne & Michaelien, 1996).

As a Basis for Studies of Self-Understanding

The RAP narratives are a convenient source of data for studies of the ability of a person to understand his or her own central relationship pattern, as described in chapter 15, this volume, and in a procedure for self-interpretation of the RAP narratives (Luborsky, 1978a).

As a Basis for the Comparison Among Diagnositic Groups

We are launched on a set of studies of RAPs in which the comparison is of the central relationship pattern of three groups: patients with major depression (Luborsky, Diguer, et al., 1996), those with schizophrenia, and normal persons (defined as without a psychiatric diagnosis on the Schedule for Affective Disorders and Schizophrenia–Research Diagnostic Criteria (SADS-RDC; Demorest, Crits-Christoph, Hatch, & Luborsky, 1997).

As a Basis for Intergenerational Comparisons

RAP narratives are being compared for the patient versus the patient's parents. The narratives are about events selected by the patient; a subset of these are narratives about the same event as told both by the patient and by the patient's parents (Waldinger, 1997a).

CONCLUSIONS

- The RAP interview produces narratives that have much in common with those produced in psychotherapy sessions (Barber et al., 1995). The format is well accepted by both patients and nonpatients.
- The RAP procedure appears to have some similarities to the Thematic Apperception Test (TAT; Murray, 1938), and its uses are often similar. Both are interviews in which narratives are elicited, but there is one major difference. The RAP narratives are told by the participant as accounts of actual experiences with actual people; the TAT stories are told as fictional narratives that are stimulated by the people and settings depicted in the TAT cards. As an assessment method, the advantage may go to the RAP interview: Conclusions based on the RAP may be less inferential than those based on the TAT because RAP narratives are based on accounts of events that more directly reveal the patient's relationship patterns.

In fact, the heavy emphasis in the past 40 years on projective techniques in diagnostic psychological testing (Holt, 1978; Rapaport, Gill, & Schafer, 1968), although it has had significant benefits, may have led to a slighting of the potential gains for accurate assessment that can be derived from narratives about actual events in the patient's present and past relationships. The RAP procedure is congruent with the trend toward giving less attention to projective tests and even to psychodiagnostic testing generally (Holt, 1967; Piotrowski & Keller, 1984).

- The RAP interview relies on a relatively natural format; it requires only doing what people like to do—tell narratives about events in relationships that have occurred between themselves and other people. For this reason the RAP interview can be used for assessing a broad range of developmental, intellectual, and cultural qualities, as is illustrated in the research studies already completed or in progress.

APPENDIX

The RAP Interview for Mr. Edward Howard: An 8-Year-Follow-up

The following are 3 of 10 relationship episodes from a RAP interview. In the left margin are the tailor-made CCRT scoring annotations by one of the judges; the parts of the text from which the inferences were derived are underlined.

RE 1: Therapist

PRS: Feelings of self-worth _____

PRS: Felt important _____

NRS: Low self-worth _____

W: To be cared about for himself _____

And uh, I was thinking//,^{RS} the therapy was the first time in my relationships that I felt like uh that I was worth something,// and and that//,^{RS} I was important in myself.// And even though it was a professional kind of relationship, it struck me uh that that was kind of strange, you know that//,^{RS} I hadn't felt that at all in my family.// Uh, but that's really how it was. That was the first time. And I guess in terms of my uh a lot of my individual growth, that//,^{W} I was somebody uh separate and an individual in my own right and that somebody cared about me just for that// and not what I could do for them or not because of who I knew or something like that . . .

RE 2: *Work Supervisor*

My first-year placement was in Law Center, and my supervisor was a man who grew up in Hungary and//[RO] as a supervisor he really showed a lot of interest in me as a professional and a person.// We spent a couple of hours doing an evaluation of . . . of my work, because of his concern he brought out a lot of things that had been going on with me and he says,//[RO] "Frankly, I've been a little concerned."// I said, "What about?"//[RO] He said, "I think you're a loaf." I said, "A loaf!" I'm not answering, "a loaf." I said, "A loaf, huh." 'Cause actually I'd been . . . //[RS] I'd been waiting for him to say something like this// because//[W] my, my worst fear was that I would be seen as a, as an ineffectual do-nothing,// you know, and since//[RS] I really worked hard to counteract this image that I had of myself and saw myself//. . . //[RS] And so he talked a little bit more about that then I figured out what he was saying.// // He wasn't saying "a loaf," he was saying "aloof." And it was his accent, and it was so weird because//[RS] that was like my worst fear.// And he said that uh, yeah, that I . . . I seem to always be walking around like absentminded, and I would never have time to talk to the staff people.//[RO] He thought that a lot of the staff like me much more than I, I liked them,// and

PRO: Showed interest in me

NRO: Express concern

NRO: Criticizes him

NRS: Fear of criticism

W: To be seen as a competent, effective worker

PRS: Tried to be competent and effective

PRS: Misunderstood

NRS: Fear of criticism

PRO: Reassures, encourages

NRS: Reject others

NRS: Fear of rejection

W: To receive approval from others
NRS: Reject others

uh, and that was kind of nice to hear but uh also it . . . //^{RS} I began to think more about how I turned people off// //^{RS} because of my feeling that they wouldn't be interested in me, like my assumption, and//^{W} working so hard to get their approval// uh,//^{RS} I ended up turning them off instead of being direct with them.

RE 3: Sister

(W): To be close with his sister

NRS: Felt cold, distant, aloof

NRO: Cried; in distress

PRO: Courageous

PRS: Empathized

NRS: Sad
NRS: Angry

NRS: Angry

Uh (pause) I don't have too many angry interactions, which is a problem. I have to work on that. Uh, I remember a sad interaction that I had when I was about 16 or 17. This . . . like//$^{(W)}$ the first time I could remember ever having any kind of nonnegative feelings for my sister// who was younger than I was.//^{RS} I always like either felt really cold and distant and uh just aloof, like I hated her guts,// but uh this time she came in in the morning off her delivery route and uh and//^{RO} she was crying 'cause her, her hands and her feet were really cold.// //^{RO} And uh and she was like a really courageous kid,// I mean, she doesn't cry, you know, and//^{RS} I just felt so bad that her fingers and toes were a little bit frostbitten,// you know.//^{RS} And uh, it made me feel really sad// //^{RS} and it made me feel angry, too some,// because I felt like she shouldn't have had to do that and and I knew that that the reason . . . I guess//^{RS} it made me angry at my parents some.//

8

WHY EACH CCRT PROCEDURE WAS CHOSEN

LESTER LUBORSKY

To measure such a complex concept as a central relationship pattern reliably and validly requires both plain luck and great care in decision making about methods of assessment. The decisions I made had profound effects on the structure of the method and on the observations derived from it. In this chapter I explain the virtues and vices of each of the many decisions about construction of the CCRT measure. The decisions are grouped into three main bunches: the database, the scoring system, and the inference level.

DATABASE DECISIONS

To Rely on Psychotherapy Sessions

There is a special virtue in using psychotherapy sessions as the database of the new measure; after all, sessions were the original data from which Freud (1912/1958a) generated the concept of a central relationship

121

pattern and, from it, his transference template. We therefore hoped that the phenomena of transference that were supposed to be present in sessions could be captured within them. For locating such a bounty, it would be worth putting up with the time and expense of transcribing and of making judgments from sessions. My approach was to use psychotherapy sessions but to try to rise to the challenge of transforming such data into objectively scorable form by means of the procedures listed in chapter 2, this volume.

My decision to use data from psychotherapy sessions to find central relationship patterns did not follow the most popular route. Workers in the field had concentrated for several decades on questionnaires about the patient's relationship with the therapist and with others, perhaps because of the difficulty of transforming data from sessions into objectively scorable measures. True, the questionnaire method could save time, but so far the gains from relying on it solely appear to have been penny-wise, because the questionnaire approach, as reviewed in chapter 20, has not convincingly captured what we were after.

To Restrict the Database to Narratives About Relationship Episodes

The decision to restrict the scoring to the narratives about relationship episodes within the sessions came early in the development of the CCRT method. As I tried to formulate the relationship patterns from whole sessions, it became obvious that the judges' inferences about transference were mainly derived from the patients' narratives about relationship interactions with people. Narratives provide rich data for the method because they are concrete examples of the patient's interactions with others and self. Thus, it seemed simpler and without significant loss of information to focus the judges' attention on relationship episodes. The narrowing of the focus to relationship episodes not only reduced the data to be inspected and scored but, more importantly, highlighted the relationship ideas and behaviors that were of most interest.

The decision to score only the relationship episodes was reinforced by the conclusion from a study of ratings of transference (Luborsky, Graff, et al., 1973). In that study, ratings of "transference as expressed to specific objects" were found to yield higher interjudge agreement than ratings of "transference as expressed in the entire segment"; that is, ratings of the entire segment without attention to rating the specific people were less reliable than ratings focused on specific people.

In light of further experience, the decision to restrict scoring to the relationship episodes appears to have been a good one, even though in principle any restriction of focus entails some loss of information. In fact, the judge can and should read the transcript of the whole session, which is easy to do because the relationship episodes are typically presented to the judge within the transcript of the whole session. The whole session can be thought of as a context for further understanding of each relationship episode. The session can be considered to be the associative context for the relationship episode in much the same sense as the dream in dream analysis, for which much of the session can be viewed as associations to the dream. As a whole, the loss entailed in the restriction to the relationship episodes is offset by a gain in simplicity of the procedure and is further offset by a crucial gain in focus because the relationship episodes provide a good basis for inferring typical relationship patterns.

Finally, I decided not to use the thought unit as an alternative to the relationship episode—at least not now. It can, however, be used as a subunit within the relationship episodes (see chapters 3 and 5, this volume). The thought unit is an operationally defined single thought (Benjamin, 1974). For the purpose of producing a database that can measure interactional patterns, however, it seemed too small and too noninteractional. The thought unit is a much smaller unit than the relationship episode; it is often about the length of an average sentence. Another unit that could have been used, patient utterances, was relied on by Schacht and Binder (1982) in their dynamic focus method. It is defined as a single uninterrupted turn at talk. It, too, appeared to be too short in comparison with the relationship episode.

To Include Behavioral Enactments of the Relationship With the Therapist

The database for the CCRT consists both of narratives told by the patient and of enactments of these. The enactments are the behavioral expressions of interactional sequences during the session in relation to the therapist. In dramatic terms, they are the central scenes within the play. Although the whole session can be considered an interaction between patient and therapist, the enactments are limited, discrete behavioral episodes within the session. I assume, so far, that in terms of CCRT content the narratives and the enactments have much similarity.

The use of enactments offers some advantages for the CCRT method. First, they are actual behavioral interactions between patient and therapist, not just narrative accounts of episodes with the therapist. Therefore, they offer an opportunity to examine the validity of the CCRTs from the narratives by a comparison with the enactments. Second, the use of enactments increases the number of *relationship episodes with the therapist*, a category that is typically sparse. One disadvantage, however, is that more work needs to be done to improve the reliability of recognition of enactments.

SCORING SYSTEM DECISIONS

To Use Guided Judgments

In the everyday relatively unguided approach to inferring the transference, the clinician is free to rely on any principle and any level of abstraction in making judgments that his or her training and intuition suggest is appropriate. But the use of unguided judgments of transference —for example, those examined by Seitz (1966)—has yielded poor and ambiguous agreement among clinicians. In contrast, measures of central relationship patterns, such as the CCRT, the Plan Diagnosis, or the Dynamic Focus, use guided clinical judgment, which gives high levels of interclinician agreement, as summarized in chapters 6 and 20, this volume. These guides specify in advance the judgment principles and levels of abstraction that should be relied on for making inferences. Holt (1978) reviewed the extensive research on unguided versus guided clinical judgments and concluded that guided approaches yield benefits for reliability and validity; measures that provide some degree of guidance to the judge produce results that are psychometrically more promising.

To Identify the Main Other Person Within Each Relationship Episode With Whom the Speaker Is Interacting

The judges who select the relationship episodes from the psychotherapy sessions also identify in each relationship episode one main other person with whom the narrator is interacting. (The agreement on this task is given in chapter 6.) A CCRT built on this basis provides an opportunity to learn the degree to which the relationship pattern in the CCRT is pervasive across many types of relationships.

An alternative decision might have been to analyze the relationship episodes grouped for each type of other person. This method would yield a separate CCRT about father (and father figures), about mother (and mother figures), about the therapist, and so on. Developing separate CCRTs in this way would have caused a practical problem: For many participants we would not have had a sufficient sample of relationship episodes about each type of other person. This was certainly the most difficult restriction faced by Fried et al. (see chapter 11, this volume) in her study comparing the CCRT for the therapist with the CCRT for other people. (A study on this topic by Crits-Christoph & Demorest, 1991, had a large number of relationship episodes per different other person but relied on one treatment only with many sessions transcribed and scored.) Fried et al. looked only at the degree of parallel between the CCRT for the therapist and the CCRT for other people; she has not yet explored the kinds of differences. When this task is done, she will probably find both a specific prototype for each type of other person, as well as what we have already found, a basic prototype that encompasses and pervades the narratives about most other persons. Such a general as well as specific pattern would be no surprise to clinicians; in fact, Freud (1912/1958a) expected both kinds of results on the basis of his observation about the characteristics of the pattern (reviewed in chapter 21).

To Rely on Three Components of Narratives: Wishes, Responses From Others, and Responses of Self

The CCRT scoring system relies on inferences based on signs in the session of central classes of components that are often reflected in clinicians' descriptions of the transference pattern. These components are often in conflict with each other. The first is the wish class: wishes, needs, and intentions; psychoanalytic theorists call these *drive derivatives*. The second is in the response class: responses from others and responses of self; psychoanalytic theorists generally consider these as containing control, executive, or ego functions (Rapaport & Gill, 1967). The wish class and the response of self class are recognizable as representatives of two of the main entities posited in psychoanalytic constructions of the "mental apparatus." The responses from other contain that part of the perceived relationship environment that the person must deal with. Clinicians tend to believe that through greater insight the patient's responses from others and of the self can become more conflict free in the course of psychotherapy because the patient's insights offer more information about the internal and external conditions affecting the possibilities of satisfaction of the wish, need, or intention. Thus, the built-in similarity of the content of the CCRT to the transference concept increases the meaningfulness of the CCRT method in clinical practice.

To Use a Theme Format That Highlights Conflicts

The format of the CCRT is set up to point to the locus of conflicts. The usual sequence of the components is wishes, followed by responses from others, followed by responses of self. Among these components, the two most prominent types of conflicts are (a) among the wishes ("I want this, but it conflicts with something else I want") and (b) between the wishes and the responses from other and of self. The second type of conflict is much more frequent.

> *Example*: The most obvious conflict for Mr. Edward Howard (see chapter 5, this volume) concerns his wish to be close, which conflicts with his expected response from others of being cut off from closeness. Although he is somewhat aware of this conflict, he is less aware of some aspects of the conflict, such as that his wish to be close conflicts with

his wish to be distant. And perhaps his wish to be distant arises because of his expectation that he will be cut off from closeness. He is probably even less aware of other aspects of the conflict and that the wish to be close, because it is so intimately associated with sexual wishes, heightens his expectation of a negative response from others.

To Judge All Responses as Either Positive or Negative

The inclusion of the qualities of the narratives for the CCRT as positive or negative followed the work of Freud (1912/1958a), who designated transference patterns as positive or negative. I have been using this aspect with considerable satisfaction since the launching of the CCRT idea (Luborsky, 1977b). The judgment of positive or negative was confined to responses from other or responses of self; wishes are not typically in themselves positive or negative. Much has been learned since then about positivity and negativity; for example, Grenyer and I (chapter 4) have shown that positivity and negativity can be reliably judged and (chapter 9) that there is a general proclivity of people toward negative narratives and therefore negative CCRTs.

To Use Both Tailor-Made and Standard Categories

In the original form of the CCRT (Luborsky, 1977b), as well as in part of its present form in this book, categories that were fashioned to suit each patient were selected by each judge in a scoring system appropriately called *tailor-made*. In the language of psychometrics, the system is *idiographic* because it outfits each patient with case-specific descriptive categories. This fine asset, however, is offset by a practical liability: The variability from patient to patient and from judge to judge in the selection and wording of tailor-made categories makes comparisons among cases problematic.

The contrasting current system based on standard categories, also discussed in this book, is *nomothetic*. It escapes the problem of variability in the wording of case formulations by asking judges to fit their formulations into the standard categories described in chapter 3. Other standard category systems for central relationship pattern measures differ in their choice of categories; for example, the Cyclical Maladaptive Pattern (Schacht & Binder, 1982; also see chapter 20, this volume) and the Quantitative Analysis of Interpersonal Themes (Crits-Christoph, Demorest, & Connolly, 1990; see chapter 20, this volume) require judges to code formulations into the categories provided by the Structural Analysis of Social Behavior (Benjamin, 1974).

In conclusion, although an idiographic approach is desirable because it is closer to the clinical process of making transference formulations, the use of standard categories provides definite benefits to the researcher, including a greater ease of establishing interjudge agreement. Yet an evaluation remains to be done of the gains from the use of standard categories and the degree to which these make up for the loss of the uniqueness of each case that is provided by the tailor-made categories. I believe, therefore, that it is advantageous to report results by both tailor-made and standard categories.

To Rely on Redundancy Across the Narratives (Pervasiveness) as the Indicator of the CCRT

From the inception of the CCRT method (Luborsky, 1977b), CCRT scores were based on their pervasiveness across narratives about REs, that is, on the proportions of the REs containing each type of component. This definition of pervasiveness was first applied to 20-minute segments of sessions from the Penn Psychotherapy Study.

The reliance on the frequency of each category to define the CCRT makes good sense as an indicator of the relationship schema reflected in the CCRT, but it also might risk missing what is salient but infrequent. This risk was noted by Howard Shevrin in his comments about my paper on the nature of the CCRT at the MacArthur Conference in 1985. This concern was also expressed in Hartvig Dahl's critique of the CCRT at the psychotherapy conference in Sweden's Skokloster Castle in April 1980; he was concerned that the formulation could be limited because of reliance on frequency and suggested it would be better to call it the main theme, not the core theme. Several findings, however, helped in coping with this concern. The main one is that the frequency with which a theme is expressed tends to be a good indicator of its importance; according to Murray (1938), the most frequently expressed theme is the most central one in the sense that it tend to be the locus of the most pervasive relationship problem and a concomitant of the greatest intrapsychic conflict.

> *Example*: The heart of Ms. Sally Simpson's CCRT illustrates the issue. Her CCRT was "I want to be given reassurance that I'm okay and even special (mentally, professionally, and sexually), but the other person will not give it and I feel rejected and defective." Her main wish to be okay or special and the responses to frustration of that wish, as reflected in her CCRT, caused her the greatest recurrent suffering. It was responsible for her need to start treatment when she did. At that time she was suffering acutely because she realized that she was not going to be special for the married man she was having an affair with and he would go back to his wife. She tried throughout the treatment to be special for the therapist and soon began to feel that she was. This theme, therefore, not only was expressed in a salient instance but was frequent.

> *Example*: The wish in the CCRT of another patient, Ms. Rachael Apfel (see chapter 12, this volume), to get a positive response, especially

from men, and to be able to cope with negative ones, was most frequent and most central. Recurrently, throughout most of the treatment, she maintained the painful expectation that she was going to be rejected. She expressed instances of this expectation in both dreams and relationship episodes.

Another reason that the theme with the highest frequency is worth designating the core theme is that it provides a framework within which to understand the network of intertwined themes. The other themes, many of them clearly subsidiary themes, can be represented as related to the core theme. Rather than considering all the other themes as subthemes, it is often more fitting to refer to them as alternative expressions of the CCRT.

Example: For Ms. Sally Simpson, her oedipal theme is a version of her CCRT. Two examples from her two early and two late sessions support this inference: (a) her wish to be special compared with the wife of the married man she was having an affair with and (b) a triangular situation evident in her relationship episodes in which a woman telephone operator was continually seen as preventing her from contacting the man.

Example: For Ms. Cathy Cunningham, her oedipal theme also appeared to be one version of her CCRT. The general version of her main wishes was "I need and want to assert myself and to get the support and attention of a man." In some sessions, especially the later ones (e.g., Session 1,028), the wish appeared as "I want and felt I must have a baby from Father" and "I want and must have a baby from you [the therapist]."

Finally, the reliance on frequency as a criterion appears not to have interfered with and even is likely to have fostered the high association of the CCRT-based results with clinically based observations about the transference as summarized in chapter 21, this volume. This type of association needs to be explored more systematically, for it offers a basis for examining the value of reliance on frequency as a criterion for assessing the CCRT.

To Allow Only One Score per Relationship Episode for Each Different Category

The score for each category is the frequency of that category on the basis of a count of the number of relationship episodes out of the total number of relationship episodes in which the category appeared (that is, its pervasiveness). Each relationship episode is allowed only one score for each different type of scoring category. The desirable effect of this decision is to emphasize the degree of redundancy of the category *across relationship episodes*.

An alternative CCRT scoring system would permit the frequency to reflect the total number of times the category appeared, regardless of how often it appeared in a relationship episode. A high score, however, that is based on a count done in this way might come from a few relationship episodes in which the category was frequent. We therefore opted for our current system, which clearly captured pervasiveness of categories across relationship episodes. But a scoring in terms of the now-rejected alternative score is worth examining in future research.

To Use Our Usual System for Counting All Scorable Components Regardless of Sequence

The decision was made to include all scorable components, not just those with an explicit, complete sequence of the CCRT components. The decision means that all types of CCRT components are counted even when there are missing components in the sequence; for example, a type of wish might be expressed with no expected response from the other to *that wish*. The decision to use all scorable components was based on the need for simplicity of scoring, the concern that sequences often might not be explicitly stated, and the expectation that the decision would provide meaningful data about the central relationship pattern.

I have covered all bases, however, by adding as an optional scoring system the designation of explicit sequences (chapter 2, this volume). Research needs to be done in which the present score-all-components system is compared with the score-only-explicit-sequences system to determine the degree of difference between the two (as my colleagues and I have briefly done in chapter 9). Since this section was initially written in 1989, further development of a sequence method has appeared (Dahlbender, Albani, Pokorny, & Kächele, in press).

INFERENCE LEVEL AND FOCUS DECISIONS

To Stay Within the Range of Moderate Inference

The decision to stay within a moderate level of inference was based on the impression that when the level of inference is high, it is hard to get agreement among judges. Yet the restriction of inference to a moderate range also means that the present guidelines for scoring appear to be adequate in terms of judges' agreement with each other (see chapter 6). Although the decision to stay within the limits of moderate inference means that some unconscious-level inferences may be excluded for some patients, fortunately the restriction of the range of inference does not mean that unconscious processes are excluded; in fact, according to one study (see chapter 15), important inferences within the usual CCRT appear to be at a restricted-awareness, or unconscious, level.

Several ideas for future research are implied by these decisions. A study should grade the degree of inference used for each score; it could then be determined whether different levels of inference are associated with different levels of reliability. Another study might investigate the types of CCRTs when no limit on inference level is imposed on the judge. This study would check systematically on the reliability of deep-level inferences and show what kinds of inferences they are. My colleagues and I are working on research to develop an "unconscious conflict" measure that extends the CCRT to include deeper levels of inference (see the brief description of this study in chapter 21).

To Add a Re-Review of the Relationship Episodes by Steps 1′ and 2′

The purpose of the re-review of the relationship episodes is to achieve a more complete scoring and formulation of the CCRT by the tailor-made system. Is the expected gain worth the effort? Why not just do a collation of the scores from Steps 1 and 2 and stop there? It would be simpler, more straightforward, and more like the coding of the original TAT stories by many quantitative scoring systems.

But the rationale for the re-review and reformulation required by Steps 1′ and 2′ comes from an enduring clinical observation, for example, by Freud (1958d, p. 112): "It must not be forgotten that the things one hears are for the most part things whose meaning is only recognized later on." A basic theme may not be discerned until a later occasion on which the same theme is re-presented; the delay followed by a further review sometimes sparks the judge's recognition of a common theme. In terms of the CCRT scoring, one may not discern a theme until the step of reviewing across relationship episodes, because much of the realization of a theme's centrality is based on the well-established clinical inference principle of attending to redundancy. The following example from Mr. Howard's treatment makes this virtue more apparent:

> *Example*: In Session 3, in RE 3 about the therapist, Mr. Edward Howard suddenly feels he has nothing to say to the therapist. A judge who reads all the REs in context reads this relationship episode immediately after reading the preceding and before reading the subsequent relationship episodes and so can readily infer that the experience of not having anything to say to the therapist could be the patient's response to this realization that the therapist did not have enough to say to him. In fact, the therapist states exactly that inference in his interpretations to the patient. The theme is so recurrent that it might well have been recognized simply on the basis of Steps 1 and 2, but the review in Steps 1′ and 2′ would clinch its recognition.

The possible criticism needs to be considered that Steps 1' and 2' open the door to the inclusion of inferences that are not inherent in the relationship episode by itself. Such a criticism is tenable, but in fact it does not correspond to the judges' experience. Steps 1' and 2' generally suggest or bolster inferences that have the same degree of cogency and range of inference as inferences derived during Steps 1 and 2. Furthermore, as the example shows, it is not only Steps 1' and 2' that are vulnerable to this criticism but also any knowledge derived from another relationship episode, even in Steps 1 and 2. To be safe from this criticism, each relationship episode would have to be scored by judges who knew only the single relationship episode being scored (as in the QUAINT system discussed in chapter 20, this volume). But such a procedure would limit the CCRT, because the inference system for the CCRT was set up to parallel the experience of the therapist, who is attentive to redundancy across relationship episodes as the usual basis for forming inferences during psychotherapy.

Nevertheless, it would be of interest to know (a) how often inferences are added by Steps 1' and 2' and (b) how often this additional review of inferences makes a difference. "Making a difference" might mean that the correlations with other measures based on Steps 1 and 2 alone are different from the correlations based on the addition of Steps 1' and 2'.

To Focus on the Patient's Perspective

The clinician's focus should be on inferring the patient's perspective in the patient's narratives, not anyone else's. The carrying out of this basic injunction fits the definition of a psychoanalytic method, as Klein (1970) described it: The intention of the clinician who is following this method is to achieve understanding of "intentionally" from the point of view of the patient.

CONCLUSIONS

- This chapter examines the rationales for and justifies each of the procedures chosen for the CCRT method. Three basic types of decisions had to be made: decisions for the database, for the scoring system, and for the inference level. I decided to focus on redundancy across narratives from psychotherapy sessions as the database for inferring the CCRT. The scoring system was based on a three-part clinical judgment of the types of wishes, needs, and intentions; responses from other; and responses of self, together with the positivity versus negativity of each response.

- The inference level was to be limited to moderate, which mainly serves to avoid very high-level abstractions.
- Now, with hindsight, I can see that the rationale for these decisions was reasonable and useful in terms of achieving adequate reliability, reported in chapter 6, and several types of validity, reported in the next major section on "Discoveries with the CCRT." Further research remains to be done to test the competing options considered for each of the decisions.

II

DISCOVERIES FROM THE CCRT METHOD

9

THE NARRATIVES TOLD DURING PSYCHOTHERAPY AND THE TYPES OF CCRTs WITHIN THEM

LESTER LUBORSKY, JACQUES P. BARBER, PAMELA SCHAFFLER, AND JOHN CACCIOLA

Each time we have told people about our book's topic, their first question has been, "And what *are* the types of narratives people tell and what *are* the types of CCRTs?" In this chapter, we begin with a description of the narratives told during psychotherapy and go on to explore the types of CCRTs extracted from them.

All psychotherapists know that narratives are often told during psychotherapy sessions and that they are clinically very informative. Although the special clinical values of narratives are evident, the narrative as a unit in psychotherapy had never been systematically investigated before; until the launching of the CCRT (Luborsky, Barber, & Diguer, 1992), its exact formal characteristics (such as frequency, length, and variety of people in them) remained unexplored territory. Because narratives are the database for the CCRT, our focus on the CCRT requires us to scrutinize the narratives themselves closely. This chapter sketches a few features of narratives that are important to the studies in this book, such as the number and completeness of narratives, the length of the narratives, and the main other people in the narratives. This chapter also examines the frequency of the types of CCRT components, such as the types of standard category CCRTs within narratives, the sequential versus the regular CCRT, the positive versus negative responses within CCRTs, and the possible significance of the diagnosis of dysthymia for CCRTs.

NUMBER AND COMPLETENESS OF NARRATIVES

Narratives are common in psychotherapy sessions: The average session in psychotherapy in the Penn Psychotherapy Study had 4.1 passably complete narratives (with a range approximately from 1 to 7 narratives per session). This average is for Sessions 3 and 5, the usual sessions in this book chosen as a basis for extracting the CCRT early in therapy, and the estimation of narratives' completeness is based on the rules outlined in chapter 2.

It is worth taking a moment to consider why patients tell so many narratives about relationships with other people within psychotherapy sessions. Although the patients themselves have not been asked this question directly, we do have explanatory leads that are based on the context in which the narratives are told: (a) Narratives are clearly useful to the patient as a means of illustrating for the therapist examples of the patient's problems. A patient may say, for instance, "I have a problem with dependency. Let me tell you this event. . . ." (b) The central relationship pattern and the conflicts within it, as this book shows, are present within the narratives and make them memorable to the patient. (c) The therapist occasionally asks for specific examples. The first and second of these leads imply that patients find they can communicate to their therapist the nature of their problems better through the narrative mode than through more direct modes of communication; Bruner (1987) made a similar point about this property of narratives.

LENGTH OF NARRATIVES TOLD DURING THERAPY SESSIONS

The length of the usual narrative is now known. A convenient measure of the length of a narrative is the number of typed lines it takes up in a session transcript. The average number of lines per narrative within the early sessions is 51.1, which is about two double-spaced pages. The range is large: 7–207 lines. These figures are based on a representative sample of 18 patients from the Penn Psychotherapy sample (Luborsky, Crits-Christoph, et al., 1988).

The main other types of persons with whom the teller of the narrative interacts most often, in a sample of 33 patients, are given in Table 1. The 33 patients are also a representative sample of the 73 patients in the Penn Psychotherapy Project (Luborsky, Crits-Christoph, et al., 1988).

The therapist is often a main other person in the patients' narratives. Of the 33 patients studied, 25 (76%) told about the therapist as the main other person in their narratives, and these 25 patients told a total of 52 narratives. Of the 10 narratives told by each patient, a mean of two of these were about the therapist.

Family members (father, mother, siblings, or other relatives) made up another frequent type of other person in the narratives. Twenty-eight (85%) of the 33 patients told narratives about family members as the main other person. The total number of narratives they told was 87, meaning almost 3 out of 10 of their narratives were about family members. Among the large number of narratives about family members, when they were broken down into subcategories, was a relatively small percentage about siblings, which is surprising in view of the importance of conflict among siblings as overwhelmingly demonstrated by Sulloway (1996).

Intimate relationships with other people are an especially frequent category for female participants. Of the 24 women in this sample, 19 (79%) told narratives about intimate relationships with others; there were 82 of these narratives, meaning that narratives about intimate relationships constituted 4 out of 10 relationship episodes. Narratives about nonintimate relationships were told less frequently. We conclude that the distribution of narratives follows the principle that the more intimate the relationship

TABLE 1
Frequency of Different Other Persons in Narratives ($N = 33$)

Person	Patients ($N = 33$) %	REs ($N = 323$) %
Therapist	76	16
Family (father, mother, siblings, or relatives)	85	27
Intimate relation (e.g., spouse)	73	29
For males (5)	56[a]	13[b]
For females (19)	79[c]	35[d]
Friends (same sex)	30	8
Friends (opposite sex)	15	2
Friends in general	15	2
Authority figures	45	7
Coworkers	15	2
People in general	21	3

Note. RE = relationship episode.
[a] 9 patients. [b] 89 REs. [c] 24 patients. [d] 234 REs.

with a type of other person, the more narratives are told about that type of other person.

That principle about intimacy is so obvious it evokes memories of Groucho Marx's routine of challenging his audiences with the question, "Who is buried in Grant's tomb?" (Grant, who else?) The rediscovery of an obvious principle catches our interest because of its reassuring fit with what was expected. The principle is consistent with the meaningfulness of narratives as our database—intimate relationships are important for people; thus, what is buried in narratives reflects meaningful data.

CCRTs OF PATIENTS

What do patients in psychotherapy want from other people, how do they expect them to respond, and how do they react? These familiar questions can be answered from the narratives patients tell about their interactions with other people in the course of psychotherapy sessions and from the CCRTs derived from these narratives. The purpose of this part of the chapter is to examine the frequency of different types of CCRT components and their patterns. Such data have never been systematically reported before for a sizable sample of patients in dynamic psychotherapy.

We also searched through the clinical writings of dynamic therapists to classify the types of descriptions of central relationship patterns or transference patterns. Although we found such a formulation in each case study, there is no summary anywhere of the frequency of different types of transference patterns.

Nor is there much about central relationship patterns in Murray's (1938) book on Thematic Apperception Test (TAT) stories. His main variables were needs and presses, with the exception of his brief suggestion of a central relationship pattern in terms of his "unity theme" (see chapter 1). The same applies to other guides to the TAT, such as Tomkins' (1947), which also presents sets of needs and presses.

We have already observed in the case examples (in chapter 5, this volume) that the CCRTs derived from the three specimen patients' narratives were very different from each other. Their diversity is apparent even when one looks only at the main wishes: Ms. Smyth's main wish was to be given support and care; Mr. Howard's was to be close and not cut off from affection; Ms. Cunningham's was to be independent and assertive. This chapter shows how common these wishes and the responses to them were among the narratives told by a sample of patients about their interactions with other people.

We did CCRT analyses on the basis of Sessions 3 and 5 in the sample of 33 patients selected from the Penn Psychotherapy Project's sample of 73 patients (Luborsky, Crits-Christoph, et al., 1988). From these sessions, approximately 10 narratives were selected (sometimes a third session was needed to reach a sample of 10 narratives). These sessions had been independently scored for their CCRT by two judges (CP and DM) using the tailor-made system (chapter 2).

We report on the rescoring of the tailor-made categories by two other independent judges (JC and PS) using the standard categories. This chapter also presents the frequency of each of the three usual CCRT components among the 33 patients.

TYPES OF TAILOR-MADE CCRTs WITHIN NARRATIVES

One of the authors (PS) summarized the tailor-made CCRT frequencies for the 33 patients as scored by two judges (CP and DM; see Table 2, first column). The table includes the frequencies, both the most frequent and next most frequent, for each patient for each CCRT component in the narratives. The summarizing judge tried to remain faithful to the tailor-made categories offered by each of the original scoring judges. Even though the tailor-made method has inherent limits that make comparisons difficult, the experience of the summarizing judge was that the categorization usually could be done in a fairly straightforward way.

We now offer an answer to the age-old question, "What do people want most from people they interact with?" The most frequent wishes are listed in Table 2 and are summarized here; in parentheses is the number of patients having each wish: to be close (13), to assert myself (10), and to get attention and interest from other (6). The next most frequent wishes expressed by patients were also to be close (5) and to assert myself (6). As would be expected, the next most frequent categories tended to be similar to the most frequent.

The most frequent responses from other were negative: rejects or criticizes me (11) and dominates or controls me (9). The positive responses from other were moderately frequent. The two most frequent negative responses of self were angry (12) and withdrawn, distant (8).

TYPES OF STANDARD CATEGORY CCRTs WITHIN NARRATIVES

To ease the task of summarizing the tailor-made scoring done by different judges, we developed the lists of standard categories presented in chapter 3, this volume. The one used here is the result of a cluster analysis of the standard categories of Edition 2, described in chapter 3.

The agreement in the translation into standard categories by the two judges is moderately good. More specifically, the kappas—that is, the

TABLE 2
Tailor-Made CCRT Categories for the Penn Psychotherapy Project Sample (N = 33) With Subsamples of Dysthymic (n = 12) and Nondysthymic (n = 21) Groups

	Percentage of Patients					
	Total Sample		Dysthymic		Nondysthymic	
Cluster	Most Frequent	Next Most Frequent	Most Frequent	Next Most Frequent	Most Frequent	Next Most Frequent
Wish						
To be close to other	39	21	50	17	33	24
To assert myself, be independent	30	45	33	75	29	29
To get attention from other	18	0	0	0	29	0
To be helped, taken care of	9	12	8	17	10	10
To be accepted	9	3	25	8	0	0
Negative responses from other						
Rejects or criticizes me	33	12	25	8	38	14
Dominates or controls me	27	15	42	17	19	14
Distant	18	6	17	0	19	10
Unhelpful or unreliable	12	0	0	0	19	0
Positive responses from other						
Close to me	21	0	25	0	19	0
Likes me	6	0	17	0	0	0
Negative responses of self						
Angry	36	24	25	25	43	24
Withdrawn, distant	24	24	33	17	19	29
Feel inadequate, helpless	21	21	33	33	14	14
Self-blaming	18	15	25	17	14	14
Positive responses of self						
Close to other	15	0	17	0	14	0
Assertive	9	0	8	0	10	0
Like other	9	0	8	0	10	0

TABLE 3
Clustered Standard Categories Within Narratives for Penn Psychotherapy Project Sample (N = 33) With Subsamples of Dysthymic (n = 12) and Nondysthymic (n = 21) Groups

	Percentage of Patients		
Cluster	Total	Dysthymic	Nondysthymic
Wishes			
1. To assert self and be independent	33	42	29
2. To oppose, hurt, or control others	18	25	14
3. To be controlled, hurt, or not responsible	24	25	24
4. To be distant and avoid conflicts	27	33	24
5. To be close and accepting	39	42	38
6. To be loved and understood	36	50	29
7. To feel comfortable and good	15	17	14
8. To achieve and help others	18	17	19
Resonses from other			
1. Strong	3	8	0
2. Controlling	36	42	33
3. Upset	27	17	33
4. Bad	6	0	17
5. Rejecting and opposing	73	58	81
6. Helpful	6	0	17
7. Likes me	6	17	0
8. Understanding and accepting	9	8	17
Responses of self			
1. Helpful	9	17	8
2. Unreceptive	42	25	52
3. Respected and accepted	6	17	0
4. Oppose and hurt others	3	0	8
5. Self-controlled and self-confident	3	8	0
6. Helpless	36	33	38
7. Disappointed, depressed, angry	45	33	52
8. Anxious and ashamed	21	0	33

chance-corrected agreement between the two judges—were .59 for wishes, .60 for responses from others, and .59 for responses of self. Table 3 reports the frequencies in standard categories for all 33 patients combined and for the two diagnostic groups within the sample.

The same age-old question can now be answered in terms of standard categories: The most frequent wishes were "to be close and accepting" (13), "to be loved and understood" (12), and "to assert self and to be independent" (11). The first and second most frequent wishes, "to be close" and "to be loved," undoubtedly have much in common.

By far the most frequent responses from others were "rejecting and opposing" (14) and "controlling" (12). By far the most frequent responses of self were "disappointed and depressed" (15), "unreceptive" (14), and "helpless" (12). Taken together, the results of these analyses show that

TABLE 4
Most Frequent Tailor-Made and Standard Clustered Categories for the
Penn Psychotherapy Project Sample (N = 33)

Tailor-Made	Percentage	Standard Cluster	Percentage
Wishes			
To be close to other	39	To be close and accepting	39
To assert myself, be independent	30	To assert self and be independent	33
To get attention from other	18	To be loved and understood	36
Responses from other			
Rejects or criticizes me	33	Rejecting and opposing	73
Dominates or controls me	27	Controlling	36
Close to me	21	Upset	27
Responses of self			
Angry	36	Disappointed, depressed, angry	45
Withdrawn, distant	24	Unreceptive	42
Feel inadequate, helpless	21	Helpless	36

much of what appeared by the tailor-made method appears again by the standard categories method (see Table 4).

CCRT SEQUENCES OF COMPONENTS FOR THE WISH TO BE CLOSE VERSUS THE WISH TO BE INDEPENDENT

We report here on one of the earliest systematic attempts to examine the sequence of the CCRT components as they appear in the patients' sessions; these results build on the earlier work of Luborsky (1984, p. 202) and Barber (1989). The usual CCRT method looks only at the frequency of CCRT components without taking into account their sequence. Because we could not look at the sequences of CCRT components that follow *all* wishes, we decided to focus only on the wish to be close and the wish to be independent. Not only are these two wishes the most common, but also they carry much theoretical weight. To make this task more realistic, we considered ratings belonging to the clusters "to be loved' and "to be close" as interchangeable because their meaning is similar (see the clustered standard categories called Edition 3 in chapter 3).

A judge (PS) did a sequence analysis for these wishes in all relationship episodes, noting the responses from others and responses of self that came just after these wishes. In many cases, we could only find either responses from others or responses of self; in a few cases we found both or neither. Because there were many relationship episodes in which several wishes were present or the same wish was present on numerous occasions, we kept the most complete sequence; when there was more than one complete sequence or there were two incomplete sequences, we kept the first identified sequence. This selection process was performed in order to keep only one main sequence for each relationship episode, that is, the most frequent combinations of wishes and responses from others or responses of self. The results of this analysis are presented separately for each of the two types of wishes.

The Wish to Be Close or Be Loved

This wish was the main wish of 13 patients. It was followed by the response from others of "rejecting and opposing" in 24.4% of the relationship episodes in which the wish itself was expressed; the sequence was in 67% of the relationship episodes in which the wish was followed by *any* responses from others.

The wish to be close or loved was followed by the response of self "helpless" or "disappointed or depressed" in 44.2% of the relationship episodes in which the wish was expressed; the sequence was in 50% of the relationship episodes in which the wish was followed by *any* responses of self. The following breakdown of the RE components makes even clearer the major sequences and subdivisions in these results:

> Wish: "To be close or loved" is in 13 of 33 patients
> ↓
> RO: "Rejecting and opposing" (in 24% of the REs with the wish)
> RS: "Helpless" or "disappointed or depressed" (in 44% of the REs with the wish)"

The wish to be close or loved was followed by the response of self "helpless," "disappointed or depressed," or "ashamed or anxious" in 62% of the relationship episodes in which the wish was expressed; the sequence was in 76% of the relationship episodes in which the wish was followed by *any* responses of self.

Regarding the complete sequence of wish, response from others, and response of self, the wish to be close or loved was followed by the response from others "rejecting and opposing" and responses of self "helpless," "disappointed or depressed," or "ashamed or anxious" in 11.6% of the relationship episodes in which the wish was expressed; the sequence was in 55.4% of the relationship episodes in which the wish was followed by any responses from others and responses of self. The findings regarding the complete sequence are even more impressive if one considers the fact that only 8 of the 13 patients had any relationship episode with such a complete sequence.

The Wish to Be Independent

This wish was the main wish of 7 patients. It was followed by the response from others "rejecting" in 25.4% of the relationship episodes in which the wish was expressed; the sequence was in 47.6% of the relationship episodes in which the wish was followed by *any* responses from others.

The wish to assert oneself and to be independent was followed by the response of self, "helpless" or "disappointed or depressed" in 42.7% of the relationship episodes in which the wish was expressed and in 47.3% of the relationship episodes in which the wish was followed by any responses of self.

The wish to assert oneself and to be independent was followed by the response of self, "helpless," "disappointed or depressed," or "ashamed or anxious" in 57% of the relationship episodes in which the wish was expressed and in 61.6% of the relationship episodes in which the wish was followed by any responses of self. The wish to assert oneself and to be independent was followed by the response of self "unreceptive" in 17.9% of the episodes in which the wish was expressed and in 19.4% of the episodes in which the wish was followed by any responses of self.

The wish to assert oneself and to be independent was followed by the responses from others "rejecting," "upset," or "bad" in 34.6% of the relationship episodes in which the wish was expressed; the sequence was in 64.3% of the relationship episodes in which the wish was followed by any responses from others. If we added the response from others "controlling," these responses from others followed the wishes in 41.5% of the relationship episodes in which the wishes were expressed and in 78.5% of the relationship episodes in which the wishes were followed by any responses from others.

However, only 3 patients had the *complete* sequence of the wish, followed by responses from others, and followed by responses of self.

COMPARISON OF THE SEQUENTIAL CCRT AND THE REGULAR CCRT

According to the frequency analysis of the CCRT, as noted earlier, the most frequent wish was "to be loved"; the more frequent responses from others were "rejecting" and "controlling"; and the most frequent of the responses of self were "disappointed and depressed," "unreceptive," and "helpless." In the sequential analysis, we found that the same wish was actually followed by a "rejecting and controlling" response from others and by a "helpless," "disappointed and depressed," or "ashamed and anxious" response of self in 8 of 13 patients who provided relationship episodes including the three CCRT components. The same analysis does not seem worth doing in this sample for the wish to be independent because only 3 patients had a complete sequence of CCRT components involving this wish in their relationship episodes.

In conclusion, our results so far suggest that the usual procedure of a mere compilation of CCRT components generally yields similar results to those obtained with a sequential analysis of the CCRT components. Recently, a more formal sequence-of-components CCRT method has been developed to enable more of such analyses (Dahlbender, Albani, et al., in press; Dahlbender, Kurth, Stübner, Kalmykova, & Pokorny, in press).

POSITIVE VERSUS NEGATIVE RESPONSES WITHIN CCRTs

We also scored each type of component for its positive or negative quality. The idea for scoring the positive or negative quality within the CCRT came from Freud's (1912/1958a) designation of positive or negative in his transference formulations. In our operational measure of positive and negative, *positive* is defined from the patient's point of view as noninterference or expectation of noninterference with the satisfaction of wishes; *negative* is defined from the patient's point of view as an interference or expectation of interference with satisfaction of the wishes. We scored each response from other and response of self as either mainly positive or mainly negative. But because wishes are not easily assigned a positive or negative rating, we did not do such scoring for wishes. A wish to be close, for example, is not in itself either positive or negative. It is its association with the responses that tends to give it a positive or negative quality.

We found that independent judges can reliably assign either a positive or negative score. The agreement of the two judges was 95% for both the responses from others and the responses of self. (The two judges used here were the two who translated the tailor-made into the standard categories.) The study by Grenyer and Luborsky reported in chapter 4, this volume, found a similar high level of agreement.

The results shown in Table 5 in terms of percentages of positive and negative CCRT responses constitute a remarkable set of findings. There is an overwhelming trend for people to tell narratives about others reflecting negative rather than positive patterns in their responses from others and responses of self: Negative responses from others and self were found in 81.5% and 88.5% of the responses, respectively; positive responses from others and self were found in only 14.4% and 10.7%, respectively. Does this phenomenon occur because these are patients in psychotherapy who might be expected to tell negative narratives? Probably not, but more data are needed, including related data from other groups, before this question is answered. Another interpretation of these results is that negative inter-

TABLE 5
Positive Versus Negative CCRT Components Related to the
Therapist or Others

Type of Responses	Therapist (52 REs)		Others (271 REs)	
	Frequency	Percentage	Frequency	Percentage
Negative responses from others	29	55.8	220	81.2
Negative responses of self	32	61.5	239	88.2
Positive responses from others	6	11.5	39	14.4
Positive responses of self	7	13.4	25	9.2

Note. RE = relationship episode.

actions are more memorable because they deal with relationship interactions that are harder to master. Remembering them and telling them are in the service of efforts at mastery (Loevinger, 1976; White, 1952). Such possible meanings of these results are discussed further in chapter 22.

We also found an interesting property of the positivity and negativity of narratives about the therapist (Table 5). Although for the narratives about the therapist (n = 52) the percentages of positive responses from other and positive responses of self are somewhat similar to each other, they are higher than in the narratives told about other people. Perhaps the relationship with the therapist is less negative; alternatively, it may be harder to tell something negative about the person one is speaking to than to tell something negative about someone not present. Freud (1912/1958a) had the latter alternative in mind when he said that it is hard to talk about aspects of the negative transference when it involves someone—the therapist—who is directly present.

DIFFERENCES IN CCRTs BY DIAGNOSIS (DYSTHYMIA AND NONDYSTHYMIA)

The main results we have reported so far are for the entire sample of 33 participants, but this group included 12 patients with dysthymia who may have differed from the remaining 21. Because of the small number of dysthymics, we discuss here only the results from the clustered standard categories (see Table 3) in which percentage differences between patients with and without dysthymia are very large (two times in size or close to it). Among the differences for the wishes, the most impressive is the larger percentage of dysthymics (25% vs. 14%) with the wish to oppose, hurt, or control others. Among the responses from others, the other is seen less often as "upset" by those with dysthymia (17% vs. 33%). Among the responses of self, "unreceptive" is less evident for the dysthymics (25% vs. 52%). In essence, patients with dysthymia more often see themselves as wishing to oppose, hurt, or control the other; they see the other as less upset; and they see themselves as more responsive (more receptive) than nondysthymic patients.

RESULTS, DISCUSSION, AND CONCLUSIONS

- A novel piece of information about relationship episodes reveals just how common they are in every psychotherapy session: We found 4.1 at least fairly complete narratives per session, on the basis of the sample from Sessions 3 and 5. Each narrative took up a mean of about 51 lines, which is approximately two double-spaced pages. The main other people with whom the narrator of the relationship episode interacted were, in the following order, family members, the therapist, and other intimate relationships.

- Certain wishes and responses were moderately frequent in the narratives told by patients during psychotherapy (in our sample of 33 patients), on the basis of either the tailor-made or the standard category methods. Because a standard category method is more likely to produce reliable results than a tailor-made method, we concentrated in this chapter on the standard category clustered results using Edition 3.

- These results were summarized in terms of the CCRT components. The two most frequent wishes expressed by our patients were "to be close" and "to assert myself and to be independent." The most frequent of the responses from other were "rejecting" and "controlling"; the most frequent of the responses of self were "disappointed and depressed," "unreceptive," and "helpless."

- We reported on a pioneer analysis of the CCRT components that followed the two most common wishes: "to be close" versus "to be independent."

- It is interesting to notice the degree to which the most common wishes are socially acceptable (see both the tailor-made and standard category results in Tables 2 and 3). Almost never is there an example of a strongly socially unacceptable wish such as to steal or to murder someone. Our impression is that this tendency to tell socially acceptable wishes has most to do with the fact that these narratives are told by the narrator about the narrator's own relationships with others;

from their own point of view, their wishes are socially acceptable. A few socially unacceptable themes tend to appear in the response of self. A paraphrase of the narrative from this point of view is that the person is saying "I want socially acceptable things and others impede me or hurt me, so I sometimes end up with socially unacceptable responses."

- It is impressive to find the high frequency of negative responses in contrast to positive responses (as we discuss further in chapters 4 and 22, this volume); it would be useful to have even more comparison groups to know how to evaluate the frequency of these responses.

- We now know from the data presented in this chapter how common the wishes and responses were for the three patients whose CCRTs serve as illustrations throughout this book. On the basis of the frequencies of the clustered standard categories (Table 3), Ms. Smyth's main wish, "to be helped," fits with only part of Cluster 3 and is therefore relatively infrequent. Mr. Howard's wish fits with the most common wish, Cluster 5, to be close and accepting. Ms. Cunningham's main wish fits with the next most frequent wish, Cluster 1, to assert self and to be independent.

- As we said at the start, there are no surveys of frequencies of types of CCRTs or types of transference patterns in clinical sources, although we have general impressions from a review of Freud's case histories (e.g., 1893–1895, 1901–1905) and many other clinical case studies.

In terms of source of the transference patterns, we know that clinicians tend to refer to negative transference as modeled on the patient's early relationship with the father or mother (as in Freud's Observation 10; see chapter 21, this volume). Examples of such interpretations are not difficult to find in the cases used for illustration in chapter 5: (a) In Mr. Howard's Session 3, for the relationship episode about the therapist, the patient describes feeling "generally unresponsive, I'm getting a headache, tense. . . ." The therapist interprets the negative relationship with the therapist by conveying the idea that the patient is expecting to be disappointed by the therapist's response (with the implication that this was the disappointment he had also felt with his mother). (b) A similar interpretation of the negative experience in the relationship with the therapist is present in the case of Ms. Cunningham. After the patient speaks about needing reassurance from her husband, the therapist says, "You didn't express wanting reassurance here yesterday." Such interpretations of the negative experience of the relationship with the therapist are not uncommon. They fit Freud's (1913/1958c) recommendations to therapists to deal with negative transference manifestations.

In terms of content of the most frequent patterns, many clinicians believe that the most common transference pattern is one involving the oedipal triangle. Yet the oedipal theme is not immediately obvious in our three main examples of early sessions (chapter 5), and it is not obvious in the other 30 cases of the Penn Psychotherapy Project sample discussed in this chapter. Instead, the oedipal theme is often indirectly expressed in the early sessions, and it becomes more directly exposed in the later sessions. This sequence of indirect expression becoming more direct later in the therapy fits the data from Mr. Howard. His CCRT derived from the early sessions reflected a strong wish for closeness and affection from his mother; the same wish appeared later in the treatment in ways that more directly reflected an oedipal theme. In addition, a version of the oedipal theme often appears in the CCRT, when it is either directly or indirectly expressed, as we saw for Ms. Cunningham in the late sessions.

■ We conclude that the two most frequent types of wishes, to be close and to be independent, are probably associated with each other in the sense that they often conflict, probably even in people in our society who do not have psychiatric diagnoses. The likelihood of spawning symptoms from this conflict is related to (a) the conflict's intensity and (b) the fears aroused by thoughts or behaviors that coincide with the expression of one or the other side of the conflict. A good example of the second source came when Ms. Cunningham (in Session 5) reached out and stroked the professor's tie to express admiration for it. This impulsive break from her usual control increased her anxiety and her symptoms of inhibition and constriction, the symptoms that had served to forestall such breaks.

This view about the likelihood of conflict between these wishes is consistent with a review by Bonanno and Singer (1990). They see the wishes "to be close" and "to be independent" as an expression of an inherent conflict between two classes of wishes: a basic desire to blend with another person versus a desire to have individuality, power, and competence. Their review implies that maladaptive behavior may appear as one moves closer to one extreme at the expense of the other. Further evidence of the meaningfulness of the conflict between these two types of wishes comes from a study (Luborsky, Crits-Christoph, & Alexander, 1990) relating CCRT wishes and repressive style measures. Participants who scored low on the Weinberger measure of repression (1990) tended to score high on the wish to receive affection (which is related to the wish to be close) and low on wishes for dominance and competitiveness (which are related to the wish for independence).

- Our findings must reflect our sample of nonpsychotic outpatients in dynamic psychotherapy (Luborsky, Crits-Christoph, et al., 1988). We still do not have data from other diagnostic groups to show the distinctiveness of the CCRT components. Although the CCRT *Newsletter* (Luborsky et al., 1997) lists 26 studies of diagnostic groups, none has yet been published. In time we will have results from at least three of such groups: (a) normal persons without any psychiatric diagnosis (Demorest et al., 1997), (b) patients with borderline personality disorder who are in dynamic psychotherapy (Lefebvre, Diguer, Morissette, Rousseau, & Normandin, 1996), and (c) patients with major depression who are in dynamic psychotherapy (Luborsky, Diguer, et al., 1996).

10

CHANGES IN CCRT PERVASIVENESS DURING PSYCHOTHERAPY

PAUL CRITS-CHRISTOPH AND LESTER LUBORSKY

In case descriptions by psychodynamic writers, it is the relationship conflicts that are pointed out as the fomenters of symptom outbreaks. When the symptoms decrease, these relationship conflicts are seen as having become less pervasive. To become less pervasive means that the relationship conflicts appear in fewer narratives about interaction with other people. This sequence of reduction in generality of relationship conflicts across relationship episodes, followed by reduction in symptoms, is illustrated in the examples we gave of improvement in patients assessed before versus after psychotherapy (chapter 5).

Example: The following CCRT emerged from a review of Mr. Howard's narratives of interactions with other people: (a) I wish not to be cut off from closeness and affection; (b) I expect the other person to cut me off from closeness and affection; (c) I respond by feeling rejected and becoming angry, self-blaming, and highly anxious, that is, by developing a symptom. In this example the main relationship conflict is

An earlier version of this chapter appeared in L. Luborsky, P. Crits-Christoph, J. Mintz, and A. Auerbach, 1988, *Who Will Benefit from Psychotherapy?* (pp. 250–262), New York: Harper-Collins. It has been adapted, revised, and printed with permission of the publisher.

between the wish and the expected response from the other person. The patient's relationship conflicts were considerably better controlled by the end of psychotherapy, although when they reappeared from time to time the patient's anxiety symptom reemerged, as in the episode reported 8 years later (described at the end of chapter 7, this volume), when the patient's supervisor at first appeared to him to be cutting him off from approval. On that occasion the fomenters of the patient's relationship conflict were reactivated and anxiety symptoms started to develop, but he showed greater mastery, for he had acquired a greater capacity to recognize the reappearance of a familiar relationship conflict and then even to see the humor in his mistaken perception that almost set off its recurrence.

The decreased pervasiveness of the conflictual relationship patterns appears to operate as a curative factor through fostering reduction of the symptoms, and the amount of change in itself is a theoretically relevant measure of the outcome of dynamic psychotherapy. One of the most significant needs of research on psychotherapy, particularly dynamic psychotherapy, is for measures of the outcome of therapy that are relevant to the theory of psychodynamic change. Both the behaviorists and supporters of the *Diagnostic and Statistical Manual* (DSM) approach have pulled the field of psychotherapy research toward the use of bare measures of overt behavior and symptoms as outcome criteria. For psychodynamic psychotherapies, the lack of a reliable and valid measure of psychodynamic change has forced researchers to rely on other types of assessment, such as general symptom inventories or global ratings of improvement. Although such measures have the virtue of simplicity and applicability to many different kinds of treatment, they are not derived from sound theory. For psychoanalytic psychotherapy, relevant measures include change in the main conflictual relationship pattern and changes in the patient's awareness of this pattern.

The work by Malan and his associates (Malan, 1963; Malan, Bacal, Heath, & Balfour, 1968) is an exception to the trend because it deals with theory-related outcome measures. Malan has argued against the reliance on behavioral manifestations alone and has developed an individualized method of assessment that is guided by psychodynamic hypotheses. In brief, his method involves (a) an initial detailed account of the patient's presenting problems, (b) a consensus formulation of a dynamic hypothesis by a group of clinicians, and (c) the specification of emotional and behavioral changes that would indicate favorable outcome for each case. Posttreatment assessment is based on a clinical interview. An account of the interview is given to the group of clinicians so that they can rate improvement on a global 9-point scale. However, problems with Malan's method have been detailed by Mintz (1981); they include the lack of reliability and validity information about the psychodynamic hypothesis and the reliance on one interviewer's account after treatment rather than independent assessment of outcome by different clinicians. Using Malan's published case reports, Mintz (1981) has also demonstrated that a large component of the Malan outcome rating is simple symptomatic improvement that can be readily assessed by nonclinician judges.

Other individualized methods of outcome assessment have been developed, such as the Target Complaints method (Battle et al., 1966) and Goal Attainment Scaling (Kiresuk, 1973), but these measures are not psychodynamically based and have been criticized on psychometric grounds (Mintz & Kiesler, 1982). Still other measures go beyond assessment of symptoms (e.g., Weiss, DeWitt, Kaltreider, & Horowitz, 1985), yet these methods do not assess the types of individual themes and conflicts that are important in psychoanalytic psychotherapy.

It is clear that the major stumbling block to the development of a measure suited to the evaluation of outcomes of psychoanalytic psychotherapy has been the lack of a reliable and valid measure of the nature of the patient's particular dynamic conflicts and themes. Without a measure of the relevant conflicts for each patient, researchers cannot determine whether improvement that is consistent with the theory and techniques of the therapy has occurred.

Several studies (Seitz, 1966; DeWitt, Kaltreider, Weiss, & Horowitz, 1983) comparing independent clinicians' formulations of patients' dynamic themes have reported a lack of consensus among clinicians in unguided judgments of such themes. But more recently, guided clinical case formulation methods that are applied to psychotherapy session material have arrived on the scene and appear to be more promising. There are 17 of these alternative methods listed in chapter 20, this volume, that have appeared since information about the Core Conflictual Relationship Theme (CCRT) method was first published in 1976.

The concept of pervasiveness as the recurrence of components across narratives is at the heart of the CCRT method, as first described by Luborsky (1976, 1977b). Because the focus of dynamic psychotherapy tends to be on themes that are maladaptive, repetitive, and inappropriately applied, we propose that one index of change in dynamic therapy is the extent to which the maladaptive theme becomes less pervasive in the relationships of a patient by the end of treatment. For the CCRT method, this concept translates into a decrease from the beginning to the end of treatment in the percentage of relationship episodes in which the maladaptive theme is present.

The purposes of the study presented here were (a) to assess the agreement of independent judges on our measure of change based on the CCRT, (b) to compare results from applying the measure to sessions early and late in treatment, and (c) to examine the relationships between the psychodynamic measure of change in the CCRT and the more conventional measures of change in self-reported symptoms (Derogatis, Lipman, Covi, Rickels, & Uhlenhuth, 1970) and change on a clinician-rated psychological health–sickness scale (Luborsky, 1962, 1975; Luborsky & Bachrach, 1974; Luborsky, Diguer, et al., 1993).

PROCEDURE

Combination of Judges' CCRT Formulations

For each case the final CCRT selected for inclusion in the study was a composite of two judges' independent CCRT formulations. It included five components: wish, negative response from other, negative response of self, positive response from other, and positive response of self. Each of the two judges' tailor-made formulations for each type of component was coded into standard categories (Edition 1) to permit direct comparisons between their formulations. This task of coding the tailor-made into the standard categories was done with greater than 95% agreement between judges.

For each case, each judge's CCRT formulation, as coded into standard categories, was examined. A composite CCRT was derived by selecting wishes and responses that were in common among the two judges' listings of the most frequent CCRT components. Frequency scores were derived for each type of component by taking the average of the different judges' frequency scores.

Finally, these average frequency scores were divided by the number of relationship episodes used for each case to derive a percentage score, which we have termed the CCRT *pervasiveness score* or the *pervasiveness of conflicts across the relationship episodes*. Because this score is a central measure in the current study, we restate it here for the sake of clarity (RE = relationship episode):

CCRT pervasiveness

$$= \frac{\text{Number of REs that include the CCRT component}}{\text{Total REs in the session or sessions}}$$

This measure is built on a theory-derived expectation of the gains from successful psychoanalytic psychotherapy: The main conflictual relationship patterns should become less pervasive across the relationship episodes because the patterns should become less stereotyped as more relationship options are opened up to thought and expression.

Although multiple wishes and responses are generally evident for each patient, the categories with the highest frequency for each of the five types of CCRT components were chosen for study. Because we were examining *change* on these components, it was necessary to use the percentage score for the same thematic category both early and late in treatment, although the same category was not necessarily the one with the highest frequency at both times (for example, if "anxious" was the most common negative response of self early in treatment, it was not always the most common response of self late in treatment). For the wish, negative response from other, and negative response of self, the early-in-treatment category with the highest frequency was selected as the focus to examine change. For the positive response from other and positive response of self, the late-in-treatment category with the highest frequency was chosen first, and then the frequency of this same component early in treatment was noted.

A modified version of the Hopkins Symptom Checklist, the Symptom Checklist (SCL; Derogatis et al., 1970), containing 85 items, was used as a general measure of level of self-reported symptoms. The measure was obtained from patients before the start of therapy and at termination. The internal consistency (Cronbach's alpha coefficient) of this measure was .96.

Patients and Therapists

The sample in this study was 33 patients chosen to approximate the range of improvement in the larger sample of 73 patients in the Penn Psychotherapy Project. The sample consisted of 8 men and 25 women, with a median age of 24 years. The *DSM-III* diagnoses included dysthymic disorder (13), generalized anxiety disorder (7), schizoid personality disorder (7), and histrionic personality disorder (4); the rest of the diagnoses are represented by only 1 to 3 patients each. All patients were nonpsychotic.

A total of 25 therapists (all psychiatrists) treated the 33 patients, with each therapist generally working with only one or two patients. The therapists ranged in age from 26 to 55 years, with a median age of 34. Thirteen of the therapists were 4th-year psychiatric residents who were supervised by experienced clinicians. Eight therapists had fewer than 10 years of post-residency experience, and four therapists had more than 10 years of post-residency experience.

Treatment, Sessions, and Judges

The patients were in psychodynamic psychotherapy, attending once or twice per week; two patients attended four sessions per week of psychoanalysis. Treatment length varied from 21 to 149 weeks, with a median length of 43 weeks.

Sessions drawn from the early and later parts of treatment were used to score the CCRT. The number of early and late sessions was a function of the number of sessions needed to obtain the minimum of 10 relationship episodes. This was generally two sessions, but for a few patients it was three or four.

The early sessions used were typically Sessions 3 and 5. For the late sessions we chose to avoid sessions close to termination so that issues related to termination (such as resurgence of symptoms) would not affect our data. On the average, the late sessions represented the point of treatment at which 90% of sessions had been completed.

Trained judges working independently were used for each task. The judges were clinical psychologists, psychiatrists, and research assistants highly familiar with the methods.

RESULTS

CCRT Pervasiveness Scores Were Highly Reliable

The agreement between judges in the pervasiveness of the main CCRT components was examined by calculating intraclass correlation coefficients for early-session data in which the same two judges had scored the cases. The results indicated relatively high agreement between the two judges; pooled judges' intraclass correlations were as follows: wish, .82; negative response from other, .90; negative response of self, .80; positive response from other, .84; positive response of self, .85. Judges' pervasiveness scores were therefore averaged for all subsequent analyses.

Measures of CCRT Change Were Low to Moderately Intercorrelated

To find the degree of intercorrelation among change scores on each of the CCRT pervasiveness measures, Pearson correlations were computed (see Table 1). Of the 10 intercorrelations, 3 were statistically significant: (a) Residual gain on the wish measure was significantly correlated with residual gain on the negative response of self scores, $r = .45$, $p < .01$ (the residual gain is the gain corrected for initial level); (b) change in pervasiveness on the positive response from other dimension was related to

TABLE 1
Intercorrelations of CCRT Pervasiveness Change Measures
(Residual Gain Scores)

Dimension	Negative RO	Negative RS	Positive RO	Positive RS
Wish	.25	.45**	−.24	−.24
Negative response from other		.28	−.52**	−.28
Negative response of self			−.22	−.16
Positive response from other				.41*

Note. Residual gain is corrected for initial level of the variable. RO = response from other; RS = response of self.
*p < .05. **p < .01.

change on the negative response from other measures, $r = -.52$, $p < .01$; and (c) change in positive response from other was related to change in positive response of self, $r = .41$, $p < .05$.

CCRT Pervasiveness Was Greatest for the Wishes

The early and late pervasiveness scores for the CCRT were moderately high (see Table 2). When we looked at each CCRT component separately, we found the wishes to be much more pervasive than the responses. This was true for the wishes at both the early (66.3%) and late (61.9%) points in the psychotherapy; the negative responses averaged only a little more than half the pervasiveness of the wishes. The positive responses were much less pervasive than the negative ones.

CCRT Pervasiveness Decreased From Early to Late in Therapy

To examine differential change across the measures, the early treatment CCRT pervasiveness and late treatment CCRT pervasiveness on each of the five CCRT measures were subjected to a two-factor repeated-measure analysis of variance (ANOVA). One factor, Measure, had five levels corresponding to the five types of pervasiveness measures (wish, negative response from other, negative response of self, positive response from other, and positive response of self), and a second factor, Time, consisted of the early–late dimension. The interaction term of primary interest, Measure by Time, addressed the question of differential change across the five CCRT measures.

The ANOVA produced statistically significant main effects for both Measure, $F(4, 128) = 93$, $p < .001$, and Time $F(1, 32) = 7.4$, $p < .01$. In addition, the Measure by Time interaction was highly significant, $F(4, 128) = 12.6$, $p < .001$, indicating that the early–late changes were not uniform across the five measures.

Table 2 presents mean early and late pervasiveness scores on each of the five CCRT measures. For each measure, the statistical significance of

TABLE 2
Mean Percentages Early and Late in Treatment for CCRT
Pervasiveness Scores ($N = 33$)

Dimension	Early	SD	Late	SD
Wish	66.3	15	61.9	25
Negative response from other	40.7	14	28.5	18
Negative response of self	41.7	14	22.8	18
Positive response from other	8.6	10	18.7	12
Positive response of self	13.4	12	19.1	16

Note. SD = standard deviation.

the early-to-late changes was tested by a paired *t* test. Small but reliable changes occurred on four of the five CCRT measures. The pervasiveness of the CCRT main wish decreased nonsignificantly from 66.3% to 61.9% over the course of treatment. Changes on the negative response from other (12.2% decrease), negative response of self (18.9% decrease), and positive response from other (10.1% increase) dimensions were all highly significant ($p < .001$, two-tailed). Change on the positive response of self score (5.7% increase) was also significant ($p = .055$, two-tailed).

Some Early-in-Therapy Pervasiveness Scores Were Related to Initial Symptoms and to Initial Health–Sickness

Pearson correlation coefficients were calculated between the five CCRT pervasiveness measures and (a) initial symptoms as measured by the total score on the Hopkins Symptom Checklist and (b) initial scores on the composite clinician-rated Health–Sickness Rating Scale (HSRS). Four of the five measures of pervasiveness yielded correlations near zero with the scores on the Symptom Checklist. But the positive response of self pervasiveness measure correlated significantly ($r = -.48$, $p < .005$) with the Symptom Checklist scores, indicating that higher symptom levels were associated with fewer positive responses of self. It is consistent with this that a significant correlation ($r = .41$, $p < .05$) was also found between the HSRS and the positive response of self pervasiveness measure. Again consistently, scores on HSRS correlated significantly ($r = -.34$, $p < .05$) with the negative response from other measure.

Change in CCRT Pervasiveness Was Moderately Correlated With Change in Symptoms and Change in Health-Sickness

The relationships between change in CCRT pervasiveness and both change in symptom levels and change in the HSRS were assessed through partial correlation analyses. The purpose of using this method was to allow for an assessment of change corrected for initial level on each type of measure. Posttreatment Symptom Checklist scores were correlated with late-in-treatment pervasiveness, with the effects of pretreatment symptom scores and early treatment pervasiveness partialed out. The same analysis was done using the HSRS.

Table 3 presents the partial correlations between change on each of the five CCRT measures and change on the Symptom Checklist and the HSRS. Of the five CCRT measures, three showed statistically significant partial correlations with the change in the Symptom Checklist, and the other two evidenced near-significant partial correlations, all in the expected direction. For change in the HSRS, only change in the pervasiveness of the negative response of self was significantly correlated ($r = -.53$,

TABLE 3
Partial Correlations of Change in CCRT Pervasiveness Measures With Change in Symptoms and Change in Health–Sickness

Dimension	Hopkins Symptom Checklist Change	Health–Sickness Rating Scale Change
Wish	.41***	−.14
Negative response from other	.34*	−.27
Negative response of self	.40***	−.53****
Positive response from other	−.32**	.11
Positive response of self	−.40***	.14

*$p = .06$. **$p = .08$. ***$p < .05$. ****$p < .01$.

$p < .01$), again in the expected direction: Improvement in HSRS was associated with less change in pervasiveness of the negative response of self.

DISCUSSION

This study provided a theory-relevant measure of psychodynamic change based on the CCRT method. Good interjudge reliability was obtained with the measure of pervasiveness of the CCRT across relationship episodes. The theory-derived expectation in relation to successful psychotherapy did emerge: The main conflictual relationship pattern did become less pervasive across the relationship episodes; the change was relatively small but consistent.

CCRT changes from early to late in treatment were found. Changes in pervasiveness were significantly correlated with changes in other outcome measures, namely changes in symptoms and changes in clinician-rated health-sickness. Each of these findings is discussed in turn.

Reliability of Pervasiveness Score

The relatively high reliability of the pervasiveness score can be attributed to several factors. First, the system calls for a two-step task: categorizing the main relationship pattern and then scoring its pervasiveness. Second, the CCRT method on which the pervasiveness measure is based is a guided clinical scoring system with demonstrated interjudge reliability (see chapter 6, this volume). A dynamic formulation method of questionable or unknown reliability clearly would be problematic as a basis for assessing change in dynamic conflicts. The concept is clear: It is the percentage of interactions with other people across narratives that contain the main relationship theme.

CCRT Pervasiveness Across the Narratives

What we have labeled Freud's (1912/1958a) Observation 9 (see chapter 21, this volume), states that there is a single central relationship pattern. One way to examine this observation is to measure the degree of pervasiveness of the CCRT components across the narratives in psychotherapy sessions. A high pervasiveness of components would be consistent with Freud's observation. The fist bit of precise evidence of this kind was presented in Table 2. It revealed that the pervasiveness percentage was especially high for the wish (greater than 60%) within the early sessions; it was only slightly lower within the late sessions, but at both early and late points the pervasiveness of the wishes was greater than that of the responses.

CCRT Pervasiveness Changes in Therapy

In terms of the pattern of changes from early to late in treatment in the pervasiveness scores, it was found that the wishes changed less than the responses. Apparently, one's wishes, needs, and intentions in relationships are relatively intractable, and yet the expectations about others gratifying or blocking one's wishes and one's emotional responses to the others' actions or expectations have more flexibility, or malleability. Through successful therapy, patients learn to recognize and cope with their wish–response patterns in ways that lead to fewer negative and more positive responses. In essence, the reduction in pervasiveness of the conflictual relationships can be seen as a theoretically crucial curative factor.

The magnitude of the changes in the pervasiveness scores during psychotherapy also raises important questions. Despite the fact that on standard outcome measures the majority of patients in the Penn Psychotherapy Project improved—65% were moderately or much improved, which is the usual percentage in psychotherapy outcome studies (Luborsky, Crits-Christoph, et al., 1988)—the dynamic changes were small on the average, and even patients who improved considerably retained some of their basic relationship components. These results have implications for theories of the curative process in psychoanalytic psychotherapy. Clinical discussions of the theory of change offer two views of what happens in the course of psychoanalysis or psychodynamic psychotherapy: One view holds that the transference patterns and the conflicts within them are resolved (see, for example, Ekstein, 1956; Davanloo, 1980); the other view (e.g., Pfeffer, 1963; Schlessinger & Robbins, 1975) holds that transference patterns and the conflicts within them remain evident even in the most successful psychotherapy, although some components of the pattern are altered. Our results clearly favor the second clinical view of change, which emphasizes the stability of the transference pattern. An early CCRT study (Baguet,

Gerin, Sali, & Marie-Cardine, 1984) of five patients also showed basic stability during group psychotherapy.

Another implication has special interest for the still very hot debate in academic psychology about traits and states. We have developed what is mostly a trait measure, the CCRT, with a wish component that is especially consistent across situations concerning parents, therapists, and others while remaining consistent across time, despite dedicated therapeutic efforts to change the patient. Our finding would be opposite to the expectations of such writers as Mischel (1968), who emphasized inconsistencies over time in personality measures, and more consonant with the writings of Block (1971, 1977), who emphasized the findings of consistencies over time.

CCRT Change Tends to Correlate With Symptom Reduction

The changes in pervasiveness found in our data, although small, apparently were meaningful, as evidenced by the significant correlations between change in CCRT pervasiveness and symptom reduction. Whether the change drives the symptom reduction or is merely a correlate cannot be rigorously answered with the current data. Assessing both dynamic and symptomatic change at multiple time points would test hypotheses about whether dynamic change precedes and predicts symptom change.

The correlations between CCRT change and symptom change were not so high, however, as to suggest that change in the CCRT is redundant with change on symptom inventories. Our data indicate that change in the CCRT provides reliable extra information that is not captured by symptom inventories or clinician ratings.

Limitations of the Measure of CCRT Pervasiveness

Despite the promising results obtained, the methods used here have certain limitations. The CCRT pervasiveness measure is based on all of the relatively complete relationship episodes that we found in the two or three sessions used at each time point. Variations in the size of this database may affect the final measure of dynamic change. For example, it may be that a larger number of episodes than the 10 early and 10 late ones used here might be necessary to obtain a more representative index of the frequency of the main relationship theme in the person's life.

Another problem was a product of the freedom given to the patient to select the main other person in the narratives told about relationship episodes. For some patients, the same type of other person may be present in several of the episodes early in treatment but not included in the episodes sampled late in treatment, a situation that potentially could bias the data through comparison of episodes from early and late points that are based on narratives about different types of other people. Of course, the simple fact that the patient chooses which episode to tell means that the group of episodes cannot be considered a representative sampling of the interpersonal interactions in the patient's life. On the other hand, similar relationship patterns tend to emerge in narratives about different other persons, and it is our impression that the main relationships in most patients' lives are covered by the sampling used here. In addition, the reliance on material as it unfolds to the clinician allows our measure to have a closer tie to the clinical theories and methods. But more research is necessary to examine the role of the patient's choice of significant other people in affecting the measures of early versus late changes in the frequencies within the CCRT.

Another limitation on our results came into view only after we applied a different method of data analysis: a rating of each relationship episode by itself after randomizing them (see the QUAINT method described in chapter 20, this volume; Crits-Christoph et al., 1994; Connolly, Crits-Christoph, Demorest, Azarian, Muenz, & Chittams, 1996). The new results indicated slightly less pervasiveness, high levels of chance pervasiveness, and the presence of multiple themes. However, a limitation may also emerge from the rating of each relationship episode by itself, because the clinician makes use of the context of other relationship episodes to help in understanding each relationship episode.

Finally, our usual index of CCRT pervasiveness is only one operational conceptual translation that might be used as an outcome measure for psychoanalytic psychotherapy or psychoanalysis. Other aspects of the psychoanalytic process, such as changes in defenses and changes in awareness of relationship patterns, need more study as criteria for improvement in psychoanalysis or psychoanalytic psychotherapy.

We also need to know how our measure of pervasiveness compares with similar measures used in the field. We have defined pervasiveness as the frequency of the types of relationship theme components across different narratives. Yet this definition is only a variation of a common one for pervasiveness, that is, the frequency of *all* instances of the types of components, regardless of whether they are in different narratives. Many TAT scoring systems use such a frequency-of-all-occurrences measure. Murray (1938) discussed the merits of the use of frequency of occurrence, regardless of how often a component appears in a particular narrative. Frequency, he argued, has much to offer as a measure; it even corresponds generally to the salience of the component.

CONCLUSIONS

The purpose of the study presented in this chapter was to examine a theory-relevant measure of change in moderate-length psychoanalytic psychotherapy in 33 patients' psychotherapy transcripts from the Penn Psychotherapy Project. The measure chosen was change in pervasiveness of the CCRT from early to late in therapy; the aim was to learn whether it was related to more usual measures of change: the self-reported change in symptoms and the clinician-rated health–sickness rating. The main results were as follows.

- CCRT pervasiveness scores showed high agreement among judges.
- There were small but meaningful changes in pervasiveness from early to late in treatment, although the changes were not uniform across the five pervasiveness measures. Essentially, wishes did not decrease significantly in pervasiveness, but responses from others and responses of self did decrease significantly. The largest changes were a decrease in negative responses of self, a decrease in negative responses from other, and an increase in positive responses from other.
- The early-in-treatment pervasiveness of the positive responses of self was significantly correlated with initial level of symptoms and clinician-rated mental health–sickness. Health–sickness ratings were significantly correlated with pervasiveness of negative responses from other. These correlations were in the expected direction.
- Change in CCRT pervasiveness from early to late in therapy was significantly correlated with change in symptoms for three of the five CCRT measures; change in health-sickness was correlated significantly with change in the negative responses of self measure. These correlations were in the expected direction.
- As a whole, these results demonstrate another aspect of validity for the CCRT method of measuring dynamic change. Beyond that, the data have implications for psychoanalytic and other theories of change and in particular lend support to clinical theories maintaining that aspects of the core conflictual relationship pattern are still apparent even after successful treatment.

11

THE PARALLEL OF THE CCRT FOR THE THERAPIST WITH THE CCRT FOR OTHER PEOPLE

DEBORAH FRIED, PAUL CRITS-CHRISTOPH, AND LESTER LUBORSKY

During much of his clinical career, Freud (1895/1955b, 1901–1905/ 1953a, 1912/1958a) observed a basic parallel in relationship patterns: Soon after psychotherapy starts, the relationship pattern with the therapist is experienced as similar to the patient's relationship pattern with other people. This observation gave rise to Freud's concept of a relationship template and to the term *transference*, a word that implies that there is a transfer of attitudes and behavior from earlier relationships with personally important people to the later relationship with the therapist as well as others.

Freud's first use of the term *transference* (1955b) focused on this parallel between the relationship with the therapist and a much earlier relationship, as the following quotation makes clear:

> In one of my patients the origin of a particular hysterical symptom lay in a wish, which she had had many years earlier and had at once relegated to the unconscious, that the man she was talking to at the time might boldly take the initiative and give her a kiss. On one occasion, at the end of the session, a similar wish came up in her about

me. She was horrified at it. . . . What had happened therefore was this. The content of the wish had appeared first of all in the patient's consciousness without any memories of the surrounding circumstances which would have assigned it to a past time. Since I have discovered this, I have been able, whenever I have been similarly involved personally, to presume a transference and a false connection had once more taken place. (pp. 302–303)

In his postscript to the Dora case Freud (1901–1903/1953a) again wrote about this parallel:

They [transferences] are new editions or facsimiles of the impulses and fantasies which are aroused and made conscious during the progress of the analysis; but they have this peculiarity . . . that they replace some earlier person by the person of the physician. To put it another way; a whole series of psychological experiences are revived, not as belonging to the past, but as applying to the person of the physician of the present moment. Some of these transferences . . . are merely new impressions or reprints. Others . . . may even become conscious, by cleverly taking advantage of some real peculiarity in the physician's person or circumstances. (p. 116)

Freud (1901–1905/1953a) showed in a further description of the treatment of Dora how literally he followed his definition of transference in terms of this parallel:

At the beginning it was clear that I was replacing her father in imagination . . . she was even constantly comparing me with him consciously, and kept anxiously trying to make sure whether I was being quite straightforward with her, for her father "always preferred secrecy and roundabout ways." But when the first dream came, in which she gave herself a warning that she had better leave my treatment just as she had formerly left Herr K's house, I ought to have listened to the warning myself. "Now," I ought to have said to her, "it is from Herr K that you have made a transference on to me. Have you noticed anything that leads you to suspect me of evil intentions similar . . . to Herr K's?" (p. 118)

Until recently all of Freud's observations about transference—and 23 of them are listed in chapter 21 of this volume—have remained unexamined by clinical–quantitative measures applied to the sessions themselves. This is a gaping gap in research in dynamic psychotherapy because the concept of transference has been in everyday clinical use for the last 100 years. The main exception, for many years, has been studies of the concept by a questionnaire approach (see chapter 20), but these were not generally taken seriously, even though they were confirmatory of a parallel, perhaps because of uncertainty about the validity of the questionnaire approach.

AIMS AND PROCEDURES

Freud's initial observation about transference—that it involves a parallel between the current relationship with the therapist and past relationships—is reexamined here by clinical–quantitative means. Thirty-five cases were drawn from the Penn Psychotherapy Project (Luborsky et al., 1988). All were outpatients who were diagnosed according to *DSM-III* as having nonpsychotic disorders, mostly personality disorders and anxiety disorders. The diagnoses were revised into *DSM-III* terms by research psychologists on the basis of case reviews. The patients were treated in psychodynamically oriented psychotherapy with a mean of 45 sessions during a mean of 41 weeks. The therapists were either psychiatric residents in supervision at the University of Pennsylvania or therapists who had completed their training and had had several years of experience.

The data for the project were transcripts of psychotherapy sessions, two sessions from early in therapy and two from late in therapy. The two early ones were generally Sessions 3 and 5, and the late ones were at approximately the 90% point in the treatment.

This study required a sufficient number of relationship episodes from the sessions to extract a relationship pattern both toward the therapist and toward other people. As is usually true, relationship episodes about other people (other people-REs) were plentiful, whereas relationship episodes about the therapist (therapist-REs) were sparse: Only a small percentage of all relationship episodes were about the relationship with the therapist—16% in the early sessions and 22% in the late sessions. With so few therapist-REs it is difficult to extract a therapist-CCRT. We therefore decided to provide the judge with the maximum information available: the therapist-REs themselves rather than the therapist-CCRTs. The basic comparison, therefore, was between the other people-CCRTs and the therapist-REs.

Not all transcribed sessions included therapist-REs. When there were none in the late sessions, only those in early sessions were used. When there were none in the early sessions, only those in late sessions were used. When both early and late sessions included therapist-REs, both sources were used for the relationship episodes and for formulating the other person-CCRTs.

The study was carried out in two phases, as explained in the following paragraphs:

Phase 1: Formulating Other Person-CCRTs

Because our interest was in the CCRT, which is based on patients' experiences with people in their lives other than the therapist, the data from the therapist-REs were deleted from the originally scored CCRTs.

Other person-CCRTs were formulated by the CCRT method using the relationship episodes that did not refer to the therapist: The number of relationship episodes that contained a specific wish, response from other, or response of self were counted; the most frequently found wishes, responses from other, and responses of self were used for the final CCRT formulation.

Phase 2: Comparing Other Person-CCRTs With Therapist-REs

Three judges familiar with the CCRT method and blind to our hypothesis were employed for this study. Each judge first read through the therapist-REs collated from the early and late sessions. They were instructed to use what they read to form a "gestalt" view of the patient. The judges then compared the group of therapist-REs with the other person-CCRTs for the patient and with the other person-CCRT formulations for 7 other patients. Pairs were judged for similarity by the method of mismatched pairs (Levine & Luborsky, 1981): A "matched" pair was composed of the therapist-REs from "Case A" and the other person-CCRT from Case A; a "mismatched" pair was composed of the therapist-REs from Case A and the other person-CCRT from a randomly chosen, different case, such as Case B, as diagrammed in Figure 1. This use of mismatched cases served as a control for chance levels of similarity. We decided to use this method and only 7 mismatched cases because a previous pilot study involving 30 cases showed that similarity ratings for 29 mismatched pairs correlated highly ($r = .9$) with similarity ratings for 7 mismatched pairs. Judges were blind to the match–mismatch design. The judges compared the CCRT components separately; that is, they examined each wish, response from other, and response of self in turn and made the comparison to the gestalt derived from reading the relationship episodes. These judges were asked to rate how well each CCRT component identified a theme of the relationship episodes, that is, to note how much similarity they saw between the CCRT component and the relationship episodes, using a 1-to-7 scale (1 = *no similarity*, 7 = *high similarity*). Data were analyzed by paired t tests for differences between means with two-tailed probability values.

The reader can readily get a sense of the judge's task by reading the case examples in chapter 5, this volume, starting with the relationship

Matched case pair:	Case A Therapist-RE
	Case A Other person-CCRT
Mismatched case pair:	Case A Therapist-RE
	Case B Other person-CCRT

Figure 1. Matched versus mismatched pairs used for similarity judgments.

episodes. Briefer impressions of the judges' task are conveyed in the following two examples:

> *Example*: Mr. Howard. Consider the similarity of Mr. Howard's therapist-RE 3 to the CCRT formulation. The relationship episode is about people being unresponsive to each other, and the patient's response is anxiety and tension. The CCRT is about the wish to be close and to get a response, with the expectation that the other person will be unresponsive and the response of self will be anxiety and tension. There is moderate similarity between this therapist-RE and this CCRT.

> *Example*: Ms. Cunningham. The therapist-RE 5 for Ms. Cunningham is about the patient's conviction that she will not get reassurance from the therapist. The CCRT contains the wish for reassurance and the expected response from other that she will not get the reassurance. Again, there is moderate similarity between this theme of the therapist-RE and this CCRT.

The kind of comparison made in these two examples is exactly the type the judges had to make for the matched samples. For the mismatched material, the same therapist-REs were presented to the judges along with the CCRT from another case. For Mr. Howard's data, the clinical judge would almost certainly see considerable similarity for the matched pair and dissimilarity for the mismatched pair.

RESULTS

Interjudge Reliability of the CCRT Was Adequate

The intraclass correlation coefficient (pooled judges) ranged from .55 to .75 for the different CCRT components, with a median of .69. These figures demonstrate adequate interjudge reliability.

Therapist-REs and Other Person-CCRTs Showed Similarity

The main finding of this study was that patients demonstrate a pervasive relationship pattern that can be discerned when they interact with the therapist as well as with other people. We found that correctly matched pairs of therapist-REs and other person-CCRTs were more similar than were mismatched pairs. This was found for all three CCRT components (wishes, responses from other, responses of self) and reached statistical significance for the wish and response of self components (see Figure 2). Averaging the ratings for wishes, responses from other, and responses of self showed that the mean similarity between other person-CCRTs and therapist-REs was 3.5 for the correctly matched pairs and 3.0 for mis-

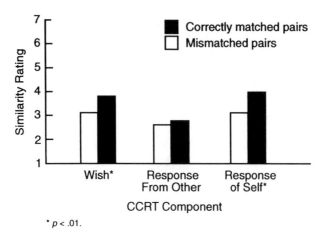

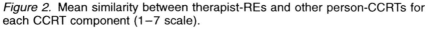

Figure 2. Mean similarity between therapist-REs and other person-CCRTs for each CCRT component (1–7 scale).

matched pairs. The difference, although apparently small, was highly significant, $t(34) = -3.51$, $p = .001$.

Similarity Was Greater for Cases With Three or More Therapist-REs

When only cases with three or more therapist-REs were examined, the findings were in the same direction but of greater magnitude: The similarity between correctly matched cases was 4.1 for the wish, 3.1 for the response from other, and 4.3 for the response of self component (mismatched cases had lower average similarity ratings, as shown, respectively, in Figures 3, 4, and 5).

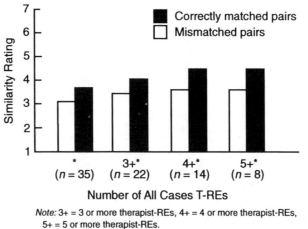

Note: 3+ = 3 or more therapist-REs, 4+ = 4 or more therapist-REs, 5+ = 5 or more therapist-REs.
*All differences significant, $p \leq .04$.

Figure 3. Mean similarity between therapist-REs and other person-CCRTs by number of therapist-REs for wishes only.

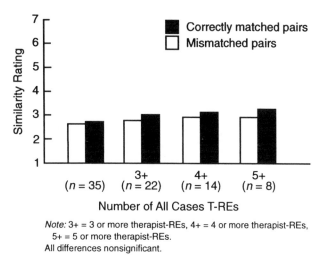

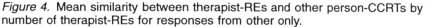

Note: 3+ = 3 or more therapist-REs, 4+ = 4 or more therapist-REs,
5+ = 5 or more therapist-REs.
All differences nonsignificant.

Figure 4. Mean similarity between therapist-REs and other person-CCRTs by number of therapist-REs for responses from other only.

This trend was maintained; that is, the more therapist-REs per case, the greater the similarity between therapist-REs and other person-CCRTs, with significantly greater similarity for the wish, response from other, and response of self components for the correctly matched pairs (as shown, respectively, in Figures 3, 4, and 5).

THE DIRECTIONS THAT LEAD FROM HERE

Increasing the Number of Relationship Episodes

Because the late sessions offered a few more therapist-REs, we used a combined sample of early and late sessions. Future work with larger subsamples should examine the possibility that the parallel between the relationship with the therapist and relationship patterns with others might well fluctuate in the course of the treatment.

We have emphasized the vital role of the number of relationship episodes in the measurement of the relationship pattern: With each increase in the number of therapist-REs, all similarity ratings rose, and more so for correctly matched pairs. It is likely, that a replication of the present study with a larger sample of therapist-REs would show the same parallel, but even more strongly.

We were struck by the concomitant increase in similarity between incorrectly matched pairs of therapist-REs and other person-CCRTs. This finding indicates that with more therapist-RE data available, a judge can discern more overlap with *any* other person-CCRT, particularly for that of the same patient but also for randomly chosen patients. This finding can

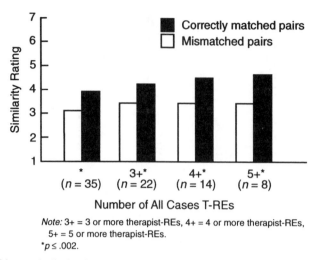

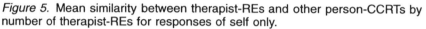

Note: 3+ = 3 or more therapist-REs, 4+ = 4 or more therapist-REs,
5+ = 5 or more therapist-REs.
*p ≤ .002.

Figure 5. Mean similarity between therapist-REs and other person-CCRTs by number of therapist-REs for responses of self only.

be understood as illuminating two points: (a) There is a degree of personal specificity to a patient's relationship pattern as expressed by the CCRT formulation (Luborsky, Mellon, van Ravenswaay, et al., 1985; see also Freud's Observation 11, chapter 21, this volume), and (b) some aspects of the CCRT may be commonly found among different patients. The specificity may lie in patients' particular combinations of the three CCRT components, so that, *taken as a whole,* the CCRT tends to be specific to each patient; but looking only at the CCRT components separately may highlight the commonly expressed aspects of relationship patterns across different patients.

Examining Concomitants of Different Other Persons

Comparing the three CCRT components separately gives researchers the ability to clarify which aspects of the relationship pattern are consistent when the "other person" changes. We found that the wish and response of self components were the most consistent, whereas the response from other component did not show this pattern. The former can be considered patient-specific components, determined mostly, by the patient's personality. The response from other, although seen through the patient's eyes, is presumably influenced to some degree by what was actually said or done by the other person; the patient's perception of this behavior may be relatively insusceptible to influence by the patient's own pattern. Our sample consisting of patients with anxiety disorders and depression was a fairly high functioning one. Perhaps patients with psychotic disorders or borderline personality structures would have more distorted perceptions of the responses from others.

Improving the Level of Similarity of Therapist-REs and Other Person-REs

Another finding to consider is that even the correctly matched pairs involving many therapist-REs had similarity ratings less than 5 on a 1-to-7 scale (7 = *highly similar*)—at best they were only moderately similar. This may be the result of the nature of the task required of the judges: to compare data as disparate as therapist-REs with a CCRT formulation. One set of data, the therapist-REs, is composed of narratives from which the judges were asked to form a gestalt sense of the patient. The other, the other person-CCRTs, is a brief summary of complex ideas: the patient's wish, the expected response from others, and the patient's response of self. It may be that even when the underlying motives and responses were quite similar, their expression in such different formats made their comparison difficult, thereby lowering the similarity ratings.

CONCLUSIONS

The results of the study reported here offer quantitative support for the initial hypotheses of the transference concept.

- A patient's relationship with the therapist has parallels with the patient's relationships with other people (Freud's Observation 4; chapter 21, this volume). We demonstrated this for the first time ever through a comparison of therapist-REs with other person-CCRTs for 35 patients: Each patient's three CCRT components (wish, response from other, response of self) were compared separately with the patient's therapist-REs considered en masse.

  In essence, this work has examined the observation of Freud's (1912/1958a) that is absolutely basic to the concept of transference and therefore vital to all psychodynamic therapies: that the patient's experience with the therapist partially parallels the pattern of experiences with other people. Through inspection of the central relationship patterns by the CCRT method, we have shown that there is a significant degree of similarity between patients' wishes and responses toward the therapist and those toward other people.

- Patients have a consistent relationship pattern, which was demonstrated by the greater similarity of correctly matched than of incorrectly matched pairs of therapist-REs and other person-CCRTs.

12

THE PARALLEL OF THE CCRT FROM WAKING NARRATIVES WITH THE CCRT FROM DREAMS

Editors' introduction: We have shown so far in this book that the Core Conflictual Relationship Theme can be reliably recognized within the narratives that a person tells. What we have not looked into until the venture in this chapter is whether the CCRT can also be reliably extracted from another kind of narrative told in psychotherapy, that is, from dreams. Although dreams provide a wealth of conscious and unconscious revelations about relationships (Freud, 1900/1953b), we do not know (a) the extent to which the CCRT can be reliably extracted from dreams and (b) when it is extracted, how much it is like the CCRT obtained from the narratives.

Study 2 of this chapter is a revised version of "Repetitive Relationship Themes in Waking Narratives and Dreams," by Popp, Diguer, Luborsky, Faude, Johnson, Morris, Schaffer, Schaffler, and Schmidt, 1996, *Journal of Consulting and Clinical Psychology, 64*, pp. 1073–1078. Reprinted by permission.

The research was partially supported by a grant from the Fund for Psychoanalytic Research (to Carol Popp); by Research Scientist Award (NIDA) DA-00168-24 and Research Scientist Award (NIMH) MH 40710-22 (to Lester Luborsky); by NIMH Clinical Research Center Grant P50NH45170 (to Paul Crits-Christoph); and by FCAR Research Grant 95-NC-1277 and SSHRCC Research Grant 410-93-1388 (to Louis Diguer).

175

On the basis of Freud's observations (for example, Observation 21; see chapter 21, this volume), we thought they might reveal parallel information. But in fact, until the studies reported in this chapter were done, we could not easily predict the degree of parallel of the central relationship patterns in the waking narratives with those in the dreams.

In this chapter we report on two studies. The first study is an evaluation of three sample cases presented in detail; we also examine the degree to which it is necessary to have the associations to the dream to understand and score the dream for the CCRT and to make the comparisons with waking narratives. The second study was to be done if the results of the first were encouraging. It was to be a precise and exact examination of the same two questions, that is, (a) can the CCRT be applied reliably to dreams, and (b) is the CCRT from dreams like the CCRT from waking narratives?

STUDY 1: THE PARALLEL OF THE CCRT FROM WAKING NARRATIVES WITH THE CCRT FROM DREAMS[a]

Carol Popp, Lester Luborsky, and Paul Crits-Christoph

The data selected for the first study were drawn from the psychotherapy of three patients, to be called here Ms. Apfel, Ms. Bauman, and Mr. Crane. Ms. Apfel's and Ms. Bauman's data were transcriptions of psychoanalytic sessions conducted by expert psychoanalysts; Mr. Crane's data were a series of dreams published by Gottschalk (1985, p. 66). The transcribed cases were selected from the Penn Psychoanalytic Collection (Luborsky, Stuart, et al., 1997) only on the basis of the availability of transcribed dreams and narratives. Diagnoses were made according to *DSM-III* criteria applied to the initial interviews. The diagnosis for Ms. Apfel was obsessive–compulsive disorder, and for the diagnosis for Ms. Bauman was dysthymia and mixed personality disorder.

Selection of Dreams, Narratives, and Judges

For Ms. Apfel (Case 1), transcripts of Sessions 2 and 3 were used to select 10 relationship episodes for the CCRT scoring. For Ms. Bauman (Case 2), the narrative CCRT formulations were based on 39 relationship episodes from five early and five late sessions. For both cases the usual

[a]Grateful acknowledgment is given to Hartvig Dahl, Merton Gill, Horst Kächele, Sydney Pulver, and George Woody for help in assembling the Penn Psychoanalytic Collection of recorded psychoanalyses administered by Lester Luborsky, Sydney Pulver, and George Woody. We thank Paul Crits-Christoph for some of the transcriptions of the waking narrative relationship episodes. Portions of this study were presented in 1995 at the international meeting of the Society for Psychotherapy Research, Vancouver, Canada.

criteria for selection of relationship episodes on the basis of completeness of content were used (see chapter 2, this volume). The 10 dreams and associations for Case 1 and the 7 dreams and associations for Case 2 were obtained from sessions in both early and late phases of treatment. Three of the 7 dreams for Case 2 were obtained from incomplete transcripts, and therefore associations were available for only 4 of these dreams. To delineate the beginnings and ends of associations, we followed the usual clinical criteria, which involve the patient's designated associations and the analyst's designations, usually adjacent to the dream, of what he or she considered to be associations to the dream. Essentially all the dreams available to us in 1987 were used for the study; that is, no discrimination was made on the basis of completeness of content or other characteristics. Psychodynamically oriented clinical psychologists served as CCRT judges. A psychiatrist and a research assistant identified the relationship episodes. The psychiatrist identified the dreams and associations. All CCRT judges were experienced in the use of the CCRT method and all worked independently.

CCRT Tailor-Made and Standard Categories

CCRT components were scored both in narratives of relationship episodes and in dreams by application of the CCRT method in the usual tailor-made fashion. When scoring the dreams for Ms Apfel and Ms. Bauman, the judges used three successive sets of clinical material: (a) the dreams alone, (b) the dreams with the addition of associations to assist in identifying CCRT components, and (c) the dreams with the addition of associations as part of the entire sessions that included the relationship episodes. For Mr. Crane, no relationship episodes were available, so that only sets A and B were given to the judges. Each of the individual tailor-made types of CCRT components were assigned a standard category from three lists of 14 wishes, 7 responses from other, and 14 responses of self (Crits-Christoph, 1987). Two research assistants working as independent judges made the assignments. Agreement between judges was 91%. Differences were resolved by a third judge. The results are given for each of the three patients separately and then summarized. Preceding each patient's results, a brief clinical sketch is provided for background.

Results

Ms. Apfel (Case 1)

At the time she came for analysis, Ms Apfel was a 31-year-old woman who had had repeated unsuccessful relationships with men. In the first session she explained the onset of her symptoms and her goals for the therapy. "I'm unmarried although I'd like to be. . . . The thing that made me seek therapy was that I was in an unusually emotional state, with crying and depression . . . and some encounter with a young man touched or culminated the whole thing." She described choosing younger men and taking a maternal role in relation to them. In a previous brief therapy, "the therapist pointed out I always set up the relationship with men or I always choose one which I could feel terrible anger against, and that I would be forbearing and accept the conditions as laid down by them meekly on the surface but meanwhile would be feeling very resentful and ill-treated." Her other symptoms included a fear that she was homosexual and a work inhibition involving years of unsuccessful attempts to finish her graduate work. Of all of her symptoms, she felt the recurrent failure with men was the most pressing. She was seen four times a week for 8 months, after which her male analyst became ill and had to stop the treatment. She resumed treatment with a female analyst and continued for 3 more years.

Wishes derived from dreams alone. Ten dreams were analyzed using the CCRT method. An example of the tailor-made wish formulations is given in Table 1, which lists the number of dreams of the 10 dreams scored in which the wishes were identified. The wishes were some of the highest frequency wishes obtained from the tailor-made application of the CCRT method to the dreams alone.

To facilitate comparisons between judges and between results that were based on different sets of clinical material, each tailor-made formation was assigned a standard category. All of the standard category wishes obtained from the dream content alone are shown in Table 2, Column A. We selected for each judge the wishes that occurred with the highest frequency. If one wish was most frequent, the wish or wishes that occurred at the second highest level of frequency was also included. Consequently, up to three components per judge were used for comparisons, as shown in Table 2, Column A. The highest frequency wishes for Judge 1 were for closeness and independence and for Judge 2 for closeness, for independence, and to be helped. Here, the judges agreed on two of the highest frequency wishes.

TABLE 1
Tailor-Made Wishes Scored From Dreams Alone for Ms. Apfel

Judge 1	Number[a]	Judge 2	Number[a]
1. To be close to, intimate with other	6	For others to be interested in me, give to me	3
2. To have sexual intimacy, physical affection	3	To show affection and concern for a woman	3
3. To reject other, get away from other	3	To do things my way	1

[a]Number of dreams and narratives, out of 10, containing the wish.

TABLE 2
Standard Category Wishes for Ms. Apfel

	A Dreams Alone		B Dreams + Assoc.		C Dreams + Session		D REs Alone	
	Judges		Judges		Judges		Judges	
Wish	1	2	1	2	1	2	1	2
1. Closeness	6[a]	3[a]	6[a]	3[a]	6[a]	2[a]	9[b]	7[b]
2. Independence	3[b]	3[b]	3[b]	3[b]	3[a]	4[a]	10[a]	7[a]
3. To be helped	2	3	2[b]	4[b]	2	1	1	5
4. Respect	2	0	2	0	4	1	1	0
5. To help others	2	1	3	0	3	0	0	0
6. To be good	0	0	0	0	3	0	0	0
7. To feel good about myself	0	0	0	0	0	2	0	0
8. To be understood	0	0	0	0	0	0	1	0
9. To avoid conflict	0	0	0	0	0	0	2	0

Note. Entries are number of dreams and narratives, out of 10, containing each wish. Assoc. = associations; REs = relationship episodes.
[a]Identified as having the highest mean frequencies for the pair of judges. [b]Identified as having the next highest mean frequencies for the pair of judges.

Wishes Derived From Dreams Plus Associations and From Dreams Plus Whole Sessions

In the clinical situation, dreams are assessed not in isolation but together with their associations and together with the entire session. Additional material was given to the judges in two sets: first, as the dream's associations, and second, as the entire sessions, including all of the relationship episodes. Results of these additions are shown in Table 2, Columns B and C. There were some changes when associations and relationship episodes were used. Judge 1 scored up to six more wishes when the additional clinical material was available. Both judges formulated some additional, entirely new wishes. There was also some change in the relative frequency of wishes. Regarding interjudge agreement on the most frequently scored wishes, there was at least one match between the most frequently occurring wishes for both sets of clinical material.

Comparisons between the formulations obtained from the three sets of clinical material (Table 2, Columns A, B, and C) can be approached by first selecting from each set the components that were identified by both judges. These include Wishes 1, 2, 3, 4, and 5. The wishes for closeness, for independence, and to be helped were obtained by both judges for all three sets of clinical material. To compare the relative frequency of occurrence, the average of the frequencies of occurrence determined by the two judges was obtained. The wish formulation for closeness occurred with the highest average frequency for all three sets of clinical material. The wish

TABLE 3
Standard Category Responses From Other or of Self for Ms. Apfel

	A Dreams Alone		B Dreams + Assoc.		C Dreams + Session		D REs Alone	
	Judges		Judges		Judges		Judges	
Responses	1	2	1	2	1	2	1	2
Responses from other								
1. Rejecting	2ᵃ	5ᵃ	4ᵇ	1ᵇ	4ᵇ	3ᵇ	0	2
2. Not trustworthy	4ᵇ	2ᵇ	5ᵃ	3ᵃ	5	0	9ᵃ	3ᵃ
3. Dislikes me	3	1	3	0	3ᵃ	5ᵃ	2ᵇ	2ᵇ
4. Are hurt	3	0	2	0	2	0	1	2
5. Accepting	3	1	3ᵇ	2ᵇ	3	1	0	0
6. Happy	2	0	2	0	2	0	0	0
7. Are attractive	0	0	0	0	0	0	0	1
Responses from self								
1. Angry	2ᵇ	1ᵇ	2ᵇ	3ᵇ	2ᵇ	1ᵇ	5ᵇ	4ᵇ
2. Uncertain	3ᵃ	2ᵃ	4ᵃ	3ᵃ	4	0	8ᵃ	4ᵃ
3. Guilty	0	3	3	1	5ᵃ	4ᵃ	1	2
4. Hurt other	4	0	4ᵇ	1ᵇ	4	0	0	0
5. Am not open	0	1	0	1	0	0	8	0
6. Dependent	0	0	0	0	0	0	3	0
7. Jealous	0	0	0	0	0	0	3	1
8. Accepted	0	0	0	1	0	0	0	0
9. Self-confident	0	1	0	0	0	1	0	0

Note. Entries are number of dreams and narratives, out of 10, containing each response. REs = relationship episodes.
ᵃIdentified as having the highest mean frequencies for the pair of judges. ᵇIdentified as having the next highest mean frequencies for the pair of judges.

for independence occurred at the level of the second highest average frequency, in all three sets.

Wishes derived from narratives. The wish formulations obtained from relationship episodes by the standard category CCRT are shown in Table 2, Column D. The wishes that were identified by both judges are Wishes 1, 2, and 3, and they are the same as the wishes identified by both judges in all three sets of clinical material used to formulate the dream CCRT. The relationship episode wishes that occur with the highest and second highest average frequency were Wishes 1 and 2, which is comparable to the dream formulations.

Responses from other and responses of self for dreams and for narratives. Results for the responses from other and responses of self are shown in Table 3. When scoring the dream-based CCRT components, Judge 1 obtained a few more formulations with the use of additional clinical material, whereas Judge 2 sometimes decreased the number of components scored. For these formulations, there was at least one match between judges for the highest frequency components for all sets of clinical material. A comparison between sets of clinical material for the highest average frequency dream-based CCRT components shows a considerable degree of consistency. The response from other of rejecting was common in all three sets, and the category not trustworthy was frequent in two sets. The responses of self of angry and uncertain were most frequent in three and two sets of clinical material, respectively. The most frequent response from other formulations obtained from the relationship episodes were not trustworthy and dislikes me. The category not trustworthy agreed with the dream formulations that were based on dreams alone and on dreams with their associations. The category dislikes me agreed with a frequent response from other formulation identified in dreams with the additional clinical material of relationship episodes. The most frequent response of self components identified in the relationship episodes were angry and uncertain; they agreed with the dream formulations for two or three sets of clinical material, respectively.

Composite CCRT formulations. To complete the present discussion, we include Ms. Apfel's composite CCRT formulation. A composite formulation can be obtained by collecting the components that occur with the highest average frequencies. Thus, the CCRT formulation obtained from the dreams alone is "I wish for closeness or independence, but the other person is not trustworthy and rejecting and then I am angry and uncertain." One of the dreams used as the basis for the CCRT is the following:

W: Independence
NRO: Not trustworthy

//I dreamt on Thursday night that ... I was in some kind of meeting// ... And it was a very long meeting//^{W} ... and I wanted to get out//^{RO} ... we were asked to go back in for another meeting, but uh, there was something about it being a trick ... //

The CCRT formulation from the narratives alone is almost identical to the one from the dreams: I wish for closeness or independence, but the other person is not trustworthy and dislikes me and then I am angry and uncertain. One of the narratives used as the basis for the CCRT is the following:

NRO: Not trustworthy
W: Independence

// And, uh, my friend, ... and I was betrayed by that [the friend] too ... // not exactly had been used but ... something like that.//^{RO} That she hadn't my best interests at heart ... //I felt betrayed. //^{W} And I was very unwilling to have another such relationship with a girlfriend ... //

Ms. Bauman (Case 2)

Ms. Bauman came for treatment at age 35 because she felt burdened by abnormal hair growth all over her body (idiopathic hirsutism). She felt it to be a stigma and a reason for social withdrawal. She avoided social activities because of anxiety about being seen and then rejected. In addition, she feared being observed to be blushing. Her mood was depressed, her self-esteem was low, and she felt lonely and full of guilt.

Her relationships with her parents remained close. She spent weekends and most of her vacations with them, but these relationships were strained because she felt overly influenced by her mother and depreciated in relation to her brothers. The same tension appeared as well in relation to other women: She felt inadequate in comparison and questioned her femininity. The tension was reinforced because she never had had heterosexual relations. She attributed this to her hirsutism and her Catholic background. She did feel competent in her profession as a teacher, but she found it hard to tolerate rivalries with the other teachers and to be assertive with other teachers, with the head of the school, and with her pupils. She felt guilty each time she was able to behave assertively. She felt too dependent for approval on people in authority. Her analysis continued for 517 sessions, with gradual improvement in most of her symptoms, especially in the depression and the feelings of guilt.

Seven dreams were present in the 10 sessions available. Summaries of the results based on the standard categories are given in Table 4, which lists only the components identified by both judges in at least one set of clinical material.

Only a few changes in the CCRT occurred when dreams were scored with the assistance of additional session material. Agreement between judges was difficult to assess because of the low number of components scored. There was some similarity of highest average frequency formulations for dreams on the basis of the three sets of clinical material. There was also moderate agreement between the dream CCRT based on that material and the CCRT based on the relationship episodes. For example, a dream CCRT formulation obtained from the dreams alone is "I wish for closeness and to be helped or for independence, but the other is rejecting and is hurt and then I feel incompetent." One of the dreams used as a basis for Ms. Bauman's CCRT is the following:

W: Closeness _____ . . . //^{W} So it was my wish . . . that I was waiting to sleep with him . . . // but it didn't work out, so I practically, as it were had
NRO: Rejecting _____ offered myself//^{RO} but was rejected.//

TABLE 4
Standard Category Wishes and Responses From Other or of Self for Ms. Bauman

Responses	A Dreams Alone Judges 1	2	B Dreams + Assoc. Judges 1	2	C Dreams + Session Judges 1	2	D REs Alone Judges 1	2
Wishes								
1. Independence	2[b]	2[b]	2	1	2	1	24[a]	18[a]
2. Closeness	3[b]	1[b]	3[b]	1[b]	3[b]	1[b]	8[b]	5[b]
3. To be helped	4[a]	1[a]	4[a]	1[a]	4[a]	1[a]	8[b]	5[b]
4. Respect	0	1	0	1	0	1	3	5
Responses from other								
1. Rejecting	2[a]	2[a]	2[a]	2[a]	2[a]	2[a]	9[a]	5[a]
2. Are hurt	2[a]	2[a]	2[a]	2[a]	2[a]	2[a]	0	0
3. Not trustworthy	2	0	2	0	2	0	8[b]	2[b]
4. Dislikes me	0	1	0	1	0	1	3	3
5. Happy	2	1	2	1	4	1	0	0
6. Accepting	0	0	0	0	0	0	1	1
Responses of self								
1. Incompetent	4[a]	1[a]	5[a]	1[a]	5[a]	1[a]	8[a]	8[a]
2. Angry	2	1	2[b]	2[b]	2	2	3	2
3. Uncertain	2	1	2	1	2	1	8[a]	8[a]
4. Hurt other	2	1	2	1	2	1	0	6
5. Dependent	2	1	2	1	2	1	7[b]	8[b]
6. Am not open	0	1	0	1	0	1	2	3
7. Guilty	0	1	0	1	4[b]	1[b]	8[a]	8[a]
8. Accepted	3[b]	1[b]	0	1	0	1	0	0
9. Self-confident	0	0	0	0	0	1	5	6

Note. Entries are number of dreams and narratives, out of ten, containing each wish or response. REs = relationship episodes. [a]Identified as having the highest mean frequencies for the pair of judges. [b]Identified as having the next highest mean frequencies for the pair of judges.

The CCRT formulation from narratives about relationship episodes is "I wish for closeness and to be helped or for independence, but the other is rejecting and not trustworthy and then I feel incompetent, guilty, and uncertain." One of the narratives used as a basis for Ms. Bauman's CCRT is the following:

W: Closeness _____ . . . //^{W} if I were to call him for once because I need him, sometime when I really want to talk to him// . . . would he actually listen?//

NRO: Rejecting _____ Would I think that was possible?//^{RO} And I have the damnable feeling that it just isn't possible.//

Mr. Crane (Case 3)

When Mr. Crane came for treatment, he was a 35-year-old lawyer. His main physical symptoms were associated with a duodenal ulcer; he had a diagnosis of peptic ulcer by a gastroenterologist. He was an intelligent, perceptive, and well-adjusted man. He had the typical conflicts reported by some members of the Chicago Psychoanalytic Institute for patients with peptic ulcers: a conflict over dependency urges versus feeling of shame. After his personal analysis, he never experienced peptic ulcer symptoms again and successfully advanced in his career. Gottschalk (1985) summarized the patient's conflicts as follows: He was experiencing separation anxiety and guilt about his desires for affiliation and care during the termination phase of his therapy. This formulation appears to be consistent with the dream CCRT results.

Table 5 shows only the dream CCRT formulations (Gottschalk, 1985). Again, a relatively small number of components were scored on the basis of this small sample of dreams. A few more wishes were scored when the judges could use the associations to the dreams.

The results showed that for the wish and response of self formulations, there was agreement between judges on the highest frequency components. A CCRT formulation that was based on the preceding dream content is as follows: I wish for independence or to be helped, but the other dislikes me and then I feel shame and guilt and am too controlling.

TABLE 5
Standard Category Wishes and Responses From Other or
of Self for Mr. Crane

Components	A Dreams Alone Judges		B Dreams + Associations Judges	
	1	2	1	2
Wishes				
1. Independence	4[a]	4[a]	4[a]	5[a]
2. To be helped	2[b]	4[b]	3[b]	5[b]
3. Closeness	0	2	3	2
Responses from other				
1. Dislikes me	2	1	2	0
Responses of self				
1. Shame	2	2	2	2
2. Guilt	2	2	2	2
3. Controlling	2	2	2	2

Note. Entries are number of dreams, out of six, containing each wish or response.
[a]Identified as having the highest mean frequencies for the pair of judges. [b]Identified as having the next highest mean frequencies for the pair of judges.

Summary and Discussion

The main findings in Study 1 were based on a comparison of dreams and narratives of three cases presented in detail.

- Dreams can be reliably judged by the use of the CCRT method. A study of two psychoanalytic cases and one published set of dreams from a psychoanalytic psychotherapy case indicates that independent judges can obtain similar CCRT formulations from dreams and from waking narratives.

    In terms of the aims of this research, the results suggest that the CCRT method can be reliably applied to dreams; that is, judges working independently can obtain similar formulations. In all comparisons between the judges in which both judges scored components with a frequency of 2 or greater, there was at least one match between the highest frequency components. Using this match as a criterion for interjudge agreement, there was agreement between judges for all three cases on the relatively more frequency scored CCRT components. Further assessment of interjudge agreement is limited at this time because of the small number of cases and the relatively small number of components scored per case.

- Dream-based CCRTs were not significantly altered by additional material from the session. An examination of the dream-based CCRT components using graded sets of clinical material indicated that the judges made some changes when additional clinical material was provided to them. However, assessment of the components with the highest average frequency showed more consistency than change between the graded sets of clinical material. Considering the importance accorded to the use of associations to arrive at an understanding of conflictual issues revealed in dreams, more differences might have been expected. However, associations are often used clinically to help in decoding the manifest content on the basis of an understanding of dream work mechanisms, such as condensation, displacement, and the meaning of dream symbols (Pulver, 1987). None of these decoding techniques were employed in deriving the CCRT themes, which were intentionally obtained at a level of inference that was no more than moderately beyond the manifest level.

- Dream-based and narrative-based CCRTs show agreement. With regard to the second aim of this research, we found that agreement is usual between the CCRTs that are extracted from dreams and those that are extracted from narratives about relationship episodes. In all comparisons, there was at least one match between dreams and narratives on the highest average frequency components. Using these matches as a criterion, we found interjudge agreement for both psychoanalytic cases between the relatively more frequently scored dream CCRT components and the relatively more frequently scored narrative CCRT components. We concluded, therefore, that there is similarity between the central, recurrent relationship patterns revealed in dreams and those revealed in waking narratives. The parallel between dreams and narratives in terms of the CCRT is consistent with the concept of a basic relationship schema that shapes similar versions of itself in each mode of expression—in dreams and in narratives.

Some studies have demonstrated the clinical observation of a parallel between waking ideation and dreams. Goldhirsh (1961) showed that the dream themes of convicts were related to the particular crime that they committed. Miller (1970) showed that the dreams of patients with depression were about being defeated, frustrated, and coerced. Beck (1967, 1971) examined the themes of waking ideation and fantasies of depressed patients and showed their similarities to the themes in dreams; one general theme common to both dream and waking life was negative outcome of an activity. The studies by Beck (1967) have much in common with our own. However, our study is focused specifically on the parallels of waking narratives and dreams on the basis of our measure of the central relationship pattern.

Two other comparable studies were reported by Greenberg and Pearlman (1975) and Greenberg (1987). Although no quantitative data were given, the authors described similarity between the manifest dream content and discussions within the analytic hours or interviews conducted, before and after the nights of the dreams. This similarity concerned issues of central import in the patients' waking lives, including the transference.

■ Refinement of the standard categories may show even greater agreement among judges. A final comment deals with the similarity of the standard category wish formulation obtained in these three cases. For all cases, the components identified with the highest average frequency were wishes for "closeness" for "independence," and "to be helped." These appear to be very common wishes. However, it is useful to note that this similarity is based on a comparison of standard category formulations, and their use may obscure differences between cases. For example, the tailor-made wish formulations derived from the dreams alone that were assigned the standard category of "independence" were these:

Ms. Apfel   Judge 1: To reject other, get away from other
             Judge 2: To be free of responsibilities, to do something illicit, to do things my way
Ms. Bauman   Judge 1: For privacy
             Judge 2: To protect my privacy
Mr. Crane   Judge 1: To get ahead of, to beat others, to intrude into others' property
             Judge 2: To compete with others, to take what I want, not to be dependent, to be alone

For each case, tailor-made descriptions appear by inspection to have congruence but also some differences. Further refinement of the standard category lists, which is an ongoing process in our group (see chapter 3, this volume), may enable more discriminating comparisons to be made between different cases and between dreams and waking narratives.

STUDY 2: THE PARALLEL OF THE CCRT FROM WAKING NARRATIVES WITH THE CCRT FROM DREAMS: A FURTHER VALIDATION

Carol Popp, Louis Diguer, Lester Luborsky, Jeffrey Faude, Suzanne Johnson, Margaret Morris, Norman Schaffer, Pamela Schaffler, and Kelly Schmidt

The learning experiences from Study 1, the pilot study of the comparison of dreams and waking narratives, encouraged us to go ahead with Study 2, which was a more exact comparison of dreams and waking narratives across a larger sample of patients, with greater focus on the same theoretically and clinically important questions as in Study 1: (a) the reliability of the CCRT in dreams and (b) the comparison of the CCRT in dreams and in waking narratives.

Method

Our research relied on psychoanalytic treatment because it is a type of psychotherapy that often involves many dreams. We were fortunate to have access to a collection of audiotapes and transcripts from the Penn Psychoanalytic Collection administered by Lester Luborsky, Sydney Pulver, and George Woody (Luborsky, Stuart, et al., 1997). The main criteria for inclusion in our sample of 13 cases were that the treatment was a psychoanalysis and that the case contained a minimum of 20 usable dreams. (We have included one case that contained only 19 usable dreams.) Although our number of cases is small, it is quite large for a psychoanalytic collection because psychoanalytic cases are difficult and expensive to collect; in total, these 13 cases consist of approximately 8,500 sessions.

Of the 13 patients, 10 were female and 3 were male. They all were in formal psychoanalysis and were treated by well-known and experienced analysts. The number of sessions in each treatment ranged approximately from 110 to 1,200. Ten cases each consisted of more than 400 sessions.

The CCRT method was performed as described in chapter 2, this volume. As the first step, transcripts of psychotherapy sessions were reviewed for the presence of waking narratives about interactions between the participant and others. These narratives were rated for the degree of detailed information given about the interaction. The ratings were performed using a 5-point completeness-of-content rating scale in which a complete narrative would contain a description of the events that occurred, the patient's wishes, the responses from others, and the responses of the self. Reasonably complete narratives—those that were 2.5 or above on the 5-point scale—were selected for CCRT scoring; they are called relationship episodes (REs). Because differences have been seen between CCRT components of early versus late phases of therapy, we selected relationship episodes separately from early and late sessions (Crits-Christoph & Luborsky, 1990). For waking narrative relationship episodes, early sessions were typically Sessions 2, 3, 4, 5, or 6. Late sessions for 9 cases were located about 75% of the way through the analysis, and late sessions for the 4 other cases were located closer to the 90% point of the completion of treatment. The total number of waking narrative relationship episodes used in this study was 346.

Although transcripts of full sessions were used to locate waking narrative relationship episodes, transcripts of full sessions were not available to locate dreams for most cases because only the dream was transcribed. The criteria for rating dreams for completeness of content were similar to those for narratives except that dreams were selected as usable if they had a completeness-of-content rating of 2.0 or above. We were able to obtain a minimum of 20 usable dreams per case from 12 cases; a 13th case included 19 usable dreams. The dreams of these 13 cases were separated into 26 sets: 13 sets of early dreams and 13 sets of late dreams. Early dreams were located, on average, in approximately the first 25% of the analytic sessions, and late dreams were located in approximately the last 37% of the sessions. Of the 26 sets, 3 sets contained only 9 dreams, and 1 set contained only 8 dreams. Dreams and narratives were almost always selected from different sessions—of the 309 dreams used in this study, only 7 dreams were located in sessions that also contained scored waking narratives.

A count of words in the dreams was made as described for the dream-related word count by Stickgold, Pace-Schott, and Hobson (1994, pp. 20–21). There were 168 early dreams that met completeness-of-content criteria; 84% of these consisted of 100 or more words, and 94% consisted of 50 words or more. Of the 141 late dreams used, 87% consisted of 100 words or more, and 96% consisted of 50 words or more.

We scored the waking narratives and dreams for the three elements called CCRT components: wishes, responses from other, and responses of self. Two methods of formulating components were used: tailor-made and standard category. Tailor-made CCRT components present the wish, response from other, and response of self in words of the CCRT judge's choice, often using the participant's own words. CCRT scoring using tailor-made components allows the CCRT judges a great deal of flexibility and results in CCRT components that can be uniquely formulated for each participant. However, tailor-made components are not optimal for many types of statistical analyses of reliability and validity. Thus, standardized lists of CCRT wishes and responses must also be used. These standardized content categories were translated by CCRT judges from the tailor-made components. The standard categories used here were selected from Edition 2 lists of the standard categories (in Barber, Crits-Christoph, & Luborsky, 1990; see also chapter 3, this volume). The lists consist of 33 wishes, 33 responses from others, and 31 responses of self categories.

Within the standard category lists, there is some overlap among the standard categories. For example, there can be some overlap in the meaning and assignment of the standard category wishes "to be independent" and "to be my own person." Because of this overlap, it was found that the standard categories could be condensed or clustered into smaller sets (Barber et al., 1990). That is, the 33 standard category wishes could be condensed into only 8 categories called CCRT standard category clusters. The 33 responses from other could be condensed into 8 response from other standard category clusters, and the 31 responses of self could be condensed into 8 response of self clusters. (These standard category clusters of Barber et al., 1990, are listed in Appendix B, chapter 2, this volume.) In this study, all the standard category CCRTs assigned by the CCRT judges were put into the appropriate standard category clusters. Finally, we determined which CCRT standard category clusters occurred most frequently and second most frequently for each set of waking narrative relationship episodes or dream narratives. The most frequent and second most frequent CCRT standard category clusters were identified because they are the most repetitive relationship patterns and they have the greatest similarity to the transference concept (Luborsky, Crits-Christoph, & Mellon, 1986; Luborsky, 1990b). To do this, we averaged the frequency scores of the two judges, ranked the frequencies, and then selected the clusters with the highest and the second highest average frequency. These are the first rank and second rank scores, respectively.

To assess reliability of the CCRT scoring, we used the weighted kappa (Cohen, 1968), which has become standard for evaluating reliability of the CCRT (Crits-Christoph, Luborsky, et al., 1988; chapter 6, this volume). This statistic allows one to estimate the agreement of judges on nominal scales with provision for agreement occurring by chance. In counting "matches" between judges, a weight of 1.0 was given when the match was based on agreement between the first rank CCRT cluster of Judge 1 and the first rank cluster of Judge 2. A weight of 0.66 was given when the match was based on agreement between the first rank CCRT cluster of Judge 1 and the second rank cluster of Judge 2. When the match was based on agreement between the second rank CCRTs of both judges, a weight of 0.33 was given. Finally, a weight of 0 was given when there was no agreement between judges for either first or second rank CCRTs.

To evaluate agreement between waking narrative and dream CCRTs paired by each case, a similar method to the preceding was used; the weighted kappa and the same weights as those used in reliability estimation were used. A further analysis was conducted using similarity scores (see chapter 6, this volume). Similarity scores weight the agreement between two judges for first and second rank CCRTs in a more graded fashion than does the preceding method and account for the occurrence of ties. A tie occurs when more than one CCRT cluster may rank equally as first (or second) rank clusters. The weights are as follows: weight of 1.0 for first rank–first rank and second rank–second rank match without any ties; weight of 0.75 for first rank–first rank match with or without ties; weight of 0.50 for first rank–second match with or without ties; weight of 0.25 for second rank–second rank match with or without ties; and weight of 0 for "none of the above" matches. The highest appropriate similarity score was assigned to each comparison. Hotelling's T^2 multivariate analysis was used to examine the similarity scores.

Results

Reliability

The reliability of CCRT scoring for the three components—wish, response from other, and response of self—in the dream reports and waking narratives was assessed by examining agreement between judges for the most frequent (first rank) and second most frequent (second rank) CCRT standard category clusters (see the section on Methods, preceding). The most frequent and second most frequent CCRT components were examined because they describe the most repetitive relationship patterns and show many similarities to the transference concept. We used Cohen's weighted kappa statistic to estimate reliability (Cohen, 1968). Table 6 shows our results. Kappas of 0.0 to 0.39 suggest poor agreement, of 0.40 to

TABLE 6
Agreement by Weighted Kappa of Two Judges in Scoring the CCRT

Component	Dreams	Narratives
Wish	.58	.67
Response from other	.70	.74
Response of self	.83	.75

0.74 fair-to-good agreement, and of 0.75 to 1.0 excellent agreement (Landis & Koch, 1970). Our results fall in the fair-to-good or excellent ranges of kappa. They indicate good agreement between judges for standard category CCRT scoring of dream reports. These values of kappa for dreams are similar to those found in this study for waking narratives (see chapter 6, this volume). Thus, the reliability of the CCRT method when applied to dreams appears comparable to the reliability of the method when applied to waking narratives.

Common Types of CCRT Components in Dreams and Narratives

We wished to know which CCRT standard category clusters were most common. In Table 7, we show the percentage of cases in which a standard category CCRT cluster appeared as the first rank, or most frequent, CCRT cluster. For example, in dreams located in early sessions, the wish cluster "to be distant," "avoid conflict" was the most common wish in 31% of the 13 cases. The wishes "to be helped, controlled;" "to be loved, understood;" and "to achieve, help others" were also found to be the most common wishes in early dreams in a relatively high percentage of cases. Similar results were seen for narratives, except that the wish "to achieve, help others" did not appear as a first rank wish in narratives. The most prevalent first rank response from other clusters in dreams and narratives were "rejects, opposes; upset;" and "likes me." The most prevalent first rank response of self clusters were "anxious, ashamed;" "sad, angry;" "happy, respected;" and "helpless." Thus, it appears that most CCRT standard clusters that presented as highest ranking CCRTs in dream reports also appeared as highest ranking CCRTs in waking narratives.

Similarity Between Dream and Narrative CCRT Components

To look at the degree of similarity between dream and narrative CCRT formulations, we compared the dreams to waking narratives paired by each case. First, we examined how often the two different sets of CCRT scorings had the same first rank or second rank standard category clusters. Table 8 shows that, for each of the three CCRT components, usually from

TABLE 7
Percentage of Cases in Which a Standard Category CCRT Cluster Appeared as the First Rank, Most Frequent CCRT Cluster

Wish

Cluster	Dreams		Waking Narratives	
	Early	Late	Early	Late
1. To assert self	0	8	0	0
2. To oppose, hurt others	0	0	15	8
3. To be helped, controlled	15	8	23	31
4. To be distant, avoid conflict	31	62	31	54
5. To be close, accept others	8	0	8	15
6. To be loved, understood	38	38	23	23
7. To feel good, comfortable	0	0	0	0
8. To achieve, help others	23	0	0	0

Response From Other

Cluster	Dreams		Waking Narratives	
	Early	Late	Early	Late
1. Strong	0	0	8	0
2. Controlling	0	8	0	0
3. Upset	54	23	23	8
4. Bad	0	0	0	0
5. Rejects, opposes me	62	62	69	92
6. Helpful	0	8	0	0
7. Likes me	8	8	15	8
8. Understands	0	0	0	0

Response of Self

Cluster	Dreams		Waking Narratives	
	Early	Late	Early	Late
1. Helpful	0	0	0	0
2. Unreceptive	0	0	0	0
3. Happy, respected	15	31	15	0
4. Oppose, hurt others	0	0	0	0
5. Self-confident	0	0	0	0
6. Helpless	0	8	0	31
7. Sad, angry	31	23	23	38
8. Anxious, ashamed	69	46	62	46

Note. $n = 13$ for dreams, $n = 13$ for narratives. The total percentage can be larger than 100% owing to ties of CCRT cluster categories for first choice rank.

TABLE 8
Number of Participants With the Same Highest Frequency Clusters in Dreams and Narratives

Early Dreams Versus Early Waking Narratives				Late Dreams Versus Late Waking Narratives			
CCRT Match	I	II	Weighted Kappa	CCRT Match	I	II	Weighted Kappa
W	5	10	.63	W	5	12	.60
RO	11	13	.91	RO	8	13	.68
RS	9	13	.79	RS	9	10	.45

Note. The numbers represent the number of participants, out of 13, whose highest frequency wish, response from other, or response of self clusters were the same for the comparison. A match in Column I means that the CCRT formulations that were compared had the same first rank, highest frequency CCRT standard category clusters. A match in Column II means that the two CCRT formulations that were compared had at least one agreement between the first rank or second rank CCRT standard category clusters. W = wish; RO = response from other; RS = response of self.

about half to more than half of the participants had the same frequency cluster. As examples, 5 of the 13 patients had the same first rank, highest frequency wish cluster in both early waking narratives and dreams, and 10 out of the 13 had at least one match between the first rank or second rank wish clusters in their early dreams and waking narratives. Similar comparisons were made between late dreams and late narratives. Cohen's weighted kappas were calculated to account for agreement between CCRTs occurring by chance. Table 8 shows kappas for comparisons between dreams and narratives. The kappas ranged from 0.45 to 0.91 and indicated considerable agreement for all three components: wish, response from other, and response of self.

Next, Hotelling's T^2 multivariate analysis was used to assess further the agreement between dreams and waking narratives of the most frequent CCRT components. The analysis was made on the similarity scores, weighting the agreements between dreams and waking narratives. The results indicated that at the early stage of psychotherapy, the similarity between dreams and waking narratives varied from one CCRT component to another, Hotelling's T^2 (2, 11) = 9.35, p = 0.04. The F statistics indicated that the similarity between dreams and waking narratives was lower for wishes than for responses of self, $F(1, 12)$ = 5.47, p = 0.04, and for responses from others, $F(1, 12)$ = 9.12, p = 0.01; response from other and response of self were not different, $F(1, 12)$ = 0.0, ns. At the late stage of psychotherapy, the similarity between dreams and waking narratives was again found to differ from one CCRT component to another, Hotelling's $T^2(2, 11)$ = 10.17, p = 0.03. The similarity between dreams and waking narratives was higher for response from other than for response of self, $F(1, 12)$ = 6.72, p = 0.02; wishes, $F(1,12)$ = 7.80, p = 0.02; response from other and response of self were not different, $F(1, 12)$ = 0.03, ns.

Negativity of Responses

The CCRT response from other and response of self can be rated as either negative or positive (Luborsky, 1990a; chapter 4, this volume). Reliability of negativity scoring was evaluated with Pearson correlations: for response from other, $r = .76$, $p = .0001$; for response of self, $r = .79$, $p = .0001$.

In early dreams, 69% of response from other CCRTs were negative (Table 9). In early narratives, 76% of responses from other were negative. Comparable assessments were made for late dreams and late narratives. The range of average percentage of negative responses was 67% to 76% for response from other and 65% to 80% for response of self. The paired t test was used to examine the negativity scores of response from other and response of self; the results indicated that the negativity of response from other early dreams versus response from other early waking narratives, of response of self early dreams versus response of self early narratives, and of response from other late dreams versus response from other late narratives was not significantly different but that the negativity of response of self late narratives was significantly different, $t(12) = 4.46$, $p = .0008$.

In summary, our comparisons of CCRT components in dreams and waking narratives show considerable agreement. The results indicate the presence of a central relationship pattern that is commonly expressed in both waking narratives and dreams. Clinically, the similarities provide a basis for application of the CCRT method to both dream and waking narratives to help find the repetitive patterns, which can be a guiding focus for the therapist.

It should be noted that we almost always selected dreams from different sessions than were used for scoring relationship episodes in waking narratives. In so doing, we chose a more demanding condition for assessment of similarity; it might be expected to be easier to find similarities if many of the dreams and waking narratives came from the same sessions, in which particular themes would predominate. The fact that we found

TABLE 9
Negativity of CCRT Components

Source of Data	Percentage of Negative Responses	
	Response From Other	Response of Self
Early dreams	69 (11)	71 (11)
Early narratives	76 (16)	79 (12)
Late dreams	66 (15)	65 (14)
Late narratives	71 (10)	80 (11)

Note. The negative and positive responses were counted, and the percentage of negative responses per total number of responses was calculated for each participant's group of early or late dreams or waking narratives. The numbers are the mean percentages of negative responses obtained by averaging over the 13 participants. Numbers in parentheses are standard deviations.

similarities between dreams and waking narratives selected from many different sessions suggests that the contents that were similar were pervasive across many sessions.

We also found that the participants tended to express more negative than positive responses and that they did so in both dreams and waking narratives. A preponderance of negative emotions in dreams has also been reported in work by Carlson (1986), Hall and Van de Castle (1966), Merritt, Stickgold, Pace-Schott, Williams, and Hobson (1994), and Rhode, Geller, and Farber (1992). Our results are similar to those of several other studies done with the CCRT, reported in chapter 4 and in this chapter. We considered the possibilities, in chapter 4, that the patients expressed more negative responses in their waking narratives because they were in psychotherapy and hence were presumably experiencing pronounced difficulties or because negative experiences were more strongly remembered or because describing negative relationship episodes might help master them. Regarding dreams, Merritt et al. (1994) invoked several possible explanations for the large amount of negative emotion in dreams, including activation of limbic areas by pontogeniculo-occipital waves and synthetic activity of cortical association systems occurring during the process of dream generation. Although the relevance of these hypotheses is not known, further investigations of negativity in either dreams or waking narratives should give consideration to the fact that considerable negativity has been found in both dreams and waking narratives.

Further studies would benefit from use of both a larger number of participants and control over the conditions of dream reporting. These circumstances are unlikely to be met using psychotherapy sessions. Finding psychotherapy cases, which usually involve one session per week, that contain 20 usable dreams would require an enormous database of patients because dreams are relatively uncommon in psychotherapy treatments. It is for this reason that we chose to study psychoanalytic cases. However, psychoanalytic cases are difficult and expensive to record because they consist of a large number of sessions; some of our cases were 1,200 sessions long. An alternative approach would be to study patients in psychotherapy, conducted once per week, in which the patients report their dreams at home on a nightly basis using controlled protocols such as described by Hobson and Stickgold (Hobson & Stickgold, 1994; Merritt et al., 1994; Stickgold et al., 1994). In this way, the number of patients could be increased and the circumstances of obtaining dream reports could be controlled.

SUMMARY AND CONCLUSIONS

- Study 2 confirms and expands on Study 1. This systematic comparative study of relationship themes in dreams is the first that is based on the CCRT and confirms and adds to the findings of Study 1. Study 2 was also supported by the finding in Study 1 that the dream association material in the sessions was not essential for the comparison with narratives.

- CCRTs of dreams can be reliably judged. Our results confirm our hypothesis that the CCRT can be reliably identified in dreams.
- The dream and narrative CCRTs are similar, even when the samples of dreams and narratives are collected from different sessions. The repetitive elements that form the CCRT in dreams can be compared with relationship themes in waking narratives in a relatively straightforward fashion. We found significant similarities between the recurrent relationship themes in dreams and those in waking narratives. The results for relationship narratives are new and imply that the narrative also has qualities that also justify its being considered a "royal road" to deeper levels of the personality.
- We also found that the similarity between dreams and narratives is highest for the responses from others. This high similarity may be of special significance and should be followed up in future analyses.
- The positive and negative quality of waking narratives and dreams can be judged reliably.
- Negativity of responses of self in late dreams is less than that of the responses of self in late narratives. This finding should also be followed up in future studies for it is contrary to what might be expected.
- The finding of similar CCRTs in the waking narratives and dreams implies similarity of CCRTs across states of consciousness. These results support the concept of a central relationship pattern that shows itself in two different states or modes of thinking: in dreams and in waking narratives.

13

THE MEASUREMENT OF ACCURACY OF INTERPRETATIONS

PAUL CRITS-CHRISTOPH, ANDREW COOPER,
AND LESTER LUBORSKY

For years a steady succession of clinical papers have shown therapists how to recognize the accuracy of interpretations. A representative one by Kubie (1952) offered these criteria: "Evidence for the accuracy of the interpretations is sought in the patient's further free associations and in the unlocking of doors to his lost memories" (p. 76). Kubie went on to provide clinical examples of this kind of match between the interpretation and the patient's associations and concluded that the tests of the accuracy of an interpretation derive from "1) the patient's associations to it, which may confirm, correct or reject it; 2) the alterations in symptoms; 3) finally, and only rarely, the increase in our ability to predict future behavior. But we need better tests than these" (p. 89). He was right; we do need better tests than these. Kubie's main test, a fit between the interpretations and the patient's verbal and repeated-in-action associations, echoed Freud's (1912/1958a, 1913/1958c,

From "The Accuracy of Therapists Interpretations and the Outcome of Dynamic Psychotherapy," by P. Crits-Christoph, A. Cooper, and L. Luborsky, 1988, *Journal of Consulting and Clinical Psychology*, 56, pp. 490–495. Reprinted by permission.

197

1914/1958e) views of how to determine the accuracy of interpretation.

Although such criteria for accuracy of the match between the interpretation and the associations are often clinically recognizable, the field lacks information about the interjudge agreement on such criteria. An early method of Luborsky's (included in Auerbach & Luborsky, 1968), intended to handle this research problem, requires ratings of the degree of convergence between the therapist's interpretations and the essence of the patient's main communications. The degree of such convergence was found to be moderately reliably judgeable (mean r of about .6), but it had a major problem: its impressionistic assessment of the patient's main communication.

The current method improved on the previous one by operationalizing further the concept of accurate interpretation by means of this new measure: convergence of the therapist's interpretations with the patient's CCRT (Crits-Christoph, Cooper, & Luborsky, 1988). The improvement is accomplished by the safer reliance on the CCRT (see chapter 6, this volume) as a measure of the patient's main communication. The improved assessment rests on the hypothesis that a cogent measure of accuracy is the extent to which the therapist's interpretations in a session deal with the main independently established CCRT components of the session.

Our initial aims in the current work were (a) to develop the improved measure of accuracy of interpretation and (b) to examine the predictive capacity of the measure for the outcome of psychotherapy. Our subsequent aims were (c) to learn whether accuracy of interpretation would predict outcome only in the context of a positive therapeutic alliance and (d) to learn the relative predictive capacity of a broader measure of the therapist's responses, the Therapist's Errors in Technique Scale (Sachs, 1983).

PROCEDURES

Of the 73 patients in the Penn Psychotherapy Project (Luborsky et al., 1988), 43 were included in this study because their transcripts were available and they roughly reflected the range of outcomes in the total sample. We applied our CCRT measure to transcripts of two sessions drawn from early in treatment (usually Sessions 3 and 5). Sets of independent judges could then rate each of the interpretations for their accuracy.

With the exception of one judge who coded interpretations and one judge who marked off relationship episodes (both trained research assistants), judges were experienced clinicians (clinical psychologists and psychiatrists) trained in each task. All judges were blind to treatment outcome and worked independently. Separate sets of judges scored each measure.

Two previously developed measures, the Helping Alliance Counting

Signs method (Luborsky, Crits-Christoph, Alexander, Margolis, & Cohen, 1983) and the Errors in Technique Scale (Sachs, 1983), a subscale of the Vanderbilt Negative Indicators Scale (O'Malley, Suh, & Strupp, 1983), were also applied to the sessions. The Errors in Technique Scale was used to examine the overlap between this scale and our measure of accuracy of interpretations. The Helping Alliance method was applied to examine whether alliance and accuracy measures contribute independently to the predictions of outcome and to test the hypothesis that interpretations have more impact in the context of a positive therapeutic relationship.

Patients

The patient sample consisted of 30 women and 13 men, ranging in age from 18 to 48 years, with a mean age of 25.2 years. About two-thirds of the patients were between the ages of 18 and 24. Descriptive characteristics of the patients are presented in Table 1. Patient diagnoses are summarized in Table 2. The majority of patients were diagnosed as having dysthymic disorder, generalized anxiety disorder, or one of a variety of personality disorders.

Therapist and Treatment Characteristics

Twenty-eight therapists participated in the research project. Each therapist usually treated one or two patients. The therapists ranged in age from 27 to 55 years, with a mean age of 35.6 years. They had between 1 and 22 years of prior clinical experience, with an average of 5.4 years. Twelve of the therapists were psychiatrists in private practice; the remain-

TABLE 1
Characteristics of Patients (*N* = 43)

Characteristic	Number	Characteristic	Number
Age		Marital status	
15–19	3	Single	29
20–24	25	Married	8
25–29	6	Divorced, separated, or widowed	6
30–34	4	Education	
35–39	4	High school degree	5
40–44	0	Some college	21
45–49	1	College degree	6
Sex		Some graduate or professional school	7
Female	30	Graduate or professional degree	4
Male	13		
Race			
Black	3		
White	40		

TABLE 2
Patient Diagnosis (*N* = 43)

Diagnosis	Number	With Axis II
DSM-III Axis I		
Atypical eating disorder	1	—
Dysthymic disorder	16	8
Ego dystonic homosexuality	2	1
Generalized anxiety disorder	11	4
Inhibited sexual excitement	2	—
Obsessive–compulsive disorder	2	—
No Axis I diagnosis	13	13
DSM-III Axis II		
Atypical personality disorder	1	
Compulsive personality disorder	4	
Histrionic personality disorder	4	
Narcissistic personality disorder	1	
Passive–aggressive personality disorder	4	
Schizoid personality disorder	8	
Schizotypal personality disorder	3	
Mixed personality disorder	1	

Note. Several patients had more than one diagnosis.

ing 16 were psychiatric residents. The residents attended weekly 1-hour individual therapy supervision sessions led by experienced clinicians.

All patients were seen in individual psychodynamic psychotherapy. Approximately two-thirds of the patients were treated at the outpatient clinic of the Hospital of the University of Pennsylvania. The rest were seen in private practice settings. Treatment length ranged from 21 to 149 weeks, with an average of 53.5 weeks.

Measures

Identifying Interpretations

Two judges (an experienced clinician and a research assistant very familiar with the task) coded therapist statements into interpretations versus all other types of responses. A response was considered an interpretation if it met at least one of the following criteria: (a) The therapist explained possible reasons for a patient's thoughts, feelings, or behavior (such as, "Yes, but one of the benefits of using drugs is that it keeps you in the role of the child"); and (b) the therapist alluded to similarities between the patient's present circumstances and other life experiences (such as, "And what's happening is that you keep getting yourself into these kinds of situations, like what happened on Saturday where you put yourself in a hell of a big rejection experience").

The judges were kept blind to treatment outcome and independently read the typed transcripts of two therapy sessions. Responses that were scored as interpretations by both judges were included in the study. If a case yielded no interpretations in the two sessions (as occurred for two patients), judges read additional sessions until agreement was reached on at least one interpretation. The number of interpretations obtained per patient ranged from 1 to 16, with a mean of 6.1.

Interrater reliability on the basis of judges' ratings for all 43 cases, was assessed for distinguishing interpretations versus other statements. The interjudge agreement was 95%; Cohen's (1960) kappa statistic, a measure of chance-corrected agreement for nominal scales, was .56 ($p < .0001$).

Combining Judges' CCRT Formulations

Two, or occasionally three, experienced clinician judges scored each of the 43 patients for the CCRT, according to the method outlined in chapter 2, this volume. For each case the final CCRT selected for inclusion in the study was a composite of the judges' independent CCRT formulations. It included the wish, negative response from other, and negative response of self (positive responses from other and positive responses of self were of low frequency in this sample). The judges' tailor-made CCRT formulations were coded into standard categories (Edition 1; see Luborsky, 1986b) by three other judges, with greater than 95% agreement.

A composite CCRT was derived by selecting the most frequent wishes and responses among the CCRT judges. The final CCRT formulation for each patient consisted of up to two wishes, three negative responses from other, and three negative responses of self.

Accuracy of Interpretations

Accuracy of interpretations as scored here represents the degree of congruence between the contents of the therapist's interpretations and the contents of a patient's CCRT. Because the CCRT is composed of three main subtypes, accuracy is conceptualized as a multidimensional concept. Consequently, the assessment of accuracy involves multiple ratings on each interpretation. A 4-point rating scale was used to assess the degree to which a clinical judge believed that the therapist's interpretation addressed a particular CCRT wish, response from other, or response of self.

The following CCRT and therapist's interpretation, drawn from one of the cases used in this study, is presented to illustrate the nature of the accuracy ratings. The patient's CCRT consisted of one wish ("to make contact with others, be close"), one negative response from other ("rejects, distant"), and three responses of self ("lonely, depressed, anxious"). One of the therapist's interpretations follows:

> Well, I'm beginning to get a picture of a—a lot of involvement that you have with this guy still, even though he's cut things off, you

PATIENT'S CCRT

Wish: To not be cut off from closeness

Response From Others: Rejects

Response of Self: Anger; self-devaluation; upset

THERAPIST'S INTERPRETATION

Naturally you feel upset now—You see me as
unresponsive to you

Figure 1. A therapist's interpretation that is highly congruent with the patient's CCRT (patient: Mr. Howard, Session 3).

haven't. And you're not able to begin replacing him yet and, uh, the emotional investment, emotional tie you've got still to him, and pretty strongly. And that's inhibiting you. Now, what's behind that, y'know, obviously he was very important to you, more important than any other guy has been. And that makes it harder to give him up. And the fact that he really is the one who decided—made the choice to break, not you, makes it harder to give him up too. I—I see some reaction: What's going on?

This interpretation was rated as accurate in regard to the wish and response from other but not for the responses of self. For the wish, the average of the accuracy of the judges' ratings for the congruence of content was 3.67; for the response from other, it was 4.0; and for the three responses of self, 1.33, 1.33, and 1.0, respectively.

Examples of interpretations from two other patients are given in Fig-

PATIENT'S CCRT

Wish 3: I want to be reassured; to get approval; to
avoid disapproval

THERAPIST'S INTERPRETATION

What strikes me . . . you went home after you left and
talked to Henry [husband] about it . . . wanting
reassurance, but not here.

Figure 2. A therapist's interpretation that is moderately congruent with the patient's CCRT (patient: Ms. Cunningham, Session 5).

ures 1 and 2 (from chapter 5, this volume). These interpretations are given here in simplified form. The one by Mr. Howard's therapist was given a high rating for accuracy (3.8); the one by Ms. Cunningham's therapist got only a moderate rating for accuracy (2.4).

For each case, three experienced clinician judges who were kept blind to treatment outcome were presented with composite CCRT formulations and interpretations that were extracted from transcripts for each case. The judges, working independently, were directed to familiarize themselves with the patient's CCRT formulation and to make ratings of accuracy on each wish, response from other, and response of self contained in that patient's CCRT formulation.

Ratings for the wishes were averaged to form a composite wish dimension for each patient. Similarly, ratings for the responses from other and responses of self were averaged to yield composites for each. For each patient, these accuracy scores were then averaged across all interpretations. Interrater reliability of the accuracy scales was computed using the intraclass correlation coefficient. On the basis of the sample of 43 cases, the pooled interjudge reliabilities were as follows: (a) .84 for accuracy with respect to the patient's wishes, (b) .76 for accuracy with respect to the patient's responses from other, and (c) .83 for accuracy with respect to the patient's responses of self.

Intercorrelations between the accuracy scales were computed to examine the overlap between these dimensions. The correlation between the wish and response from other scales was .68. Virtually no correlation was found between the response of self and wish ($r = .07$) or between the response of self and response from other scales ($r = .04$). Given the sizable correlation between the wish and response from other components, these two dimensions were combined into a composite dimension to avoid problems of multicollinearity of predictors (Cohen & Cohen, 1975) in subsequent multiple regression analyses.

Errors in Technique Scale

The Errors in Technique subscale of the Vanderbilt Negative Indicators Scale (O'Malley et al., 1983) is a set of 10 items, all of which are hypothesized to be inversely related to beneficial treatment outcome (Sachs, 1983). The 10 items are (a) failure to structure or focus the session, (b) failure to address maladaptive behaviors or distorted apperceptions, (c) insufficient examination of potentially harmful behavior or attitudes, (d) failure to address signs of resistance, (e) failure to examine the patient–therapist interaction, (f) superficial interventions, (g) poorly timed interpretations, (h) destructive interventions, (i) inappropriate use of silence, and (j) inflexible use of therapeutic techniques. Possible ratings for each item range from 0 (*errors not present or within normal limits*) to 5 (*strong evidence for errors*).

In Sachs's (1983) study of negative factors in short-term therapy, interrater reliability was calculated for the Errors in Technique Scale. Of the original 10 items, 7 had adequate levels of interrater reliability (>.60). The average interrater reliability of the 7 scales was .73. The level of internal consistency (coefficient alpha) was .46 (p. 559). In addition, the scale was significantly correlated in the expected direction with treatment outcome ($r = -.56, p < .01$) in a sample of 18 male college students in brief therapy.

For each case in the present study, two experienced clinician judges (including the author of the scale) independently listened to the tape recordings while reading the typed transcripts of the first 30 minutes of each of two early therapy sessions. To reduce the complexity of the task, each 30-minute segment was divided into two 15-minute segments, which were separately rated on the 10 items of the Errors in Technique Scale. The ratings of each item were averaged across the two segments, and then the scores of the two sessions were combined. Of the original 10 items on the scale, only 6 had some variance; these were summed to form a final scale score. The 6-item version of the Errors in Technique Scale used in the current study had a mean of 5.5 (out of a possible 30 points) and a standard deviation of 3.4.

On the basis of the sample of 43 cases, the pooled interjudge reliability (intraclass correlation) of the 6-item scale was .61. Additionally, the level of internal consistency of the scale, as assessed by Cronbach's alpha, was .60.

Helping Alliance Counting Signs Scale

The Helping Alliance Counting Signs method (Luborsky, 1976; Luborsky, Crits-Christoph, et al., 1988) was applied by two experienced clinician judges to the first 30 minutes of each of the two early sessions for each patient. The score for positive helping alliance signs was selected for use in this analysis because this measure had proved to be the most successful predictor of outcome in the comparison of the 10 most improved and 10 least improved cases from the Penn Psychotherapy Project. The pooled judge reliability of this measure (intraclass correlation = .57) was lower than expected and appeared to be a function of one judge's scoring many more indicators of a helping alliance than the other judge. Nevertheless, we combined the two judges' scores for a final helping alliance measure.

Treatment Outcome

Test and interview evaluations were conducted for the 43 patients when they began therapy and again when they terminated treatment. From these data two outcome measures were devised: residual gain (meaning a gain corrected for initial level) and rated benefits (meaning a composite rating of improvement; Luborsky, Crits-Christoph, et al., 1988).

RESULTS

The Average Level of Accuracy of Interpretations Was Low

Table 3 gives the means and standard deviations of the accuracy dimensions. It can be seen that the average level of accuracy was low, yet enough variability was present to allow for relationships with other variables to emerge.

The mean level on a 5-point scale of the different component measures ranged from 1.49 to 1.81. It might be argued on clinical grounds that this is not really low, because clinicians may give piecemeal, partial interpretations. (What would be of interest, therefore, would be to examine the level of accuracy of the top 20% so that we would know how accurate the level is for the most accurate interpretations; we should also do an initial study on what follows the most and least accurate of interpretations.)

The Predictors of Accuracy Were Unrelated to Each Other

The relationships among the predictors were examined as a preliminary to the prediction of outcome. An intercorrelation matrix for the four predictors is given in Table 4. None of the correlations attained statistical significance.

Accuracy of the Wish Plus Response From Other Was the Best Predictor of Outcome

Multiple regression analyses were performed using the two accuracy measures (wish plus response from other, and response of self), the Errors in Technique Scale, and the Helping Alliance Scale as predictors, and rated benefits and residual gain as outcome criteria. Simple correlations between each predictor and the two outcome measures are given in Table 5, as well as partial correlations (each variable controlling for the others) and a multiple correlation combining the predictors.

Most striking is the fact that the accuracy on the wish plus response

TABLE 3
Means and Standard Deviations for Accuracy Dimensions ($N = 43$)

Accuracy Dimension	Mean	Standard Deviation
Wish (W)	1.81	.56
Response from other (RO)	1.49	.38
Response of self (RS)	1.69	.41
W + RO	1.65	.43

Note. Accuracy dimensions were rated on a 1-to-4 scale, with 1 indicating *no congruence* between the content of the interpretation and the patient's CCRT and 4 indicating *high congruence*.

TABLE 4
Intercorrelations of Predictors

Predictor	1	2	3	4
1. Accuracy of wish + response from other	—	.06	.12	−.11
2. Accuracy of response of self		—	.17	−.21
3. Helping Alliance Scale			—	−.08
4. Errors in Technique Scale				—

from other scale is the best predictor of outcome, yielding statistically significant results in all cases (both outcome measures and simple and partial correlations). The Errors in Technique subscale and the accuracy on the response of self scale were not significantly related to outcome. The Helping Alliance measure correlated significantly with both outcome measures, as we expected on the basis of a study by Luborsky, Crits-Christoph, et al. (1983), which included a sample of 20 patients that overlapped with the sample of 43 used here. In addition, the Helping Alliance Scale demonstrated a significant partial correlation with residual gain and a near-significant correlation with rated benefits. Thus, the predictive effects of accuracy of interpretations and Helping Alliance Scales appear to be independent.

The Impact of Accurate Interpretations Was Not Limited to When the Alliance Was Positive

To test the reasonable hypothesis that accuracy interacts with helping alliance (that is, that accurate interpretations have an impact only when the therapeutic alliance is positive), cross-product terms between accuracy on the wish plus response from other and helping alliance were entered after main effects in the multiple regressions. These interactions were nonsignificant.

TABLE 5
Prediction of Outcome by Accuracy, Helping Alliance, and Errors in Technique Measures ($N = 43$)

Predictor	Simple Correlations		Partial Correlations	
	Rated Benefits[a]	Residual Gain[b]	Rated Benefits[a]	Residual Gain[b]
Accuracy of wish + response from other	.38*	.44**	.36*	.43**
Accuracy of response of self	.16	.07	.07	−.02
Helping Alliance Counting Signs	.31*	.36*	.26	.35*
Errors in Technique Scale	−.21	−.10	−16	−.04
Multiple R			.49*	.54**

[a]Ratings of improvement. [b]Gain corrected for initial level.
*$p < .05$. **$p < .01$.

Because one item ("failure to address maladaptive behaviors or distorted apperceptions") of the Errors in Technique Scale overlapped conceptually with the concept of accuracy of interpretation, it was of interest to examine the correlations of this item with the accuracy scales. For both accuracy scales, the correlations were nonsignificant ($r = -.11$ for wish plus response from other; $r = -.19$ for response of self).

DISCUSSION

Congruence of Interpretations With the CCRT

We developed a reliable measure of the accuracy of therapists' interpretations that is based on their congruence with the Core Conflictual Relationship Theme, and we examined its relationship to the outcome of dynamic psychotherapy, Accuracy of therapists' interpretations was assessed from two early-in-treatment sessions of 43 patients receiving moderate-length therapy. The results indicated that accuracy with respect to the main wishes and responses from others that were contained in the relationship themes was significantly related to outcome, even when we controlled for the effects of general errors in therapist technique and the quality of the helping alliance. The hypothesis that accurate interpretations have their greatest impact in the context of a positive helping alliance was not confirmed. The main findings have provided new information about the validity of the CCRT.

It is important to note that the interrater reliability of the accuracy of interpretation scales was reasonably high compared with the general levels of reliability usually found in psychotherapy process research. The specific nature of the rating task (the scales were tailored to each patient's CCRT) and the use of experienced clinical research judges probably contributed to the reliability level. By combining the ratings made on all interpretations identified in each of two complete therapy sessions, as well as averaging the ratings over three judges, a robust measure was constructed.

The major hypothesis of this research received strong support: A statistically significant and moderately strong relationship was found between accuracy of interpretations (for the wish plus response from other dimension) and treatment outcome. In a later study of compatibility of interpretations using the Plan Diagnosis (Norville, Sampson, & Weiss, 1996) with seven patients in therapy, a high correlation was found with outcome at the end of therapy and 6-months after therapy ended. In the study reported in this chapter, larger and more diverse groups of patients and therapists were examined, allowing for the first systematic investigation of the relationship between accuracy of interpretations and treatment outcome.

Our results suggest that the therapist's *technical* performance in dynamic psychotherapy has an impact on outcome. The overall pattern of results also suggests that a specific technique factor, not a more general one, accounts for the finding. The predictive strength of accuracy of interpretation on the wish plus response from other dimension was not accounted for by other variables such as errors in technique or quality of the therapeutic alliance.

The approach used in the current study has possible implications for research concerning the effects of other treatment techniques on psychotherapy outcome (Frank, 1979; Orlinsky & Howard, 1978, 1986). Assessing the "quality" or "skillfulness" of the treatment techniques under investigation, as we did, may be necessary before documented relationships between treatment techniques and outcome are observed. This type of research strategy has recently been advocated by a few psychotherapy researchers (e.g., Schaffer, 1982, 1983; Silberschatz, Fretter, & Curtis, 1986) and has now been confirmed by the significant association of competence and outcome reported by Barber, Crits-Christoph, and Luborsky (1996).

It is of interest that accuracy with respect to the wish plus response from other, rather than accuracy with respect to the response of self, predicted treatment outcome. It appears that correctly addressing the patient's stereotypical patterns of needs and wishes, the responses of others, is an effective strategy. In contrast, limiting the focus of interpretations to the patient's usual responses of self (typically, feeling states and symptoms) in interpersonal situations may offer more limited benefits. It may be that the responses of self are closer to awareness than the wishes and expected responses from others. It also may be that the wishes and expected responses from others capture the main facets of relationship conflicts that are antecedent to and lead to symptoms; they often are, in the language of cognitive–behavioral therapy, dysfunctional attitudes.

Noninteraction With the Helping Alliance

The helping alliance predicts outcome significantly, but it is independent of and noninteractive with accuracy. The finding suggests that the greater the accuracy of an interpretation, the more it is beneficial, regardless of the state of the alliance. The lack of a significant interaction between accuracy of interpretation and the quality of the therapeutic alliance was surprising, given the clinical lore that a strong alliance is necessary for patients to tolerate and make use of interpretations. Perhaps this association would emerge with more severely disturbed patients than the ones used here, particularly if there were a higher frequency of poor alliances present. In our study, only three therapist–patient dyads showed no signs at all of a positive alliance. It is of interest, however, that Crits-Christoph,

Barber, & Kurcias (1993) showed that the accuracy on the wish plus response from other strongly predicted changes in the helping alliance.

Nonsignificant Relationship With the Errors in Technique Scale

The results for the Errors in Technique Scale are discrepant with the findings in Sach's (1983) study, which showed a significant inverse relationship between errors in technique and outcome. There are a few possible reasons for the nonsignificant finding for errors in technique in the current research. For one, the relatively limited reliability of the Errors in Technique Scale may partly explain the results. The limited reliability may have been a function of the generally low level of errors in this sample (four items did not occur and several others occurred infrequently). In addition, items on this scale may be more appropriate for time-limited psychotherapy. The treatment in Sachs's (1983) study was specified as brief therapy (a maximum of 6 months), whereas open-ended therapy was used in the current research (mean length of about a year).

Limits of Correlational Findings

Interpretation of the main findings in the study is subject to the inherent limitations of all correlational research. First, the direction of the relationship between interpretations of the wish plus response from other dimension and treatment outcome is not clear. For example, it is possible that patients who are making good progress in treatment are more likely to elicit accurate interpretations from their therapists, particularly if they are becoming aware of their own relationship patterns and can articulate these issues during the sessions. However, the fact that the finding was observed very early in treatment (usually by the fifth session) provides some support for the opposite position—that accuracy leads to favorable outcome.

It is also possible that an alternative hypothesis, or "third variable," accounts for the relationship between accuracy and treatment outcome. For example, the complexity of a patient's CCRT may influence both accuracy and outcome. Perhaps therapists are more likely to make accurate interpretations with patients who have less complicated, and therefore easier to discern, relationship patterns. These patients may improve in treatment, not as a result of the impact of accuracy but simply because patients with less complicated relationship patterns may make greater treatment gains. An informal inspection of the CCRTs in the sample, however, did not reveal any major differences in the complexity of the relationship patterns.

Another alternative hypothesis is that the therapist uses accurate interpretation more often on patients who are healthier psychologically (that is, exhibiting lesser psychiatric severity). We know that there is a trend for patients with better psychological health to show greater improvement in psychotherapy (Luborsky, Crits-Christoph, et al., 1988).

It should be mentioned that focusing interpretations on issues that are not captured by the patient's CCRT may also be important. For example, it would be interesting to learn whether focusing on defenses is related to patient improvement. (The CCRT does not require the judge to infer types of defenses.) Inspection of the interpretations in the sample did not reveal any consistent differences among therapists in focusing on defense mechanisms. In fact, with only a few exceptions, the content of the interpretations appeared to fit the structure of a typical CCRT formulation: wishes, responses from others, and responses of self. Formal research in this area is clearly needed.

A further caveat is in order here. Our use of the word *accuracy* is only shorthand for convergence of the interpretation content with the CCRT content. Our measure of accuracy is not based on an external criterion of validity—if such a criterion is even possible—and it does not deal with the larger concept of the *adequacy* of the interpretation, that is, accuracy plus timing and tact.

CONCLUSIONS

The net gain from our new measure of accuracy was these three findings:

- Our operational measure of accuracy of interpretations was based on their congruence with the Core Conflictual Relationship Theme. The measure turned out to be reliable and it showed validity in terms of a significant correlation with outcomes of psychotherapy.
- Accuracy with respect to the congruence of the main wishes and responses from others with the interpretations was significantly related to outcome even after controlling for the effects of errors in therapist technique and the quality of the helping alliance.
- The hypothesis that accurate interpretations would have their greatest impact in the context of the positive helping alliance was not confirmed.

Where do these findings lead in terms of clinical and research directions? We believe that the present operational definition of accuracy has advantages over our early measure and that both of the accuracy measures have advantages for research and clinical practice over the clinical definition from which they sprang. In clinical terms, our findings imply that an effective interpretation tends to be a therapist response that presents to the patient a part of the patient's relationship pattern, both what is wished for and the expectations from others. In addition, the selection of the part of the patient's relationship pattern that is presented in interpretations should not be too far removed from the patient's awareness (Bibring, 1954; Freud, 1912/1958d).

It is fitting here to reassure clinical readers that, on the basis of applying the measure to the sample of sessions from the Penn Psychotherapy Project, we found that therapists already tended to make interpretations that were consistent with our measure. The content of the usual interpretations appeared to fit the structure of the typical CCRT formulation: wishes, responses from others, and responses of self. Yet the therapists in the sample were doing what they understood to be dynamic psychotherapy as it existed before the era of psychotherapy manuals.

Several other operational recastings of the clinical concept of interpretation have been suggested, as we mentioned earlier. One of the best known is that proposed by Weiss et al. (1986), in which accuracy of interpretation is evaluated by the congruence of the interpretation with the patient's "unconscious plan" as measured by the Plan Diagnosis method (Rosenberg, Silberschatz, Curtis, Sampson, & Weiss, 1986). We expect many more operational measures to be generated in the next few years for the concept of accurate interpretation, and clinicians and researchers will be able to choose from these the best for their purpose.

In future studies of the accuracy of interpretations, we intend to apply our method to a larger number of sessions than the two early ones used in the present study. It is likely that the predictability of accuracy will be heightened by the increase in number of sessions. We will also learn then how consistent the therapist's behavior is and whether it is equally predictive at different points in the treatment.

Our accuracy finding, if replicated, could have several implications for the teaching of the practice of psychodynamic psychotherapy. For example, therapists could be trained in formulating their patients' CCRTs and in correctly addressing these issues in their interpretations. Assuming that the therapist in this study are representative of the general population of psychodynamic clinicians, the relatively low mean scores for accuracy in this study's sample of therapists suggests that there is much room for improvement in the quality of therapists' interpretations. These findings further imply that when the improvement occurs, it will be associated with improved patient outcomes.

14

SELF-UNDERSTANDING OF THE CCRT

PAUL CRITS-CHRISTOPH AND LESTER LUBORSKY

In psychotherapy most patients need to increase their self understanding as a way to help achieve their treatment goals. This proposition is clinically accepted as central among the curative factors in dynamic psychotherapies (Luborsky, 1984). Both the clinical views and the quantitative studies of the relation of insight to treatment outcomes, as reviewed by Crits-Christoph, Barber, Miller, and Beebe (1993), stress this factor. Yet few quantitative studies exist of the association of self-understanding with the outcome of psychotherapy. The studies reviewed by Luborsky et al. (1988) have provided the following results: Of three studies that measured insight pretreatment (Raskin, 1949; Stein & Beall, 1971; Zolik & Hollon, 1960), the last two showed significant prediction of outcomes; but of two studies in which the level of insight was measured during psychotherapy (Rosenbaum, Friedlander, & Kaplan, 1956; Morgan, Luborsky, Crits-Christoph, Curtis, & Solomon, 1982), neither showed a significant prediction of outcome. Therefore, it is a fair verdict that self-understanding measures have tended to vary in their significance as predictors. The studies are weak in other ways as well. Several investigators relied on single-item ratings of

An earlier version of this chapter appeared in L. Luborsky, P. Crits-Christoph, J. Mintz, and A. Auerback, 1988, *Who Will Benefit From Psychotherapy?* New York: HarperCollins. It has been adapted, revised, and printed with permission of the publisher.

insight and did not present reliability data; only two of the studies were based on psychodynamic psychotherapy; and all of the measures of self-understanding were unguided clinical ratings—each judge defined insight as he or she saw fit.

In contrast, the measure of self-understanding that we have begun to develop is a guided clinical rating. The judge assesses the extent to which the patient has developed self-understanding relative to a specific, independent criterion: the Core Conflictual Relationship Theme. Because guided clinical ratings have generally been found to have better predictive validity than unguided ratings (Holt, 1978), our use of a guided clinical rating represents a potential methodological advance.

The purpose of the present study was to develop a method that would allow us to assess the extent to which patients in the Penn Psychotherapy Project acquired self-understanding of their central relationship patterns. If we could develop such an operational measure, we could then examine a main theory of psychoanalytic psychotherapy: that improvement is related to gains in this form of self-understanding.

PROCEDURE

Patients and Sessions

The sample used for this study consisted of the same 43 patients used in the study of accuracy of interpretation (see chapter 13, this volume). These 43 were a subset of the total sample of 73 patients in the Penn Psychotherapy Project (Luborsky et al., 1988).

Two sessions drawn from the early part of treatment were used to score our measures of self-understanding and also to score the CCRT. The CCRT method was generally scored on Sessions 3 and 5, but occasionally a third session was needed to obtain the minimum number of 10 relationship episodes needed for the method. For the ratings of self-understanding, only the two sessions that contained the most relationship episodes were used.

Trained judges working independently were used for each task. The judges were clinical psychologists, psychiatrists, and research assistants highly familiar with the methods.

Measures

The CCRT Measure

The CCRTs represented a composite of individual judges' CCRTs; they were composed of up to two wishes, three responses from other, and three responses of self.

Self-Understanding of the CCRT

The items that constituted the self-understanding rating scale were derived mostly from the principles provided in Luborsky's (1984) manual for supportive—expressive psychoanalytic psychotherapy. The items tap the patient's self-understanding in different areas. Ratings, each on a 5-point scale from *none* to *very much*, were made of self-understanding of (a) the CCRT in general, (b) the CCRT in relationship to the therapist, (c) the CCRT in relationship to parents, and (d) the CCRT in relationship to each of two main other people discussed by the patient within each session; these people were the most frequent topics of relationship episodes.

For each of these areas, separate ratings were made for each wish, response from other, and response of self present in each patient's CCRT. The ratings of all wishes, responses from others, and responses of self were averaged for each patient to create four final scores corresponding to the four areas listed previously.

The judges who rated self-understanding were given the following information for each patient: (a) transcripts of two early sessions, (b) a list of the two main other people for each session, and (c) the CCRT formulation. Judges read each transcript and then rated the session as a whole on the self-understanding scale items. This operational measure of self-understanding reflects a clinical judge's rating of the degree of convergence of what the patient is aware of understanding in a session with what independent clinical observers have judged to be the CCRT.

Health—Sickness Rating Scale

The Health—Sickness Rating Scale (HSRS) (Luborsky, 1975; Luborsky, Diguer, et al., 1993) was included so that we could examine gains in self-understanding controlling for the patient's general level of psychological health. This control was considered necessary because the level of self-understanding might be a function of psychological health.

Outcome Measures

Two composite outcome measures were employed: measures of change (corrected for initial level) and ratings of benefits (see Luborsky et al., 1988).

RESULTS

Reliability of Judging Self-Understanding Was Good

Interjudge reliability was assessed for the four scores from the self-understanding scale (global, therapist, parents, other people) and a total

TABLE 1
Interjudge Reliability of the Self-Understanding Scale

Self-Understanding Scale Item	Pooled Judges' Intraclass Correlation
Global	.77
Therapist	.87
Parents	.89
Other People	.87
Total (sum of subscales)	.85

combining the four subscales, using the intraclass correlation coefficient. The results are given in Table 1. It can be seen that interjudge reliability was quite good. Scores for the two judges were combined for subsequent analyses.

Level of Self-Understanding Was Low

The 1-to-5 rating scale defined an average level as 2.5; according to this definition, the mean levels shown in Table 2 were generally low. The mean level of self-understanding in Session 3 was compared with that in Session 5 to assess whether there was any noticeable increase in self-understanding over these early sessions. Means, standard deviations, and the results of paired t tests on each of the four subscales are shown in Table 2. In general, the level of self-understanding of the CCRT was low in these early sessions; it remained at about the same level from Session 3 to Session 5 except for a small but significant decrease in self-understanding toward the therapist. No other significant changes were found.

Level of Self-Understanding Predicted Outcome; Change in Self-Understanding Did Not

Prediction of outcome of psychotherapy was performed in two ways. First, level of self-understanding (averaging Sessions 3 ad 5) was correlated

TABLE 2
Mean Self-Understanding for Session 3 and Session 5 ($N = 43$)

Self-Understanding Scale Item	Session 3	SD	Session 5	SD	Paired t Test
Global	2.21	(.7)	2.31	(.9)	.7
Therapist	1.66	(.9)	1.33	(.5)	2.4*
Parents	2.31	(1.1)	2.13	(1.1)	.9
Other people	2.50	(.7)	2.74	(.8)	1.6
Total score	2.16	(.5)	2.12	(.5)	.4

Note. Self-understanding was rated on a 5-point scale.
*$p < .05$.

with the two outcome measures. Because it might be expected that the healthier patients would display more insight, these correlations were done controlling for patients' pretreatment level of health–sickness using the HSRS. Second, change in self-understanding from Session 3 to Session 5, correcting for initial (Session 3) level of self-understanding by regression analysis, was correlated with outcome, again partialing for pretreatment scores on the HSRS. Although this is a short period of time to assess gain in insight, and there were no significant increases in insight over this period, previously reported results (see chapter 13, this volume) had indicated that the therapist's interpretations in these sessions had an impact on outcome. It might be possible, therefore, to detect trends toward increasing self-understanding in patients who improve the most in treatment.

The results of the predictive analyses are given in Table 3. *Change* in self-understanding from Session 3 to Session 5 yielded no significant partial correlations with the two outcome measures. *Level* of self-understanding of CCRT, however, produced two significant relationships with outcome: (a) Self-understanding of the CCRT in relation to the therapist correlated with rated benefits (.31, $p < .05$), and (b) self-understanding of the CCRT in relation to other people demonstrated a significant partial correlation with residual gain (.34, $p < .05$).

SUMMARY, DISCUSSION, AND CONCLUSIONS

The Findings and Their Meaning

- The results provide evidence that our measure of self-understanding of specific relationship themes can be rated reliably.
- We found evidence that there are associations between the *level* of self-understanding and outcome. These associations between our measure of self-understanding and outcome are small, however, and we are not able to decide at this time on the relative merits of two possible interpretations of the results: (a) that self-understanding is hard to operationalize in a meaningful way or (b) that any measure of it will achieve low associations with outcome because clinical theory about the necessity of self-understanding is not well founded.
- Several methodological issues lead us to be cautious in interpreting our findings. The specific hypothesis that *gain* in self-understanding is related to more favorable outcome was not confirmed, although we believe that this hypothesis was not given an adequate test. It probably is necessary to evaluate change in self-understanding over a longer period of treat-

TABLE 3
Prediction of Outcome From Level of and Change in Self-Understanding ($N = 43$)

Self-Understanding Scale Item	Outcome Measures	
	Rated Benefits	Residual Gain
Level (Session 3 + Session 5)		
Global	.03	.16
Therapist	.31*	.29
Parents	−.28	−.30
Other people	.22	.34*
Total	.04	.12
Change from Session 3 to Session 5		
Global	.06	.11
Therapist	.23	.25
Parents	−.23	−.22
Other people	−.07	.11
Total	−.07	.04

Note. Coefficients are partial correlations, controlling for Health–Sickness Rating Scale score and, in the case of change in self-understanding, for Session 3 level.
*$p < .05$.

ment than two early sessions. To evaluate change over a longer period of time on a specific criterion (that is, the CCRT), it would be necessary for that criterion to be equally relevant to both the early and later points in therapy. In the case of the treatments studied here, this condition may not have applied: The relatively large number of sessions on the average (mean number of sessions was 53.5 for the 43 patients) meant that it was likely that some change in the content of the clinical material and even some change in the CCRT would occur over therapy. In a brief focal dynamic therapy, it might be a simpler task to track level of self-understanding of the same content over the course of the whole treatment.

Although the significant results for *level* of self-understanding are promising, the correlational nature of the study limits inferences about the causal role of self-understanding. Statistical control of one major variable, psychological health–sickness, allows us to rule out one potential third variable as an explanation of the results, yet other third variables may well exist.

■ To the extent that we can speculate from these data, it is of interest that ratings of self-understanding of the CCRT in relation to the therapist and to other people were predictive but self-understanding of the CCRT in a global sense or in relation to parents was not. The major importance of the relationship pattern with the therapist is of course evident in many clinical theories of psychodynamic psychotherapy (Luborsky, 1984; Strupp & Binder, 1984). The data may be more consistent with a focus on the "here and now" relationships of the patient and less on the past parental relationships, although we did not specifically code each relationship for past versus present.

The Search for Better Operational Measures

The only measure that has been partially examined in this chapter is the degree of convergence of the patient's self statements with the independently established CCRT. Other reasonable types of operational measures can be derived from the clinical observations reported by Luborsky (1984, pp. 124–25) about the kinds of improvements in self-understanding that develop in the course of psychotherapy. The gains are observed to appear in five stages. (a) Early in psychotherapy, the patient reports involvement in relationship interactions with the therapist and other people, but there is relatively little ability to recognize the patient's own usual relationship pattern. (b) Later in therapy, the experience of having one's own increasingly familiar pattern becomes clearer to the patient. The effect of this recognition of one's own pattern is that the patient is better able to distinguish between what he or she brings to relationship problems and what the external circumstances bring. (c) The patient develops a healthy respect for how deeply embedded in his or her personality the central relationship problem is. It leads, as one patient said, to an appreciation of its "slippery power to reappear." (d) The recognition of having one's own central relationship pattern leads to other developments, including a greater understanding of how the pattern might have originated, usually in relation to interactions with the parents. (e) It is also crucially beneficial that the recognition lead to a range of new ways of dealing with and mastering the relationship problems in the patterns.

An example of the benefits provided by a greater understanding of the pattern is exemplified by the following words of Mr. Howard in Session 83, with which he describes his feelings about the therapist: "I felt bad because of distrusting our relationship. I saw an article that makes me distrust you. I realize that I distrust everybody." It is clear in this abbreviated example that the patient became more distrustful on seeing the article. But it is also clear that the patient was able to distinguish the two sources of distrust: the article and his central relationship pattern, which included a readiness to distrust.

It might be useful to compare a set of measures that is based on these clinical observations with an expanded operational measure of self-understanding of the kind reported in this chapter. The set would be composed of rating scales that reflect the degree to which the patient experiences each of the five stages listed previously. Finally, in future studies we plan to try a self-report approach (described in chapter 15, this volume) but using as part of a postsession questionnaire items that include the five stages of self-understanding as well as the patient's reports of their own capacity to see the degree of self-applicability of the four specific relationship themes of the CCRT: global, therapist, parents, and other people.

- The data presented in this chapter have taken us by a new route one step toward testing aspects of the clinical concepts of dynamic psychotherapy. This study examined our experiences in investigating an operational measure of the role of self-understanding in psychotherapy and offers suggestions about where to look in future studies for the therapeutic "action" in the patient's level of and change in self-understanding during psychotherapy.

15

THE PERSPECTIVE OF PATIENTS VERSUS THAT OF CLINICIANS IN THE ASSESSMENT OF CENTRAL RELATIONSHIP THEMES

PAUL CRITS-CHRISTOPH AND LESTER LUBORSKY

In carrying out the CCRT method, clinical judges extract relationship patterns from narratives about interactions with other people. Although the clinical judges do the task with reliable and valid results, some of the procedures have drawbacks. A major one is that making transcripts of psychotherapy sessions to be scored by clinical judges is extremely time consuming. Then the clinical judges themselves spend, on the average, about 1½ to 3 hours to score one session. Thus, large-scale research with the CCRT method is difficult; and the other transference-related measures generally require even more time (see chapter 20).

AIM

Our purpose in this study is to examine the possibility of obtaining CCRT information directly using a self-report method. Although there will always be a role for clinician-derived measures in data sets when self-report questionnaires are not available (for example, with psychotherapy tapes) or need to be amplified, the practical advantages of a self-report measure for research could be great. In addition, a comparison of self-reported relationship patterns with clinical judge-scored patterns may tell more about the nature of a core conflictual theme in terms of which aspects are typically conscious and which may not be fully in awareness. According to psychodynamic theories, some part of a conflictual pattern is generally outside of a patient's awareness. It is not known, however, how much the CCRT or the other judge-scored measures discussed in chapter 20 routinely assess major aspects of a conflictual relationship pattern that are unconscious.

We proceeded with the development of a self-report CCRT measure well aware of the potential pitfalls of self-report methods. One main problem is that people may be inaccurate in their reporting of their own behavior (Nisbett & Wilson, 1977) for a variety of reasons. For example, when the frequency of occurrence of a behavior is very low, people are less likely to be able to describe retrospectively what went on in the situation in which it was expressed. Social desirability effects can also distort self-report measures.

On the other hand, it seems likely that important parts of some major relationship patterns are readily available to conscious self-report. Such relationship themes can be part of highly redundant patterns, so that interpersonal interactions with friends, parents, colleagues, and others that might contain such themes occur with high frequency for most people. The ability to observe and describe such patterns may be an important individual difference variable, however, perhaps highly correlated with psychological mindedness or interpersonal awareness. Self-knowledge about interpersonal patterns may also be acquired through feedback from other people concerning such patterns.

PROCEDURE

The data collection centered on a comparison of the following three main measures:

Self-Report CCRT Questionnaire (SR-CCRT); (Crits-Christoph, 1986). In this questionnaire participants simply rate on a 1-to-5 scale each of a number of wishes and responses on how typical those wishes and responses are of their relationships. In addition, respondents are asked to describe in a sentence or two what their main conflicts are.

Self-Interpretation of RAP Narratives (SI-RAP). This instrument is the self-interpretation (SI-CCRT) of the RAP interview (see chapter 7). During the RAP interview, participants are asked to relate detailed episodes of actual interactions with other people, including what happened and what was said during the interaction. The instructions ask for reports of interactions that were emotionally involving and included a significant other person (such as parents, friends, or lovers). The self-interpretation procedure comes after all of the narratives have been told. After telling each of the narratives, subjects are asked to rate each of a number of wishes and responses on the degree to which the wishes and responses apply to their behavior in the reported interaction. They are also asked to describe what conflict, if any, was present for them in each interaction. We elicited 10 such narratives in the current study.

Standard Clinician-Judged CCRT of RAP Narratives (CCRT). This measure is the standard CCRT measure scored by a clinical judge from the RAP interview.

Although each of the three measures assessed all three CCRT components (wishes, responses from other, and responses of self), this presentation is reduced to a single focus only on the results for the wishes. Two groups of subjects were used for these studies. The first sample consisted of 70 University of Pennsylvania undergraduates who completed the SR-CCRT Questionnaire. One week later, 30 of these students were readministered the questionnaire to assess test–retest reliability.

The main comparison of the SR-CCRT Questionnaire, SI-RAP, and clinical judge-scored CCRT was performed on the second sample, consisting of 16 patients. These patients were all receiving psychotherapy at the outpatient psychiatry clinic at the University of Pennsylvania.

RESULTS

Self-Report CCRT Questionnaire (SR-CCRT)

The item pool for the SR-CCRT measure was drawn from the standard categories list, Edition 1, of wishes developed as an aid in reliability studies (see chapter 3, this volume). These 18 wishes (see Exhibit 1) were distilled from the set of wishes obtained empirically by clinical judges who applied the CCRT method to a different sample of 16 patients.

Retest Reliability Was Moderate; Internal Consistency Was Marginal

Test–retest correlations were computed for each of the 18 wish items. The results (see Table 1) indicated that item reliability ranged from .24 to .90, with a median reliability of .61. Although the test–retest reliability results were adequate, the internal consistency (Cronbach's alpha) coefficients were marginal. Subsequent analyses were performed at both the item and factor levels.

EXHIBIT 1
Wishes Rated in the CCRT Self-Report Questionnaire

1. To assert my independence and autonomy
2. To dominate; to impose my will or control on others
3. To overcome other's domination; to be free of obligations imposed by others; to not be put down
4. To win in competition with another; to be better than the other person
5. To win someone's affection or attention, through competition with another person
6. To submit, to give in, to be passive
7. To make contact with others, to be close, to be friends
8. To receive affection, to not be deprived of continued affection
9. To be receptive (to open up) to others
10. To please the other person
11. To avoid hurting the other person
12. To get sexual gratification
13. To receive acceptance; to be respected, recognized, approved, vindicated, reassured; to maintain self-esteem
14. To be fairly treated
15. To get help, care, protection, and guidance from others
16. To achieve, be competent, be successful
17. To hurt the other person, to get back at the other; to express anger, hostility, or resentment to the other person
18. To exert control over myself

Note. Wishes are from Edition 1 Standard Categories (see chapter 3, this volume).

Three Factors Were Found

The existence of higher order dimensions within the set of 18 items was examined by factor analysis (principal components analysis, varimax rotation) using the responses of the 70 students. Inspection of the successive solutions indicated that a three-factor solution was most appropriate. Table 2 gives the factor loadings and reliability statistics for the three factors.

Interpretation of the factors was straightforward. The first factor contained wishes related to giving and getting affection and intimacy in relationships and was labeled Wish for Closeness. The second factor consisted of the wishes (a) to dominate, (b) to be better than the other person, and (c) to get back at the other person. This factor was described as a Competition dimension. The third factor, Independence, was characterized by high loadings on wishes related to independence, achievement, overcoming others' domination, and desire to be treated fairly. The factors were scored by summing the salient items as listed in Table 2.

Self-Interpretation of the RAP Interview

The Self-Interpretation of the RAP (SI-RAP) procedure (Luborsky, 1978b) yielded patients' ratings of the 18 wishes for each of the 10 rela-

TABLE 1
Reliability of Self-Report CCRT Questionnaire on Wishes

Wish Item	Test–Retest Correlation
1. To assert myself	.61
2. To dominate	.72
3. To overcome domination	.73
4. To be better than others	.66
5. To win attention	.53
6. To submit	.62
7. To be close	.60
8. To get affection	.24
9. To be receptive	.70
10. To please	.72
11. To avoid hurting	.90
12. To have sex	.64
13. To get acceptance	.61
14. To be treated fairly	.34
15. To get care	.40
16. To achieve	.50
17. To hurt	.57
18. To exert control	.47

tionship episodes. Of initial interest was the extent to which patients were consistent in their self-ratings of themes across 10 items. For example, if a patient described a relationship episode as containing a wish for closeness, was the patient more likely to rate this wish as present in other relationship episodes as well? Put another way, can we construct a scale of a patient's

TABLE 2
Factor Analysis of Wishes

Factor Loadings	Closeness	Competition	Independence
7. To be close	.75		
8. To get affection	.68		
9. To be receptive	.68		
10. To please	.66		
11. To avoid hurting	.59		
15. To get care	.50		
2. To dominate		.66	
4. To be better than others		.70	
17. To hurt		.70	
1. To assert myself			.62
3. To overcome domination			.65
14. To be treated fairly			.60
16. To achieve			.72
Reliability			
Internal consistency	.67	.52	.60
Test–retest	.71	.74	.82

Note. Loadings are listed only for the variables that defined the subscales. Five variables did not load on any of the three main factors.

characteristic level of experienced wishes by aggregating over the multiple episodes?

Consistency Over Narratives Was High

This question was answered by computing Cronbach's alpha coefficient for each of the 18 wishes, considering the 10 replications to be analogous to items on a test. Table 3 presents the results. It can be seen that the internal consistencies of the aggregate scores were all reasonably high, with the exception of the wish for sex item. The low (.40) value for wish for sex is not surprising, given that this item focuses more on a particular behavior than on a general psychological need or intention (such as a wish to be close to others) that might be manifested behaviorally in many different ways. In addition, the RAP test requested narratives about a variety of people (for example, parents) for whom a conscious wish for sexual gratification and a narrative about it would be unusual. The high internal consistencies for the other wishes indicate that these patients perceived the same themes to be present in many relationships.

Correlation With the Self-Report CCRT Was Poor

Table 4 presents the correlations between the aggregate scores from the RAP (averaging over the 10 episodes for each wish) and the corresponding wish rating from the SR-CCRT Questionnaire. One would expect

TABLE 3
Self-Interpretation of RAP: Consistency of Wishes Across
10 Relationship Episodes

Wish Item	Internal Consistency
1. To assert myself	.80
2. To dominate	.86
3. To overcome domination	.66
4. To be better than others	.84
5. To win attention	.88
6. To submit	.91
7. To be close	.85
8. To get affection	.88
9. To be receptive	.83
10. To please	.88
11. To avoid hurting	.85
12. To have sex	.40
13. To get acceptance	.81
14. To be treated fairly	.88
15. To get care	.81
16. To achieve	.86
17. To hurt	.74
18. To exert control	.81

Note. Internal consistency was computed using Cronbach's alpha.

TABLE 4
Correlations Between Self-Report and
Self-Interpretation

Wish Item	Correlation
1. To assert myself	−.03
2. To dominate	.41
3. To overcome domination	.54*
4. To be better than others	.58*
5. To win attention	.23
6. To submit	−.14
7. To be close	−.15
8. To get affection	−.18
9. To be receptive	.18
10. To please	.16
11. To avoid hurting	−.21
12. To have sex	.19
13. To get acceptance	.05
14. To be treated fairly	−.11
15. To get care	−.25
16. To achieve	−.06
17. To hurt	.43
18. To exert control	−.14
Factor	
Closeness	−.14
Competition	.79*
Independence	.20

*$p < .05$.

that if a patient rated a specific wish highly, for example, the item Wish "to assert myself," in many different relationship episodes on the RAP, the patient also would rate this wish as typical of relationships on the SR-CCRT Questionnaire. The results in Table 4 indicate that the two measures were generally not correlated, however. An exception was the Competition factor, for which there was a .79 correlation between the Self-Report CCRT and the Self-Interpretation of the RAP scores. The items constituting this factor (Items 2, 4, and 17) as well as Item 3 (wish to overcome domination) showed modest correlations.

There may be several reasons for the general lack of correlation between the levels of the same wish in the two tests. (a) The process of telling RAP narratives and then interpreting them probably leads to increased self-awareness about one's relationship patterns. The Self-Report CCRT questionnaire was completed, therefore, before the self-interpretation process was initiated. Completion of the Self-Report questionnaire after the Self-Interpretation RAP may yield more agreement. (b) The narratives about relationship episodes chosen by the patient for the RAP interview may not be representative of the patient's typical interactions with others. For example, a bias toward remembering problematic interactions rather than typical interactions would lead to a lack of concordance between the two measures. (c) Finally, social desirability effects are likely to be more pronounced for questions asking about "your typical needs and desires" than for questions about specifically exemplified interactions, thereby leading to disagreements.

Clinical Judge's Scoring: Comparisons With Self-Report and Self-Interpretation

To facilitate comparison of the three methods, we first selected for each patient the first and second most frequent wishes as scored by the clinical judge. These wishes were then translated into the wordings used in the list of 18 wishes. These wishes had average frequencies of 7.6 and 4.4, respectively, out of the 10 RAP episodes. We then examined the patient's ratings on the same wishes from the Self-Report CCRT Questionnaire. For example, if the clinical judge identified the wish to dominate others as the most frequent wish from the RAP, we examined the patient's ratings on this wish, that is, how much this wish was typical of the patient's relationships in general (Self-Report CCRT Questionnaire) and, on the average, how much this wish applied to the RAP episodes (Self-Interpretation of RAP). In deriving the patient's self-interpretation mean ratings on the wishes the clinical judge scored, we chose to include only episodes in which the clinical judge identified the wish as being present. Thus, we asked the question: When a clinical judge infers a main wish to be present in a relationship episode, to what degree does the patient rate this wish as applicable to the same relationship episode? We were also concerned with the possibility that patients have a general sense of the nature of their main wishes, which may be similar to that of the clinician, but that they do not choose the identical wish that the clinician identified. For this reason, we turned to the subscales that emerged from the factor analysis of the Self-Report CCRT Questionnaire completed by the student sample. We speculated that average score of the patients on the particular subscale containing the wish item identified by the clinician would provide an index of whether the patient was in the ballpark in designating which wishes applied to his or her relationships.

Patients Tended to Give High Ratings to Wishes Identified by the Clinicians

Table 5 displays the results comparing the SR-CCRT and the SI-RAP with the clinical judge's CCRT scoring. It can be seen that patients generally rated highly the wishes that were identified by the clinicians. For example, the main wish identified by the clinician was rated, on the average, 4.0 on the 5-point scale (5 = *very typical of me*) of the Self-Report CCRT Questionnaire. but it is conceivable that patients rate all wishes highly and therefore were not making the same discrimination that was

TABLE 5
Comparison of Patient's Report With Clinician-Identified Wishes

Measure	Mean Rating for Wish Identified by Clinician	Mean Rating for Other Wishes	Significance (*p* Value)
Main wish			
Self-Report			
Item	4.0	3.5	.04
Subscale	3.5	3.5	*ns*
Self-Interpretation			
Item	3.7	2.7	.001
Subscale	3.5	2.8	.001
Secondary wish			
Self-Report			
Item	3.7	3.6	*ns*
Subscale	4.0	3.7	*ns*
Self-Interpretation			
Item	3.6	2.7	.004
Subscale	3.3	2.8	.06

Note. Ratings were made on a 1-to-5 scale, in which 5 = *very typical of me.*

made by the clinician. The column Mean Rating for Other Wishes in Table 5 allows a comparison of the patients' ratings of the wish identified by the clinician with the patients' ratings of other wishes not identified by the clinical judge. The statistical significance of these comparisons was tested with a paired *t* test.

Although patients tended to rate many other wishes as applicable, discrimination among the wishes was apparent. This was particularly true for the Self-Interpretation RAP, on which, for example, patients rated the clinical judge's main wish 1 point higher on the rating scale than they rated other wishes (3.7 vs. 2.7, *p* < .001).

However, the Self-Report-CCRT Questionnaire provided poorer discrimination, especially for the secondary wish identified by the clinical judges. Examination of subscale scores did not improve discrimination for either the Self-Report CCRT Questionnaire or the Self-Interpretation of the RAP.

Because mean comparisons can obscure important individual differences, we inspected each patient's ratings in comparison to the clinician's CCRT. Fourteen patients showed ratings consistent with the mean differences. Two patients, however, had somewhat lower ratings for the main wish that the clinician identified than for other wishes. Whether this reflects a selective lack of awareness of an important wish or is simply a chance finding with less than perfectly reliable measures is not known.

Finally, we compared the patients' description of their main conflicts (written out as part of the Self-Report CCRT Questionnaire and Self-Interpretation of the RAP tests) with the clinician's description of the main conflict in the CCRT. In only 25% of the cases did the patients' descriptions from either measure reasonably match the content of the clinician's description of a conflict. In most of the mismatches, the patients attributed the "conflict" to problematic people in their lives, whereas the clinician saw the conflict as intrapsychic (for example, as a conflict between wishes).

SUMMARY AND DISCUSSION

For this initial study of patients' versus clinicians' evaluations, only the wish component of the CCRT was examined. Three procedures for assessing a patient's main wishes within the CCRT were compared: (a) the Self-Report CCRT Questionnaire composed of 18 standard category wishes, (b) the Self-Interpretation of the RAP test, and (c) the clinician's interpretation of the RAP test. The SR-CCRT Questionnaire is a newly developed procedure that has been shown to have adequate test–retest reliability and to be composed of three main factors. The SI-RAP test (Luborsky, 1978a) has been further developed by the inclusion of ratings of the standard categories for the CCRT.

- The results suggest that, typically, patients are able consciously to report on the Self-Report CCRT Questionnaire the same wishes that are identified by a clinical judge.
- Although this is an important finding that increases our understanding of the CCRT method, for several reasons it would not be accurate to conclude that self-report measures are interchangeable with clinician-scored measures. First, despite statistically significant differences between patients' ratings of the clinician-identified wish versus other wishes, patients did not make as large a discrimination between important or relevant wishes and unimportant or less relevant wishes. The use of the mean of "all other wishes" as a comparison for patients' ratings of the main clinician-identified wish does not indicate that the patient's rated the clinician's wish the highest. In fact, other wishes were often rated by the patient equally highly (of course, many wishes were rated lower by the patient, thus bringing the mean of "all other wishes" down).
- It seems likely that patients vary in the extent to which they are aware of their main wishes, even if most tend to be aware of them. Two patients in this study showed particularly

low awareness of the main wish. Without knowing a priori which patients give accurate self-reports (that is, are aware of the CCRT), a self-report measure might be misleading. In future research, patients with low self-awareness could be evaluated by other tests (such as repressive style measures) before their assessment with self-report or clinician methods.

- Although patients often are aware of the wish component of the CCRT, other aspects of the CCRT may be less available to conscious self-report. In fact, our results indicated that patients do not usually describe the main conflict in the same way the clinician does. It might be important to provide patients with specific questions about their conflicts, including an item defining a conflict in the way the clinician formulated it for each patient, rather than relying only on open-ended questions as we did here. In addition, although it is expected that relatively high awareness of the other components of the CCRT (responses from other and responses of self) will be obtained, the *sequence* of particular wish → response from other → response of self that defines the thematic nature of the CCRT may not be evident to many patients. Our data suggest that the method of inquiry affects the types of self-report information given. The Self-Interpretation measure which consists of questions anchored to specific accounts of interpersonal interactions, yielded better discrimination than did the general Self-Report CCRT Questionnaire. The use of the Self-Interpretation measure requires that a RAP interview be performed (usually lasting about one-half hour), followed by a self-interpretation phase (lasting 1 hour). The hoped-for time advantage of a 5-minute questionnaire does not seem to be achievable at this stage. Further research experimenting with different instructions in a self-report questionnaire may allow better congruence with clinician-based measures. In fact, further research has yielded an expanded and improved central relationship questionnaire (CRQ) (Barber, 1993).

CONCLUSION

Our overall conclusion is that although patients are conscious of many of the individual components of the CCRT, a better discrimination of more versus less important wishes is achieved by the clinician. In addition, clinician formulations of conflict do not agree with patients' open-ended descriptions of their conflicts.

16

STABILITY OF THE CCRT FROM AGE 3 TO 5

LESTER LUBORSKY, ELLEN LUBORSKY, LOUIS DIGUER,
KELLY SCHMIDT, DOROTHEE DENGLER, JEFFREY FAUDE,
MARGARET MORRIS, PAMELA SCHAFFLER,
HELEN BUCHSBAUM, AND ROBERT EMDE

Starting in the late 1970s, the advent of a reliable operational measure of central relationship patterns in psychotherapy gave backing to the view of a stable, distinctive, central relationship pattern for each person (L. Luborsky, 1976, 1977b; L. Luborsky & Crits-Christoph, 1990; L. Luborsky, Mellon, van Ravenswaay, et al., 1985; L. Luborsky et al., 1986). This new measure of the Core Conflictual Relationship Theme showed some stability over a period of approximately 1 year of psychotherapy (Crits-Christoph & Luborsky, 1990). But early-in-life consistency on this new measure was not examined until the present study.

If the CCRT method could be applied to very young children's narratives, a study might reveal whether a central relationship pattern appeared in their narratives about close relationships with their parents. We

This chapter is a modified version of "Extending the Core Conflictual Relationships Into Childhood," by Luborsky, Luborsky, et al., 1995, in *Development and Vulnerability in Close Relationships* (pp. 287–308), Mahwah, NJ: Lawrence Erlbaum Associates. Copyright 1996 by Lawrence Erlbaum Associates, Inc. Reprinted by permission.

planned to score the CCRT in children's narratives at age 3 and repeat the same scoring of the CCRT with the same children at age 5 to see the consistency of the relationship patterns over time. Beyond the study at ages 3 and 5, we also planned to compare these relationship patterns with those of adult groups whose narratives were scored by the same standard CCRT categories.

BACKGROUND OF RELATED RESEARCH

Three distinct scores have been tapped so far for evaluating children's relationship patterns in their very early years: (a) clinical retrospection on the basis of adults' narratives about their early childhood, (b) infancy research with direct observations of early relationships, and (c) narratives told by young children.

Clinical Retrospection

The retrospection method has had a long history in clinical practice. The method relies on early memories for reconstructing scenes, usually traumatic ones, that may have prefigured the current relationship pattern. There is impressive clinical evidence that some early traumatic scenes act like a template so that later episodes contain replications of components of the earlier scene (as suggested by Reiser, 1984). Tomkins's (1987) script theory similarly places emphasis on the replication of scenes, as illustrated in the case presentation by Carlson (1986). Such a concept of a long-lasting consistency of relationship patterns is also suggested by the famous 30-year longitudinal study of Monica, a young child with a gastric fistula (Engel & Reichsman, 1956).

Infancy Research

Research on relationship patterns in infancy has mushroomed in the last 2 decades. The two methods that have been increasingly used are the study of the mother–infant exchange and the study of attachment patterns. The microanalysis of the mother–infant exchange has revealed much about the structure of the interactions (Tronick, 1982); the enduring meaning of this exchange for personality development has been examined by Stern (1985, 1989) and by Beebe and Lachmann (1988).

A systematic comparison of developmental changes in coping styles (E. Luborsky, 1987), based on videos of 30 mother–child pairs of children at age 1 and 2, gave specific evidence for the expected greater differentiation of coping styles at age 2.

Dahl and Teller (1993) cited a dissertation (Davies, 1989) describing twelve 3-year-olds involved in 10 interactions with each of their mothers and 10 interactions with each of two other children. Similar "frames" were found in each child's interactions with his or her mother compared with those of the other children; the frames were also different for each child.

Research based on attachment theory (Bowlby, 1969, 1973) has provided a means of examining different patterns of attachment (Ainsworth, Blehar, Waters, & Wall, 1978) at 1 year and more recently beyond 1 year. The linking of Bowlby's (1969, 1973) concept of internal working models of relationships with attachment patterns has extended knowledge of the age range of attachment behavior and located the bonds between internal representations and behavior (Bretherton, 1995; Bretherton, Ridgeway, & Cassidy, 1990; Main, Kaplan, & Cassidy, 1985).

Important work on delineating relationship patterns is represented by Sroufe (1983) and by Sroufe and Fleeson (1986), who pointed out that continuity and coherence in attachment patterns remain evident in the early years and beyond.

Narratives Told by Young Children

Very young children who are just becoming verbal can tell narratives, but they find it difficult to do so consistently unless they are given considerable structure and assistance. Providing these children with a set of interesting stimulus pictures is a technique for stimulating narratives, as in Bellak's (1954) Children's Apperception Test (CAT) derived from Murray (1938). Yet even with the CAT it is difficult to elicit organized narratives regularly before age 3 or 4. Buchsbaum and Emde (1990), partly on the basis of work by Bretherton, Prentiss, and Ridgeway (1990), initiate the narratives using a story-stem and a doll family. Such devices have the effect of extending to earlier ages the ability of children to provide coherent narratives consistently.

PROCEDURE

Subjects

In our study, twenty-six 3-year-old children were evaluated. These children from Denver or its vicinity had been in an earlier study of normal development (Buchsbaum & Emde, 1990). They were firstborn and normal at birth, and 16 were female. The parents were white, middle-class, and married; 25 of the 26 couples were still married at the time of the study. Eighteen of the mothers had full-time jobs, and their children were in day care. Fourteen of the children had a younger sibling and the mothers of two of them were expecting a second child.

After their third birthday, these children were interviewed briefly in their home, where they told four narratives to provide them with preliminary practice. Seven to 10 days later, they were interviewed and videotaped in the laboratory by a different interviewer. For the analyses involving a comparison of age 3 with age 5, we restricted our sample to the 18 children who took part at both times.

A Doll Family Story Method For Collecting Narratives

The basic data from each of 25 children from Buchsbaum and Emde's (1990) sample of 3-year-olds were based on the use of a doll family story method. Each child told 10 videotaped narratives in the laboratory. The duration of the session was from 25 to 30 minutes. For each narrative, the experimenter presented a stimulus story-stem peopled with a doll family— a father, mother, and two children of the same gender as the child—in which an upsetting event that had just happened was related.[1] The experimenter then inquired about what would happen next, after the event in the story-stem. For example, one of these stimulus story-stems is called "The Lost Car Keys"; the experimenter starts the narrative by saying that the keys to the family car were lost. The doll mother accuses the doll father of losing the keys; the doll father denies this. The child is then asked, "What happens next?" Like the lost key story, most of the other stimulus stories are conflictual in content. An example of data from the lost key story is given in Figure 1, and the scoring of the wishes in that story is shown in Figure 2.

Basically, the doll family story procedure is a guided and prompted method of eliciting narratives. A scene is set by the experimenter's stimulus story, and at each stage of the child's narrative the child is prompted to explain what happened next. The procedure is much like that of the Thematic Apperception Test (TAT; Murray, 1938), but in the TAT a pictorial scene is presented, and the narrator creates a story about it. In contrast, the relationship episodes told for the Relationship Anecdotes Paradigm (RAP) interview (L. Luborsky, 1990b) or in psychotherapy (L. Luborsky & Crits-Christoph, 1990) are intended by the narrator to be about actual events. In Buchsbaum and Emde's (1990) method of guided narratives, the child's presentations of what the dolls do or say appear to contain a variable mixture of depictions of relationship events that have occurred along with fantasies about these relationships.

---

[1] At 36 months, the 10 story-stem events were about spilled juice, toilet, monster, car keys, argument, ice cream, naps, restraint of aggression, departure/reunion, couch, and moral dilemma. At 60 months, the story-stems were about ice cream, monster, sad, car keys, argument, nap, bicycle, clean room/new toy, departure/reunion, couch, and Band-Aid (6 of the 10 story-stems were the same). The fuller account of the story-stem can be found in a chapter by Buchsbaum and Emde (1990).

"Lost Car Keys" Story

	Tailor-made	Top Standard Categories	Top Clusters
E: Mom and Dad look for the car keys?			
C: Un-huh. //And . . . and . . . and then Jane comes into the room.// //And . . . and Jane says, "How about you talk about it." (Brings dolls together.)//	PRS: facilitates dialogue between parents	#7: am open #9: am helpful	1: helpful
E: And then what happens after Jane says that?			
C: Well, //then Susan comes in (reaches for Susan, brings to other dolls)// //and they all sit down and talk about it.//	W: to help parents solve problem	#12: to help others #17: to avoid conflict	8: to achieve and help others 4: to be distant and avoid conflict
E: So, they all sit down and talk about it. What are they talking about?			
C: Well, //they're two are having a little talk (moves Jane and Susan together)// and //they're two having a little talk (faces Mom and Dad).//	PRS: sisters discuss sharing PRO: parents talk about lost key	#7: am open #15: am independent #11: are open #18: are cooperative	1: helpful 5: self-controlled 8: understanding 6: helpful
E: And they're talking about . . . what are they talking about?	W: to open communication	#9: to be open #11: to be close to others	5: to be close and accepting
C: Well, //they're talking about the car keys (touches Mom and Dad)//, and //they're talking about playing (touches Jane and Susan)//.			
E: And they're talking about playing?			
C: Like . . . like . . . like sharing and stuff.			

Figure 1. The story told by Constance at age 5, to the "Lost Car Keys" stem. The ratings of the wishes are given in Figure 2. The double slashes (//) in the story mark off each thought unit to be scored. PRS = positive response from other; W = wish.

Standard Category: Wishes	Ratings of Thought Units	
	To help parents solve problems	To open communication
1. TO BE UNDERSTOOD	1	1
2. TO BE ACCEPTED	1	1
3. TO BE RESPECTED	1	1
4: TO ACCEPT OTHERS	3	2
5. TO RESPECT OTHERS	3	3
6. TO HAVE TRUST	3	2
7. TO BE LIKED	1	1
8. TO BE OPENED UP TO	4	4
9. TO BE OPEN	1	1
10. TO BE DISTANT FROM OTHERS	1	1
11. TO BE OPEN TO OTHERS	4	4
12. TO HELP OTHERS	5[a]	4[b]
13. TO BE HELPED	1	1
14. TO NOT BE HURT	1	1
15. TO BE HURT	1	1
16. TO HURT OTHER	1	1
17. TO AVOID CONFLICT	5[b]	5[a]
18. TO OPPOSE OTHER	1	1
19. TO HAVE CONTROL OVER OTHER	1	1
20. TO BE CONTROLLED BY OTHER	1	1
21. TO HAVE SELF-CONTROL	1	1
22. TO ACHIEVE	1	1
23. TO BE INDEPENDENT	1	1
24. TO FEEL GOOD ABOUT MYSELF	1	2
25. TO BETTER MYSELF	1	1
26. TO BE GOOD	1	2
27. TO BE LIKE OTHER	1	1
28. TO BE MY OWN PERSON	1	1
29. TO NOT BE OBLIGATED	1	1
30. TO HAVE STABILITY	5	4
31. TO FEEL COMFORTABLE	4	3
32. TO FEEL HAPPY	4	3
33. TO BE PROTECTED	3	3

Figure 2. A sample of the ratings by judge MM on the standard categories of wishes for Constance for the Lost Car Keys story (see Figure 1).

[a]Top choice.

[b]Second choice.

Data Analyses

Transcripts of the narratives were made from videos of the interview and were CCRT scored by the method described in chapter 2, this volume. First, a specially trained text-preparation judge marked the transcript with the CCRT-scorable thought units and the type of component to be scored for each thought unit. Second, trained CCRT judges (EL, PS, KS, and MM) inferred the tailor-made categories of each of the thought units and rated them for all of the Edition 2 standard categories (Appendix A, chapter 2) listed (on the form provided in Appendix B, chapter 2, with 34 wishes, 30 responses from others, and 31 responses of self).

For the present analysis of results, only a single judge's scores for each child were used, which allowed the transcripts to be apportioned for scoring among the three judges. The use of only one judge per case appeared justified by the moderately high level of agreement in scoring among judges, as is discussed in the results section.

An Example of a Scored Narrative

To help explain the data analysis, we include the scored story told by 5-year-old Constance after hearing the lost car keys story-stem, along with the nondirective promptings by the experimenter (see Figure 1). The first ruled column on the left has the tailor-made scores, that is, the judge's own inferences about each marked-off thought unit. The middle column contains the top (most frequent) standard categories, and the column on the right contains these top categories expressed in terms of clusters.

As shown in Figure 2, each judge starts with the thought unit's tailor-made inferences and rates each one on all of the standard categories. The rating reflects the degree to which the judge believes the standard category is expressed in the thought unit. In this example, two of the thought units and their tailor-made inferences are named in the heading of the columns, and the ratings from 1 to 5 (with 5 being the highest) for each of 33 standard categories given in each column.

One judge's ratings of the wishes in the story by Constance are given in Figure 2. Constance is clearly a child of our psychotherapy era for she believes in conflict resolution by means of the people talking things over. That ethos can be seen as reflected in the thought unit's tailor-made inference: "to help parents solve problems." This judge gave a score of 5 to the standard category "to avoid conflict." Judges identified their top choice by putting a circle around a rating and their second choice by putting a square around it. The standard category ratings in each column were summed across the narratives, which allowed us to locate the most pervasive across-narratives standard categories expressed in the form of clusters.

Compliance of 3- and 5-Year-Olds With the Narrative-Telling Task

As the first step in the analysis of results, the narratives were scored for the degree to which the child complied with the request to tell a narrative. This information was useful to us in two ways: (a) We could limit our sample to children who provided narratives that were complete enough to score, and (b) we would have an estimate of the degree to which the children included in our sample were willing or able to comply with the request to tell narratives. We rated compliance on a 5-point well-defined scale; the scale points were defined as follows: Point 1: The child does not respond to any of the stimulus stories despite additional prompting. Point 2: The child may begin to engage in responding to the stimulus story in a superficial way, but there is no attempt to develop it. Point 3: The child makes an initial attempt to deal actively with the stimulus story but breaks this off entirely or is distracted from creating an ending or resolution. Point 4: The child directly engages the doll in the content of the child's story; the child needs prompting but tends to be responsive to this prompting. Point 5: The child becomes actively involved with the stimulus story, needs little prompting, and works effortfully and agreeably within the stimulus story format to find a satisfactory resolution or outcome.

At 3 years of age, 21 of the 25 children were able to comply sufficiently to be included in the sample. At age 5, all of the children complied sufficiently to be included. For the 18 children who were included at both age 3 and age 5, the average compliance rating for age 3 was 3.49 and for age 5 was 3.96, showing that, as a whole, the compliance at age 3 was fairly good and that it improved only moderately by age 5.

We also found that at age 3 the ratings of compliance differed across the 10 stories. We used a repeated-measures analysis of variance for the mean ratings of the 10 stories and found a significant difference across the 10 stories, $F(9, 180) = 2.14$, $p < .05$, two-tailed.

Two of the stories at age 3 were of special interest because the children were markedly less compliant in completing them; they were the exclusion–departure story and the reunion story. The average rating of compliance for these two stories was compared with the average of the other eight stories using a paired t-test procedure. The means were significantly different, $t(20) = 2.73$, $p < .05$, two-tailed, and the difference was in the predicted direction, that is, lower compliance was evident for these two stories. These story themes of departure and reunion prompted more disruption in compliance with storytelling than did the other themes, although some of them were also conflictual. This inadvertent finding dovetails with the use of Ainsworth's Strange Situation in attachment research (Ainsworth et al., 1978). The departure–reunion sequence in both cases seems to activate stress reactions.

Although children of both age groups could tell a story and adequately follow directions, an interesting shift was noted concerning how they handled a conflict element within a story. When a story-stem was not how a 3-year-old child wanted it, he or she sometimes changed the original story line and looked for a solution there. The 5-year-olds did not change the story-stem. Instead they were likely to have the main character do something else about the problem, including having the main character pretend or hide their character's agenda.

RESULTS

Do the Judges Agree in Scoring the CCRT?

As noted earlier, the level of agreement among judges was generally satisfactory and supported our decision to rely on the scoring of only a single judge in later analyses. Three types of agreement were examined for the CCRT scoring of the children's narratives. First, agreement was based on scoring by two judges (JF and DD) with a subsample of 12 of the 25 children at age 3 (Dengler, 1990). The two judges exactly agreed in their composite CCRT scores for 75% of the items. Second, from the sample of the 18 children in the present study for whom we had data at both age 3 and age 5, we used the 3-year-olds ($n = 10$) who were rated by two judges (EL and PS). These judges agreed on the wishes (W) of 7 of the 10 children, on the responses from other (RO) of 10 of the 10 children, and on the responses of self (RS) of 9 of the 10 children. (Agreement is defined as a match between the two judges in identifying the same cluster of each child with the highest average sum of standard categories.) Finally, a weighted kappa measure of agreement was also computed by assigning 1.0 to instances in which both judges gave the same first choice to each component; other partial matches were assigned weights of .66 or .33. These weighted kappas for each CCRT component were: W = .33, RO = .69, and RS = .60 (for comparisons with other studies see chapter 6, this volume). The lower kappas, especially for the wishes, appear to be largely attributable to the very low variability. The kappas are therefore not as representative of the reliability as the agreement percentages.

How Pervasive Are the Clusters of CCRT Standard Categories Within Narratives at Age 3 and Age 5?

Our interest was in which clusters of standard categories were most pervasive, that is, which reappeared most often across each child's 10 narratives. Pervasiveness was scored for each of the three components that made up the central relationship pattern that is measured by the CCRT: wishes, responses from others, and responses of self.

Our judges rated the narratives for each scorable thought unit for every standard category using the 1–5 scale, with a high rating indicating that the standard category was strongly reflected in that thought unit. In our analysis, we summed the ratings given to each thought unit for each of the approximately 30 standard categories. The lists of standard categories were then simplified by cluster analysis in Edition 3 to only eight clusters (see chapter 3, this volume). Our tables of results reflect the frequency of highest and next highest cluster scores for each child; a cluster score is the mean of the sums for the standard categories within each cluster.

For each of the three components (W, RO, RS), just one or two cluster scores among the eight clusters had a high frequency. For example (see Table 1), the wish "to be loved, understood" was presented in the narratives among the 18 children as highest or next highest 10 times at age 3 (28%) and 15 times at age 5 (42%). Similarly, the wish "to feel good and to be comfortable" was presented 15 times for the 18 children at age 3 (42%) and 12 times at age 5 (33%).

Among the responses from other component scores (see Table 2), the most frequent in the narratives was "helpful" (both at age 3 with 15 [42%] and at age 5 with 16 [44%]) and "understands" (with 16 [45%] at both age 3 and age 5). The responses of self (see Table 3) that were most frequent were in the clusters "self-confident" and "helpful." (At age 3, the frequency of "helpful" was 7 [19%] and at age 5 it was 16 [44%]. The increase at age 5 of "helpful" was one of the largest increases from age 3 to age 5.)

Is There a Core Relationship Theme for Each Child?

For examining this question of a single versus several CCRTs for each child, the most telling data were the rankings of the frequency profiles of the eight clusters of the CCRT components for each child. Our reasoning was that the more each child's profile concentrated on just a few clusters, the more we can conclude that the concept of a core theme for each child is a cogent one. The data from the profiles, both at age 3 and at age 5, tended to be consistent with this concept of a core theme. A telling illustration of this concentration can be seen in the rankings of each child's pervasiveness on each cluster. Most children had a high pervasiveness within their top two clusters, with the remaining six clusters having considerably less pervasiveness. The drop in mean pervasiveness from the top two to the remaining six was about one third. This drop was about the same at age 3 as at age 5 and about the same for wishes and responses of self, but the drop from responses from others was very small.

TABLE 1
Comparison of Children at Ages 3 and 5 for the Number of Times Highest or Next Highest for Each Wish Cluster (N = 19)

	Wish Cluster								
Age (years)	To Assert Self 1	To Oppose, Hurt Others 2	To be Controlled or Hurt 3	To Avoid Conflict 4	To be Close, Accept Other 5	To be Loved, Understood 6	To Feel Good, Comfortable 7	To Achieve, Help Others 8	Total[a]
3	4	0	0	5	1	27.7% 10	41.6% 15	1	36
5	5	0	0	2	2	41.6% 15	33.3% 12	0	36

[a]The totals are because each of the 18 children has a highest and next highest cluster.

TABLE 2

Comparison of Children at Ages 3 and 5 for the Number of Times Highest or Next Highest
for Each Response From Other Cluster ($N = 18$)

Age (years)		Responses From Other Cluster							Total[a]
	Strong 1	Controlling 2	Upset 3	Bad 4	Rejects, Opposes 5	Helpful 6	Likes Me 7	Understands 8	
3	0	2	0	1	1	41.6% 15	1	44.4% 16	36
5	0	2	0	0	0	44.6% 16	2	44.4% 16	36

[a]The totals are 36 because each of the 18 children has a highest and next highest cluster.

TABLE 3

Comparison of Children at Ages 3 and 5 for the Number of Times Highest or Next Highest
for Each Response of Self Cluster ($N = 18$)

Age (years)	Helpful 1	Unreceptive 2	Respected 3	Oppose, Hurt Others 4	Self-Confident 5	Helpless 6	Sad 7	Anxious, Ashamed 8	Total[a]
				Responses of Self Cluster					
3	19.4% 7	1	3	5	38.8% 14	4	0	2	36
5	44.4% 16	1	6	3	27.7% 10	0	0	0	36

[a]The totals are 36 because each of the 18 children has a highest and next highest cluster.

How Constant Does Each Child's Profile of Clusters Remain From Age 3 to Age 5?

The profile of clusters remains relatively constant from age 3 to age 5 (even though 4 of the 10 story-stems were different at the two ages). The Spearman rank correlations between cluster scores at age 3 and at age 5 are high: W, .84 ($p < .01$); RO, .89 ($p < .01$); RS, .74 ($p < .05$). The components of the CCRT that have the most similarity from age 3 to age 5 are the wishes and responses from others (the same W, 83.4%; the same RO, 94.5%; the same RS, 72.3%).

> *Example, John:* John's responses from other and responses of self remained consistent from age 3 to age 5. At age 3, the story-stem given to him was about spilled juice; in John's continuation of the story he has the mother clean up the juice (RO), and John then says, "Yum, yum" as he eats the meal she provides (RS). At age 5, the story-stem given to him is about falling off his bike while going to get ice cream; John has the mother give the child a Band-Aid (RO), and then the child picks up his bike and rides off again (RS).

How Constant From Age 3 to Age 5 Were the Highest Clusters of the CCRT Patterns?

We now look at the pervasiveness from age 3 to age 5 of the combined patterns of the CCRT components, that is, the wish, response from others, and response of self together, rather than singly. Specifically, we examined each child's combination of his or her three top frequency clusters for the wish, response from others, and response of self. In this measure, the highest number that can be the same is three: one for the same highest frequency cluster for the wish, one for the same response from others, and one for the same response of self.

> *Example, Robert:* In this example, the wish and the response from others stayed the same from age 3 to age 5. At age 5, the most pervasive wish was still "to feel good and comfortable" and the most pervasive response from the doll parents was still "to be helpful." The one component that changed for Robert was the response of self: At age 5 his most pervasive response of the doll child was to be "self-confident" and "assertive." Robert's sameness score was 2.

We found across the groups of children that there was considerable consistency in the highest clusters from age 3 to age 5: The mean sameness of the highest clusters for the 18 children at age 3 and again at age 5 was 2.5. Sixty-one percent of the children had a score of 3. Twenty-eight percent had a score of 2, and 11% had a score of 1.

The consistency over time is greatest for the wish (10 children with the same wish), next for the response of others (8 children), and least for the response of self (3 children). This preponderance of consistency over time for the wish is similar to the finding for adult groups (see chapter 10, this volume), for whom wishes were found to have more consistent pervasiveness than the responses over a mean time of 1 year.

How Positive and How Negative Were the Relationship Patterns at Ages 3 and 5?

Central relationship patterns can be classified as positive or negative, after Freud's usual practice of labeling the transference as positive or negative (e.g., Freud, [1912/1958a]; see also chapter 4, this volume). Positive or negative classifications imply satisfaction of wishes (positive responses from others or of self) or lack of satisfaction of wishes (negative responses from others or of self). With this concept in mind, we classified as positive or negative the CCRT patterns of each child at age 3 and age 5. Positive and negative responses from other and of self were counted for all scored thought units for each child (Table 4).

Our sample of relatively high-functioning Denver children showed very low percentages of negative responses and very high percentages of positive responses, both at age 3 and at age 5 (see Table 4). For example, the responses from others at age 3 were 31% negative, and at age 5, 29% negative. The responses of self at age 3 were 37% negative, and at age 5 they were 23% negative.

When we describe the level of these negative responses of the children as *very low*, we base our evaluation on our main experience with adult patients (L. Luborsky & Crits-Christoph, 1990; see chapter 4, this volume). In contrast, the adults' level of negative responses is very high: The Penn Depression Study sample and the Penn Outpatient Department patient sample (Luborsky et al., 1988) had levels of 72% and 73%, respectively (see Table 4). These higher percentages of negative responses may be attributable to the fact that we have studied groups of adults and adults tend to have more negative responses.

An additional obvious explanation is that the adults were patients, and patients tend to have a high percentage of negative responses. For evidence we cite two unpublished papers reporting studies of normal German adults. One of these papers reports work with normal college students (15 men and 15 women) at the University of Göttingen in Germany (Cierpka et al., 1992). In this sample (Table 4) 43% of the responses of self were negative for women, and 42% were negative for men. The other sample consisted of 35 normal women from Ulm, Germany (Dahlbender, 1992); the negative responses from others amounted to 57%, and the negative responses of self, 48%. A likely implication of these studies is that normal adults are less negative than patients but much more negative than children.

TABLE 4
Postive and Negative CCRT Responses (Percentages)

Component	Positive	Negative	Neutral
Denver Nonclinical Children (N = 18)			
RO Age 3	69	31	
RO Age 5	71	29	
RS Age 3	63	37	
RS Age 5	77	23	
Penn Depression Patients[a] (N = 30)			
RO, RS (combined)	21	72	7
Penn OPD Patients[a] (N = 20)			
RO, RS	19	73	
Göttingen Nonclinical[b] (N = 30)			
RS	35	43	21
Ulm Nonclinical[c] (N = 35)			
RO	38	57	5
RS	47	48	9

Note. RO = responses from others; RS = responses of self; OPD = Outpatient Department
[a]Luborsky & Crits-Christoph (1990, p. 225)
[b]Cierpka et al. (1992)
[c]Dahlbender (1992)

Are There Gender Differences in Central Relationship Patterns at Ages 3 and 5?

The commonalities across the frequencies of the eight clusters for boys versus girls were much more impressive than the differences. This was true for all three CCRT components. Because there were only 11 girls and 7 boys, however, high percentages are needed to reveal the few differences. For example, under the wish "to be loved and understood," at age 3 there were two top or next-to-top frequency clusters for the boys (that is, the total number of top or next-to-top clusters is 14 for the seven boys, and 2 out of 14 would be 14%). By comparison, at age 3 there were eight top or next-to-top clusters for the girls (this would be 8 out of 22 = 36%; 22 is the number of top or next-to-top clusters for 11 girls).

The wish "to be loved and understood" was more frequent for girls, but it is hard to test whether 36% for girls is significantly greater than the

14% for boys. At age 5, the comparable figures are 36% for boys and 45% for girls, but the figure for girls is probably not significantly larger.

The differences between boys and girls in response from others clusters were small; the differences in response of self clusters were also small.

SUMMARY, DISCUSSION, AND CONCLUSIONS

- *Compliance with the task of telling narratives.* Both the 3-year-olds and the 5-year-olds were able to comply and tell moderately complete narratives when provided with story-stems.
- *Pervasiveness of the CCRT.* Originally we asked, is there a pervasive central relationship pattern in the narratives about close relationships at age 3, and if there is, does it continue at age 5? The answer to both questions is *yes,* on the basis of both (a) a high level of pervasiveness of CCRT components across each child's set of narratives at age 3, and (b) the number of these pervasive CCRT components that reappeared at age 5 (with a high percentage of similar components at the two ages).

  The two most pervasive clusters were the wish "to be loved and understood" and the wish "to feel good and comfortable." The two most pervasive responses from others were "helpful" and "understands"; the two most pervasive responses of self were "self-confident" and "helpful." The *combination* of the wish, response of other, and response of self also showed high stability from age 3 to age 5. The most impressive changes from age 3 to age 5 were that (a) the wish "to be loved, understood" increased slightly, and (b) the response of self of being "helpful" increased markedly, possibly reflecting greater maturity and responsibility.

  These findings are new, and as new findings tend to do, they lead to questions even harder to answer: Is the CCRT pattern at age 3 likely to continue to reappear at even later ages through adolescence and adulthood? To answer this question, we need to reevaluate children at later times. Waldinger et al. (1997) are assessing the CCRT through interviews with adolescents at age 14 and then again at age 23 on the basis of longitudinal data collected by Stuart Hauser, Gil Noam, Sally Powers, Alan Jacobson, and Joseph Allen.
- *Positive versus negative quality of the CCRT pattern.* Positivity and negativity are meaningful modifiers of the central relationship pattern. We found that both at age 3 and at age 5

the CCRT's were overwhelmingly positive. Further research is needed to learn whether this is a representative finding to be taken at face value as a characteristic of the developmental stage of this age group. Older people and people who are patients tend to have more negative responses. In interpreting the results concerning positive and negative responses in narratives, several factors must be taken into account:

1. Most of the CCRT research so far has been with adults who are patients. Both of these conditions are associated with an increase in the number of negative responses.

2. The type of narratives the children told may have contributed to the positivity of their responses. These narratives are partly fictional rather than accounts of actual events, and fictional accounts may be particularly prone to idealization. In contrast, the narratives collected from adults are intended to be descriptions of actual events (L. Luborsky, 1990a).

3. This sample of Denver children may have been especially healthy. We need, therefore, to study other groups of children. From such studies, we may still emerge with the conclusion that the preponderance of positive responses is a typical early developmental characteristic. We are told by Seligman (1975), by Seligman, Kamen, and Nolen-Hoeksema (1988), and by Seligman (1991), for example, that children are more optimistic than adults in their style of explaining the causes of negative events.

4. We need to check our assumption about the relationship patterns we found—that the normal adult groups are not unduly affected by differences in cultural backgrounds, such as between American and German groups.

- *Gender differences in CCRT patterns.* Gender similarities clearly are more prominent than gender differences in the CCRT components. The only difference that may be gender related is an increase at age 3 for the girls in the wish "to be loved and understood," which *may* go along with the slight decrease at ages 3 and 5 in the wish "to feel good and comfortable." These gender differences may involve differences in relatedness to others, a characteristic that is thought by some (e.g., Gilligan, 1982), to be found more commonly in women than men. A larger and older body of research based on the work of Witkin (1949) has shown similar differences, for example, that females are more responsive to the "field" than males and that, among ways of showing this, females are more attentive to faces of other people.

WHAT IS NEXT IN THIS LINE OF RESEARCH?

We found that children at the early ages of 3 and 5 already have a pervasive pattern in close relationships, and that pattern is mostly positive. To get more perspective on this finding, a study should be done with data from children that also includes narratives about actual events, which would allow for better comparisons with our adult data.

The vulnerabilities of each child in close relationships are likely to be associated with each child's most pervasive central relationship pattern; when special stresses give rise to symptoms, they should appear as part of that pattern. We have begun to examine this premise for the few children in this sample who experienced traumatic conditions, and Waldinger (1997b) is examining a group of children who experienced rejecting conditions in their early environment.

The CCRT patterns we have found at ages 3 and 5 may be similar to patterns described as "attachment patterns," and "internal working models" (Bretherton, 1995; Bretherton, Ridgeway, & Cassidy, 1990; Main, Kaplan, & Cassidy, 1985), or as "transference patterns." Its relation to transference gets support from the work of Fried, Crits-Christoph, and Luborsky (1990c; also see chapter 11, this volume), who showed that the relationship episodes about the therapist provide a CCRT that is much like the CCRT derived from the relationship episodes about other people. This parallel is a crucial one, perhaps even more central than many of the rest of the 23 facets of Freud's definition of transference (see chapter 21). Our next broad agenda is to examine more systematically the relations among these differently labeled concepts. We will then be able to examine the overlap among different researchers' apparently different but probably similar conceptual models.

Our results on age-related themes may be linkable to Piagetian and other "transformational psychologies." The themes we uncovered may be related to stages of development (Loevinger, 1976). Only longitudinal analysis will be able to differentiate core themes that remain across the life span from those that change over time (Noam, 1991).

17

STABILITY OF THE CCRT FROM BEFORE PSYCHOTHERAPY STARTS TO THE EARLY SESSIONS

JACQUES P. BARBER, LESTER LUBORSKY, PAUL CRITS-CHRISTOPH, AND LOUIS DIGUER

We come now to an issue about the sources of the CCRT: Is it primarily a quality that the patient brings to therapy or a product of the therapist's responses to the patient? Some understanding of this issue might be achieved by examining the stability of the CCRT between a time before the therapist is met to a time after the treatment has started.

Psychoanalytic data is mostly inferred from what patients say and from their behavior. Because these data require inference to be understood, the therapist's interpretation of these words and other behaviors is likely to play a major role in determining their significance (Eagle, 1983). The therapist's theoretical stance is likely to influence how he or she interprets the patient's words and other behaviors. These interpretations, in turn, influence the patients, who are prone to accept their therapists' interpretations for a variety of reasons. Thus, argued Grunbaum (1984), patients' data

This chapter is a reedited version of an article by Barber et al. (1995) from the *Journal of Consulting and Clinical Psychology*, 63, 145–148. Reprinted with permission.

obtained from therapy sessions may be contaminated by the therapists' theoretical point of view and indoctrination and, therefore, cannot be used to validate the underlying theory of treatment. In other words, Grunbaum (1984) claimed that clinical data has little, if any, scientific value because it tends "in any case to be artifacts of the analysts' self-fulfilling expectations, thus losing much of their evidential value" (Grunbaum, 1986, p. 217). Although Grunbaum referred to psychoanalysis proper, his criticism applies also to contemporary psychoanalytic theories (Eagle, 1983), to dynamic psychotherapy, and to other therapies. This critique has the power to undercut the use of treatment sessions as a way of validating the scientific aspect of the theory, because

> if the patient's responses are merely a result of brainwashing, then Freudian analysis might have beneficial emotional effects not because it allows the patient to acquire genuine self-knowledge, but because of suggestion operating as a placebo under the guise of non-directive therapy. (Grunbaum, 1986, p. 221)

The comparison of CCRTs obtained through narratives from therapy sessions with those obtained from clinical interviews conducted before the therapist is even met might begin to address this criticism (Luborsky, 1986a). To the extent that the CCRTs obtained from interviews preceding psychotherapy are similar to the ones extracted from therapy sessions, we can be confident that the clinician's influence on the patient's central relationship pattern, at least in the early sessions of therapy, is not as pervasive as Grunbaum has suggested and that psychodynamic psychotherapy (and other therapies) may be something more than suggestion.

METHOD

We compared a measure of the central relationship patterns before the treatment started with a measure obtained after it started. A review of such measures developed in the last 15 years has been reported (see Barber & Crits-Christoph, 1993; also see chapter 20, this volume). The Core Conflictual Relationship Theme method, the oldest of these measures, is the one we selected. Its interjudge reliability has been shown to be fair to good (weighted kappas of .60 to .71) across eight samples (see chapter 6). Various findings have supported its validity by showing that the CCRT method assesses a construct that is consistent with many characteristics of the transference pattern described by Freud (1958a) and discussed in chapter 21, this volume.

Nineteen patients (15 women, 4 men; mean age, 40, $SD = 9.6$) participated in a study involving 16 sessions of time-limited supportive–expressive dynamic psychotherapy for depression (Luborsky, 1984; Luborsky, Mark, et al., 1995). Eight patients were never married, and 4 were divorced, separated, or widowed. Patients either were referred from other clinics within the hospital of a major Northeastern medical center or had responded to advertising in the community. Only patients with a Research Diagnostic Criteria diagnosis of major depression without psychotic features, brain impairment, or current drug or alcohol abuse were entered into the study. Patients needed to have been diagnosed using the Schedule for Affective Disorders and Schizophrenia (Endicott & Spitzer, 1978) on two consecutive interviews spaced 1 week apart before entering treatment. At the second intake interview, the average level of depressive symptoms as measured by the Beck Depression Inventory was 28 (SD = 7.5); patients' average score on the Health–Sickness Rating Scale was 49.0 (SD = 6.1). Eleven patients had at least one probable or definite coexisting personality disorder diagnosis. A more complete description of the larger sample may be found in articles by Diguer, Barber, and Luborsky (1993) and by Luborsky, Diguer, et al. (1996).

The Core Conflictual Relationship Theme Method

The Core Conflictual Relationship Theme method (see chapter 2, this volume) describes the relationship pattern that is most pervasive across narratives using the following steps: (a) Relationship episodes are delineated in the transcribed material; (b) independent judges read each relationship episode in the transcript and identify each of three components (wishes, responses from others, and responses of self); (c) for each component, the types with the highest frequency across all relationship episodes are identified and combined constituting a preliminary CCRT formulation; (d) on the basis of this preliminary CCRT formulation, the same judge re-identifies, when needed, the types of wishes, responses from others, and responses of self; (e) the judge can change the original rating on the basis of the recount of all wishes, responses from others, and responses of self. In addition, judges were asked to translate their tailor-made scoring into standard categories. It has been reported, in a sample of 35 psychotherapy patients, that interjudge agreement as measured by weighted kappas was .70 for responses from others and .61 for wishes and responses of self (Crits-Christoph, Luborsky, et al., 1988).

The RAP Interview Method

The difficulty and expense of extracting narratives from sessions, as well as their possible contamination by therapists' suggestions, have led researchers to use alternative data obtained from clinical interviews. Luborsky (1990b; see chapter 7, this volume) developed the Relationship Anecdotes Paradigm (RAP) interview to collect such interpersonal narratives from which CCRTs could be extracted. It has been assumed that a CCRT formulation based on narratives told during RAP interviews conducted by an independent researcher or clinician is similar to one obtained from therapy sessions. The present study has investigated this assumption by examining such a comparison.

Instructions for administration of the RAP interview (see chapter 7) require the participant to tell at least 10 incidents or events, each about an interaction between the participant and another person. Those interviews are recorded and then transcribed. The CCRTs are extracted from the interviews in the same manner as they are extracted from therapy sessions. The mean time usually required to tell 10 episodes is about 30 minutes.

Procedure

The patients in the present study were seen in supportive–expressive dynamic psychotherapy for 16 sessions by four different experienced therapists (Diguer et al., 1993). The therapists participated in the training phase of a treatment development project. The RAP interviews were given by a research assistant before therapy began. Sessions 3 and 5 were transcribed, but for the two patients from whom we found fewer than 10 complete relationship episodes, Session 4 was added. The transcribed RAP interviews and therapy sessions were then rated by two different teams of two judges. Each judge worked independently, used the standard categories (Barber et al., 1990; chapter 3, this volume), and followed the CCRT scoring manual (see chapter 2). All judges were experienced psychodynamic clinicians who had been trained in the CCRT method by Lester Luborsky.

Because there are many standard categories (35 wishes, 30 responses from others, and 31 responses of self) with some having similar meanings (e.g., wish to be understood vs. to be respected vs. to be accepted), assessing the judges' agreement on the most frequent standard categories would have been too stringent a criterion for calculating reliability; that is, we did not want to say that if one judge decided that the main wish was "to be understood" and the other judge thought it was "to be accepted," the interjudge agreement was 0. In addition, there were many cases in which different standard categories were high in frequency; that is, more than two or three standard categories were the most frequently used by one judge for a specific patient. To resolve these two problems, we used Barber et al.'s (1990) grouping of the standard categories into eight clustered standard categories for each CCRT component. All standard category ratings were recorded by the research assistant in their appropriate clusters. For all analyses involving the clustered standard categories, the two most frequent ratings for each CCRT component from each judge were chosen.

RESULTS

Reliability of the CCRTs Derived From the RAP Interviews

All 19 RAP interviews were rated by two independent judges. the degree of interjudge agreement on the clustered standard categories is presented in the top tier of Table 1. To correct for chance agreement, we followed Crits-Christoph, Luborsky, et al.'s (1988) use of the weighted kappa (Cohen, 1968) for assessing interjudge reliability of the rating for each of the three CCRT components. In contrast to regular kappa, weighted kappa allows different weights for different levels of agreement; that is, a higher weight can be given if agreement between the two judges occurred on the most frequent clustered standard categories, a lower weight if the second highest rating from one judge matched the most frequent rating of the other judge, and the lowest weight if judges agreed only on the second most frequent ratings. More specifically, the two most frequent clustered standard categories of wishes (or responses from others or responses of self) for each patient from one judge were compared with the two most frequent wishes of the other judge. If the most frequent wish rated by each judge matched, a weight of 1.0 was given; if the most frequent clustered standard wish category of one judge matched the next most frequent of the other judge, a weight of .66 was given; and if only the two second most frequent categories matched, a weight of .33 was given. Crits-

TABLE 1
Interjudge Agreement and Reliability for the CCRT From the RAP
Interview and Therapy Sessions, and Comparisons of CCRTs From
RAP Interview Versus Therapy Sessions

Variable	Agreement Between Judges	Weighted Kappa	
		Clustered Categories	Standard Categories
CCRT from RAP interviews			
Ws	84	.68	—
ROs	100	.60	.56
RSs	89	.65	—
CCRT from Sessions 3 and 5			
Ws	94	.81	—
ROs	100	.64	.77
RSs	88	.73	—
Comparing CCRT from session to CCRT from RAP			
Ws	77	.52	—
ROs	100	1.00	—
RSs	77	.40	—

Note. CCRT = Core Conflictual Relationship Theme; RAP = Relationship Anecdotes Paradigm; ROs = responses from others; RSs = responses of self.

Christoph, Luborsky, et al. (1988) used identical weights. This computation was performed separately for wishes, responses from others, and responses of self. The results are in the second column of Table 1. All of these kappas were in the acceptable range.

The high degree of agreement but only fair size of kappas is likely due to the narrow range of categories of CCRT components, especially responses from others, that these patients displayed. Seventeen patients (89%) were rated as having the response from others of "rejecting and opposing," one had the response from others "understanding or accepting," and one patient's response from others was "upset." Because the judges used only three of the eight clustered standard categories for the responses from others, we recalculated the degree of agreement and the weighted kappa for the responses from others using the 30 standard categories instead of the eight clusters. Using the standard categories, we observed that all response from others standard categories were used at least once by one of the two judges. The weighted kappa obtained using the 30 standard categories was .56 (shown in the third column of Table 1).

Reliability of the CCRTs Derived From Therapy Sessions

Two other independent judges rated the CCRTs from the sessions for the 17 of the 19 patients who entered treatment and for whom audiotapes were available (see the middle tier of Table 1). The adequate reliability coefficients found in the present study for the CCRT components derived from therapy sessions replicate Crits-Christoph, Luborsky, et al.'s (1988) findings in another moderate-sized sample. Again, the same problem outlined in the previous section occurred with the responses from others from the sessions (16 of 17 patients had the clustered standard categories response from others of "rejecting," whereas the other patient's response from others was "like me"). We therefore recalculated the weighted kappa for the responses from others using the standard categories; as presented in Table 1, the kappa was adequate. As in the ratings from the RAPs, these two different judges used all 30 response from others standard categories at least once.

Correspondence Between CCRTs From RAPs (Before Therapy) and CCRTs From Sessions

To compare the two sets of ratings, we needed first to combine the ratings from each independent team of judges. In the cases in which there was agreement between the two judges who scored the RAPs, the categories that were agreed on were used in the comparison with the CCRT from sessions, and vice versa. In the cases in which there was no agreement between the two judges, the clustered category that was the most frequently rated across relationship episodes by any of the two judges for a specific patient was selected for comparison with the clustered category from the other team of judges. The same process was used for the second most frequent category. The results from this comparison were summarized in part in a previous review of the CCRT (Luborsky et al., 1992).

The comparison of the CCRT ratings from the RAP interviews and the therapy sessions for the 17 patients indicated a relatively high level of agreement between the two methods of deriving the CCRT, suggesting a relatively high level of similarity between the CCRT obtained from pre-treatment data and the CCRT obtained from sessions early in treatment (see the bottom tier of Table 1). Thus, even when we corrected for chance agreement, we found a moderate-to-high level of correspondence between the CCRTs derived from the two different sources of material. In other words, moderate alternate-form reliability was found for the wishes and responses from self across the two methods of deriving narratives for CCRT formulations. In regard to the responses from others, the two methods yield excellent alternate-form reliability when one uses the clustered standard categories. From a psychometric point of view, one needs to realize that the "alternate forms" and the "responses" (patients' narratives) are very different in the two methods, at least on the surface. As an anonymous reviewer noted, this lack of perfect match between the two "forms" may have reduced the reliability estimates.

CONCLUSIONS

- These results support the conclusion that the relationship themes that emerge early in treatment are quite similar to the themes that emerge during an independent interview, with a person other than the therapist, that precedes the therapy. These findings are likely to increase researchers' confidence that the RAP interview can be used to determine patients' psychodynamic themes independently of treatment.
- In response to Grunbaum's (1984) critique, we have presented preliminary empirical evidence that the CCRT in early sessions of psychodynamic therapy is not likely to be primarily the result of therapists' influence. At the same time, our data do not indicate that the CCRTs obtained before treatment and early in treatment are identical. The present findings are especially meaningful to the extent that the CCRT indeed measures the complex and controversial but central psychoanalytic concept of transference. Indeed, Fried et al. (1992) showed that the CCRT expressed in the relationship with the therapist is similar to the CCRT expressed

in other relationships. Additional studies are needed to replicate our preliminary findings using material from before and during psychoanalytic sessions.

- One major limitation regarding the generalizability of the results of this study is that it is based on a sample of patients who had received a diagnosis of major depressive episode in accordance with the *Diagnostic and Statistical Manual of Mental Disorders* (3rd ed.; *DSM-III*, American Psychiatric Association, 1980). It may be, for example, that the restricted range of responses from others obtained in the present sample is characteristic of depressed patients but not of other groups of patients; that is, depressed patients tend to see others as rejecting. Thus, replication in larger samples as well as in heterogeneous groups of patients is recommended.

- Other factors could have affected the results of this study. The correspondence between pretreatment and early-in-treatment CCRTs may be due to the relatively severe state of depression in which the patients presented at the time. Depression may have influenced the content of the narratives in a convergent direction at both times; that is, in the two kinds of narratives, depressed patients may tend to perceive others as "rejecting" or include others who "are rejecting" or cause others to reject them. The kappa coefficient, however, was intentionally used to deal with this base-rate problem.

- It is also possible that the judges' use of only two or three clustered standard categories for the responses from others indicates some problems with the current version of the clustered standard categories.

- At least 1 month had passed between the RAP interview and the third treatment session. During this month, many changes may have occurred (e.g., slight changes in the CCRT and moderate relief of depression) that could have lowered the reliability estimates. Therefore, the two procedures may be even more similar than the results suggest.

18

THE MEASUREMENT OF MASTERY OF RELATIONSHIP CONFLICTS

BRIN F. S. GRENYER AND LESTER LUBORSKY

MEASUREMENT OF MASTERY

A special gift to the clinician from the CCRT method is its capacity to describe the central relationship conflicts. But what the clinician also needs is a method that shows the level of mastery of these central relationship conflicts. That is the agenda of this chapter.

One of the central propositions in the psychoanalytic theory of change in psychotherapy is that symptoms arise after the activation of relationship conflicts. This proposition has been supported by two strands of research: first, studies that reveal the structural pattern of these conflicts using the Core Conflictual Relationship Theme method (see chapters 2

This chapter is a revised version of an article by Grenyer and Luborsky (1996) from the *Journal of Consulting and Clinical Psychology*, 64, pp. 411–416. Reprinted with permission.

This chapter was supported in part by an APRA–Australian Research Council award, Research Scientist Award MH 40710-22, National Institute on Drug Abuse Grants 2 KO5 DA00168-23A 24 and RO-I DA0785, and National Institute of Mental Health Clinical Research Center Grant MH 45178. Acknowledgment is made to the Penn Psychotherapy Research Project for providing access to data and support. Our thanks are also extended to Vera Auerbach, Mary Carse, Annalisa Dezarnaulds, Louis Diguer, Suzanne Johnson, Nigel Mackay, Richard Rushton, Kelly Schmidt, and Nadia Solowij.

and 9 and other chapters of this book); second, studies that link these relationship conflicts with the emergence of symptoms (as was shown in Luborsky, 1996). When patients seek psychotherapy, it is often because they are overwhelmed by relationship conflicts and consequent symptoms; the almost universal goal in psychotherapy is to promote mastery over these problems (Liberman, 1978). Therefore, the goal of our study was to assess changes in the mastery of the core interpersonal conflicts over the course of psychotherapy and examine their relation to changes in symptoms.

Mastery is defined as the acquisition of emotional self-control and intellectual self-understanding in the context of interpersonal relationships (Grenyer, 1994). Gains in mastery come about as part of the working-through process. We propose that the conflictual relationship narratives in psychotherapy are partly told in the service of mastery, just as Freud wrote that children's repetitive games were attempts to master traumatic situations (Freud, 1920/1955a). In addition, Freud was the first to make the connection between patterns in the patient's narratives about conflictual problems outside of therapy with the kind of problems experienced within therapy. To our knowledge, there have been no previous attempts to measure the process of mastery of the conflicts in psychotherapy. However, research with the CCRT presents some findings that need to be considered in relation to mastery (Crits-Christoph & Luborsky, 1990; also see chapter 10, this volume). We expected that the repetitive maladaptive relationship conflicts would become less pervasive over the course of therapy, that is to say, the CCRT pattern would become more positive and include a wider range of relationship patterns indicating greater flexibility in emotional response to conflicts. The results reported in chapter 10 supported the hypothesis, with the striking finding that despite the decrease in pervasiveness, much of the CCRT patterns were still evident, supporting the view that central relationship patterns tend to remain recognizable over a psychotherapy.

Although the changes in the positive and negative components of the CCRT provide some indication of changes in the quality of the pattern and in its pervasiveness (see chapters 4, 8, and 10), the CCRT is limited in its scope as a measure that reflects mastery. The Mastery Scale was therefore constructed, which can be applied to the same database of narratives of relationship episodes but also focuses on quantifying degrees of mastery. Table 1 shows a brief summary of the Mastery Scale; for the full scale including scoring conventions and practice examples, consult Grenyer (1994).

The content of the scale was developed on the basis of our definition of mastery from our review of the literature and after the intensive study of verbatim transcripts of two successful pilot cases of dynamic psychotherapy applying a task-analysis approach (Rice & Greenberg, 1984). Task analysis is a structured discovery-oriented approach to studying psycho-

TABLE 1
Mastery Scale, Version I

Level and Score	Components
Level 1. Lack of impulse control	
1A	Expressions of being emotionally overwhelmed
1B	References to immediacy of impulses
1C	References to blocking defenses
1D	References to ego-boundary disorders
Level 2. Introjection and projection of negative affects	
2E	Expressions of suffering from internal negative states
2F	Expressions indicative of negative projection onto others
2G	Expressions indicative of negative projection from others
2H	References to interpersonal withdrawal
2I	Expressions of helplessness
Level 3. Difficulties in under-standing and control	
3J	Expressions of cognitive confusion
3K	Expressions of cognitive ambivalence
3L	References to positive struggle with difficulties
Level 4. Interpersonal awar-eness	
4M	References to questioning the reactions of others
4N	References to considering the other's point of view
4O	References to questioning the reaction of the self
4P	Expressions of interpersonal self-assertion
Level 5. Self-understanding	
5Q	Expressions of insight into repeating personal-ity patterns of self
5R	Making dynamic links between past and pres-ent relationships
5S	References to interpersonal union
5T	Expressions of insight into interpersonal relations
Level 6. Self-control	
6U	Expressions of emotional self-control over conflicts
6V	Expressions of new changes in emotional re-sponding
6W	References to self-analysis

Note. For the full details of this scale, consult Grenyer (1994).

therapy transcripts to reveal recurrent patterns of clinical importance. We were interested in dynamic concepts that were likely to indicate self-control and self-understanding, such as having insight into common personality traits, making links between past and present ways of relating, the development of tolerance for thoughts and feelings, and the ability to self-analyze and monitor internal states. These were identified by Luborsky as among the key curative factors in dynamic therapy (Luborsky et al., 1988). We saw, just as Gottschalk had some 25 years earlier, that psychological constructs could be reliably and validly located, classified, and measured within the patient's speech (Gottschalk, Winget, & Gleser, 1969).

The Mastery Scale has three broad levels. Scores 1 and 2 relate to failures of mastery manifested by problems such as cognitive disturbances. Scores 3 and 4 relate to the struggle to improve, such as the self-questioning of perceptions of relationship conflicts. Scores 5 and 6 demonstrate high levels of mastery, for example, having awareness of one's transference patterns and being able to derive pleasurable experiences from relationships. Self-control was accorded a higher rating than self-understanding on the basis of Freud's well-known view that intellectual self-understanding by itself does not guarantee therapeutic change (Freud, 1958c). Mastery is gained when one not only understands a situation but also feels in control.

We evaluated the following hypotheses: (a) that patients rated as showing greater gains in mastery will have larger gains on measures of general functioning and symptoms than patients showing fewer gains in mastery and (b) that changes in mastery will parallel changes in the components of the CCRT. The first hypothesis is important because dynamic theory holds that improvements in the mastery of interpersonal conflicts are associated with higher levels of functioning as judged by independent assessors.

METHOD

Forty-one patients (29 female, 12 male; mean age, 25; range, 18–48) were chosen as a representative sample from the group of 72 patients who participated in the Penn Psychotherapy Project (Luborsky et al., 1988). Twenty-six patients were single, 7 were married, and 6 were divorced or separated (with 2 with missing data). Five had graduated from high school only, 19 had completed some college education, 6 had completed college, and 11 were undertaking or had completed a graduate degree. The sample had a mixed diagnostic picture according to the criteria of the *Diagnostic and Statistical Manual of Mental Disorders* (3rd ed.; *DSM-III*, American Psychiatric Association, 1980). Fifteen had primary diagnoses of dysthymia, and 11 had generalized anxiety disorders; the rest of the primary and secondary diagnoses were mainly Cluster A (8 schizoid, 3 schizotypal), Cluster B (4 histrionic, 1 narcissistic), and Cluster C (3 compulsive, 3 passive-aggressive) Axis II personality disorders.

Treatment was based on weekly individual time-unlimited psycho-analytic psychotherapy with a mean treatment length of 54 weeks (range, 91–149 weeks). Therapy was conducted by 31 psychiatrists (mean age, 36; range, 26–56). Of these, 17 were psychiatric residents, 9 had up to 10 years of postresidency experience, and 5 had more than 10 years of experience. The residents saw their patients in an outpatient clinic, and the postresidents saw their patients in private practice. Thirty of the therapists were married, and 23 had children. The orientation of the group was divided between "psychodynamic eclectic" (21 adherents) and "Freudian analytic" (10 adherents).

Verbatim transcripts of psychotherapy sessions collected during the Penn Psychotherapy Project for each patient formed the database. These were mainly transcripts from early in therapy (generally Sessions 3 and 5) with two or three transcripts from late in therapy (when treatment was 90% completed). Narratives of interactions (relationship episodes, REs) served as the units for the analysis of mastery. Relationship episodes had been identified from the transcripts of early and late sessions in an earlier CCRT study (Luborsky, 1977b, 1990a). There were usually 10 relationship episodes from early in therapy and 10 relationship episodes from late in therapy, and they were randomized among sessions and patients. The relationship episodes were divided into grammatical clauses (whether independent or dependent) by marking off the claused speech units with a slash according to the conventions adopted by Gottschalk et al. (1969). The following is an example of three marked clauses, with Mastery Scale scores in parentheses: /I'm afraid of myself (2E)/because it's a father–lover sort of thing (5Q)/ It's also this hangover from when I was real young (5R)/. To facilitate the process of scoring, one prescoring judge read all the relationship episodes and identified all the clauses that could be scored with the Mastery Scale, a technique also used in CCRT research to control for possible disagreement about location (as opposed to scoring disagreement).

All the data were scored twice. Each relationship episode was independently scored by two of a pool of four trained judges. Each judge was given a random portion of the total number of relationship episodes to score. No individual judge scored the same relationship episode twice. Judges were not informed of which patient told the relationship episode, the time in therapy at which the relationship episode occurred, treatment outcome status, or other clinical variables. Judges were trained in the methods of scoring to an interrater reliability of greater than .90. One of the 23 Mastery Scale categories from 1A to 6W was assigned to each of the codable clauses by the judges. Each of the 23 category choices comes with its own built-in score ranging from 1 to 6 to represent one of the six levels in the scale. These scores were used in the compilation of statistics. We calculated Mastery Scale scores for each relationship episode by summing all the scores and dividing by the number of scorable clauses to arrive at a mean score per narrative. These scores were then used to calculate average levels of mastery for each patient early and late in therapy.

Outcome measures were collected at the beginning and at the termination of therapy by an independent assessor using the Health–Sickness Rating Scale (HSRS; Luborsky, 1962) and the Control and Insight ratings of the Prognostic Index (Luborsky et al., 1988); by the therapist's composite rating of patient satisfaction, success, and improvement; and by patient self-report with the Hopkins Symptom Checklist (SCL; Derogatis et al., 1970) and a rating of improvement on the primary target complaint identified by the patient at the start of therapy (Battle et al., 1966). The response of self and response from other components from late in therapy were used. To obtain a score late in therapy that reflected the overall degree of *positivity–negativity* for each of the two CCRT components (response of self and response from other) for each patient near termination, we subtracted the sum of the negative responses from the sum of the positive responses and divided that by the total number of responses.

RESULTS

Interjudge agreement was uniformly high, with correlation coefficients among the four independent judges as follows: A versus B, $r = .75$ ($n = 187$ REs scored in common); A versus C, $r = .77$ ($n = 161$); A versus D, $r = .81$ ($n = 89$); B versus C, $r = .79$ ($n = 149$); B versus D, $r = .85$ ($n = 127$); C versus D, $r = .89$ ($n = 81$). The judges' Mastery Scale scores were therefore averaged in all subsequent analyses.

To investigate changes in Mastery Scale scores across the 41 patients over the course of therapy, we performed a paired t test between early and late scores. The change in mastery was highly statistically significant, $t(40) = 4.94$, $p > .0001$. The effect size was large (1.35). When compared with the published effect sizes in other psychotherapy studies, the changes detected by the Mastery Scale can be considered to be of clinical significance (Lambert & Bergin, 1994). Thus, the trend in this psychotherapy sample was for patients to display greater levels of self-understanding and self-control in their interpersonal relations late in therapy.

Pretreatment–posttreatment change estimates were corrected for initial levels by the calculation of residual gain scores for the Mastery Scale and other outcome variables in which change estimates were required. The relationships between Mastery Scale change scores and outcome variables were calculated and appear in Table 2. Significant relationships were found among Mastery Scale change scores and observer, therapist, patient, and

TABLE 2

Pearson Correlations Between Mastery Scale Residual Change Scores
and Clinical Outcome Scores

Rating	r
Observer ratings of outcome	
Health–Sickness Rating Scale residual change score	.51***
Prognostic Index, Control item	.30
Prognostic Index, Insight item	.01
Therapist ratings of outcome	
Therapist rating of patient satisfaction, success, and improvement	.47**
Therapist rating of patient achieving insight	.12
Patient ratings of outcome	
Rating of change of primary target complaint	.59***
Symptom Checklist residual change score	−.53***
CCRT outcome ratings	
CCRT: Response of self late in the therapy	.37*
CCRT: Response of other late in therapy	.06

Note. N = 41. CCRT = Core Conflictual Relationship Theme.
*p < .05. **p < .01. ***p < .001.

CCRT ratings of outcome. Figure 1 shows the HSRS residual change scores plotted against the Mastery Scale residual change scores.

Figure 2 shows the percentage of change in the frequency of Mastery Scale categories appearing in narratives from early to late in psychotherapy for all 41 patients. To illustrate these typical changes in mastery from early to late in therapy, we briefly describe one patient. Ms. Simpson, a 24-year-old divorced graduate student with no children, was seen in weekly therapy for 41 weeks with the goal to help change her difficult "personality pat-

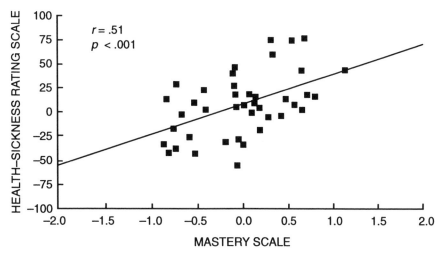

Figure 1. Distribution of Health–Sickness Rating Scale residual change scores versus Mastery Scale residual change scores for all 41 patients.

THE MEASUREMENT OF MASTERY OF RELATIONSHIP CONFLICTS   267

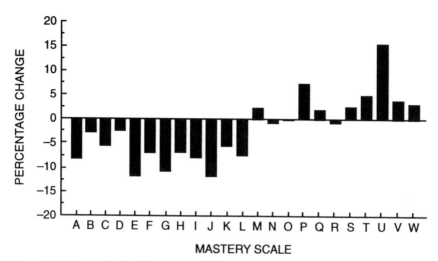

Figure 2. Change in the frequency of Mastery Scale categories appearing in narratives late in psychotherapy, expressed as percentage change from early in therapy. Data are for all 41 patients. Dimensions indicative of poor mastery (Categories A–L) show a reduction in appearance in narratives late in therapy, whereas interpersonal awareness, self-understanding, and self-control dimensions (Categories M–W) show a corresponding increase in appearance late in therapy. Data at 0% indicate no change in the percentage of appearance of categories from early to late in therapy.

terns." Her psychodynamic therapist was a 31-year-old married psychiatric resident. Early in therapy, she expressed suffering (2E) that was due to conflictual interactions with others, which led to her avoiding relationships (2H). When in close relationships, she felt worthless and guilty (2F) and encouraged men to hit her (1D). Toward the end of therapy, she could see (5Q) that her global view that "men are evil" was due to unconscious hostility toward an abusing person from her childhood (5R). She began to struggle free from these bonds (4P) and enjoy relationships (5S) in a new way (6V). These conflictual patterns also appeared within the early transference relationship with her therapist. Toward the end of therapy, she could express with confidence to her therapist that "you basically seem good to me now" (6V), thus showing some mastery over her interpersonal problem.

SUMMARY, DISCUSSION, AND CONCLUSIONS

This chapter is a departure from the theme of the book in that it is only partly on the subject of the CCRT method; its focus is on the Mastery Scale, which can be used to complement the CCRT. The study used the same clinical sample as in the studies discussed in the rest of this book, that is, a sample from the Penn Psychotherapy Project. The Mastery Scale, like the CCRT, uses the narratives within psychotherapy transcripts to quantify gains in mastery of core interpersonal conflicts and symptoms.

- The results show that theoretically relevant and central psychodynamic variables can be reliably measured directly from the content of verbal communications that patients give in therapy. The high interrater reliability obtained for the Mastery Scale was achieved in part because the judging task was highly structured, obviating disagreement that can result from methods based on the usual unguided, complex inferential judgments. Judges did not assess levels of mastery per se; the corresponding scores were already built into the category choices. This method of content analysis has proved to be a powerful way of identifying underlying constructs (Gottschalk et al., 1969).

- The fundamental conclusion of this study is that established maladaptive interpersonal patterns for meeting needs and wishes can be better mastered (understood and controlled) during the course of more successful psychotherapy. The primary hypothesis was that patients who were rated as showing greater gains in mastery would have greater gains on measures of general functioning and symptoms than patients showing lesser gains in mastery. The HSRS is an important global outcome measure of functioning (Luborsky et al., 1993); a slight revision of the HSRS, the Global Assessment Scale, constitutes Axis V of *DSM-III* and *DSM IV*. Changes in HSRS were significantly related to changes in mastery (Figure 1); patients who are sicker are less able to see the interpersonal dynamics of their predicament and tend to react with more helplessness and pain to problems in getting their needs met. Perhaps of most interest, the patient's own judgments of changes in their main complaint (that is, a target symptom) paralleled changes in the mastery of interpersonal conflicts found in their narratives. These changes were related not only to changes in reported symptoms but also to the fulfilling of the patient's main goal in therapy.

- The second hypothesis was that changes in mastery would parallel changes in components of the CCRT. We found that mastery was significantly related to the response of self, which suggests that our scale is tapping important aspects of the measure and may be seen as complementary to the CCRT method. We hypothesized that the response of other would also be related to mastery because the ability to elicit positive responses from others should be a part of gains in mastery.

When we rescored the data from 20 patients using a finer grained measure of positivity and negativity (see chapter 4, this volume), the results were essentially the same: Changes in the CCRT-RS dimension significantly paralleled changes in mastery, but changes in the CCRT-RO dimension were not significantly related to mastery. That we did not find such a relationship is less surprising in retrospect because the Mastery Scale specifically limits scoring to self-statements and self-reflections on others, whereas in the CCRT statements made by others are scored. For example, direct quotations of others in narratives are considered scorable in the CCRT but not in the Mastery Scale.

- It is noteworthy that both the observer Insight and Control ratings from the Prognostic Index (Luborsky et al., 1988) and the therapist's rating of insight failed to show a relationship with mastery (Table 2). It may be that the Prognostic Index and therapist measures suffer in validity because of the demands made on judges' scoring patterns (Luborsky et al., 1988). In addition, our scale subsumes insight and control into a single concept, mastery, which is different in important ways from either variable.

- Further inspection of the change data for the individual categories of the Mastery Scale (Figure 2) reveals some interesting findings. In general, psychotherapy leads to a diminution in three of the lower levels of mastery: lack of impulse control, introjection and projection of negative affects, and difficulties in understanding and control (from Categories A–L). This indicates that there is a general reduction in distress and confusion in interpersonal relationships over the course of psychotherapy. As predicted, certain dynamic variables showed an amplification over therapy, such as expressions of self-control (6U), which showed a large (16.5%) increase. It is noteworthy that a few dynamic variables showed no change (e.g., making dynamic links between past and present relationships [5R]). This could be partly attributed to the infrequent appearance of this category: Only 6.5% of narratives in therapy contained scorable clauses for this category. It may be that this category is dynamically important in therapy but that our method is not sensitive enough to reveal its significance. As indicated by the modest percentage changes in Figure 2, we have found support for the view that psychotherapy does not completely eliminate relationship conflicts but helps people to gain mastery over them. Our case study of Ms. Simpson illustrates the clinical relevance of the scale's categories.

The major strength of the present study is that important variables have been systematically scored from the content of the patient's verbal communications and linked to central outcome variables in therapy. We recognize, however, that what we have gained in predictive power has been at the expense of specificity. Our concept and measurement of mastery is broad and reflects many separate cognitive and affective psychological constructs such as mood, hope, anxiety, helplessness, and locus of control. We did not set out to investigate such specific interrelationships, but we subsumed aspects of these constructs within our view of mastery. We also recognize that our measurement of mastery may not include some factors that are important to the concept, such as the assessment of the degree to which an insight statement is salient to the person's core problems. But our limitation was also our strength: We have avoided complex and possibly unreliable methods of scoring, and in so doing, we may have forgone some subtle therapeutic factors; yet the method devised is robust and captures an important dynamic change variable.

III

CLINICAL USES OF
THE CCRT

19

THE EVERYDAY CLINICAL USES OF THE CCRT

LESTER LUBORSKY

Ever since the bright day in 1975 when the idea for the CCRT was conceived, I and then others have been learning about its capacities for helping therapists and patients who are in dynamic as well as other psychotherapies. The CCRT method has shown clear advantages over the usual, unguided clinical methods. Its assets come both from its guided method of formulation and from the evidence of its consequent reliability (see chapter 6, this volume). Clinicians whose formulations are guided by the CCRT method, therefore, are likely to be blessed with more interclinician concordance than those who are not so aided.

As I explain and illustrate in this chapter, each of the triad of tasks of therapists in dynamic and related psychotherapies can be helped by the CCRT method. These tasks, as outlined in my 1984 manual, include (a) listening to the patient's communications; (b) figuring out formulations, often about the conflicts within the CCRT; and (c) giving interpretative responses selected from the CCRT. The therapist then listens further, aided by the feedback circuit from the patient's response to the therapist's previous response, and then gives further interpretations. The chapter begins with detailed explanations of the *uses of the CCRT in dynamic psychotherapy*.

Subsequently, I discuss *the ways that different systems of psychotherapy result in different choices of interpretations.* Lastly, I discuss *how therapists can learn to rely on the CCRT to help with their tasks in psychotherapy.*

THE USES OF THE CCRT IN DYNAMIC PSYCHOTHERAPY

As a Guide to Formulations and Interpretations

My account of the applications of the CCRT method to the basic triad of therapeutic tasks will sound familiar to psychodynamic clinicians, even those who are not acquainted with the CCRT method. In fact, the following example of the application of the principle took place before CCRT was ever invented:

> *Example:* Mr. Howard (see chapter 5, this volume) was a college student who came to treatment because of his extreme proneness to anxiety and guilt. In Session 3 he told a series of narrative, in the first of which, at the age of about 13, he asked his mother a question about sex, and his mother frustrated him by saying that he was getting too old for that. This was followed by a second narrative from about the same age in which his mother turned down his wish to get into bed with his parents on a cold night; she explained that it was okay for his younger brother but not for him, because he was now too old for that. The third narrative was an enactment with the therapist of a similar relationship pattern: The patient had become anxious, developed a headache, and explained that he was becoming "unresponsive" to the therapist. The therapist used the information from the two antecedent relationship episodes to formulate a relationship pattern and then to interpret to the patient that the patient was expecting *the therapist* to be unresponsive to the patient's wishes.

The therapist in this example had been listening to the patient's relationship episodes. He based his formulation and then his interpretation on one CCRT component of these episodes: the patient's expected response from the other person. The therapist's inference about the patient's expected response appeared to be based on the three relationship episodes, especially the third, in which there was an enactment of the pattern in relation to the therapist. Another way to describe the therapist's technique is that the therapist's interpretation of the content of the relationship episodes had a high degree of convergence with the CCRT. Such convergence as a basis for interpretation is desirable, as demonstrated in chapter 13, this volume, on accuracy of interpretation.

The conventional style of using the CCRT for deciding on interpretations is demonstrated in the example from the treatment of Mr. Howard (see chapter 5): The therapist includes within the interpretation a recurrent facet of the CCRT derived from the relationship episodes. Both within sessions and over time, parts of the CCRT that are incorporated in interpretations help patients to build up a concept of their recurrent CCRT pattern. This conventional style might be called a *piecemeal presentation of parts of the therapist's CCRT formulation*.

Another, more focused style is used less commonly by some therapists: After several sessions of piecemeal presentation of parts of the CCRT, the therapist suggests trying to make a joint formulation of the central relationship pattern that guides the patient's conduct of relationships. The therapist introduces the joint task by a comment such as, "Let's try making a sketch of the pattern that we hear in the events that you tell me about in your relationships. In the last few episodes, what is it that you wanted from the other person?" After that part is agreed on, the patient and therapist concentrate on the question, "What is it that you tend to expect from the other person?" After that is agreed on, the therapist asks, "How is it that you react?" A further procedure might have benefits for some patients: The therapist may say, "I will write this out and you can write this out, so that we can examine together how well they fit." The method might be called a *joint patient–therapist construction of the CCRT formulation*. The method has something in common with the system used by adherents of the cognitive–analytic school, as reflected, for example, in work by Ryle (1990, 1991). This unusual patient–therapist system of joint construction of the CCRT seems especially useful for patients who have a hard time, with the usual piecemeal presentation of the therapist's formulation, becoming aware of the pattern in the conduct of their relationships.

In fashioning an interpretation, it can be helpful to choose language that will minimize the patient's defensiveness; generally, the greater the defensiveness the less a patient can use an interpretation. Language should be used in which sympathy for and recognition of the patient's typical responses are conveyed, along with the CCRT-related content (consistent with suggestions by Wachtel, 1993). In the case of Mr. Howard described earlier, a therapist's interpretation might be "When you experienced rejection of your wish for closeness, it actually felt like there was nothing you could do about it, at *that* time in your life." This interpretation clearly contains parts of the CCRT, but the language chosen for the interpretation conveys sympathy for and understanding of why the patient felt so helpless and anxious at *that* time in his life.

As an Aid to Maintaining a Treatment Focus

The treatment focus is kept on the therapist's and patient's attention to the CCRT for providing formulations and interpretations. The CCRT for each patient may change some from session to session, but typically it does not change drastically, so that it offers a fairly consistent focus. Therapists find such a focus especially useful for brief therapy; in fact, according to Koss and Butcher (1986, p. 650), short-term therapies are more focused than long-term therapies.

One gain to the therapist from reliance on the CCRT as the treatment focus is that it offers a framework from which to select interpretations. The patient also benefits because a focused treatment tends to increase the patient's motivation and concentration of effort, which may "hothouse" the growth toward the specific goals of the treatment. This may be why it has been found that changes that are related to the specific goals of treatment are greater than changes in general outcome measures (Luborsky et al., 1988): The interpretative focus can serve as a motivator because the target for change has been made explicit. The patient then puts more concentrated effort into changes that are within his or her defined targets of the treatment. It happened that way in the treatment of Mr. Howard: The therapist tended to focus on the patient's wish not to be cut off from affection and closeness and on his recurrent expectation that he would be cut off from these qualities. The patient spent a lot of time in the course of the treatment suffering from the experience of that theme but also in trying to deal with it. He became familiar with his own readiness to experience the wish and his negative expectations of other people's responses. In his follow-up (see chapter 7, this volume) many years later, he confirmed how familiar he had become with that theme and the extent to which his gain in familiarity with it mitigated his self-blame and anxiety when he experienced it.

As a Help in Choosing a Part of the CCRT for Each Interpretation

Less is sometimes more. There is no special gain from using the entire CCRT every time one needs to draw on it for an interpretation. My colleagues and I have discovered guides to the selection of components of the CCRT for making interpretations; these were noted in our presentation of results in chapter 13 on the predictive value of accuracy of interpretation. We found that accuracy based on the use in interpretations of the response of self was not correlated with outcome but that accuracy based on interpretation of the wish plus response from other was correlated with better outcomes (note that because the wish and response from other were highly correlated, they were combined). These findings led to the conclusion that, in terms of potential benefit for the patient, interpretations that combine the wish and response from other are effective in the sense that they are associated with the patient's greater benefit from treatment.

Further guidelines for fashioning interpretations come from observations of the interpretative behavior of effective therapists. A clinical analysis of these observations suggests two principles: (a) One should choose the aspect of the CCRT that is most involved in conflict, or most related to the patient's main source of suffering and symptoms; and (b) one should choose the part of the CCRT the patient is most responsive to and seems able to use best in effecting change. The second principle is much like the recommendation to listen to the patient's responses after trial interpretations.

> *Example, Ms. Cunningham:* An example of the complexity of making a choice from within the CCRT is derived from Ms. Cunningham's Session 5 (see chapter 5, this volume). The therapist interpreted her wish for reassurance, which was part of her CCRT in that session, even though in the CCRT it was only the third-ranked wish in order of frequency in the session; the more frequent wishes were "to dominate and control" and "to overcome the other's domination." But the therapist may have decided to make the interpretation on other clinical grounds, such as the second of the two principles listed above, that the patient should be able to use the interpretation in effecting change.

As a Help in Timing Interpretations

The therapist's familiarity with the CCRT in a session eases the tracking of the meaning of what is unfolding in the patient's communications and in that way helps to ensure the best timing for an interpretation. The exact timing of an interpretation requires a sensitive clinical judgment of favorable conditions. First, the theme that is to be interpreted must be experienced by the patient; second, it must be near to awareness; and third, it must be impeding the treatment. These judgments by the therapist form the basis for the classical principles of timing, which are based on when the transference has become a resistance and the patient shows that related ideas are near to awareness (Bibring, 1954).

> *Example, Mr. Howard:* The example given earlier from the treatment of Mr. Howard also provides an illustration of a therapist's application of the principles of timing. In the third session the patient told two relationship episodes dealing with fear of being cut off from closeness and affection from his mother; then, in a third episode with the therapist, he stopped talking freely and referred to himself as being "unresponsive." The therapist, therefore, inferred that transference material was involved in this resistance behavior and decided that this was a good moment for making an interpretation about the transference.

As a Clue to the Conflicts Sparking the Formation of Symptoms

It can be useful to the therapist and therapeutic to the patient to understand the conditions connected with the onset of the symptoms (see chapter 15 in Luborsky, 1996). The format of the CCRT helps to locate these conditions. Symptoms, in CCRT terms, emerge from (a) conflicts between wishes and (b) conflicts between wishes and expected responses from others. When these conflicts become more intense, the symptoms are more likely to appear in the responses of self. Ms. Smyth's depression (see chapter 5, this volume) was most likely to worsen when this conflict was experienced: a greater intensity of the wish to end nonsupportive relationships and to get support but with the expectation that the other person would be rejecting and unsupportive. Mr. Howard's symptoms were more likely to worsen when the following conflict heated up: greater intensity of the wish to be close and receive affection and not experience a loss of relationships but with the expectation that the other person will reject his wish, followed by the responses of resentment, self-blame, and anxiety. Ms. Cunningham's symptom of inhibition increased, along with her conflicts around experiencing reduced control and intensification of her wish to be in control but with her expectation that the other person would not give her what she wants.

A more exact assessment of the preconditions of symptoms can be achieved by a related method called the *symptom-context method* (Luborsky, 1996). That method can begin to be used directly after a symptom materializes in a session. When a series of recurrent episodes of symptoms has occurred, their context can be further inspected, and it is possible to identify their typical antecedents. A comparison of the two methods, the symptom-context and the CCRT, has revealed that similar conflicts are found through each method (Luborsky, 1996; Luborsky et al., 1985b).

As a Supplement to DSM Diagnoses

Patients nowadays tend to come to psychotherapists with already determined diagnoses, and more and more often these are based on the DSM family of diagnoses. But these diagnoses tend not to be very helpful to the therapist for the conduct of the psychotherapy. The major exceptions are diagnoses that include psychotic features, for these usually imply the need for a greater use of supportive techniques, the reduced use of expressive techniques, and the possible use of pharmacotherapy (Luborsky, 1984).

The DSM diagnoses by themselves are empty of content about the patient's psychodynamics, as pointed out by Karasu and Skodol (1980) and Auerbach and Childress (1988). Such diagnoses do not give information about the patient's typical relationship patterns and the conflicts within them. In contrast, I suggest a simple but informative addition: to supplement the DSM diagnosis with the CCRT. Such supplementation would reveal more about the association between the two classes of diagnostic information, the DSM diagnosis and the central relationship pattern.

As a Special Aid in the Functioning of Inpatient Units

The CCRT can have a vital place in the proper functioning of inpatient treatment units, helping professionals and other workers keep focused on treatment goals rather than only on custodial or diagnostic goals. The recommended treatment procedures are the following (Luborsky, van Ravenswaay, Ball, Steinman, Sprehn, & Bryan, 1993): The initial conference of the treatment team includes the completion of a CCRT. One of the members of the team brings to the conference a set of narratives told by the patient about relationships and constructs a CCRT from them. The team then discusses the logical treatment goals for the patient, derived from the CCRT, to be achieved during the patient's stay. Each of the team members agrees on these goals, so that in their contacts with the patient they are able to be as helpful as possible toward achieving them. Because the initial team has agreed on these goals, the team members' treatment aims can have a concerted impact on the patient. Before the patient leaves the inpatient unit, one of the team members reviews with the patient his or her accomplishments in terms of these goals.

THE DIFFERENT CONSEQUENCES OF DIFFERENT PSYCHOTHERAPEUTIC SYSTEMS ON THE INTERPRETATIVE FOCUS

Although virtually all exponents of brief psychotherapies advocate consistency of interpretative focus, the method of finding the focus differs for each type of psychotherapy. The emphasis on maintaining a focus is found even in long-term psychotherapy and in psychoanalysis, but there the urgency for maintaining it tends to be less strong. The following discussion of different systems of therapy shows their somewhat different methods for finding the focus as well as the consequences of each method.

Dynamic Therapy

In this therapy the selection of an interpretative focus necessarily requires that the therapist make a prior psychodynamic formulation. This formulation often involves an aspect of the central relationship pattern. In the example we gave from Ms. Cunningham's Session 5 (see chapter 5, this volume), the therapist must have considered it noteworthy that the patient needed reassurance and, possibly, that she wanted reassurance from him but that she did not think she could get it from him or from anyone. As his main interpretation in that session, the therapist said, "You expressed a wish to your husband for reassurance but not here." The patient responded by acknowledging that she did not think she would get it here.

In making that main interpretation, the therapist was following a body of traditional wisdom about what to focus on in an interpretation that represents two well-established criteria: (a) that the content should be close to awareness and (b) that the content should be related to the patient's current symptoms in the sense that the symptoms are impeding the patient at the moment. In Freud's words, the therapist should "wait until the transference . . . has become a resistance" (1913/1958c, p. 139).

CCRT-Guided Dynamic Therapy

Even with the preceding two criteria, clinical practice in dynamic therapy is a relatively unguided system in contrast to the guided systems that use the CCRT or one of the other relationship pattern measures (see chapter 20, this volume). Of course, the guided and unguided systems often coincide in their implied formulations and consequent interpretations, as was seen in the example from Mr. Howard's therapy presented at the beginning of this chapter.

A consequence of relying on the CCRT for finding the focus in a dynamic therapy is that the focus selected in this way differs from patient to patient depending on the particular CCRT for each patient. The differences among patients derive from the empirical grounding of the CCRT method: In this format the content of the therapy is not determined in advance. This patient-specific appropriateness of the focus is likely to increase the patient's inclination to recognize that when interpretations are made, he or she has been listened to and understood.

These and other advantages are offered by the CCRT-guided short-term dynamic psychotherapy described by Book (in press); it offers the only fully recorded and fully published CCRT-guided psychotherapy manual, together with vividly illustrated recommended techniques for drawing on the CCRT.

Davanloo's Therapy

In contrast to the appropriate diversity of focus when the CCRT is used, in some forms of brief psychotherapy the focus of interpretations is fairly uniform across all patients. In Davanloo's (1978) brief psychotherapy the focus of interpretation is likely to be on understanding the patient's current situation in terms of the patient's passivity as a way to deal with anger. This was noted in one sample by Gustafson (1986): "All interviews of Davanloo discover this passivity" (p. 175).

Sifneos's Therapy

In Sifneos's (1979) brief psychotherapy the focus of interpretation across patients typically is on understanding the patient's current situation in terms of the parallels between the early and the current oedipal triangle themes.

Mann's Therapy

In Mann's (1973) 12-session psychotherapy a uniform focus is recommended for all patients, that is, to improve the patient's self-image. According to Mann, however, the focus is different from the "central complaint," and Mann's formulations differ from patient to patient because the relationship problems that determine the poor self-image differ from patient to patient.

Cognitive Therapy

In some nondynamic therapies the need for a focus is also evident. In one of these, cognitive therapy (Beck 1989), the therapist selects and then maintains a focus on individually specified dysfunctional attitudes. Until recently, the therapist was not provided with a systematic method for selecting these attitudes, but there are now systems for deriving them (for example, Persons, 1989).

PROCEDURES FOR THERAPISTS TO LEARN TO RELY ON THE CCRT IN PSYCHOTHERAPY

The general orientation given to a therapist who is about to learn the CCRT method is that the formulation of the CCRT by the therapist during each therapy session has much in common with the formulation of the transference; however, the CCRT offers more explicit and precise guidelines for this kind of inference making. These guidelines state that the therapist listens to the patient's communications, especially to each relationship episode as it is told, and notes the types of relationship components that are most redundant across the episodes; these become part of the CCRT. Then, from time to time, the therapist uses pieces of the CCRT in the interpretations. The therapist can also occasionally prepare formulations of the CCRT from past sessions; such reviews can ease the making of formulations during subsequent sessions.

Some of the requirements of rigorous research scoring of the CCRT are unnecessary for its clinical use during psychotherapy sessions. As an example, for clinical use of the CCRT there is no need to restrict the choice of relationship episodes to the complete ones used for research purposes, and it is not necessary to have them all included. My strong impression is that the incomplete relationship episodes have similar, although unexpressed, CCRT components to the complete ones, although this comparison has not yet been studied systematically.

Instruction in the CCRT During Supervision

Learning to use the CCRT in the course of psychotherapy is best done during individual or group training in psychotherapy. The instructor teaches by showing example after example of how the therapist formulates the central relationship pattern and then how it is used in helping to shape the therapist's interpretative responses. In the course of supervision sessions, when the therapist presents process notes (preferably along with a sample of tape recordings or videotapes), the supervisor can review the formulation in terms of the CCRT and point out how it is done. That kind of repeated instruction through example is the mainstay of the clinical training in the use of the CCRT.

A special format for intensive training in dynamic psychotherapy that has proved to be satisfying to its members consists of an hour and a quarter session, and a 1-year participation in a four-therapist peer supervision group (Luborsky, 1990c). Four therapists are a good size for a training group: In 60 minutes two therapists have 30 minutes each to present and to have their presentation discussed. During the second 6 months of the year, the other two therapists present their treatments for discussion. The aim of this group training is for the therapist to learn how to carry out supportive–expressive dynamic psychotherapy following the manual by Luborsky (1984) with related readings and to help supervise other therapists in their learning. Each of the peer therapists-in-training helps the presenting therapist in treating the patient by following the methods of the treatment manual by Luborsky (1984). A seasoned therapist acts as a group leader, largely by filling the role of an orchestrator of the group. The training, in contrast to individual supervision, comes in large part from the peer therapists, who provide their versions of the formulation to compare with the presenting therapist's version and who suggest the kinds of interpretations that would follow from the formulation.

Scoring Practice Sets of Relationship Episodes

An efficient method of improving skills in scoring the CCRT is through practice scoring of a graded series of cases. Each of the practice cases consists of a set of brief relationship episodes selected from a session of a different patient. After each practice case is scored, the therapist is given feedback about the scoring until the therapist achieves an adequate level of performance.

Practice With CCRT-Based Interpretations During Tape Playbacks

A set of sessions can serve for practicing CCRT-based interpretations during playback sessions. As in the research method studied extensively by Strupp (1973), when the tape is stopped, the therapist-in-training must fill in the interruption with the most appropriate CCRT-based interpretation. Therapists find this method helpful because of its similarity to a live session with its requirement to construct interpretations immediately.

Instructions for Your Self-Analyzed CCRT

Write a series of narratives, each about an interaction between you and another person. Think of events that were meaningful to you, either in a good or bad way, recently or in the past. For each event tell when it occurred, whom it was with, and what happened. For each event give *some* of the conversation—what the other person said and what you said. For writing each event, 4 or 5 minutes should be enough. The main other person might be father, mother, other relatives, friends, people you work with, anyone. It does not matter what events you choose. Ten of these narratives about events ought to be enough. After writing these, score them by the CCRT procedures. After having gone through this self-analytic process yourself, it will be easier to see what is being tapped by the CCRT.

Format for Self-Analyzed CCRT (underline thought-units to be scored for wishes, responses from others, and responses of self)

#1. Other person: _____
    Relationship Episode:

#2. Other person: _____
    Relationship Episode:

#3. Other person: _____
    Relationship Episode:

etc.

Figure 1. Instructions and format for self-analyzed CCRT.

Training Through a Self-Reported and Self-Analyzed CCRT

A more direct deeper appreciation of what is measured by the CCRT can be gained by getting a "free self-analysis"—an analysis of one's own narratives for their CCRT (Luborsky, 1980). Many people who have tried the self-analysis say that it gives them the surprise that comes with recognition of the familiar: a quick re-viewing of the central relationship pattern that they had become familiar with during their personal intensive psychotherapy or psychoanalysis. The reader can try the self-analysis by writing at least 10 relationship episodes and scoring them, following the instructions provided in Figure 1.

Training in the CCRT During Psychiatric Residency: A Survey of Therapists' Benefits

Therapists have reported their impressions about their own training experiences. They show considerable consensus about the usefulness of the CCRT in training for and in carrying out psychotherapy. Their reports were derived from a mail questionnaire study by Fried (1989) of 53 therapist respondents who had some exposure to the CCRT in the course of their training. Most of these were psychiatrists who had completed residency in the previous 10 years. These are samples of the therapists' responses on a few of the questions:

> In answer to a question about the extent to which they use the CCRT in their psychotherapy practice, on a scale of *not at all, minimally, somewhat, frequently,* or *continually,* of 47 respondents, 28 chose *frequently* or *continually* and 11 others chose *somewhat.*
>
> In answer to a question about when they think of a patient's CCRT, of 43 respondents, 34 said *during the session* and 31 said *while mulling over a case.*
>
> In answer to a question about how the CCRT compares with other ways to learn how to do dynamic psychotherapy, of 43 respondents, 22 said it was *very helpful and more than most of the other ways of learning* to practice psychotherapy.

CONCLUSIONS

■ The main advantage of CCRT-based clinical formulations over unguided clinical formulations comes from their guided, uniform format and, consequently, the greater agreement obtained among clinicians. The CCRT method helps with the usual tasks facing dynamic psychotherapists: (a) The CCRT is valuable for its assistance in making formulations about the central relationship patterns and as the centerpiece for decision making about the treatment focus. The therapist should use the CCRT as a basis for fashioning appropriate interpretations because it is desirable to have a convergence of the CCRT with the interpretations derived from it (see chapter 13, this volume). (b) Within the CCRT it is desirable to concentrate on interpretations that include the wish and the expected response from others (see chapter 13). (c) The CCRT is helpful in the timing of interpretations; it assists the therapist in becoming aware of the central relationship pattern so that interpretations can be made when clinical indications are favorable. (d) The CCRT is of special help when a prominent symptom appears because the format of the CCRT reveals the conflicts that are associated with that symptom. (e) The patient's CCRT should be a routine qualifier to the *DSM* diagnosis.

- A comparison was given of the value of relying on the CCRT for finding the focus in dynamic therapy versus relying on the interpretative systems within other psychotherapies. My conclusion is that reliance on the CCRT results in a more patient-specific central relationship pattern formulation for each patient, rather than the relatively uniform formulations across patients that are produced by overreliance on a particular theory of therapy.

- The main methods of becoming skillful in the use of the CCRT during psychotherapy sessions include (a) the use of the four-therapist peer supervision training group, (b) graded experience in the scoring of CCRTs on practice cases, (c) practice in making CCRT-based interpretations during playback sessions, (d) a self-analysis by the therapist of self-reported and self-analyzed CCRTs, and (e) practical and theoretical experience with the CCRT during professional training.

20

ALTERNATIVE MEASURES OF THE CENTRAL RELATIONSHIP PATTERN

LESTER LUBORSKY

The CCRT measure is the first reliable central relationship pattern measure when judged from psychotherapy sessions. Such measures are in a class that has expanded dramatically in the last dozen years. In this chapter I describe each of the measures to help potential users decide which might best meet their research or clinical needs. The chapter ends with (a) a review of controlled comparisons among these observer-judged measures and (b) an evaluation of the questionnaire methods that also claim to be measures of transference patterns.

Seventeen measures, including the CCRT, now make up the membership of this class of observer-judged central relationship pattern measures. These are named in Table 1, which also portrays their almost yearly proliferation. Each of measures to be included in the class must fulfill these criteria:

1. The database for scoring the measure must be a sample of the person's relationship interactions selected from psycho-

This chapter is a revised version of an article by L. Luborsky, P. Crits-Christoph, and J. Mellon (1986) from the *Journal of Consulting and Clinical Psychology, 54*, pp. 39–47. Reprinted with permission.

TABLE 1
Central Relationship Pattern Measures Based on Sessions

Year	Researchers	Method
1976	Luborsky	Core Conflictual Relationship Theme (CCRT)
1977	Weiss, Sampson, Caston, & Silberschatz; Caston	Plan Diagnosis (PD)
1979	Benjamin	Structural Analysis of Social Behavior (SASB)
1979	M. Horowitz	Configurational Analysis (CA)
1981	Teller & Dahl	Frame method (Frame)
1981	Carlson	Tomkins's Script Theory
1982	Gill & Hoffman	Patient's Experience of Relationship With Therapist (PERT)
1982	Schacht & Binder	Cyclical Maladaptive Pattern (CMP)
1984	Grawe & Caspar	Plan Analysis (PA)
1985	Kiesler et al.	Impact Message Inventory (IMI)
1986	Bond & Shevrin	Clinical Evaluation Team
1986	Maxim	Seattle Psychotherapy Language Analysis Schema (SPLASH)
1987	Kiesler	Psychotherapy and Interpersonal Transactions (CLOPT, CLOIT)
1989	Perry, Augusto, & Cooper	Idiographic Conflict Summary (ICS)
1989	L. Horowitz, Rosenberg, Ureno, Kalehzan, & O'Halloran	Consensual Response Formulation (CRF)
1990	Crits-Christoph, Demorest, & Connolly	Quantitative Analysis of Interpersonal Themes (QUAINT)
1992	Demorest & Alexander	Personal Scripts

therapy sessions or from other interviews and based on either (a) narratives or thought units about the interactions or (b) actual behavioral samples of the interactions.

2. The most central pattern, defined as the most pervasive across relationship interactions, must be extracted from these relationship interactions.

3. The extraction of this pattern must be derived partly through clinical judgment and not be limited to self-report questionnaires.

4. The reliability of the measure must have been shown or preliminary research on reliability must be in progress.

Here we give only a short sketch of each measure, but we include references so the reader can find out more about them. For about half of the methods, longer accounts can be found in a process research handbook (Dahl, Kächele, & Thomae, 1988), in a guide to psychodynamic treatment research (Miller, Luborsky, Barber, & Docherty, 1993), in a volume on person schema studies (M. Horowitz, 1991), in an evaluation of some of these measures (Barber & Crits-Christoph, 1993), and in accounts of comparisons of seven of these measures applied to a specimen patient interview (Luborsky, Popp, Barber, & Shapiro, 1994).

SKETCHES OF THE ALTERNATIVE METHODS

Plan Diagnosis

The Plan Diagnosis (PD) method grew out of a particular psycho-analytic theory of therapy developed by Weiss (1986) and empirically tested by Weiss et al. (1986). The method has enabled clinicians to develop comprehensive and reliable case formulations that include these four components: the patient's *goals* for therapy, the inner *obstructions* (pathogenic beliefs) that prevent or inhibit the patient from attaining goals, the ways the patient is likely to *test* the therapist to disconfirm pathogenic beliefs, and the *insights* that will be helpful to the patient. The method has been applied to the study of psychoanalysis (Caston, 1977, 1986; Curtis & Silberschatz, 1989) and a variety of brief psychotherapies (Curtis & Silberschatz, 1989; Curtis, Silberschatz, Sampson, Weiss, & Rosenberg, 1988; Perry, Luborsky, Silberschatz, & Popp, 1989; Rosenberg et al., 1986). The Plan Diagnosis method has been studied as a measure of therapist accuracy (Silberschatz, 1986; Silberschatz, Curtis, Fretter, & Kelly, 1988; Silberschatz et al. 1986) and of therapy process and outcome (Nathans, 1988; Norville et al., 1996; Silberschatz, Curtis, & Nathans, 1989). These studies have demonstrated the value of the Plan Diagnosis method by showing that accurate interventions lead to patient progress and to favorable patient outcome.

In all of these studies, reliabilities (intraclass correlations) have averaged in the .7 to .9 range for each of the plan components: goals, obstructions, tests, and insights (Curtis & Silberschatz, 1989; Rosenberg et al., 1986). The method has also been reliably used by investigators outside of the Mount Zion Psychotherapy Research Group, for example by Collins & Messer (1988), who came up with somewhat different findings.

Structural Analysis of Social Behavior (SASB)

The essential Structural Analysis of Social Behavior (SASB) model was presented by Benjamin (1974); the first applications to psychotherapy sessions came later (Benjamin, 1979). The model has been applied to family interactions (Benjamin, 1977) and to dyadic interactions (Benjamin, 1979), as well as to interventions in psychotherapy (Benjamin, 1982).

The SASB can be used to trace the sequence of the patient's associations during a session (Benjamin, 1986b). It can track moment-to-moment changes in associations, as well as provide a dynamic formulation about conflicts. For this purpose sessions are scored by trained SASB coders after the session has been divided into codable units that are defined as single thought units. Such thought units usually consist of a subject and verb as well as any modifying clauses. Each unit has only one speaker. The referent is the "identified other," usually another person. Three types of judgments are then made: the focus of the message, whether the message is friendly or unfriendly, and the interdependence. The focus, affiliation, and interdependence judgments are combined to reach the SASB classification.

The SASB method is one of the oldest and psychometrically most sophisticated methods; much information is available about its validity and high levels of reliability (Benjamin, 1994), As an example, kappas for process codes of family therapy ranged from .74 to .91 with a mean of .81 (Benjamin, 1986b).

Configurational Analysis

The Configurational Analysis (CA) method (M. Horowitz, 1979, 1987) appears to estimate some of the same basic relationship patterns as the CCRT, but it involves a more encompassing method called the Role Relationship Models Configuration (RRMC; M. Horowitz, 1991). For this method, the data from process notes and transcripts of sessions are examined from three interrelated points of view: states, relationship patterns, and information (M. Horowitz, 1987, 1989, 1991). The point of view that has most in common with the CCRT is the one for the analysis of relationships, which includes the RRMC approach. The CA approach offers a conceptual model for intrapsychic conflict about relationships and the scripts for interactions between self and other. The five basic elements are (a) the roles and traits of self schemas; (b) the schema of the object person; (c) the aims from each toward the other, often beginning as the wish for action or expressed emotion from the self; (d) the response of the other; and (e) the reactions of self. These have been illustrated and compared with the CCRT (M. Horowitz, Luborsky, & Popp, 1991). In the RRMC method, four types of role relationship models are placed in a configuration about a specified type of object relationship. Thus, there are desired, dreaded, compromise–maladaptive, and compromise–adaptive role relationship models.

Evidence has been provided for the satisfactory reliability of the RRMC in four cases (M. Horowitz & Eells, 1993) and later, in more detail, for two new patients by independent configurational analysis teams (Eells, Horowitz, Singer, Salovey, Daigle, & Turvey, 1995; M. Horowitz, Eells, Singer, & Salovey, 1995).

Frame

This method is based on identification of "frames." A frame is a recurrent, structured sequence of events that represents a person's significant wishes and beliefs (Teller & Dahl, 1981, 1986). The events may include mental and other behaviors such as acting, perceiving, believing, knowing, wishing, and feeling. The most important relationship among the events is their sequential order, for example, expresses anger → feels rejected → withdraws. Dahl (1988) proposed that frames (a) are represented in the mind in a nonverbal code as described in Bucci's (1985) dual code system of mental representations; (b) are structured sequences of emotions and defenses (Dahl, 1978); (c) are the residues of early object relations (Gedo, 1979); (d) endure over time; (e) appear across conflicts, objects, and situations; (f) can interact with each other; (g) can account for a wide spectrum of repetitive, neurotic, maladaptive behavior and, in principle, normal, adaptive behavior; (h) permit specific predictions of wishes and beliefs; and (i) provide the framework for a theory of change that is independent of any particular theory of how to bring about the change (Dahl, 1988; Dahl & Teller, 1984, 1993).

Dahl and Teller (1993) described three methods for identifying frames. In Method A judges use the patient's narratives first to construct *prototypes* and second to find *instantiations* (repetitive examples) both with different objects and in different situations. Method B uses patients' own inductive generalizations about their behaviors as prototypes; judges then search for instantiations as in Method A. Method C (Leeds & Bucci, 1986) uses an objective procedure to discover the repetitive sequences of events. With this method Davies (1989) found frames in the play of 3-year-olds that were consistent for each child with two other children and reflected the child's interactions with his or her mother. Further reliability studies are in progress.

Script Theory

Carlson (1981) drew from Tomkins's (1987) script theory of personality to identify particular analyses that constitute a developing relationship pattern measure. The theory posits that an enduring set of relationship patterns are repeated throughout a person's life (Demos, 1995). Carlson described the script as "the individual's rules for predicting, interpreting, responding to and controlling experiences governed by a family of related scenes" (1981, p. 502). Tomkins's (1987) theory also identifies one "nuclear scene," and sometimes several, that manifests these rules; this scene is interpreted as a pattern-setter for later relationship episodes. Carlson (1981) gave a cogent example of a person's nuclear scene that recurred after 30 years, and Carlson's (1986) follow-up provided empirical study of analogues as reflected in transference dreams. Reliability information is being developed.

Patient's Experience of the Relationship with the Therapist (PERT)

Gill and Hoffman (1982a, 1982b; Hoffman & Gill, 1988a, 1988b; Gedo, 1993) provided a coding scheme for studying transcripts of audio-recorded psychotherapy sessions. The scheme includes codes for several types of communications regarding what the authors named the Patient's Experience of the Relationship With the Therapist (PERT). At the heart of the scheme is the coding of disguised allusions to the relationship in associations that are manifestly about other matters. There is also a code for explicit references to the relationship and one for readily observable events in the interaction that are not spoken about but that may affect the patient's experience of the immediate interaction. These explicit references and unspoken events serve as bases for the coding of disguised allusions to the relationship. The system also has a component that requires a rating of the degree to which the therapist's interventions deal with the main aspects of the patient's experience of the relationship, both latent and manifest. The coding scheme emerges from a conception of the therapeutic process in which the therapist is viewed as a significant codeterminator of the transference (Gill, 1982; Hoffman, 1983). Hoffman and Gill (1988b) recently discussed their view of the differences between the CCRT and the PERT. They suggested that the PERT is "more geared toward the tracking, not only of transference themes, but also of *resistance as it affects nuances of communication during the course of the session*" (pp. 92–93).

Gill and Hoffman (1982b) first reported some preliminary reliability data. In a more recent study employing an adapted version of the scheme (Gabbard et al., 1988), reliability was demonstrated for some of the therapist variables.

Cyclical Maladaptive Pattern (CMP)

This method offers guidelines for formulating the pattern that provides a treatment focus for the therapist's interventions; the method was therefore first called the Dynamic Focus method by Schacht and Binder (1982) and Schacht et al. (1984). The shift in label to the Cyclical Maladaptive Pattern (CMP) was intended to stress the observation that the pattern shows a self-perpetuating cycle. The system's components, as illustrated by Henry, Schacht, and Strupp (1986), include (a) acts of self, (b) expectations of others, (c) consequent acts of others toward self, and (d) consequent acts of self toward self. These components appear to be similar to the components of the CCRT. Acts of self, for example, include the wishes. The expectations of others and consequent acts of others toward self are both included in the responses from others in the CCRT system. Consequent acts of self toward self are similar to the responses of self in the CCRT system.

The CMP continues to be used in its original form. But to increase reliability and theoretical coherence, however, the CMP has another form that includes the measurement methods of the Structural Analysis of Social Behavior, which is called the SASB-CMP. Consequently, the reliability should be the same as that achieved by the SASB. This new-generation system reorganizes the information into three categories—(a) interpersonal acts, (b) introjective acts, and (c) expectancies—using procedures described by Schacht et al. (1984).

Plan Analysis (PA)

The Plan Analysis method is based on observable, often verbal behavior as well as nonverbal behavior (Grawe & Caspar, 1984). In its concern for nonverbal behavior it differs from the other measures, including the CCRT, which are usually based on verbal behavior. The Plan Analysis method emphasizes the interactional plans that are in conflict with each other. It also includes intrapsychic elements of a client's functioning from an instrumental point of view. The instrumental function of action is considered in terms of these two questions: What is the behavior for? Which means are used for a particular purpose? In essence, the sources of information for the analysis are (a) the behavior of the person, especially the nonverbal behavior and interactions; (b) the emotions and action tendencies that the patient triggers in other persons; and (c) the behavior and the emotions considered from a reactive perspective, that is, negative emotions that arise when important plans are threatened and positive emotions that arise when plans are favored. Therapies based on Plan Analysis have especially helpful therapeutic relationships owing to the individualized interpretations made by the therapist and richness of technical procedure (Grawe, Caspar, & Ambühl, 1990).

Promising reliability studies have been done, mainly in a descriptive qualitative mode (Caspar, 1989). Two studies have recorded agreement between plan analyses. In each, videotapes were used with a single patient with different judges judging the tapes (Theus, 1987, as reported by Caspar, 1995). In both, some degree of satisfactory case conceptualization was shown.

Impact Message Inventory, Form IIA (IMI)

This measure, developed by Kiesler et al. (1985), yields characterizations of the interpersonal behaviors of interactants, including patients and therapists, empirically derived from Lorr and McNair's (1965) version of the Interpersonal Circle (which provides 15 categories of behavior that overlap substantially with the 1982 Interpersonal Circle's 16 categories). Scores are obtained from an interactant's (B) report of the feelings, action tendencies, and cognitive attributions evoked in him or her during interactions with another person (A); resultant scores characterize the interpersonal behavior pattern of Person A. In the psychotherapy context, Impact Message Inventories (IMIs) filled out by therapists or observers (Bs) on patients (As) use reports of objective "countertransference" by Bs to characterize the transference patterns of As. In particular, when the measure is applied by clinical judges who are the observers (Bs), the measure qualifies for membership in the class of central relationship pattern measures.

The widening sphere of utilization of narratives as a basic unit in psychotherapy sessions is illustrated by McMullen and Conway (1997). They scored relationship episodes for 20 cases of short-term dynamically oriented psychotherapy involving the self and others for 2 early, 2 middle, and 2 late sessions for 20 cases. These narratives were coded on Kiesler's (1983) version of the Interpersonal Circle. The most successful cases were those that showed increasing friendly–submissive portions of the circumplex in their portrayal of self. In contrast, the least successful cases were in the hostile half of the circumplex.

Internal consistency reliabilities for the 15 scales are high, with coefficients tending to be .80 or higher. Additional information on reliability and results of more than 40 empirical studies can be found in Kiesler's research manual (1987b). A more recent light-scale circumplex version (Kiesler & Schmidt, 1993) has excellent psychometric properties and is routinely recommended to researchers and clinicians.

Clinical Evaluation Team

In this system (Bond & Shevrin, 1986b), the database includes transcripts of diagnostic interviews and psychological tests. In making the relationship pattern formulation, the clinical judge is not tied to a confined system. Indeed, clinicians have the wide latitude usually involved when they are asked to produce a relatively free-form diagnostic formulation. The only constraints placed on clinicians are that they are asked to describe (a) the patient's conscious experience and understanding of his or her presenting symptom (usually a social phobia) and (b) their inferences as to the unconscious conflict that might underlie and cause the symptom. Although most systems rely on frequency, the Clinical Evaluation Team method allows much more freedom for weighting information according to clinically inferred salience, not only in terms of frequency but also in terms of what seems omitted, what seems especially significant because of vivid associations, and other signs. Each clinical judge has an opportunity to interact with the group of other judges to arrive at a consensus formulation. Data on reliability are not yet available.

The Seattle Psychotherapy Language Analysis Schema

This method, called the SPLASH (Maxim, Straus, & Rosenfarb, 1986; Maxim, 1986), analyzes verbal texts in terms of short units. Each unit of the patient and the therapist is coded by speaker and text line number. The interpersonal message between speaker and listener and the frame of reference (that is, the view that Person X has of Person Y and a particular frame of reference for Person X) are also coded. In each unit, five main variables are coded: (a) object, viewpoint, and frame of reference under discussion; (b) affects; (c) impulses; (d) coping strategies; and (e) interpersonal message. It takes about 40 hours of practice to achieve about 90% accuracy. It takes about 35 hours to score a 30-page session, which is a little over an hour per page. Clearly this is a system for research and not easily adapted to everyday clinical use. The method offers a description of the interaction, but its main purpose is to illuminate change across different therapeutic situations. A companion coding scheme, Metacommunication of Interactive Sequences in Therapy (Maxim & Sprague, 1989), analyzes the knowledge that is metacommunicated by the spoken utterance. A therapy session is divided into discussion topics of its manifest content. A maladaptive patient belief is identified for each discussion topic and represents a specific version of the session's CCRT. Knowledge structure categories of plans, strategies, and interactive processes are coded for patient and therapist as they are used to address the patient's belief. This additional coding takes 20 more minutes per page.

Coders-in-training have to achieve a minimum kappa of .7 on each category code before they start coding text for research. After coding one session, each coder is given a separate five-page section of text to code to test for drift. One or two training sessions are sufficient to correct for drift in a particular category type.

The Check List of Psychotherapy Transactions–Revised (CLOPT-R) and the Check List of Interpersonal Transactions–Revised (CLOIT-R)

These measures by Kiesler (1987a), called the CLOPT-R and the CLOIT-R, are derived from the latest version of the Interpersonal Circle (Kiesler, 1983). They are used as a self-report for interactants' (patients' and therapists') ratings of each other and for observer ratings of psychotherapy sessions. These observer ratings qualify the method as a central relationship pattern measure. It yields a profile of interpersonal behavior as represented by the 16 categories of the Interpersonal Circle, as well as indexes of the degree of complementarity present in patient–therapist dyads. Important clinical applications have been made to analysis of prototypical interpersonal behaviors of *DSM-III-R* personality disorders and to complementarity and therapeutic alliance in outpatient therapy dyads.

Although reliabilities vary for the different versions of the measure, internal consistency reliabilities for the 16 scales are moderately high, tending to range from .50 to .80 with a median in the mid-.60s. Additional information on reliability and validity can be found in the work of Kiesler, Goldston, and Schmidt (1991), who also recommended that researchers and clinicians routinely score a psychometrically improved light-scale version of this circumplex measure.

Idiographic Conflict Formulation (ICF)

This method (Perry, 1994; Perry & Cooper, 1989) includes the assessment of four components (along with a statement of the evidence for the assessment): conscious and unconscious wishes and fears, symptomatic and avoidant outcomes resulting from conflicting wishes and fears, specific stressors to which the patient is vulnerable, and the patient's best level of adaptation to the conflict. A standardized list has been made of 40 wishes and 39 fears that can be used for scoring the first two components of the Idiographic Conflict Formulation (ICF) method. These wishes and fears are arranged according to the Eriksonian hierarchy of psychological development. Because each motive is placed within one of the eight developmental stages (e.g., Stage 1, trust versus mistrust), an overall developmental score can be obtained by weighting each wish or fear by its stage, then taking an overall weighted average. This calculation yields one number, which represents the mean developmental stage for the person's wishes (or fears). Comparing assessments across several points in time then allows the detection of change in an individual's developmental level with treatment or with time.

The method offers reliability evidence based on two independent formulations of 20 cases, using paired comparisons for the similarity of correctly matched versus mismatched pairs of formulations. The mean similarity of correctly matched pairs, assessed by a 7-point scale, was 4.41, significantly higher ($p < .001$) than mismatched formulation pairs either with the same diagnoses (3.05) or with different diagnoses (2.91).

Consensual Response Formulation

In this method (L. Horowitz et al., 1989), a videotape of an evaluation interview is presented to a group of clinicians, each of whom writes a dynamic formulation. Then the formulations are divided into thought units. The most frequent thought units across clinicians are collected into a composite formulation called a Consensual Response Formulation (CRF). The focus of the method, therefore, is on the clinicians' consensual observations and inferences. One validity study found that formulations with a higher proportion of interpersonal content were associated with greater improvement (L. Horowitz et al., 1989). In another validity study, naive clinicians, reading only the consensual formulations, were able to anticipate correctly the interpersonal problems that were discussed in the treatment, achieving a mean chi-square of 22.2 ($p < .001$). These results confirmed the earlier finding (L. Horowitz et al., 1988) that patients with primarily interpersonal problems are especially suitable for brief dynamic psychotherapy.

The replicability of the method was established by having another group of clinicians repeat the entire Consensual Response Formulation procedure; corresponding formulations had an 80% overlap in content. In addition, 100% of the judges were able to match the replicated formulation correctly to the original formulation of the same case.

Quantitative Analysis of Interpersonal Themes (QUAINT)

The Quantitative Analysis of Interpersonal Themes (QUAINT) method employs the CCRT structure of wishes, responses from other, and responses of self. However, the QUAINT method differs from the CCRT in that (a) it uses a broad vocabulary of reliable categories derived from the Structural Analysis of Social Behavior (Benjamin, 1974, 1986a, 1986b), which covers interpersonal behaviors defined across dimensions of affiliation, interdependence, and activity–passivity; (b) the method assesses the patient's narratives separately and in random order, rather than in the context of other narratives; and (c) the method uses a cluster analysis approach to determine the coherent, multiple themes apparent across each patient's narratives.

A precursor to the method is presented by Crits-Christoph, Demorest, and Connolly (1990), and the fully developed method, with associated reliabilities, is presented by Crits-Christoph, Demorest, Muenz, and Baranackie (1994). The QUAINT has been used to examine the degree of consistency in themes across narratives (Crits-Christoph et al., 1994) and to explore the nature of themes with therapist versus themes with other people (Connolly et al., 1996).

Personal Scripts

A clinical–quantitative script method derived from Tomkins's script theory is reflected in the work of Demorest and Alexander (1992), who outlined a method for deriving personal scripts from narrative reports. Emotional experiences or scenes are first identified, and then scripts are extracted from them by a two-step process of abstraction and sequencing. Abstraction involves translating the literal elements of a specific scene into the abstract form of a generic script (e.g., "father" becomes "intimate male authority"); sequencing involves deriving the order of events that the script seeks to predict (e.g., the self approaches with interest → the other rejects with disgust → the self withdraws with sadness). Using this method, they found that people display the same scripts within two different types of narrative imagery: autobiographical reports and projective test responses. Reliability has been established for both the abstraction and sequencing tasks of script translation (Demorest & Alexander, 1992; Demorest & Siegel, 1996).

COMPARISONS AMONG METHODS OF MEASURING CENTRAL RELATIONSHIP PATTERNS

Because most central relationship pattern measures have come on the scene in the last 2 decades, the measures differ widely in the quality of their reliability and validity data. The oldest, the CCRT, has been one of the pacesetters; it is among the most advanced psychometrically in terms of information about reliability and validity. The Structural Analysis of Social Behavior (Benjamin, 1979) is also one of the most advanced, for it represents years of ingenious research development. Significant advances also have been shown by the PD, Frame, CLOPT-R and CLOIT-R, and QUAINT methods.

Most of these diverse methods appear to have commonalities in their basic categories. One of these is in the broad duality of impulse versus executive functions, for example, on one side, wishes, needs, and goals, and on the other side, responses from others and responses of self.

Quantitative research on the commonalities among central relationship pattern measures has begun, with studies comparing one measure with another measure, usually on a single case, by the paired-comparisons method. These studies are by Luborsky (1988a; CCRT, PERT, Frame); M. Horowitz et al. (1991; RRMC and CCRT); Johnson, Popp, Schacht, Mellon, and Strupp (in press; CCRT and CMP); Kächele, Luborsky, & Thomae (1988; CCRT and PERT); and Perry, Luborsky, et al. (1989; CCRT, ICF, and PD). The consistent finding from these comparisons of measures is that there are significant similarities among the measures. A larger scale study (Mackenzie, 1989) compared 12 patients on four measures: the Inventory of Interpersonal Problems (L. Horowitz, Weckler, & Doren, 1983), the Relationship Anecdotes Paradigms interview (see chapter 7, this volume), the Structural Analysis of Social Behavior, and the Repertory Grid (Kelly, 1955). The results from all four methods were translated into uniform terms on the basis of the SASB. Each method was shown to have uniqueness as well as areas of overlap.

A more recent and more complete set of illustrations and comparisons of most of these measures applied to the same patient interview has been reported (Luborsky, Popp, Luborsky, & Mark, 1994); it includes the CCRT, Configurational Analysis, the Plan Formulation method, the SASB-CMP, the Consensual Response Formulation (CRF), Idiographic Conflict Formulation method, and Frames. All of these central relationship pattern measures were compared with each other by a paired-comparisons method by Luborsky, Popp, and Barber (1994), who showed the methods to be moderately similar; the most similar of all were the CRPF, the SASB-CMP, the CCRT, and the Frame methods.

The decision to use a particular measure may depend on a practical matter—the time it takes to use the measure. In terms of time for scoring, the methods generally are expensive. The CCRT based on relationship episodes drawn from psychotherapy sessions or on the RAP interviews takes about 1.5–3 hours per session to score properly, using the combined tailor-made plus standard categories procedure described in chapter 2, this volume. New scoring systems have been developed for the CCRT that cut down on the time required, such as a decrease in the number of forms needed, but the time estimates for the CCRT still place it among the least time consuming of the observer-judged central relationship pattern measures. Of course, the CCRT can be applied by the therapist in everyday practice in the course of a session with no extra time taken (using procedures described in chapter 19).

QUESTIONNAIRE MEASURES OF TRANSFERENCE PATTERNS

The questionnaire methods in this review were intended to be measures of the transference pattern. To achieve an operational version of the concept of transference, Chance (1952) developed a questionnaire measure of the similarity between the patient's description of a significant parent and the patient's description of the therapist. In Fiedler's studies (e.g., Fiedler & Senior, 1952), transference was defined in terms of a comparison of the patient's description of the ideal person with the patient's prediction of the therapist's self-description and by both of these with similar measures completed by the therapist.

In Apfelbaum's (1958) method, transference was intended to be tapped by a Q-sort questionnaire on the patient's expectations about the qualities of the therapist who would later be assigned to the patient. The patients were grouped in terms of three types of expectations reported in their preassignment Q sort: Cluster A (therapist will give nurturance), Cluster B (therapist will be a model), and Cluster C (therapist will be a critic). Each of these expectations tended to be maintained until the end of treatment, as indicated by high test–retest reliability. Such stability was considered by Freud (1912/1958a) to be a characteristic of transference.

Rawn (1958, 1981) developed Q-sort-based scales and applied them to four sessions of one patient's analysis. He took the unusual further step of comparing these results with those from clinical observations and noted signs of convergence. Crisp (1964a, 1964b, 1966) continued this line of research with Q sorts of questionnaire items. The items rated were about father and therapist figures; the estimate of transference was based on a comparison of these ratings. One finding indicated that attitudes toward the therapist, as measured by the questionnaires, tended to change with or to precede changes in symptoms. Subotnick (1966a, 1966b) developed the method further using two separate sets of Q sorts: attitudes toward parents and attitudes toward the therapist at various points in therapy. Similarity was found between the attitudes toward parents and therapist (there were high loadings on the factors common among the Q sorts).

These six sets of studies used the questionnaire approach, usually in the form of the Q-sort method; they are a good sample of this type of study. Studies based on the questionnaire approach, however, suffer from questionable validity: The questionnaires may not measure the same construct measured by the clinically inferred transference pattern. It is not clear that a person's responses on a questionnaire reveal the nature of the transference pattern in the way that a clinical judge would assess it from sessions or other interview data. Consequently, this oldest line of quantitative transference research has not gained much acceptance. Measures derived from questionnaires need to be compared with measures of transference based on psychotherapy sessions. The research reported in chapter 15, this volume, has suggested that there is some degree of association of the two. In the event that the two approaches turn out to agree substantially, my colleagues and I will have to acknowledge that the advent of objective transference measures was much earlier than was recognized in the review of the field by Luborsky and Spence (1978). In fact, Barber (1993) is constructing a questionnaire measure of the central relationship pattern that holds promise for bridging the gap between the early and present research.

SUMMARY, DISCUSSION, AND CONCLUSIONS

- This chapter summarized the qualities of each of 16 alternative measures that appeared after the CCRT method was fashioned (Luborsky, 1976, 1977b) and that fit the class of central relationship pattern measures.
- Alternative measures have appeared steadily since 1976, with a new one every few years since then. However, the steady

progression may have come to a stop in 1992 with the work of Demorest and Alexander; whether this is a stop or just a long pause remains to be seen.

- Many of the measures have common elements with the CCRT. Clearly, when the CCRT method is being considered, a researcher has two options: to use it or to reject it and try to devise a better measure. Most researchers have used an existing measure, but an impressive number of researchers have decided to develop their own measure.

- The few comparisons of the different measures with each other have suggested a moderate overlap among them and implied that they indeed are alternative measures.

- Although most of these alternative measures require more psychometric development, each of them is thought to have special virtues.

- One of the virtues claimed for more and more of these measures in the course of their development is that they can help the therapist during the therapy to make an accurate transference formulation and, on well-timed occasions in the therapy, they are of pivotal help in guiding the therapist's interventions. The measures that claim these benefits include the CCRT, Patient's Experience of the Relationship With the Therapist, Plan Diagnosis, Structural Analysis of Social Behavior, Configurational Analysis, Cyclical Maladaptive Pattern, and Quantitative Analysis of Interpersonal Themes.

- Another genre of alternative approaches to measuring central relationship patterns is that of questionnaires to measure the transference pattern. Work in this genre appears to have started in about 1952 and continued until now, with several promising findings uncovered. Although questionnaires have the appearance of simplicity, what they measure needs to be shown to be similar to what is measured by the session-based clinical judgment method.

IV

WHAT'S NOW AND
WHAT'S NEXT

21

THE CONVERGENCE OF FREUD'S OBSERVATIONS ABOUT TRANSFERENCE WITH THE CCRT EVIDENCE

LESTER LUBORSKY

Freud's many observations about transference have never before been brought together in one place. In this chapter, 23 observations—apparently all that he made—are assembled. Most of these observations are given in his 1912 paper (1958a), a few in his earlier work in the postscript to the Dora case (1901–1905/1953a), some even before that in his "Studies in Hysteria" (1895/1955b), and some spread over his works in 1915, 1917, and 1937. From the wide range of these dates it is obvious that Freud had a career-long wish to solve the puzzles inherent in his transference concept and to explore its clinical applications.

One by one Freud's observations are compared in this chapter with evidence from the Core Conflictual Relationship Theme method. Most of that evidence has been assembled from the University of Pennsylvania Center for Psychotherapy Research; some of it has drawn on collaborations with researchers at the University of California at San Francisco's MacArthur Foundation program for the study of conscious and unconscious mental processes; and some of it has come from longer collaborations with faculty at the University of Ulm (Germany), Department of Psychotherapy.

This chapter is the latest in the succession of ever more complete reports on the convergence of Freud's observations with CCRT evidence; the first was by Luborsky (1977b); the next was by Luborsky et al. (1985); and the next three were by Luborsky et al. (1986); Luborsky and Crits-Christoph (1990); and Luborsky, Crits-Christoph, Friedman, Mark, and Schaffler (1991). The achievement of the present chapter is that it surveys all findings that fit the topic of Freud's observations about transference and, most comprehensively of all of the chapters, helps in understanding transference as illuminated by findings from the CCRT method.

Freud's concept of transference became more differentiated over time. His early use of the term *transference*, as in his Dora case (1901–1905/1953a), concentrated on what was directly implied by the idea of transference: the transfer of attitudes and behaviors derived from early parental relationships to the current one with the therapist. In his Dora case report Freud gave an example of a formulation of the transference pattern derived from his famous psychotherapy with Dora, an 18-year-old woman he diagnosed as having hysterical symptoms. Freud believed that her transference pattern was based on her relationship with her father and with her father's close "friends," Frau K and Herr K—Frau K and her father were lovers. Dora's central relationship pattern (in simplified clinically derived CCRT form) was "I wish for love from my father, but I see that father's love is for Frau K rather than for me" (meaning that his response is that he rejects me for Frau K and he also rejects me by throwing me to Herr K). Dora's responses of self to this negative response from father included her hysterical symptoms and an inclination to take revenge on men by cutting herself off from them. Only belatedly did Freud recognize her inclination; it came at the end of the psychotherapy when the patient abruptly broke off the treatment with him. Because this case was so instructive to Freud about the nature of transference, we draw on it to explain further his concept.

By the time of his 1912 paper, Freud had observed a wide range of characteristics of what he called then the transference "template"; this word is more easily understood as a translation of the German word than as "stereotype plate," rendered by Strachey in his translation of Freud (1912/1958a). In that article Freud surveyed his many observations about this template much as a naturalist would in describing a natural phenomenon. One of his main conclusions was that the transference template is a central relationship pattern that serves as a prototype, or a schema for guiding, shaping, and conducting subsequent relationships.

TABLE 1
Freud's "Transference Template" Observations and the CCRT Evidence

Freud's Observation	CCRT Evidence
1. Wishes toward people are prominent	+
2. Wishes conflict with responses from other and of self	+
3. Especially evident in erotic relationships	+?
4. Partly out of awareness	+?
5. Originates in early parental relationships	+
6. Comes to involve the therapist	+
7. May be activated by the therapist's perceived characteristics	R
8. May distort perception	R
9. Consists of one main pervasive pattern	+?
10. Subpatterns appear for family members	+?
11. Distinctive for each person	+?
12. Remains consistent over time	+
13. Changes slightly over time	+
14. Shows short-term fluctuations in activation	R
15. Accurate interpretation changes expression of pattern	+
16. Level of insight is associated with change in the pattern	+?
17. Can serve as resistance	R
18. Symptoms may emerge during its activation	+?
19. Is expressed in and out of therapy	+
20. Positive vs. negative patterns are distinguishable	+
21. Is similar in different modes (dreams and narratives)	+
22. Improvement means greater mastery of the pattern	+
23. Innate disposition plays a part	R

Note. + = study with positive results; +? = preliminary study with positive results; R = remains to be studied.

FREUD'S OBSERVATIONS COMPARED WITH CCRT EVIDENCE

This chapter reviews the whole range of Freud's observations about the transference template—numbered 1 through 23 in Table 1—mostly from his 1912 article but also from his other articles on transference. Under each observation, two pieces of information are given: (a) the essence of the observation and (b) the CCRT evidence that is consistent or inconsistent with it.

> 1. *The "instincts," "aims," and "impulses" that the person wishes to satisfy in relation to other people are prominent in the pattern.* This observation is about the nature of a main drive component in Freud's transference template. Along with the preceding terms, Freud used the term "libidinal cathexes," which are to be satisfied in relations with other people during the "conduct of the erotic life" (1901–1905/1953a, p. 116).

Although Freud's terms are not specifically defined in his articles, his uses of them implies that the CCRT's "wishes, needs, and intentions" are concrete versions of his terms. It is consistent with his observation that clinical judges who apply the wish categories to the narratives find these categories to be very prevalent; for example, as reported in chapter 10, this volume, the main wishes are pervasive in more than 60% of the narratives both early and late in psychotherapy. This pervasive category of wishes is also reliably judgeable (see chapter 6). Our conclusion is that if wishes, needs, and intentions are similar to the terms Freud used, we have found considerable evidence for this parallel.

> 2. *Wishes to others conflict with responses from others and responses of self.* The arousal of a wish tends to become part of a conflict in which the responses from others and responses of the self become active. The three components of Freud's transference concept clearly emerge from a review of the examples of transference that he provided. In one of his early examples (1895/1955b), a woman's transference is described as including a thought about her wish that Freud give her a kiss. This thought is followed by her responses of self of extreme anxiety, sleeplessness, and inability to work. In a later example from the Dora case (1901–1905/1953a), the transference pattern began with a wish for love from her father and from Herr K, followed by her response of feeling rejected because father's love was not for her but for Frau K, followed by responses from herself of feeling rejected and then rejecting men and experiencing dissociative symptoms.

The CCRT's conceptual categories are congruent with Freud's basic categories for what he referred to as the *mental apparatus*. The CCRT is based on a similar conflictual dichotomy: wishes (wishes, needs, intentions), which conflict with responses (responses from others and of self). The counterpart to our categories might be considered to be Freud's conflictual dichotomy: id impulses (wishes, drives, instincts), which conflict with ego responses (the executive functions of defense and action). It is difficult to construct a precise test of the degree of this congruence between Freud's dichotomy and that of the CCRT. It is easier to demonstrate that the CCRT scoring system components of wishes and responses typically have a high frequency of association and that the association is typically conflictual. The conflicts among the wishes and responses were especially evident in the special analysis, in chapter 8, this volume, of the sequences of wishes and responses for the wish to be close versus the wish to be independent.

> 3. *The central relationship pattern is especially evident in erotic relationships.* Freud (1912/1958a) stated that the pattern applies

to the "conduct of . . . erotic life" (p. 99). As an obvious example, this observation fits his account of the relationship pattern in the Dora case (1901–1905/1953a).

No systematic study of this distinction between erotic and nonerotic relationships has yet been done. In the few patients we have examined, it is clear that a CCRT is found in both erotic and nonerotic relationships, but there appears to be a greater concentration of pervasive components of the CCRT within the erotic relationships, for example, within the Dora case and within the Mr. Howard case (see chapter 5, this volume).

4. *The central relationship pattern is partly out of awareness.* The transference concept is used by Freud (1912/1958a) in two senses that imply states of reduced awareness: (a) as a template consisting of largely unconscious memory systems of past relationships and (b) as the activations of these memory systems in the experience of the relationship with the therapist, implying that before the activation they had been in reduced awareness. In both instances a large portion of the pattern is considered to be out of awareness. In the second instance, for example in the Dora case, Freud (1901–1905/1953a) referred to the expected activation of the transference in the treatment in blaming himself for not having dealt with the patient's reduced awareness of her pattern: "I neglected the precaution of looking out for the first signs of transference" (p. 118).

This observation appears to fit with the CCRT data, but more systematic methods are needed to define degrees of lack of awareness. Some beginning methods are already launched. In one method (see chapter 15), there is a comparison of judgments that are based on the CCRT with those based on the patient's self-interpretation of narratives; it reveals that the clinician using the CCRT has a more differentiated focus than the patient about the central relationship pattern. Another method (Luborsky & Popp, 1989) for recognizing unconscious conflicts within the CCRT also shows promise: the provision of a set of inference cues to point to ideas that are out of awareness.

5. *The central relationship pattern originates in the early relationships with parental figures.* This observation, repeatedly presented throughout Freud's writings, implies that there should be a parallel between the early relationship patterns with the parents and the current ones with other people. The parallel can also be between a later representation of the earlier parental figures (such as Herr K in the Dora case) and the therapist.

There is some evidence for this observation (Luborsky et al., 1985) based on a comparison of CCRTs from relationship episodes involving memories of events about the early parental figures with CCRTs from relationship episodes about other people in the present. The similarity of the patterns across these two lifetime eras was evident (mean similarity rating on a 7-point scale was 6.4); as would be expected, the similarity for purposely *mismatched* CCRTs was much lower (mean similarity was 3.6). The degree of similarity of the early and late relationship episodes does not prove causality but is consistent with the supposition that the later pattern was prefigured by and may have originated in the earlier one.

The current CCRT pattern, when traced back in time, may be found to show concrete correspondences with early traumatic scenes in terms of the recurrence of theme components as well as of fragments of the traumatic scenes (Carlson, 1981; Reiser, 1984). Further evidence of a parallel between the very early relationship patterns with the parents and the current relationships is seen in the findings of Main and Goldwyn (1984). They used the Adult Attachment Interview to measure adults' recollections of their own childhood attachment to their mother. They found a parallel between a mother's early childhood relationships and her current relationships with her own children: Mothers who distorted their recollections of their own childhood relationship with their parents had attachments to their own children with basic similarities to the ones they experienced with their own parents; in contrast, mothers who realistically recalled poor relationships and who were able to forgive their mothers had secure attachments with their own children. As a whole, however, research on the influence of very early relationship events on later personality development reveals a deficiency of evidence, according to a review by Kagan (1996).

6. *The central relationship pattern affects the relationship with the therapist.* It is basic to Freud's (1912/1958a) concept of transference that with the start of therapy the therapist becomes "attached to" one of the templates, and the patients' relationship pattern comes to involve the patient's "perceptions" of the therapist.

An operational CCRT translation of Freud's observation about transference requires that the main pattern in relation to other people also be found within the relationship episodes about the therapist. The study of this clinically expected convergence of the pattern with other people and with the therapist reported in chapter 11, this volume, yielded the first systematic confirmation of this observation based on psychotherapy sessions.

7. *The central relationship pattern can be activated by similarities the patient perceives in the current relationship in the therapy.* This

observation deals with two conditions for the activation of the patient's pattern. In Condition 1, some aspects of the transference are just a substitution, a "new impression or reprint," as Freud (1901–1905/1953a) called it. Such "reprints" may be merely the *distortion of the perception of the current relationship*, which is experienced as a replica of the past relationship. In Condition 2, other activations of the template may be aroused and "may even become conscious" on the basis of *finding a similarity in the therapist's "person or circumstances"* (p. 116). He added to this another basis for such therapist-stimulated arousal of transference, "some detail in our relations" (p. 118). It may be a detail, but its meaning to the patient is not unimportant.

No studies with the CCRT or with any of the alternative methods discussed in chapter 20 have focused exactly on these two conditions for the arousal. However, the most pertinent collection of data derives from a version of Condition 2: instances of "negative fit" (Singer & Luborsky, 1977), in which *the patient's behavior actually stimulates the behavior of the therapist in ways that fit the patient's negative transference expectations.* These are common patient-stimulated countertransference experiences, as described by Hoffman and Gill (1988a). In the Dora case the correspondences of the patient's transference template and the therapist's behavior were thought by Freud to have been coincidental (Condition 1) rather than based on behaviors of the therapist that were elicited by the patient's transference.

8. *The central relationship pattern may distort perception.* It is clear that Freud (1895/1955b) thought of the activation of transference as setting off a distortion in perception. Other observations have the same implication: Observation 6, that the process involves the therapist; Observation 7, that the therapist's characteristics may activate it; and even Observation 15, that interpretations of the pattern can benefit the patient by correcting the distortion. Observation 7 states that the distortion involves perceiving the therapist as having an attribute that the therapist does not have or magnifying an attribute that the therapist does have. In both cases the distortion also involves identifying the therapist as similar to an earlier person to whom the patient is attached (Freud, 1895/1955b or 1905/1960).

It is not easy to construct an operational measure of the distortion of perception in relation to the activation of transference. One possible measure of distortion might be the degree of parallel between the patient's perception of the therapist and the patient's perception of other people, although as stated in chapter 11, this volume, not all such parallels can be justified as distortion.

9. *The concept of the transference template emphasizes that there is one main relationship pattern.* Freud (1912/1958a) said there was only one main pattern. However, he must not have been completely sure because he added, "or several such."

We reported evidence in chapter 10 for the existence of a highly pervasive central relationship pattern across each session especially in terms of the wishes. But to determine whether there is one main pattern requires operational definitions. In CCRT terms it might be that for each patient there is one high-frequency theme and other themes with much lower frequency. This translation implies that for the one high-frequency theme the components of the self–other interactions are highly pervasive across different relationship episodes. We found this to be true in a sample of 8 patients (Luborsky et al., 1985, 1986); for example, the wish with the highest pervasiveness was much more pervasive across the narratives than its runner-up in the order of frequency. Another example of stepped-down rankings of frequencies of CCRTs appeared in the rankings of the pervasiveness of each cluster for each child at Age 3 and 5, reported in chapter 16. Most children had high pervasiveness for their top two clusters and much lower pervasiveness in their remaining six clusters.

This emphasis both in Freud's observations and in the CCRT data on one main pattern needs to be considered in relation to the work of others, who posit multiple schemas (e.g., Crits-Christoph & Demorest, 1991; M. Horowitz, 1987; J. Singer, 1985). However, the emphasis of the CCRT on one main pattern is only relative; the CCRT analysis typically turns up several other, less frequent patterns along with the main one. The observation that the CCRT has one main pattern is often misunderstood by people who have not used the CCRT extensively. Such people at times ask, "How can that be? I often see other themes." Further experience with the CCRT would make it plain to them that although the scoring reveals a variety of themes, only the most frequent one is designated the CCRT.

Another factor that needs to be considered is the method of CCRT scoring of the narratives. Was it the usual method as spelled out in chapter 2, this volume, or was it another method? More precisely, was it a system that allows for scoring the relationship episodes in the context of other relationship episodes in the session, or was it a scoring system that evaluates each relationship episode one by one after they have been randomized? In the latter case, it is likely that more variety in CCRTs would be discovered, because the clinical judge is not given the usual opportunity to know the larger context of other relationship episodes in which each relationship episode occurs. The function of the other relationship episodes may be to allow the judge to see a component that is revealed only opaquely in the relationship episode being judged and may not be noticed without the other relationship episodes. (In addition, even with the usual CCRT method, described in chapter 2, it is important to know the degree to which the judge followed the recommendation for scoring both Phase 1 and Phase 2, and then Phase 1' and Phase 2', that is, the degree to which the judge considered and then reconsidered the scoring, taking into account the whole set of relationship episodes.)

> 10. *Specific subpatterns appear for each family member.* In the same article referred to in the previous section, Freud (1912/ 1958a) also noted that the pattern is not tied to a "particular prototype." Instead, there are several common "prototypes"; the principal ones are the "father-imago," "mother-imago," and sometimes brother- or sister-imago. It follows from the nature of these prototypes (although it is not directly stated in the 1912 paper) that each specific prototype forms from the memories of experiences in relation to a significant family figure. In the Dora case, Freud (1901– 1905/1953a) thought of the main prototype in the transference pattern as the father and a father figure (Herr K). He noted from time to time that there was another pattern in Dora's relationships: the one involving Frau K and Dora's mother.

Evidence for specific CCRT prototypes has been extensively examined in one case (Crits-Christoph & Demorest, 1991) in which there were indications of subpatterns. It would be helpful if researchers collected narratives about each of the family members to permit separate CCRTs for each. My strong impression at this time is that there is both a main CCRT, which is general across different other people, and some partially specific subpatterns for a few significant other people.

> 11. *The central relationship pattern is distinctive for each narrator.* Freud (1912/1958a) stated that "people have their own special transference pattern. ... each individual ... has acquired a specific method of his own in the conduct of his erotic life" (p. 99).

Evidence for the distinctiveness of each person's main pattern compared with that of other people is based on the CCRTs in a small sample of 8 patients (Luborsky et al., 1985, 1986). The distinctiveness is especially striking when the entire CCRT pattern, based on all three components, is compared among people, rather than when each component is compared among people. A larger study of the degree of distinctiveness of each person's pattern is needed.

12. *The central relationship pattern tends to be consistent over time.* Freud (1912/1958a) referred to the pattern as "constantly repeated—constantly reprinted afresh—in the course of the person's life." The term *template* fits best with this observation, for it implies that there is a pattern serving as a prototype for shaping replicas in later editions.

There is no evidence about the degree of consistency over the course of the person's life, but there is evidence for the consistency of the pattern during approximately 1 year of treatment (see chapter 10, this volume). For example, for 33 patients whose pattern was measured early in treatment, on the average the main wish was evident across 66% of the early relationship episodes and across 62% of the late relationship episodes. For the future, a longitudinal study extending the studies of Dengler (1990) and Luborsky, Luborsky, et al., (1995; also see chapter 16) of children's narratives at ages 3 and 5, and continued into later life, could help establish the degree of consistency of the CCRT.

13. *The central relationship pattern changes slightly over time.* In Freud's (1912/1958a) words, the pattern is "certainly not entirely insusceptible to change" (p. 100). The wording of Freud's observation implies that he believed the pattern had considerable stability but also some plasticity over the long term.

In fact, it was found (see chapter 10) that whereas wishes had considerable stability in their pervasiveness across the person's narratives over time, they also showed a slight (nonsignificant) decrease from the early to the late period in psychotherapy. Even larger changes were shown in pervasiveness of the negative responses from others (from 41% to 29%) and negative responses of self (42% to 23%). These decreases were expected because most of the patients had improved, and the degree of improvement was associated with the degree of decrease in these two negative components.

14. *The central relationship pattern shows short-term fluctuations in activation.* This observation involves the very short-term changes in activation of the pattern, often during a session, as distinguished from the long-term changes referred to in Observation 13. This Observation 14 is based partly on the effects of Observation 7, that the therapist's characteristics may activate the pattern.

Changes in activation of the pattern are commonly observed within sessions as well as across sessions. Examples of such changes are not difficult to find: For Mr. Howard, within Session 3 (see chapter 5, this volume), the relationship episode about the therapist reflects greater activation of the pattern and reflects a within-session increase in activation. The therapist response to that relationship episode implies that the therapist was aware of the activation. When the patient began to be markedly unresponsive, distant, and tense during the session, the therapist offered the interpretation that the patient expected the therapist to be more responsive. The interpretation was timed to coincide with the greatest activation of the transference pattern in the session. There has been little operational translation of this basic observation about within-session activations. Only the work of Gill and Hoffman (1982b) has shown an attempt to score such changes in activation.

15. *Interpretation changes the expression of the central relationship pattern.* Through interpretations that focus on the transference pattern, the pattern becomes altered. An absence of such interpretation was the "defect" Freud (1901–1905/1953a) decided was responsible for the premature breaking off of treatment by Dora. He wrote the following:

> I did not succeed in mastering the transference in good time. . . . when the first dream came, in which she gave herself the warning that she had better leave my treatment just as she had formerly left Herr K's house, I ought to have listened to the warning myself. 'Now,' I ought to have said to her, 'it is from Herr K that you have made a transference onto me. Have you noticed anything that leads you to expect evil intentions . . . similar to Herr K's?' (p. 118)

There is some evidence that is exactly on target in supporting the observation: Interpretations with greater focus on the pattern reflected in the CCRT—"accurate" interpretations—were more strongly associated with benefit to the patient (see chapter 13, this volume). There is also some evidence that bears generally on this observation; for example, a greater number of interpretations that combine present and past relationships have been reported in a review of studies (Luborsky et al., 1988) to be positively related to outcome of therapy. Although the number of interpretations is a factor in changing the central relationship pattern, as shown by Piper, Azim, Joyce, and McCallum (1991), the accuracy of the focus of the interpretations is also important.

16. *Insight into the central relationship pattern can benefit the patient.* Accurate interpretations help the patient to gain insight into the pattern, which in turn leads to a reduction of the intensity of transference or to greater mastery of it and to ultimate benefits to the patient. "One must allow the patient time to become conversant with this resistance . . . to work through it, to overcome it" (Freud, 1914/1958e, p. 155).

The evidence from the CCRT research shows mixed results about the benefits of insight (see chapter 14, this volume). The measure of self-understanding or insight used was the convergence of (a) the patient's self-descriptions with (b) the independently established CCRT. The assumption within this operational measure is that the more these two converge, the greater the self-understanding. The first result was consistent with the theory: The *level* of self-understanding in an early session was significantly correlated with the patient's benefits from the treatment. The second finding was not confirmatory of the theory: The *gain* in self-understanding was not significantly correlated with the patient's benefits from the treatment. However, the operational measure in the study that was chosen for examination of gains—that is, change from Session 3 to Session 5—did not seem to fit well with the theory; therefore, better operational measures are needed.

Operational measures of this observation, and of Observation 15 on the benefits of interpretation of the pattern, have also been successfully tried by the Mount Zion psychotherapy research group (Norville et al., 1996; Silberschatz et al., 1986) but with a focus on the immediate impact of convergent interpretations. The authors defined self-understanding operationally as the convergence of the interpretations with their measure of the Plan Diagnosis (as described in chapter 20, this volume). In contrast to our study, which was based on benefits received by the time of the termination of the treatment, their measure of impact on the patient was an immediate one; that is, a sample of the session just after the interpretation as rated by independent judges. They found that the greater the convergence of the interpretation with the Plan Diagnosis, the more beneficial was the immediate impact on the patient, in terms of greater experiencing of affects and greater insight.

17. *The central relationship pattern can serve as a resistance.* Freud (1912/1958a) considered it surprising and "a puzzle why in analysis transference emerges as the most powerful resistance to the treatment" (p. 101). "Every single association, every act of the person under treatment must reckon with the resistance and represents a compromise between the forces that are striving towards recovery and the opposing ones [from the transference]" (p. 103). For example, when Dora viewed Freud (1901–1905/1953a), her therapist, as acting like her father, and this piece of the transference was not interpreted, the transference served as a resistance, and the treatment became ineffectual and was aborted by the patient.

Empirical studies must be designed to examine the hypothesis that the transference is the most powerful resistance. But the puzzle might become somewhat less puzzling if one considered that the pattern reflects traitlike attitudes in the relationship patterns to self and to others; in that light, it is not surprising that there is resistance to changing them.

> 18. *Symptoms may emerge when the pattern is activated.* The Dora case (Freud, 1901–1905/1953a) provides examples of the observation that the conflicts that are active during the telling of a patient's memories constitute a context conducive to the appearance of symptoms. Dora's hysterical symptoms emerged following the activation of her central relationship patterns, in particular of the erotically related ones.

In the CCRT research, we have found many examples that fit Freud's observation. The conflictual relationship pattern, expressed in terms of the CCRT format, forms the context for the appearance of the symptoms, with the symptoms typically included in the response of self component of the CCRT. The appearance of a symptom during a psychotherapy session can be greeted, therefore, as an opportunity to examine its context and learn more about its meanings, as shown systematically for the first time by Luborsky (1996).

> 19. *The pattern expressed within therapy is similar to the pattern expressed outside of therapy.* The point of this observation is that the template is a general pattern and not confined to expression in the treatment. Freud's (1912/1958a) observation was exactly that: "It is not a fact that transference emerges with greater intensity and lack of restraint during psychoanalysis than outside" (p. 101).

There is evidence for the expression of the pattern outside of the treatment from a small-sample study of narratives that were told during an interview conducted by a person other than the therapist compared with narratives that were extracted from treatment sessions (van Ravenswaay et al., 1983). Following the proposed plan by Luborsky (1986a), a larger, more controlled study (Barber et al., 1995) showed this parallel: A RAP interview before treatment conducted by a person other than the therapist revealed similar CCRTs to those found in early therapy sessions.

> 20. *Positive and negative patterns are distinguishable.* Freud (1912/1958a) generally used the term *positive* to refer to "affectionate" feelings and *negative* to mean "hostile" feelings. Positivity was further divisible into transference of (a) "friendly or affectionate" feelings and (b) feelings that have erotic sources (p. 105). Yet in the most general terms, Freud commonly used this distinction of positive or negative to mean the expectation or nonexpectation of a "frustration of satisfaction" (p. 103).

It is difficult to come up with exactly specified operational translations of the terms *positive* and *negative*, yet what Freud meant is clear enough to guide in making the distinction between positive and negative instances in sessions. My colleagues and I (see chapter 4, this volume) tried an operational measure of a CCRT component that is related to Freud's definition: the positive or negative responses from other and the positive or negative responses of self. These appear to be appropriate measures, because when they are positive or negative they brand the whole pattern as positive or negative. We found that when each judge identified the same response from other or the same response of self, there was 95% agreement on whether it was positive or negative. A more precise scoring of positive and negative, allowing two degrees of severity for positive and two degrees for negative, also showed high agreement between judges and evidence of validity (see chapter 4).

One of the side benefits of having scored the CCRT components for their positive or negative quality was the knowledge acquired about their relative frequency. For virtually every patient, the number of negative responses far exceeded the number of positive ones (see chapters 4, 7, and 16). This is true both for the narratives told spontaneously in the course of psychotherapy and for the narratives told on request as part of the RAP interview. Possibly the high frequency of negative responses in narratives derives from the need to remember and to talk about negative or traumatic events or the need to *master* negative or traumatic events (as discussed in chapter 22).

21. *The pattern is expressed similarly through different expressive modes.* A similar pattern can appear in a variety of modes of expression: in behavior, in narratives about relationships, and in dreams. Although this observation was not explicitly stated, it was clearly exemplified in Freud's 1912 paper (1958a) and in the Dora case (1901–1905/1953a), in which two dreams were analyzed to show the patient's main relationships to parents and others.

In my initial study (Luborsky, 1977b), the main CCRT was found to appear similarly in both dreams and narratives. In chapter 12, independently scored CCRTs within dreams and within narratives were found to be significantly similar in three preliminary cases, and the trend was the same in an expanded study of the dreams and narratives of 13 patients in psychoanalysis.

22. *Greater improvement in dealing with the pattern implies greater mastery of the pattern, although the pattern itself remains evident.* Several of Freud's observations dealt with the pervasive therapeutic aim to give the patient greater freedom, control,

and even mastery over neurotic conflicts. Among these are the following: Observation 4 concerns lack of awareness of aspects of the transference, which needs to be overcome by the treatment. Observation 8 deals with distortions of perception, which need to be overcome in the course of treatment. Observation 15 deals with the use of interpretation to overcome deficits in knowledge of the negative transference. Observation 16 fits with the aim of the treatment to give greater insight into the conflicts, especially those related to the transference. In Freud's writings, there are numerous instances in which treatment was aimed at recovering memories in the service of mastery. For example, Freud (1920/1955a, p. 35) discussed the way that neurotic patients try to achieve resolution of their conflicts through "mastering or binding." At the end of one of his successful cases, Freud said, "In these last months of his treatment he was able to reproduce all the memories and to discover all the connections which seemed necessary for understanding his early neurosis and mastering his present one" (Freud, 1937/1964, p. 217).

Luborsky (1977b, 1984) noted that when patients improve, there is a shift toward greater mastery of the pattern. This finding was much more fully examined by Grenyer and Luborsky (1996) and is discussed in chapter 18, this volume, where it is revealed to be a predictor of outcome in psychotherapy.

> 23. *Innate disposition plays a part.* Freud (1912/1958a) observed that the factor of constitution plays a conjoint role with the factor of early experience: "We assume that the two sets regularly act jointly in bringing about the observed result" (p. 99). The interaction differs in individual cases because experience and constitution operate jointly in determining the pattern.

Freud's observation seems applicable on the basis of modern knowledge of genetics, but relevant data on heritability of the CCRT are not available. A collection of RAP interviews (see chapter 7) from a source like the Danish adoption registry, with data from adoptive and biological parents and children, probably could make such a contribution.

DISCUSSION

The Nature of Freud's Observations

What kinds of observations are these 23 that led Freud to the concept of the transference template? They are a varied bunch, with some overlap.

They deal with the origin, function, and activating stimuli of the transference template, as well as with measures that may reduce or contain the expressions of the template. This diversity makes it difficult to characterize the observations as a set. Rather than having been theoretically inferred, most of the observations appear to have been empirically based and derived from Freud's own experience in making inferences about patients' relationship patterns. They reflect Freud's penchant for carefully collecting observations about mental phenomena (Holt, 1965). He showed this observational style early in his career when, working in Breucke's physiology laboratory, he described the structure and function of specimens he viewed under the microscope. The basic observations he made about the transference template deserve special attention for they form the "durable core of Freud's empirical science, . . . it is the [psychoanalytic] method, the observations and the immediate inferences drawn from them that count in the end . . . it provides a solid and dependable base upon which to build" (Reiser, 1986, p. 8).

Freud's style was to marshal his observations from time to time so that they might lead to concepts about the operation of deep structures. Although in the course of theorizing he recurrently resolved to restrain his attraction to concepts that were too inferential and too metapsychological, he often gave in to the temptation (Holt, 1989). Fortunately, with the transference template he came to a middle-level, clinically grounded concept (1912/1958a) of a mental representation of knowledge about patterns of relating to other people that guides the conduct of relationships.

In this chapter the focus is on the diversity in Freud's concept of transference, as stated in his specific observations and as illustrated by the transference formulations in his case examples. But much work on his observations remains to be done to fulfill the research agenda as well as to deal with comparisons with the long line of clinical and theoretical definitional clarifications by others written over the years; among these authors are Arlow and Brenner (1964), Curtis (1983), Waelder (1936), Spitz (1956), Greenacre (1954), and Nunberg (1951), as well as many others.

The Correspondence of Freud's Observations With CCRT Evidence

To compare Freud's observations about his transference template with parallel evidence from the CCRT, each of Freud's observations had to be expressed in an operational form that could be examined using CCRT data derived from psychotherapy or psychoanalytic sessions. So far, researchers have been able to make this comparison for 18 of the 23 observations (see Table 1). For 11 of the 18 observations, studies showed a good correspondence between Freud's observations and the CCRT evidence (marked with a plus sign): Observations 1, 2, 5, 6, 12, 13, 15, 19, 20, 21, and 22 (the five underlined have the most supportive studies). For 7 of the 18, there is pilot data with results that are mixed but look promising (marked with a plus sign and question mark). For a few of the 5 observations that remain to be studied (marked with R), it probably will be possible to work out operational measures and proceed with a study. The overall conclusion for now is that researchers have found a degree of correspondence for 18 of the 23 observations and that performance implies some success for the comparisons.

The 23 observations can be subgrouped on the basis of two broad principles: (a) the breadth of the pattern and (b) the stability of the pattern. Four of Freud's observations relate to the breadth of the pattern. These observations include the fact that there is one main pattern (Observation 9); that after treatment is begun, the pattern soon involves the therapist (Observation 6); that the pattern is present both in and out of therapy (Observation 7); and that the pattern also emerges in different modes of expression, including waking narratives and dreams (Observation 21).

The second broad principle in the observations is stability over time, a principle that qualifies transference as a personality structure. According to Rapaport (1951), a personality structure is an entity with a slow rate of change. The observations about transference clearly fit this principle: It has some consistency over time (Observation 12); it also shows consistency from the time of its early parental origins to late in life (Observation 5); and its stability is especially localized in the remarkable long-term persistence of the wishes toward people (Observation 1).

Another encompassing generalization about the 23 characteristics of Freud's concept of transference is the degree to which these characteristics are like the general characteristics of psychological schemas of the kind that Knapp (1991) defined as "an enduring symbolic framework that organizes constellations of thought, feeling, memory, and expectation about self and others" (p. 94). Such self–other person schemas are considered by Knapp to have (a) pervasiveness, (b) concreteness, (c) tenacity, (d) urgency, (e) simultaneity of existence of many elements of patterning, and (f) plasticity of outward manifestations, including shifts in awareness. All of these appear to be represented in Freud's observations about the concept, although by slightly different names.

Is there at this point enough evidence that the transference template and the CCRT can be thought of as similar conceptually? Mostly, yes. Although more evidence should be and will be assembled, the evidence pulled together in this chapter shows that the two concepts have much in common.

A further principle for making conclusions about the commonality of the concept of the transference and the CCRT evidence has emerged from the congressional debates in 1988 and 1989 about whether each of various proposed tax measures was really a disguised tax. The opinion of the op-

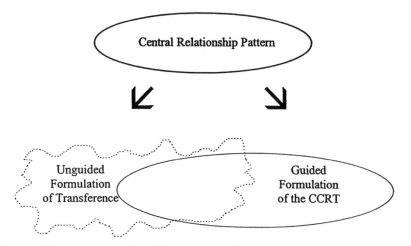

Figure 1. The central relationship pattern in the transference and in the CCRT.

position was often: "If it looks like a duck and it talks like a duck, then it *is* a duck!" Applying this principle then, is it proper to say about the CCRT that if it looks like transference and talks like transference, then it *is* transference? Yes, almost, but not exactly. As the diagram in Figure 1 shows, the similarities and differences can be simply stated: (a) It is fitting to say that a clinician's transference formulation is the clinician's unguided estimate of the central relationship pattern. (b) A clinician's formulation in CCRT terms is probably a largely overlapping but guided version of the central relationship pattern.

CONCLUSIONS

- In the course of Freud's perennial attempts to specify his transference concept, he made 23 observations about its nature.
- A key element in the strategy of our research was the translation of each of Freud's observations about transference into its most tenable operational definition to simplify and objectify the comparison with the CCRT evidence.
- For 18 of these 23 observations, research with the CCRT has found some convergence of the two versions of the central relationship pattern: Freud's transference template and the CCRT. Because researchers have found a reasonable operational measure for the majority of Freud's observations, it has been possible to examine convergence with the evidence

from the CCRT, and the results of the comparison have demonstrated a meaningful kind of validity for the CCRT.

- The benefit from using the CCRT method is that it enables clinicians to achieve consensus in their session-based judgments about this complex concept, a sought-after feat that had repeatedly suffered defeat before the advent of the CCRT method.

22

WHERE WE ARE IN UNDERSTANDING THE CCRT

LESTER LUBORSKY

Just tell a set of narratives about events that have happened to you in relation to other people, either recently or in the past. Then call on this guide to the CCRT method to help you trace through the set of narratives to find the red threads of the central relationship patterns within them. The pattern that will be revealed is much like the one typically called the *transference* by Freud (1912/1958a) and other psychoanalysts. That, in brief, is a satellite's snapshot of the large contours of what is presented in this book.

This chapter re-views what has been seen in this book so far but with a limited focus on where to build around the two largest formations supporting the CCRT in its present, mature state: the areas of reliability and validity. Construction should be on the dozen or so highest priority topics that must be developed to promote the continued maturation of the CCRT method. Roughly, the first half dozen of these topics are in the area of reliability and the second half dozen are in the area of validity.

HOW MUCH MORE RELIABLE IS THE CCRT METHOD THAN THE USUAL CLINICAL METHOD?

For an assessment method like the CCRT to be useful, clinicians and trained research judges must be able to follow its procedures with at least moderate interjudge agreement. As chapter 1, this volume, details, it took years of trying this and that and a dash of luck to come up with a reliable system. The now considerable evidence that the CCRT can be judged reliably (see chapter 6) makes it the first clinically judged measure of a central relationship pattern derived from psychotherapy that shows satisfactory levels of reliability. The secret of my success in creating a reliable measure of this complex concept was the reliance on the principle of *guided* clinical judgment: The CCRT provides all judges with the same basic system for scoring so that all judges can follow it in making inferences about the central relationship pattern. Therefore, the CCRT method is consistent with Holt's (1978) principle that guided clinical judgments have a better chance than unguided ones of achieving both interjudge agreement and successful predictive performance.

In summary, the reliability of the CCRT method is superior to that of the unguided clinical method, as found in the research by Seitz (1966) and DeWitt et al. (1983). Yet a more exact comparison of the two approaches is needed. One study in this area is already in progress (Friedman & Luborsky, 1996); it compares a set of cases evaluated by the same clinicians first using the usual clinical judgment method and then using the CCRT method. The authors already can see the expected advantage, but they hope to be able to specify the amount and kinds of advantages.

DO TAILOR-MADE OR STANDARD CATEGORIES WORK BETTER?

The mainstay of the original form of the CCRT was the tailor-made scoring system, in which each of the clinical judges makes inferences about each patient's narratives using descriptive categories that fit each patient best. The main asset of the tailor-made method is that categories are fashioned to fit each person. But some of its categories, therefore, are likely to be unique to each person and some overlap ambiguously with each other. Naturally, with this system researchers continually came up against perplexities in computing interjudge agreement for categories.

To deal with the problem, my colleagues and I tried scoring systems with sets of standard categories, as we report in chapter 3, this volume. In these systems each time a judge wishes to make a particular kind of inference about a thought unit, the judge is instructed to use an appropriate word in the standard category list. In that way, each judge uses the same words for the same concept as the other judges. Judges were able to do this task relatively rapidly and with significant agreement with each other (see chapter 6). In effect, the main assets of the standard category system are that (a) it relies on the use by each judge of the same categories, and (b) it is easy to find the degree of agreement among judges.

More comparisons of the tailor-made and standard category methods are needed. These studies should teach researchers for which special purposes it is better to use the tailor-made categories first and then translate them into standard categories versus for which purposes it is justified to use the shorter procedure of omitting tailor-made categories and inferring standard categories directly. After experience with both the tailor-made and the standard category methods (see chapters 2 and 5), our opinion is that, because of their different assets, both methods used in succession contribute more than either system by itself; use of the tailor-made system should be followed by application of the standard categories.

There is a problem that lessens the adequacy of the translation from tailor-made to standard categories: From time to time there appear to be meanings in the tailor-made categories that are not captured well in the existing standard categories. Research efforts will in time move toward expanding the standard category list to lessen the frequency of its shortfalls in meaning.

MIGHT THE TRANSFERENCE BE A MERE PRODUCT OF SUGGESTION BY THE THERAPIST?

The possibility of the therapist's contaminating the patient's transference pattern through suggestion is a crucial defect of reliance on sessions according to Grunbaum (1984), that prevents research on psychotherapy sessions from being able to prove anything. In essence, he argued that because the content of the session is vulnerable to the therapist's influence, research can prove nothing using data from sessions. This argument reflects the all-or-nothing reasoning of a logician. In contrast, this now age-worn issue was examined by Freud (1914/1958e), who believed that there were ways to minimize the possibility of the therapist's suggestion effects and ways to judge the therapist's distortion of the patient's transference; for example, when a patient *begins* treatment with a behavior in the session that is remembered as a repetition of any early experience, the therapist is not likely to have suggested it.

Despite this controversy, there is a huge and growing body of empirical studies of psychotherapy sessions focusing on the many initial factors that influence their outcomes (Luborsky et al., 1988; Orlinsky, Grawe, & Parks, 1994). The findings of these studies support the view that even though the therapist might have the power to influence the patient through suggestion and other means, there are aspects of the patient that are relatively stable and thus less subject to influence. The CCRT may be one instance of a facet of personality that is resistant to change, with the wishes within the CCRT the most constant of the CCRTs components over time.

A demonstration of the stability of the CCRT would involve getting narratives from the patient *before* the patient even meets the therapist and comparing these with narratives obtained *after* a few early sessions with the therapist, as was done by Barber et al. (1995). The CCRTs were extracted from each set independently to determine the degree of similarity of the data sets from before with those from after the therapy started. We found considerable consistency between these data sets regardless of the other types of changes that were stimulated by the therapy.

Another design also provides results that bear on the question: use of data from a patient who had two different therapists in sequence so that a comparison can be made of the CCRTs with each therapist. Only one such example with one patient, Ms. Apfel (see chapter 12, this volume), was available (Luborsky, 1988b, 1996). This patient's analysis was interrupted by the illness of her first analyst, and she continued with a second analyst. An examination of the context of her momentary forgettings showed a similar CCRT context for the first and second analyst.

IS THE CCRT FROM THERAPY NARRATIVES SIMILAR TO THE CCRT FROM RAP NARRATIVES?

Although clinicians are inclined to believe that narratives told during psychotherapy sessions are more revealing than those told as part of a special narrative-telling interview, such as the Relationship Anecdotes Paradigm (RAP) interview, the two data sources appear to give similar results in terms of the CCRT. My colleagues and I studied a group of depressed patients (Eckert et al., 1990) from whom we obtained both spontaneously told narratives from their psychotherapy and requested narratives from a RAP interview. As was expected by Luborsky (1986a), the CCRTs from RAP narratives told to someone other than the therapist before treatment started were not significantly different from the CCRT from early session narratives (Barber et al., 1995). This study contributed to the knowledge of the reliability of the RAP, as well as to allaying the concern that some have expressed (e.g., Grunbaum, 1984) that the content of the transference pattern is a product of suggestion on the part of the psychotherapist or psychoanalyst.

ARE RAP NARRATIVES ABOUT "REAL" EVENTS SIMILAR TO "STORIES" FROM THE TAT?

The Thematic Apperception Test (TAT), used extensively in personality assessment for the last 60 years (Murray, 1938), entails asking the person to make up stories about a standard set of pictures. My colleagues and I rely instead on RAP (Relationship Anecdote Paradigms) narratives that are intended to be about real events and are not stimulated by a set of pictures. Some similarity of TAT and RAP narratives should be present, but it will be only slight. It is easier for people to tell about events that happened to them than to compose stories in response to pictures. In addition, narratives about real events offer more information to the evaluator revealing what the patient knows about his or her relationships and also provide the therapist with more reliable information about the patient's life.

WOULD BEHAVIORAL ENACTMENTS OF RELATIONSHIPS REVEAL MORE THAN THE USUAL NARRATIVES ABOUT RELATIONSHIPS?

Narratives about relationship events naturally tend to be told from the perspective of the teller of the narrative. Direct observations of actual relationship events would be expected to yield additional or different information from narratives about these events. The differences among viewers of events can be so great at times as to warrant their being called a "Rashomon" experience, meaning that the perceptions of the viewers differ drastically (Mintz, Auerbach, Luborsky, & Johnson, 1973). It is because of our group's interest in this comparison that we have collected direct observations of relationship interactions by means of examining "enactments." These are brief behavioral relationship interactions with the therapist that occur in psychotherapy sessions (described in chapter 2, this volume). They are identified within the session by the same judge who identifies the narratives. They are a special category of the relationship episodes with the therapist in which the therapist and patient engage in a discrete, delimited enactment of an episode of interaction. They can also be used as part of the database for the CCRT, although there are not many included so far. When enough enactments have been collected, we will compare these with the narratives told about the relationship with the therapist.

WHAT WOULD BE LEARNED FROM SCORING *SEQUENCES* OF CCRT COMPONENTS?

In chapter 2, I offered another scoring option from Luborsky (1984): to record the exact sequence of the CCRT components as they are presented within each narrative. This option might give a better picture of the interactional sequences than the current method of simply counting all wishes, responses from other, and responses of self. Only a little information has been systematically collected on this option. In the one comparison we did (see chapter 9) of the actual sequence method with the usual CCRT method, we found that the two methods yielded similar CCRTs. But of course more evidence is needed because the issue is so basic to the usual CCRT method. In another study, Mitchell (1995) has shown that sequences that entail a larger percentage of interactions with people indicate a higher degree of psychological health.

ARE DEFENSES CLASSIFIABLE WITHIN THE RESPONSES OF SELF?

A frequent question from audiences after presentations about the CCRT is, "How does the CCRT deal with defenses?" The answer is that it could but it does not; there is not yet a formal place for defenses in the scoring system, although it is clear that the response of self component is the logical place for including judgments of defenses. It is noteworthy that clinical judges, even when using the tailor-made category system, virtually never list defenses. Perhaps they would if they were instructed on the desirability and method of doing so. If one is to examine categories of defenses in relation to the CCRT, one should include a sample of the most frequent and recognizable defenses within the standard categories list (drawing from Perry & Cooper, 1989, or from Vaillant, 1977). Good candidates for such categories are denial, projection, and isolation, because they are likely to be reliably recognizable.

One study has been done, however, on the CCRT in relation to a repressive defensive style. Luborsky, Crits-Christoph, and Alexander (1989) found that people who are classed as repressors tend to express wishes having to do with closeness; patients who are classed as isolators tend to express wishes that have to do with independence and autonomy. These findings for defensive style suggest the potential value of the inclusion of categories in the CCRT that measure defenses.

HOW CAN THE OBSERVATION BE TESTED THAT THE TRANSFERENCE IS "PARTLY OUT OF AWARENESS"

My colleagues and I began studying the awareness of the CCRT with the work reported in chapter 15, this volume, about the patients' versus the clinicians' interpretations of the narratives. Our reasoning was that patients might be less aware of some aspects of their CCRT than the clinicians were. Surprisingly, there is considerable parallel between the patients' understanding of their own CCRT and the clinician's understanding of that CCRT. But the parallel primarily appears in terms of the recognition of many of the same types of components by the patients and the clinicians. What the clinicians apparently do better than the patients is to identify the relative degrees of importance of the types of components; all this and more is discussed in chapter 15.

This question is examined in another way as well in chapter 15: by the first of the questionnaire methods for assessing the CCRT. The patient fills out a CCRT relationship questionnaire that contains the same categories that are used for standard scoring of CCRTs. An improved version of the CCRT relationship questionnaire is being tried (Barber, 1993).

This kind of exact comparison of the relationship questionnaire and the narrative-based CCRT needs to be continued. The CCRT method takes a lot of time; in contrast, the questionnaire methods are relatively brief. Questionnaires conceivably might be developed that can identify the kind of pattern identified by the CCRT and do the job more easily. Another candidate among the questionnaire methods is the Inventory of Interpersonal Problems (L. Horowitz et al., 1983, 1988; also see chapter 20). This questionnaire consists of about 90 self-report items about the patient's main interpersonal problems. The questionnaire even asks the patient to pick the 5 items that are most pressing: It is these 5 problems that might be most related to the CCRT.

I have in progress another, very different approach to measuring reduced awareness: a method of identifying unconscious conflicts within the CCRT (Luborsky, 1987). The method provides the judge with (a) the CCRT, (b) the session transcripts on which the CCRT is based, and (c) a set of principles about how to make inferences about the type and degree of reduced awareness for each aspect of the CCRT. For example, the first of these principles is that the most unconscious wishes may be found to be the opposite of the most expressed wishes in the CCRT. An instance of this principle in the CCRT for Mr. Howard follows: The most expressed (and conscious) wish is "to be close"; a more unconscious, opposite wish is "to be distant." The larger set of principles that serve as a guide to making inferences of this kind is helpful to the judges and appears to be responsible for some of the agreement in their inferences about the aspects of the CCRT that are in reduced awareness.

WHY RELY ON NARRATIVES ABOUT RELATIONSHIPS AS THE BASIS FOR THE CCRT?

The decision to use narratives as the database for the CCRT was a crucial choice and a blessed event for the CCRT; it has demonstrated that narratives offer a viable road to both the conscious and unconscious basic conflictual relationship patterns. The narrative can now claim to be worthy of sharing with the dream the classic title of "the royal road" (Freud, 1900/ 1953b); as Lyman Wynne (personal communication, 1988) noted, "The CCRT method by relying on the pattern derived from narratives about episodes in relationships represents the first systematic use of narratives that establishes them as on a par with the systematic use of dreams." We even have been able to show, by direct comparison (see chapter 12, this volume), that there is a parallel in terms of CCRT content between narratives and dreams. Narratives are, therefore, an informative mode of communicating to the therapist the nature of one's central relationship pattern and the conflicts within it. Beyond that discovery, the focus on the narrative has led to an entirely new kind of observation about the frequency of such narratives in the course of psychotherapy sessions (see chapter 9).

The choice of narratives for deriving the CCRT was based on a lucky observation. The first chapter of this book tells the story of how my idea for the CCRT took shape, at least for the part of the choice that was in my awareness. "New" ideas reflect more of the intellectual atmosphere than we know, it may be more than just good luck, because the fashion for the study of narratives could have played a part. The atmosphere in the last two decades has been increasingly charged with enthusiasm about the properties of narratives, and that ambience could have had some undercover influence on my attraction to narratives. Although it is true that what is absorbed and used in making discoveries shows signs of passive intake of these trends of the times, that is not the whole story. The rest of the story is, as Pasteur observed, that *Fortune favors the prepared mind.*

To demonstrate that the present era has had a permeating preoccupation with narratives, a brief sample follows of recent works on four facets of narratives.

Characteristics of Narratives

Narratologists, such as Labov (1972) and Chapman (1980), agree that narratives have the following characteristics: (a) two kinds of time are distinguishable in a narrative: the time sequence of plot events (the story time) and the presentation time of the story in the text (the discourse time); (b) the events have a time sequence, which means that there is more than one event in the narrative; and (c) the subject of the narrative is implicated in several different events in the negative. Another contribution on narratives (Toolan, 1989) explored the whole range of narrative types—written and spoken, literary and nonliterary—and showed what systematic attention to the language can reveal about the narratives themselves, their tellers, and their audience.

The Truth Value of Narratives

This is a highly active frontier of exploration about narratives. The truth value of narratives told during psychotherapy is of concern to many writers on the topic. Their views fall on two sides of a controversy. On the one side are the "empirical optimists," who believe that parallels in such narratives with actual events can be found out and are worth trying to find out, for example, Edelson (1984, 1988), Reiser (1984), and my research group. On the other side are those who might be called the "hermeneutists," who believe that the truth is not easily found out or that trying is not worth the effort. The kind of truth that matters, according to this viewpoint, is the presence of an inner consistency of the meanings within the narratives. Spence's book (1983b), *Narrative Truth and Historical Truth*, takes up this issue and resolves it in favor of the "narrative truth" alternative. Spence (1983a) wrote that "we are all the time constructing narratives about our past and our future, and . . . the core of our identity is really the thread that gives meaning to our life" (p. 480).

The Revelations of Narratives About Modes of Thought

Narratives about oneself have been Bruner's (1987) focus of investigation in the current phase of his multifaceted career. He described two distinct modes of thought: a narrative mode and a logical argument mode. The narrative mode uses stories about oneself, which are seen as guides for structuring experience, and thus narratives are a fundamental form of communication with others and with the self. In contrast, the logical argument mode generates a view of the mind as computerlike. That mode leaves out what is retained in narratives about the self: beliefs, desires, intentions, expectations, and emotions.

The Interpretability of Narratives

For at least 3 decades some influential literary critics have been carrying on an enthusiastic romance with a deconstructionist view of narratives. Their view is a rejection of what they believe is the aim of older literary critics, of trying to find the meanings in narratives. These current critics believe there is no meaning in narratives—that meaning is only assigned by the reader. This radical view is an extension of Husserl's (1960) concept of the "phenomenological attitude" (and related philosophers' concepts, as reviewed by Murphy, 1938), in which one tries to see a phenomenon for what it is in itself, through an unprejudiced phenomenological reduction. This current view has been extended and disseminated by Derrida (1977).

Our findings with the CCRT have a lesson to teach the literary critics who hold the current view of the inherent nonmeaningfulness of narratives. The lesson is that their basic premise is much too broadly applied. CCRT research has shown that readers can, in fact, agree fairly well with each other about certain major meanings of narratives; one of these is the central relationship patterns within the narratives. The deconstructionist's assumption that readers do not agree may have some factual basis *only* when readers provide interpretations of meanings without any prior agreed-on guidelines for making their inferences. As in the time-worn narrative about the blind men examining the elephant, the unguided readers may be looking at different parts of the narrative or looking at the same part but judging according to different guidelines. The findings based on the CCRT method imply that reader agreement increases considerably when readers are looking at the same part and guided by the same method; for the CCRT, the raters are directed by the relationship episode markers to the exact location of the relationship episode.

Beyond that basic lesson, the CCRT findings also have limitations that favor a restricted form of deconstructionism! There are central parts of narratives that allow inferences about their central relationship pattern, but undoubtedly there are crucial parts of narratives that cannot be judged with agreement. These usually are parts that require high levels of inference, such as, at what points in the play is Hamlet mad, and at what points is he feigning madness? How do we understand Lear's last words? With these parts of narratives, even guided systems such as my own would have a hard time yielding agreement among different judges. *So, it is this distinction between what can and what cannot be agreed on that is lost sight of in deconstructionist circles.*

HOW DID EACH PERSON'S CCRT ORIGINATE AND WHY IS IT SO PERSISTENT?

This book started with a discussion of the history of how the CCRT measure came to be born. Now I begin to end it with how the theme in the CCRT originates and becomes a pervasive schema—a much more mysterious origin to trace. This venture turns into an adventure—a search for the factors that explain the origins and persistence of the CCRT. So far I have managed remarkable restraint in resisting being drawn into metapsychological speculation, a temptation that Freud himself had a hard time with. Even the recapitulation of the research results in the previous chapter was limited to evidence about the CCRT in comparison with Freud's observations about transference.

But in this section, I give in to a bit of boldness by taking off on a speculative flight that allows more perspective on the sources of the CCRT. Although the flight will be over the mostly familiar terrain of Freud's observations about the transference versus the CCRT evidence, from that great height one can make out the contours of four or more formative and maintenance factors for the central relationship pattern and for that concrete version of it, the CCRT.

Source Factor 1: Learning the Pattern From Parental Figures

A central relationship pattern is discernible very early in a child's development, and the pattern may owe much to learning from the parental figures. The earliest systematic examination of such a pattern has been in narratives told by 3-year-old children who have become 5 year olds, reported in chapter 16, this volume. Sroufe's (1983) method discerned such patterns even earlier through behavioral observations. There is not yet much data on how early the central relationship patterns begin as evaluated through narratives and on the consistency of these patterns through the later years (Kagan, 1996). The expectation, on the basis of Freud's observation 12 (see chapter 21), is that there is considerable consistency of the pattern from early childhood until late in life. So far, the CCRT evidence is based mainly on the narratives told in adulthood that contain the earliest memories. It has been found that these are thematically consistent with narratives told about current events.

The transference concept implies that the early relationship patterns owe their start to the interactions with the parents and other early caregivers and clearly must become generalized to other people. In fact, both Freud's Observation 9, that the pattern is a general one, and the similar CCRT findings emphasize that the pattern is expressed to and probably has generalized to a variety of other people. Rereading the narratives from any of the sessions about a variety of different people reminds one of this fact (see chapter 5).

How the early learning of the pattern comes about deserves more investigation. The pattern appears to be acquired through four modes, the first three of which follow: (a) Repeated experiences in interactions with the parents set up expectations about parental contingent responses (Stern, 1985; Tronick, 1982); (b) the parents directly teach some aspects of the pattern; and (c) the child learns some aspects of the pattern through identification with the parents. In these modes of acquisition of the pattern, motives are the wish to please as well as the wish to avoid displeasing the parents; both wishes are widely prevalent, as emphasized by Weiss, Sampson, and the Mount Zion Psychotherapy Research Group (1986); these wishes are based partly on love and partly on fear and guilt. The three modes of acquisition appear to be built on and interact with a fourth one, the more biological capacities, such as for empathy, as shown by Brothers (1989), and for temperament, as shown by Kagan (1989).

Source Factor 2: Needing to Gratify Certain Pressing Wishes

Each person's central relationship pattern includes the recurrent inclination to gratify certain wishes toward other people and to the self. These wishes have an urgency to be expressed and satisfied, given half a chance, as stressed in George Klein's (1970) observations about "peremptory ideation." The persistence of such wishes is increased because of hoped-for positive responses and fears of negative responses from other people and from the self. The findings about the pervasiveness of each person's central wishes (see chapter 10, this volume) indicate that each person has certain high-frequency wishes expressed in many kinds of relationship interactions. For each of the three patients discussed in chapter 5, the two highest frequency wishes were as follows: For Ms. Smyth the two most urgent and related wishes were to end nonsupportive relationships and to get support and caring; for Mr. Howard the two most pressing wishes were to be close and receive affection; for Ms. Cunningham the two most pervasive wishes were to be in control and to be reassured. For each of these patients, these wishes were both prominent initially and evident at the end of treatment.

Source Factor 3: Repeating of Traumatic Ideas and Scenes

After observing the strong inclination for the repetition of traumatic ideas and scenes, Freud (1920/1955a, 1914/1958e) hit on the descriptive and yet explanatory concept of the "repetition compulsion," the need to repeat, reexperience, and reenact traumatic memories. There are many reliable and recurrent reports of observations that are consistent with this concept, for example, the soldier who has a close call with death and then repeatedly dreams of the event. The concept is applicable to data from a variety of investigators of the repetition of traumatic scenes: Reiser (1984), Tomkins (1987), M. Horowitz (1986), Loevinger (1976), and Marmar and Horowitz (1988).

There are bases for repetition of themes that fit with the concept of the repetition compulsion because they imply an automatic component to the repetition. One of these is repetition based on the presence of a prior schema. Cognitive psychologists, such as Fiske and Dyer (1985), have reported research findings about the carryover of schemas; these findings show that a schema, once learned, sets the stage for interpreting later events in a similar way. The schema gradually becomes more unconscious and generalizes. The person shows some learning about when to apply the schema and when not, but much of the application to later experiences is automatic, as noted in the even broader brain-based schema theory reviewed by Arbiv (1995).

The repetition of themes may also be based on the schema's getting its start through emotion-laden events. Emotion-laden events are especially prone to repetition when events of a similar nature are expected. There may even be an arrangement in the brain such that emotion-laden memory is triggered with a minimum of conscious control. The research of Le Doux, Romanski, and Xagoraris (1989) suggests that a focal point for cognition, the hippocampus, can be involved in the activation of emotions before cognitive processes take place. Their research suggests that there exist alternative nerve pathways leading from the thalamus to the amygdala that deal with emotions without going through the cortex. Their resultant point of view is that because the original schema was emotion-laden, arousal and repetition without conscious control can more readily occur.

Source Factor 4: Repeating in the Service of Mastery

The inclination to repeat ideas or scenes that fit into the pattern could serve as more than the need to repeat the memory of traumatic events (Source Factor 3); the repetition could also be part of an effort to find ways to master traumas (as suggested by Mayman, 1978). Competence in and control over one's life and relationship problems is a vital human need (White, 1952). The conclusion is consistent with the work of Seligman (1980; and Seligman et al., 1984) on explanatory style in response to negative events: A pessimistic style is associated with decreased mastery (helplessness) and consequent depressive symptoms.

The need to repeat in the service of gaining mastery may be related to our findings about the CCRT, specifically, the relative frequency of negative versus positive components of the CCRT, noted in relation to Freud's observation about positive and negative transference patterns (see chapters 4 and 21, this volume). The existence of a higher frequency of negative than positive components of the CCRT could be fueling the person's preoccupation with the need to solve the negative, and therefore upsetting, relationship conflicts. The negative components point to where the source of threat lies, and much of the content of the narratives can be thought of as an effort to rehearse the event and find ways of coping with it. In positive components there is less threat; they tend to portray situations in which one's coping has worked out well. The shift from the negative to the positive components of the CCRT during the course of successful psychotherapy also could be taken to imply that the level of masterful coping has increased (see chapters 4 and 18).

Some evidence for the potency of the need for mastery can also be found from studies of the effects of interpretation on the transference (Observation 15). Interpretations, especially of the negative transference, tend to have the effect of changing the pattern in the direction of greater mastery. From this point of view, the effects of accurate interpretations can be thought of as giving more support to the side of the patient that is attempting to master the traumatic aspects of the CCRT. Freud's (1901–1905/1953a) reflections about the premature interruption of treatment by his patient Dora contained his hypothesis that if he had interpreted Dora's negative transference with its fearful expectation that his behavior toward her would be like Herr K's, she would have been able to continue her therapy with Freud. Without the interpretation, the patient was merely repeating and not mastering her pattern. But through the interpretation, Freud expected that she would have been able to see her fear-inducing misidentification of Freud with Herr K and, through this awareness, would have been able to go beyond repetition to mastery.

In summary, my aim of launching on a wide-ranging search for the origins of the CCRT and of the transference template has brought out four powerful sources and maintainers of the central self–other relationship pattern. These four are the learning of the pattern from the parents, the persistence of wishes to gratify certain impulses, the need to continue to repeat the traumatic parts of the pattern, and the need to master the conflicts within the pattern. A fifth factor must also play a significant role in maintaining the pattern: the person's wish to avoid risking displeasing the parent or parent figure by altering the old pattern because an alteration would hurt the parent or the parent might retaliate. There is much evidence for this factor; for example, Weiss, Sampson, and the Mount Zion Psychotherapy Group (1986) stressed the need to please the parent by maintaining the pattern. Also, a related theory by Benjamin (1994) stressed that development of the symptom can serve to take account of the parent's needs; that is, it is based on consideration of the parent's feelings. A sixth factor may also have a significant role: The primacy of a once-established schema may have a part in maintaining the pattern in its original form (Fiske & Dyer, 1985). And a seventh factor may have a shaping role: a person's birth order (Sulloway, 1996). In fact, all of these sources and maintainers of the schema may collaborate in starting and then maintaining the pervasive expression of the central relationship pattern as measured by the CCRT. In further fact, as this exposition is completed, my appetite to fill out this sketch of source factors continues to grow; already the many factors have begun to form the germinal cell of a personality theory about the nature of the construction of the inner and interpersonal world of each person (Luborsky, 1997).

HOW MUCH DOES THE CCRT CORRESPOND WITH THE TRANSFERENCE?

For the CCRT to fit in the same family as the transference pattern requires that we reexamine the CCRT's validity. *Validity* is the extent that a measure measures what it is supposed to measure. For the CCRT measure, a useful expectation is that the CCRT will be found to be associated with phenomena that are meaningfully related to the concept of a transference-like central relationship pattern following the logic of the nature of clinical inference as presented by Benjamin B. Rubinstein (Holt, 1997). It was stated in chapter 21, this volume, that there is no single definition of transference but rather a variegated assemblage of at least 23 qualities associated with the concept. A measure of validity, therefore, is the number of correspondences between these qualities and the CCRT evidence. The following is a partial listing of some of the already confirmed transference-based meaningful predictions about the CCRT measure:

1. The CCRT should reveal a general pattern across relationships with different types of people. In fact, the CCRT is pervasive across narratives about different other people and it maintains its pervasiveness late in treatment as well (see chapter 10).

2. The CCRT should have a prominent emotional dimension. Such a dimension is strongly represented by the positive and negative dimension. In fact, that dimension is reliably scorable and it changes during treatment in a small, although clinically meaningful, way (see chapter 4).

3. The CCRT, as implied by the results of Number 1 in this list, should show a parallel pattern for the relationship with the therapist and for the relationship with other people: A careful study has shown that this is true (see chapter 11).

4. The CCRT should appear in similar form in different modes of expression. In fact, the pattern is similar in dreams reported in sessions and in waking narratives (see chapter 12).

5. The CCRT should show changes in response to interpretations so that the more fully the therapist focuses on it in the interpretations, the more benefit the patient might receive from the therapy; in fact, my group found just that (see chapter 13).

6. The CCRT should appear not only within psychotherapy but outside of psychotherapy as well. The only study that gives solid evidence for this is one by Barber et al. (1995; see chapter 16), which shows a significant parallel of the CCRT from RAP narratives told before the treatment starts with the CCRT from narratives told in the early sessions.

7. A CCRT-like pattern should appear in young children, and it should show stability over time (see chapter 16).

8. The CCRT should show some results in common with other central relationship pattern measures. In every instance in which this has been examined, patterns were discovered for components that were in common among the different measures (see chapter 20).

9. The CCRT should behave in ways that fit Freud's observations that led him to his concept of the transference template. In fact, when my colleagues and I were able to translate Freud's observations into operational terms in the CCRT, we found the parallel was confirmed; the trend so far confirms a convergence of the majority of Freud's 23 observations about transference with the CCRT evidence—at least for the 18 observations for which a translation seemed possible (see chapter 21).

These confirmations should lead to more serious attention in psychology, psychiatry, and social work to Freud's concept of the transference pattern. But it is not clear to what degree this will happen. The rejection and acceptance of psychoanalytic concepts such as transference have a curious history. This history may have parallels with the response to other revolutionary concepts like Darwin's theory of evolution. As the embryologist Karl Ernst von Baer noted (Gould, 1977), every major theory that wins acceptance goes through three stages: It is first condemned as untrue; it is then branded as against religion; and ultimately it is dogmatically embraced. The history of acceptance of the concept of transference approximately fits these stages. It did go through a stage in which it was considered untrue, and some people have remained in that stage, caught up in the current fashion of rejection of dynamic concepts. There were some people who considered it contrary to religion; they are not a very active opposition now. Finally, for some psychoanalytic practitioners it has become dogma; for some of these people, it would even be considered a violation of the concept to construct a measurement method for it. But in time the evidence of the CCRT's validity reported in this book should garner even greater recognition of the usefulness of the concept and even greater acceptance of the discoveries achieved through its operational measurement. More and more clinicians will then use the CCRT in treating their patients, and more and more studies will examine it.

The inclination to accept the findings of the research, at least for the dynamic audience, should be fortified by the strategy of our research style. The essential attribute of the style is its reliance on data from psychoanalytic and psychotherapy sessions for examining Freud's basic observations about the transference pattern. This examination of sessions through operational measures contrasts with the style of much past research on Freud's theories, especially that which relies on analogue or experimental recreations of the phenomena suggested by Freudian theory (as reviewed by Fisher & Greenberg, 1977, 1996); the obvious weakness of such analogues is feebleness in showing that they in fact capture the intended phenomena. The obvious strength of relying on psychoanalytic and psychotherapy sessions is the appropriateness of the database: It is the milieu from which the basic clinical concepts such as transference were generated, as stressed by Rapaport (1960), Schlesinger (1974), Holzman (1985), and Eagle and Wolitsky (1989).

CONCLUSIONS

- The essential narrative in this book is about the successful translation of a key clinical concept into a key clinical–quantitative operational measure of the clinical concept. The concept is that there is a schema for the central relationship pattern that can be found in a series of narratives told by persons about themselves in relation to other people or in relation to themselves.

- The Core Conflictual Relationship Theme is the reliable measure of this schema; the measure can be reliably scored in a set of narratives from each person.
- About a dozen areas for additional research that will continue the maturation of the CCRT method are listed in this chapter and chapter 21.
- A wealth of validity data implies that the Core Conflictual Relationship Theme has much in common with Freud's concept of the transference template, as reported in this chapter and in chapter 21.
- I have taken a flier into speculation about the factors that contribute to the origin and maintenance of the CCRT: (a) the learning of the pattern from parental figures, (b) the push of persistent wishes, (c) the need for repetition of the traumatic parts of the pattern, and (d) the need to master conflicts. Three other factors also have a role: (e) the fear of displeasing and the wish to please parental figures, (f) the confinement by the rut of the preestablished schema, and (g) the influence of birth order.
- The CCRT method has a host of effective clinical applications in the conduct of psychotherapy and in diagnosis.
- Like all "better mouse trap" discoveries, the CCRT, as discussed in this much revised volume, has both contributed to our knowledge about the central relationship pattern and raised an array of new questions, some of which will soon be answered through the more than 150 ongoing CCRT studies that have spread worldwide in the last 7 years.

REFERENCES

Ainsworth, M., Blehar, M., Waters, E., & Wall, S. (1978). *Patterns of attachment.* Hillsdale, NJ: Erlbaum.

Aldenderfer, M. S., & Blashfield, R. K. (1984). *Cluster analysis.* Beverly Hills, CA: Sage.

American Psychiatric Association. (1980). *Diagnostic and statistical manual of mental disorders* (3rd ed.). Washington, DC: Author.

American Psychiatric Association. (1990). *Diagnostic and statistical manual of mental disorders* (4th ed.). Washington, DC: Author.

Apfelbaum, B. (1958). *Dimensions of transference in psychotherapy.* Berkeley: University of California Press.

Arbiv, M. (1995). Schema theory. In M. Arbiv (Ed.), *Brain theory and neural networks* (pp. 830–834). Cambridge, MA: MIT Press.

Arlow, J. (1961). Ego psychology in the study of mythology. *Journal of the American Psychoanalytic Association, 9,* 371–393.

Arlow, J. (1969a). Fantasy, memory, and reality testing. *Psychoanalytic Quarterly, 38,* 28–51.

Arlow, J. (1969b). Unconscious fantasy and disturbances of conscious experience. *Psychoanalytic Quarterly, 38,* 1–27.

Arlow, J., & Brenner, C. (1964). *Psychoanalytic concepts and the structural theory.* Madison, CT: International Universities Press.

Aron, B. (1949). *A manual for analyses of the Thematic Apperception Test.* Berkeley, CA: Berg.

Auerbach, A., & Childress, A. (1988). Diagnosis in assessment for psychotherapy, *Current Opinion in Psychiatry, 1,* 293–298.

Auerbach, A., & Luborsky, L. (1968). Accuracy of judgments of psychotherapy and the nature of the "good hour." In J. Shlien, H. F. Hunt, J. P. Matarazzo, & C. Savage (Eds.), *Research in psychotherapy* (Vol. 3, pp. 155–168). Washington, DC: American Psychological Association.

Baguet, J., Gerin, P., Sali, M., & Marie-Cardine, M. (1984). Evolution des themes transferentials individuels dans une psychotherapie de groupe [Evolution of individual transferential themes in a psychotherapy group]. *Psychotherapies, 1–2,* 43–49.

Barber, J. P. (1989). *Analyzing CCRT sequences for its most frequent wishes.* Center for Psychotherapy Research, University of Pennsylvania. Unpublished manuscript.

Barber, J. P. (1993). *The Central Relationship Pattern Questionnaire.* Unpublished Version 4.5. University of Pennsylvania Medical School, Philadelphia.

Barber, J. P., & Crits-Christoph, P. (1993). Advances in measures of psychodynamic formulations. *Journal of Consulting and Clinical Psychology, 61,* 574–585.

Barber, J. P., Crits-Christoph, P., & Luborsky, L. (1990). A guide to the standard categories and their classification. In L. Luborsky & P. Crits-Christoph (Eds.), *Understanding transference: The CCRT method* (pp. 37–50). New York: Basic Books.

Barber, J. P., Crits-Christoph, P., & Luborsky, L. (1996). Effects of therapist adherence and competence on patient outcome in brief dynamic therapy. *Journal of Consulting and Clinical Psychology, 64,* 619–622.

Barber, J. P., Luborsky, L., Crits-Christoph, P., & Diguer, L. (1995). A comparison of core conflictual relationship themes before psychotherapy and during early sessions. *Journal of Consulting and Clinical Psychology, 63,* 145–148.

Bargh, J. A., Chaiken, S., Govender, R., & Felicia, P. (1992). The generality of the automatic attitude activation effect. *Journal of Personality and Social Psychology, 62,* 893–912.

Battle, C., Imber, S., Hoehn-Saric, R., Stone, A. R., Nash, C., & Frank, J. D. (1966). Target complaints as criteria of improvement. *American Journal of Psychotherapy, 20,* 184–192.

Beck, A. T. (1967). *Depression: Clinical, experimental, and theoretical aspects.* New York: Hober.

Beck, A. T. (1970). *Depression: Clinical, experimental, and theoretical aspects* (Rev. ed.). New York: Hober.

Beck, A. T. (1971). Cognitive patterns in dreams and daydreams. In J. Masserman (Ed.), *Science and psychoanalysis: Vol. 19. Dream dynamics.* New York: Grune & Stratton.

Beck, A. T. (1989). Cognitive therapy for depression and panic disorder. *Western Journal of Medicine, 151,* 9–89.

Beebe, B., & Lachmann, F. (1988). Mother–infant mutual influence and precursors of psychic structure. In A. Goldberg (Ed.), *Frontiers of self-psychology: Progress in self-psychology* (Vol. 3, pp. 3–26). Hillsdale, NJ: Analytic Press.

Bellak, L. (1954). *The Thematic Apperception Test and the Children's Apperception Test in clinical use.* New York: Grune and Stratton.

Benjamin, L. S. (1974). Structural analysis of social behavior. *Psychological Review, 81,* 392–425.

Benjamin, L. S. (1977). Structural analysis of a family in therapy. *Journal of Consulting and Clinical Psychology, 45,* 391–406.

Benjamin, L. S. (1979). Use of structural analysis of social behavior (SASB) and Markov chains to study dynamic interactions. *Journal of Abnormal Psychology, 88,* 303–319.

Benjamin, L. S. (1982). Use of structural analysis of social behavior (SASB) to guide intervention in psychotherapy. In D. Kiesler & J. Anchin (Eds.), *Handbook of interpersonal psychotherapy.* New York: Pergamon Press.

Benjamin, L. S. (1986a). Adding social and intrapsychic descriptors to Axis I of DSM-III. In T. Millon & G. Klerman (Eds.), *Contemporary directions in psychopathology* (pp. 599–638). New York: Guilford Press.

Benjamin, L. S. (1986b). Operational definition and measure of dynamics shown in the stream of free associations. *Psychiatry, 49,* 104–129.

Benjamin, L. S. (1994). SASB: A bridge between personality theory and clinical psychology. *Psychological Inquiry, 5,* 273–316.

Bernal, G., & Baker, J. (1979). Toward a metacommunicational framework of couple interactions. *Family Process, 18,* 293–302.

Bibring, E. (1954). Psychoanalysis and the dynamic psychotherapies. *Journal of the American Psychoanalytic Association, 2,* 745–770.

Block, J. (1971). *Lives through time.* Berkeley, CA: Bancroft Books.

Block, J. (1977). Advancing the psychology of personality: Paradigmatic shift for improving the quality of research. In D. Magnussen & N. S. Endler (Eds.), *Personality at the crossroads* (pp. 37–63). New York: Wiley.

Blos, P. (1941). *The adolescent personality: A study of individual behavior for the commission on secondary school curriculum.* New York: Appleton-Century-Crofts.

Bonanno, G., & Singer, J. (1990). Repressive personality style: Theoretical and methodological implications for health and pathology (pp. 435–470). In J. Singer (Ed.), *Repression and dissociation: Defense mechanisms and personality styles.* Chicago: University of Chicago Press.

Bond, J., Hansell, J., & Shevrin, H. (1987). Locating a reference paradigm in psychotherapy transcripts: Reliability of relationship episode location in the Core Conflictual Relationship Theme (CCRT) method. *Psychotherapy, 24,* 736–749.

Bond, J., & Shevrin, H. (1986a). *The Clinical Evaluation Team method.* Unpublished manuscript.

Bond, J., & Shevrin, H. (1986b). *Similarities and differences between two methods of formulating a patient's psychodynamically relevant schemata.* Unpublished manuscript, University of Michigan, Ann Arbor.

Book, H. (in press). *How to practice brief psychodynamic psychotherapy: The CCRT method.* Washington, DC: American Psychological Association.

Bowlby, J. (1969). *Attachment and loss: Vol. 1. Attachment.* New York: Basic Books.

Bowlby, J. (1973). *Attachment and loss: Vol. 2. Separation.* New York: Basic Books.

Bretherton, I. (1995). A communication perspective on attachment relationships and internal working models. *Monographs of the Society for Research in Child Development, 60*(2–3), 310–329.

Bretherton, I., Prentiss, C., & Ridgeway, D. (1990). Family relationships as represented in a story-completion task at thirty-seven and fifty-four months of age. In J. Bretherton & M. W. Watson (Eds.), *Children's perspective on the family: New directions for child development* (Vol. 48, pp. 85–105). San Francisco: Jossey-Bass.

Bretherton, I., Ridgeway, D., & Cassidy, J. (1990). Assessing internal working models of the attachment relationship—An attachment story completion task for 3-year-olds. In M. Greenberg, D. Cichetti, & E. M. Cummings (Eds.), *Attachment during the pre-school years* (pp. 273–308). Chicago: University of Chicago Press.

Brothers, L. (1989). A biological perspective on empathy. *American Journal of Psychiatry, 146,* 10–19.

Bruner, J. (1987). *Actual minds, possible worlds.* Cambridge, MA: Harvard University Press.

Bucci, W. (1985). Dual coding: A cognitive model for psychoanalytic research. *Journal of the American Psychoanalytic Association, 33,* 571–607.

Buchsbaum, H., & Emde, R. (1990). Play narratives in 36-month-old children: The portrayal of early moral development and family relationships. In A. J. Solnit, P. Newbauer, S. Abrams, & A. S. Dowling (Eds.), *The psychoanalytic study of the child* (Vol. 45, pp. 129–155) New Haven, CT: Yale University Press.

Carlson, R. (1981). Studies in script theory: I. Adult analogs of a childhood nuclear scene. *Journal of Personality and Social Psychology, 40,* 501–510.

Carlson, R. (1986). After analysis: A study of transference dreams following treatment. *Journal of Consulting and Clinical Psychology, 54,* 246–252.

Caspar, F. (1989). *Einfuhrung in die Plananalyse* [Introduction to plan analysis]. Berne, Switzerland: Huber.

Caspar, F. (1995). *Plan analysis: Toward optimizing psychotherapy.* Seattle, WA: Hogrefe & Huber.

Caston, J. (1977). Manual on how to diagnose the plan. In J. Weiss, H. Sampson, J. Caston, & G. Silberschatz (Eds.), *Research on the psychoanalytic process: Vol. 1. A comparison of two theories about analytic neutrality* (pp. 15–21). San Francisco: Psychotherapy Research Group, Department of Psychiatry, Mount Zion Hospital and Medical Center.

Caston, J. (1986). The reliability of the diagnosis of the patient's unconscious plan. In J. Weiss, H. Sampson, & the Mount Zion Psychotherapy Research Group (Eds.), *The psychoanalytic process: Theory, clinical observations, and empirical research* (pp. 241–255). New York: Guilford Press.

Chance, E. (1952). The study of transference in group therapy. *International Journal of Group Therapy, 2,* 40–53.

Chapman, S. (1980). *Story and discourse.* Ithaca, NY: Cornell University Press.

Cierpka, M., Zander, B., Krannich, S., Reich, G., Ratzke, K., Hombburg, H., Staats, H., & Seide, L. (1992, June). *Differences in conflictual relationship themes of male and female students.* Paper presented at the annual meeting of the Society for Psychotherapy Research, Berkeley, CA.

Cohen, J. (1960). A coefficient of agreement for nominal scales. *Educational and Psychological Measurement, 20,* 37–46.

Cohen, J. (1968). Weighted kappa: Nominal scale agreement with provision for scaled disagreement on partial credit. *Psychological Bulletin, 70,* 213–220.

Cohen, J., & Cohen, P. (1975). *Applied multiple regression/correlational analysis for the behavioral sciences.* Hillsdale, NJ: Erlbaum.

Collins, W., & Messer, S. (1988, June). *Transporting the Plan Diagnosis method to a different setting: Reliability, stability, and adaptability.* Paper presented at the annual conference of the Society for Psychotherapy Research, Santa Fe, NM.

Connolly, M. B., Crits-Christoph, P., Demorest, A., Azarian, K., Muenz, L., & Chittams, J. (1996). The varieties of transference patterns in psychotherapy. *Journal of Consulting and Clinical Psychology, 64,* 1213–1221.

Crisp, A. (1964a). An attempt to measure an aspect of transference. *British Journal of Medical Psychology, 37,* 17–30.

Crisp, A. (1964b). Development and application of a measure of transference. *Journal of Psychosomatic Research, 8,* 327–335.

Crisp, A. (1996). Transference symptom emergence and social repercussion in behavior therapy: A study of 54 treated patients. *British Journal of Medical Psychology, 39,* 179–196.

Crits-Christoph, P. (1986). *Assessing conscious and unconscious aspects of relationship themes from self-report and naturalistic data.* Paper presented at the MacArthur Workshop on Person Schemata, Palo Alto, CA.

Crits-Christoph, P. (1987). *Development of a set of rating scales to assess CCRT dimensions of wishes, responses from other and responses of self.* Unpublished manuscript.

Crits-Christoph, P., Barber, J. P., & Kurcias, J. S. (1993). The accuracy of therapists' interpretations and the development of the therapeutic alliance. *Psychotherapy Research, 3,* 25–35.

Crits-Christoph, P., Barber, J. P., Miller, N., & Beebe, K. (1993). Evaluating insight. In N. Miller, L. Luborsky, J. P. Barber, & J. Docherty (Eds.), *Psychodynamic treatment research: A handbook for clinical practice* (pp. 407–422). New York: Basic Books.

Crits-Christoph, P., Cooper, A., & Luborsky, L. (1988). The accuracy of therapists' interpretations and the outcome of dynamic psychotherapy. *Journal of Consulting and Clinical Psychology, 56,* 490–495.

Crits-Christoph, P., & Demorest, A. (1988). *List of standard categories (Edition 2).* Unpublished manuscript, University Pennsylvania School of Medicine, Philadelphia.

Crits-Christoph, P., & Demorest, A. (1991). Quantitative assessment of relationship theme components. In M. Horowitz (Ed.), *Person schemas and maladaptive interpersonal behavior.* Chicago: University of Chicago Press.

Crits-Christoph, P., Demorest, A., & Connolly, M. B. (1990). Quantitative assessment of interpersonal themes over the course of a psychotherapy. *Psychotherapy, 27,* 513–521.

Crits-Christoph, P., Demorest, A., Muenz, L., & Baranackie, K. (1994). Consistency of interpersonal themes for patients in psychotherapy. *Journal of Personality, 62,* 499–526.

Crits-Christoph, P., & Luborsky, L. (1990). Changes in CCRT pervasiveness during psychotherapy. In L. Luborsky & P. Crits-Christoph (Eds.), *Understanding transference: The CCRT method* (pp. 133–146). New York: Basic Books.

Crits-Christoph, P., Luborsky, L., Dahl, L., Popp, C., Mellon, J., & Mark, D. (1988). Clinicians can agree in assessing relationship patterns in psychotherapy: The Core Conflictual Relationship Theme Method. *Archives of General Psychiatry, 45,* 1001–1004.

Crits-Christoph, P., Luborsky, L., Popp, C., Mellon, J., & Mark, D. (1990). The reliability of choice of narratives and of the CCRT measure. In L. Luborsky & P. Crits-Christoph (Eds.), *Understanding tranference: The CCRT method* (pp. 93–101). New York: Basic Books.

Curtis, H. (1983, May). *Toward a metapsychology of transference.* Paper presented to the annual meeting of the American Psychoanalytic Association, New York.

Curtis, J. T., & Silberschatz, G. (1989). *The Plan Formulation method: A reliable procedure for case formulation.* Manuscript submitted for publication.

Curtis, J. T., Silberschatz, G., Sampson, H., Weiss, J., & Rosenberg, S. E. (1988). Developing reliable psychodynamic case formulations: An illustration of the Plan Diagnosis method. *Psychotherapy, 25,* 256–265.

Dahl, H. (1978). A new psychoanalytic model of motivation: Emotions as appetites and messages. *Psychoanalysis and Contemporary Thought, 1,* 373–408.

Dahl, H. (1988). Frames of mind. In H. Dahl, H. Kächele, & H. Thomae (Eds.), *Psychoanalytic process research strategies* (pp. 51–66). New York: Springer-Verlag.

Dahl, H., Kächele, H., & Thomae, H. (Eds.). (1988). *Psychoanalytic process research strategies.* New York: Springer-Verlag.

Dahl, H., & Teller, V. (1984). The characteristics, identification, and application of frames. *Psychotherapy Research, 4,* 253–276.

Dahl, H., & Teller, V. (1993). Characteristics and identification of frames. In N. Miller, L. Luborsky, & J. Docherty (Eds.), *Doing research on psychodynamic therapy.* New York: Basic Books.

Dahlbender, R. (1992, June). *Intra- and inter-subjectivity in RAP interviews of young women.* Paper given at the annual meeting of the Society for Psychotherapy Research, Berkeley, CA.

Dahlbender, R., Albani, C., Pokorny, D., & Kächele, H. (in press). The central relationship pattern (CRP): A structural version of the CCRT. *Psychotherapy Research.*

Dahlbender, R., Kurth, R., Stubner, S., Kalmykova, K., & Porkorny, D. (in press). Das zentrale beziehungskonflikt thema in der selbst-beurteilung: Der zentrale Beziehungs-muster (ZBM-) Fragebogen [The central relationship conflict theme in self-assessment: The Central Relationship Pattern Questionnaire]. *Gruppenpsychotherapie und Gruppendynamik.*

Dahlbender, R., Volkert, M., Torres, L., Pokorny, D., Frevert, G., Reichert, S., & Kächele, H. (1992). *Intra- and inter-subjectivity in Relationship Anecdotes Paradigm (RAP) interviews.* Paper presented at the annual meeting of the Society for Psychotherapy Research, Berkeley, CA.

Davanloo, H. (1978). *Basic principles and techniques in short-term dynamic psychotherapy.* New York: Spectrum.

Davanloo, H. (1980). A method of short-term dynamic psychotherapy. In H. Davanloo (Ed.), *Short-term dynamic psychotherapy*. New York: Jason Aronson.

Davies, J. (1989). *The development of emotional and interpersonal structures in three-year-old children*. Unpublished doctoral dissertation, Derner Institute for Advanced Psychological Studies, Adelphi University, Garden City, NJ.

Demorest, A. P., & Alexander, I. E. (1992). Affective scripts as organizers of personal experience. *Journal of Personality, 60*, 645–663.

Demorest, A. P., & Crit-Christoph, P. (1989). *A quantitative comparison of interpersonal themes in fantasy versus reality*. Paper presented at the meeting of the Society for Psychotherapy Research, Toronto, Canada.

Demorest, A. P., Crits-Christoph, P., Hatch, M., & Luborsky, L. (1997). *A comparison of interpersonal scripts in clinically depressed versus non-depressed individuals*. Manuscript submitted for publication.

Demorest, A. P., & Siegel, P. F. (1996). Personal influences on professional work: An empirical case study of B. F. Skinner. *Journal of Personality, 64*, 243–261.

Demos, V. (Ed.). (1995). *Exploring affect*. Cambridge, England: Cambridge University Press.

Dengler, D. (1990). *Anwendung des zentralen beziehungskonfliktsthemas auf narrative von dreijahrigen und suche nach zusammenhängen mit fähigheit zur problemslösung* [Use of central relationship themes from narratives of 3-year-olds and a search for relationship with ability in problem solving]. Dissertation zu Erlangung des Doktorgrades der Medizin der Facultät für Klinische Medizin der Universität Ulm.

Derogatis, L. R., Lipman, R. S., Covi, L., Rickels, K., & Uhlenhuth, E. H. (1970). Dimensions of outpatient neurotic pathology: Comparison of a clinical vs. an empirical assessment. *Journal of Consulting and Clinical Psychology, 34*, 164–171.

Derrida, J. (1977). *Of grammatology*. Baltimore: Johns Hopkins University Press.

DeWitt, K. N., Kaltreider, N., Weiss, D. S., & Horowitz, M. J. (1983). Judging change in psychotherapy: Reliability of clinical formulations. *Archives of General Psychiatry, 40*, 1121–1128.

Diguer, L., Barber, J. P., & Luborsky, L. (1993). Three concomitants: Personality disorder, psychiatric severity, and outcome of dynamic psychotherapy of major depression. *American Journal of Psychiatry, 150*, 1246–1248.

Eagle, M. N. (1983). Recent developments in psychoanalysis. In R. S. Cohen & L. Laudan (Eds.), *Physics, philosophy, and psychoanalysis* (pp. 31–56). Dordrecht, The Netherlands: D. Reidel.

Eagle, M. N., & Wolitsky, D. (1989). The idea of progress in psychoanalysis. *Psychoanalysis and Contemporary Thought, 12*, 27–72.

Eckert, R., Luborsky, L., Barber, J. P., & Crits-Christoph, P. (1990). The CCRT in patients with major depression. In L. Luborsky & P. Crits-Christoph (Eds.), *Understanding transference: The CCRT method* (pp. 222–234). New York: Basic Books.

Edelson, M. (1984). *Hypothesis and evidence in psychoanalysis*. Chicago: University of Chicago Press.

Edelson, M. (1988). *Psychoanalysis: A theory in crisis*. Chicago: University of Chicago Press.

Eells, T. D., Horowitz, M., Singer, J., Salovey, P., Daigle, D., & Turvey, C. (1995). The role relationship models method: A comparison of independently derived case formulations. *Psychotherapy Research, 5*, 161–175.

Ekstein, R. (1956). Psychoanalytic techniques. In D. Brower & L. E. Abt (Eds.), *Progress in clinical psychology* (Vol. 2, pp. 79–99). New York: Grune & Stratton.

Endicott, J., & Spitzer, R. L. (1978). A diagnostic interview: The Schedule for Affective Disorders and Schizophrenia. *Archives of General Psychiatry, 35*, 837–844.

Engel, G., Jr., & Reichsman, F. (1956). Spontaneous and experimentally induced depression in an infant with gastric fistula: A contribution to the problem of depression. *Journal of the American Psychoanalytic Association, 4*, 428–452.

Erikson, E. H. (1959). Identity and the life cycle. *Psychological Issues* (Monograph No. 1).

Fiedler, F., & Senior, K. (1952). An exploratory study of unconscious feeling reactions in fifteen patient–therapist pairs. *Journal of Abnormal and Social Psychology, 47*, 446–453.

Fisher, S., & Greenberg, R. (1977). *The scientific credibility of Freud's theories and therapy*. New York: Basic Books.

Fisher, S., & Greenberg, R. (1996). *Freud scientifically reappraised: Testing the theories and the therapy*. New York: Wiley.

Fiske, S., & Dyer, L. (1985). Structure and development of social schemata: Evidence for positive and negative transfer effects. *Journal of Personality and Social Psychology, 48*, 839–852.

Frank, J. (1979). Present status of outcome studies. *Journal of Consulting and Clinical Psychology, 47*, 310–316.

French, T., & Wheeler, D. R. (1963). Hope and repudiation of hope in psychoanalytic therapy. *International Journal of Psychoanalysis, 44*, 304–316.

Freud, S. (1953a). Fragment of an analysis of a case of hysteria. In J. Strachey (Ed. and Trans.), *The standard edition of the complete psychological works of Sigmund Freud* (Vol. 7, pp. 15–122). London: Hogarth Press. (Original work published 1901–1905)

Freud, S. (1953b). The interpretation of dreams. In J. Strachey (Ed. and Trans.), *The standard edition of the complete psychological works of Sigmund Freud* (Vols. 4 and 5). London: Hogarth Press. (Original work published 1900)

Freud, S. (1955a). Beyond the pleasure principle. In J. Strachey (Ed. and Trans.), *The standard edition of the complete psychological works of S. Freud* (Vol. 18, pp. 7–64). London: Hogarth Press. (Original work published 1920)

Freud, S. (1955b). Psychotherapy of hysteria. In J. Breuer & S. Freud, *Studies on hysteria. In J. Strachey (Ed. and Trans.), *The standard edition of the complete psychological works of Sigmund Freud* (Vol. 2, pp. 255–305). London: Hogarth Press. (Original work published 1895)

Freud, S. (1955c). Studies on hysteria. In J. Strachey (Ed. and Trans.), *The standard edition of the complete psychological works of Sigmund Freud* (Vol. 2., pp. 3–305). London: Hogarth Press. (Original work published 1893–1895)

Freud, S. (1958a). The dynamics of the transference. In J. Strachey (Ed. and Trans.), *The standard edition of the complete psychological works of Sigmund Freud* (Vol. 12, pp. 99–108). London: Hogarth Press. (Original work published 1912)

Freud, S. (1958b). Observations on transference-love. In J. Strachey (Ed. and Trans.), *The standard edition of the complete psychological works of Sigmund Freud* (Vol. 16, pp. 431–447). London: Hogarth Press. (Original work published 1915)

Freud, S. (1958c). On beginning the treatment (further recommendations on the technique of psycho-analysis). In J. Strachey (Ed. and Trans.), *The standard edition of the complete psychological works of Sigmund Freud* (Vol. 12, pp. 121–144). London: Hogarth Press. (Original work published 1913)

Freud, S. (1958d). Recommendations to physicians practicing psychoanalysis. In J. Strachey (Ed. and Trans.), *The standard edition of the complete psychological works of Sigmund Freud* (Vol. 12, pp. 111–120). London: Hogarth Press. (Original work published 1912)

Freud, S. (1958e). Remembering, repeating and working through. In J. Strachey (Ed. and Trans.), *The standard edition of the complete psychological works of Sigmund Freud* (Vol. 12, 145–156). London: Hogarth Press. (Original work published 1914)

Freud, S. (1960). Jokes and their relation to the unconscious. In J. Strachey (Ed. and Trans.), *The standard edition of the complete psychological works of Sigmund Freud* (Vol. 8, pp. 9–258). London: Hogarth Press. (Original work published 1905)

Freud, S. (1964). Analyses terminable and interminable. In J. Strachey (Ed. and Trans.), *The standard edition of the complete psychological works of Sigmund Freud* (Vol. 23, pp. 216–253). London: Hogarth Press. (Original work published 1937)

Fried, D. (1989). *The benefits of the CCRT for training in psychotherapy: A survey of practitioners.* Unpublished manuscript.

Fried, D., Crits-Christoph, P., & Luborsky, L. (1990). The parallel of narratives about the therapist with the CCRT for other people. In L. Luborsky & P. Crits-Christoph, *Understanding transference: The CCRT method* (pp. 147–157). New York: Basic Books.

Fried, D., Luborsky, L., & Crits-Christoph, P. (1992). The first empirical demonstration of transference in psychotherapy. *Journal of Nervous and Mental Disease, 180,* 326–331.

Friedman, S. H., & Luborsky, L. (1996). Enhancing agreement of dynamic formulations: Comparison before versus after training in the Core Conflictual Relationship Theme (CCRT) method. Unpublished manuscript.

Gabbard, G., Horowitz, L., Frieswyk, S., Allen, J., Colson, M. D., Newsome, G., & Coyne, J. L. (1988). The effect of therapist interventions on the therapeutic alliance with borderline patients. *Journal of the American Psychoanalytic Association, 36,* 697–727.

Gedo, J. (1979). Theories of object relations: A metapsychological assessment. *Journal of the American Psychoanalytic Association, 27,* 361–373.

Gedo, P. (1993). A micro analytic method for tracing transference references: Gill and Hoffman's PERT coding scheme and its elaborations. In N. Miller, L. Luborsky, & J. Docherty (Eds.), *Doing research on psychodynamic therapy.* New York: Basic Books.

George, C., Kaplan, N., & Main, M. (1985). *The attachment interview for adults.* Unpublished manuscript, University of California, Berkeley.

Ghannam, J. (1987, June). *Representation of self and other from clinical transcripts: A quantitative approach for characterizing schemas.* Paper presented at the meeting of the Society for Psychotherapy Research, Ulm, West Germany.

Gill, M. (1982). The analysis of transference: Vol. 1, Theory and technique. *Psychological Issues* (Monograph No. 54).

Gill, M., & Hoffman, I. (1982a). Analysis of transference: Studies of nine audiorecorded psychoanalysis sessions. *Psychological Issues* (Monograph No. 54).

Gill, M., & Hoffman, I. (1982b). A method for studying the analysis of aspects of the patient's experience of the relationship in psychoanalysis and psychotherapy. *Journal of the American Psychoanalytic Association, 30,* 137–167.

Gilligan, C. (1982). *In a different voice: Psychological theory and women's development.* Cambridge, MA. Harvard University Press.

Goldhirsh, M. (1961). Manifest content of dreams of convicted sex offenders. *Journal of Abnormal and Social Psychology, 63,* 643–645.

Gottschalk, L. A. (1985). *How to understand and analyze your own dreams.* Corona Del Mar, CA: Art Reproductions Press.

Gottschalk, L. A., & Gleser, G. (1969). *The measurement of psychological states through the content analysis of verbal behavior.* Berkeley: University of California Press.

Gottschalk, L. A., Winget, C. N., & Gleser, G. C. (1969). *Manual instructions for using the Gottschalk-Gleser Content Analysis Scale: Anxiety, hostility, and social alienation—Personal disorganization.* Los Angeles: University of California Press.

Gould, S. J. (1977). *Ever since Darwin: Reflections in natural history.* New York: Norton.

Graff, H., & Luborsky, L. (1977). Long-term trends in transference and resistance: A quantitative analytic method applied to four psychoanalyses. *Journal of the American Psychoanalytic Association, 25,* 471–490.

Grawe, K., & Caspar, F. (1984). Die Plan Analyse als Konzept und Instrument für die Psychotherapie Forschung [Plan analysis as a concept and instrument for psychoanalytic research]. In U. Bauman (Ed.), *Psychotherapie: Makro-und mikro Prespectiven* (pp. 177–197). Göttingen, Germany: Hogrefe.

Grawe, K., Caspar, F., & Ambühl, H. (1990). Die Berner therapie-vergleichs studie [The Berner comparisons of therapies study]. *Zeitschrift für Klinische Psychologie, 19,* 362–376.

Greenacre, P. (1954). The role of transference. *Journal of the American Psychoanalytic Association, 2,* 671–684.

Greenberg, R. (1987). On the importance of wearing two hats: Dream researcher and psychoanalyst. *Journal of the American Academy of Psychoanalysis, 15,* 321–330.

Greenberg, R., & Pearlman, C. (1975). A psychoanalytic continuum: The source and function of dreams. *International Review of Psychoanalysis, 2,* 441–448.

Grenyer, B. F. (1994). *Mastery Scale I: A research and scoring manual.* Wollongong, Australia: University of Woolongong.

Grenyer, B. F., & Luborsky, L. (1996). Dynamic change in psychotherapy: Mastery of interpersonal conflicts. *Journal of Consulting and Clinical Psychology, 64,* 411–416.

Grunbaum, A. (1984). *The foundations of psychoanalysis: A philosophical critique.* Berkeley: University of California Press.

Grunbaum, A. (1986). Précis of *The Foundations of Psychoanalysis: A Philosophical Critique. Behavioral and Brain Sciences, 9,* 217–228.

Guitar-Amsterdamer, H., Stahli, R., Schneider, H., & Berger, E. (1988). Können komponenten konfliktiver beziehungsmuster in einem psychotherapeutischen gesprach reliabel identiziert werden? [Can components of conflictual relationships in a psychotherapy session be reliably identifed?]. In L. Luborsky & H. Kächele (Eds.), *Der Zentrale Beziehungskonflict—Ein Arbeitsbuch [The CCRT —A workbook]* (pp. 60–78). Ulm, Germany: PSZ Publications.

Gustafson, J. (1986). *The complex secret of brief psychotherapy.* New York: Norton.

Hall, C. S., & Van de Castle, R. L. (1966). *The content analysis of dreams.* New York: Meredith.

Heider, F. (1958). *The psychology of interpersonal relations.* New York: Wiley.

Henry, W. P., Schacht, T. E., & Strupp, H. H. (1986). Structural analysis of social behavior: Application to a study of interpersonal process in differential psychotherapeutic outcome. *Journal of Consulting and Clinical Psychology, 54,* 27–31.

Hobson, J. A., & Stickgold, R. (1994). Dreaming: A neurocognitive approach. *Consciousness and Cognition, 3,* 1–15.

Hoffman, I. The patient as interpreter of the analyst's experience. *Contemporary Psychoanalysis, 19,* 389–422.

Hoffman, I., & Gill, M. (1988a). Critical reflections on a coding scheme. *International Journal of Psychoanalysis, 69,* 55–64.

Hoffman, I., & Gill, M. (1988b). A scheme for coding the patient's experience of the relationship with the therapist (PERT): Some applications, extensions, and comparisons. In H. Dahl, H. Kächele, & H. Thomae (Eds.), *Psychoanalytic process research strategies*. New York: Springer-Verlag.

Holt, R. R. (1965). Freud's cognitive style. *American Imago, 22*, 163–179.

Holt, R. R. (1967). Diagnostic testing: Present situation and future prospects. *Journal of Nervous and Mental Disease, 144*, 444–465.

Holt, R. R. (1978). *Methods in clinical psychology: Vol. 2. Prediction and research*. New York: Plenum Press.

Holt, R. R. (1989). *Freud reappraised*. New York: Guilford Press.

Holt, R. R. (Ed.). (1997). *Psychoanalysis and the philosophy of science—Collected papers of Benjamin B. Rubinstein*. New York: Guilford Press.

Holzman, P. (1985). Psychoanalysis: Is the therapy destroying the science? *Journal of the American Psychoanalytic Association, 33*, 725–770.

Horowitz, L. M., Rosenberg, S. E., Baer, B. A., Ureno, G., & Villasenor, V. S. (1988). Inventory of interpersonal problems: Psychometric properties and clinical applications. *Journal of Consulting and Clinical Psychology, 56*, 885–892.

Horowitz, L. M., Rosenberg, S., Ureno, G., Kalehzan, B., & O'Halloran, P. (1989). Psychodynamic formulation: Consensual Response Method and interpersonal problems. *Journal of Consulting and Clinical Psychology, 57*, 599–606.

Horowitz, L. M., & Vitkus, J. (1986). The interpersonal basis of psychiatric symptoms. *Clinical Psychology Review, 6*, 443–469.

Horowitz, L. M., Weckler, D., & Doren, R. (1983). Interpersonal problems and symptoms: A cognitive approach. In P. C. Kendall (Ed.), *Advances in cognitive–behavioral research and therapy* (Vol. 2, pp. 82–127). New York: Academic Press.

Horowitz, M. J. (1979). *States of mind: Analysis of change in psychotherapy*. New York: Plenum Press.

Horowitz, M. J. (1986). *Stress response syndromes*. Northvale, NJ: Jason Aronson.

Horowitz, M. J. (1987). *States of mind: Analysis of change in psychotherapy* (2nd ed.). New York: Plenum Press.

Horowitz, M. J. (1989). Relationship schema formulation: Role relationship models and intrapsychic conflict. *Psychiatry, 52*, 260–274.

Horowitz, M. J. (Ed.). (1991). *Person schemas and maladaptive interpersonal behavior*. Chicago: University of Chicago Press.

Horowitz, M. J., & Eells, T. D. (1993). Case formulations using role-relationship model configurations: A reliability study. *Psychotherapy Research, 3*, 56–68.

Horowitz, M. J., Eells, T. D., Singer, J., & Salovey, P. (1995). Role relationship models for case formulation. *Archives of General Psychiatry, 53*, 627–632.

Horowitz, M., Luborsky, L., & Popp, C. (1991). A comparison of the Role Relationship Models Configuration and the Core Conflictual Relationship Theme.

In M. J. Horowitz (Ed.), *Person schemas and maladaptive interpersonal behavior* (pp. 197–212). Chicago: University of Chicago Press.

Husserl, E. (1960). *Cartesian mediations: An introduction to phenomenology* (D. Cairns, Trans.). Dordrecht, The Netherlands: Martinus Nijhoff.

Johnson, M. E., Popp, C., Schacht, T. E., Mellon, J., & Strupp, H. S. (in press). Converging evidence for identification of recurrent relationship themes: Comparison of two methods. *Psychiatry*.

Kächele, H., Luborsky, L., & Thomae, H. (1988). Übertragung als structur und verlaufsmuster—zwei methoden zürfassung dieser aspekte [Transference as structure and process pattern—Two method versions of these aspects]. In L. Luborsky & H. Kächele (Eds.), *Der zentrale beziehungskonflikt*. Ulm, Germany: PSZ-Verlag.

Kagan, J. (1989). Temperamental contributions to social behavior. *American Psychologist, 44*, 668–674.

Kagan, J. (1996). Three pleasing ideas. *American Psychologist, 51*, 901–908.

Karasu, T. B., & Skodol, A. (1980). VIth Axis for *DSM-III*: Psychodynamic evaluation. *American Journal of Psychiatry, 197*, 607–610.

Kelly, G. A. (1955). *The psychology of personal constructs* (Vol. 1). New York: Norton.

Kernberg, O., Burnstein, E., Coyne, L., Applebaum, A., Horowitz, L., & Voth, H. (1972). Psychotherapy and psychoanalysis: Final report of the Menninger Foundation's Psychotherapy Research Project. *Bulletin of the Menninger Clinic, 36*, 1–275.

Kiesler, D. J. (1983). The 1982 interpersonal circle: A taxonomy for complementarity in human transactions. *Psychological Review, 90*, 185–214.

Kiesler, D. J. (1987a). *Check List of Psychotherapy Transactions—Revised (CLOPT-R) and Check List of Interpersonal Transactions—Revised (CLOIT-R)*. Richmond: Virginia Commonwealth University.

Kiesler, D. J. (1987b). *Research manual for the Impact Message Inventory*. Palo Alto, CA: Consulting Psychologists Press.

Kiesler, D. J., Anchin, J. C., Perkins, M. J., Chirico, B. M., Kyle, E. M., & Federman, E. J. (1985). *The Impact Message Inventory: Form II*. Palo Alto, CA: Consulting Psychologists Press.

Kiesler, D. J., Goldston, C. S., & Schmidt, J. A. (1991). *Manual for the Check List of Interpersonal Transactions—Revised and the Check List of Psychotherapy Transactions—Revised*. Richmond: Virginia Commonwealth University.

Kiesler, D. J., & Schmidt, J. A. (1993). *The Impact Message Inventory: Form IIA Octant Scale Version*. Palo Alto, CA: Mind Garden.

Kiresuk, T. (1973). Goal attainment scaling at a county mental health service. *Evaluation, 1*, 12–18.

Klein, G. (1970). *Perception, motives and personality*. New York: Knopf.

Knapp, P. (1991). Self–other schemas: Core organizers of human experience. In

M. J. Horowitz (Ed.), *Person schemas and maladaptive interpersonal behavior patterns.* Chicago: University of Chicago Press.

Koss, M., & Butcher, J. (1986). Research on brief psychotherapy. In S. Garfield & A. Bergin (Eds.), *Handbook of psychotherapy and behavior change* (pp. 627–670). New York: Wiley.

Kubie, L. (1952). Problems and techniques of psychoanalytic validation and progress. In E. Pumpian-Mindlin (Ed.), *Psychoanalysis as science* (pp. 46–124). Stanford, CA: Stanford University Press.

Labov, W. (1972). *Language in the inner city.* Philadelphia: University of Pennsylvania Press.

Lambert, M. J., & Bergin, A. E. (1994). The effectiveness of psychotherapy. In A. E. Bergin & S. L. Garfield (Eds.), *Handbook of psychotherapy and behavior change* (pp. 143–149). New York: Wiley.

Landis, J., & Koch, G. (1970). The measurement of observer agreement for categorical data. *Biometrics, 33,* 159–174.

LeDoux, J., Romanski, L., & Xagoraris, A. (1989). Indelibility of subcortical emotional memories. *Journal of Cognitive Neuroscience, 1,* 238–243.

Leeds, J., & Bucci, W. (1986). *A reliable method for the detection of repetitive structures in a transcript of an analytic session.* Paper presented at the meeting of the Society for Psychotherapy Research, Wellesley, MA.

Lefebvre, R., Diguer, L., Morissette, E., Rousseau, J. P., & Normandin, L. (1996). *The borderline and their Core Conflictual Relationship Themes.* Paper presented at the annual meeting of the Society for Psychotherapy Research, Amelia Island, FL.

Levine, F. J., & Luborsky, L. (1981). The Core Conflictual Relationship Theme method: A demonstration of reliable clinical inferences by the method of mismatched cases. In S. Tuttman, C. Kaye, & M. Zimmerman (Eds.), *Object and self: A developmental approach* (pp. 501–526). Madison, CT: International Universities Press.

Liberman, B. L. (1978). The role of mastery in psychotherapy: Maintenance or improvement and prescriptive change. In J. Frank, R. Hoen-Saric, S. Imber, B. Liberman, & A. Stone (Eds.), *Effective ingredients of successful psychotherapy* (pp. 35–72). New York, Brunner/Mazel.

Loevinger, J. (1976). *Ego development.* San Francisco: Jossey-Bass.

Lorr, M., & McNair, D. M. (1965). Expansion of the interpersonal behavior circle. *Journal of Personality and Social Psychology, 2,* 823–830.

Luborsky, E. (1987). *Stability and transformation of coping and affect from 12 to 23 months of age.* Unpublished doctoral dissertation, New York University, New York.

Luborsky, L. (1962). Clinicians' judgments of mental health: A proposed scale. *Archives of General Psychiatry, 7,* 407–417.

Luborsky, L. (1967). Momentary forgetting during psychotherapy and psychoanalysis: A theory and research method. In R. R. Holt (Ed.), *Motives and thought:*

Psychoanalytic essays in honor of David Rapaport. Madison, CT: International Universities Press.

Luborsky, L. (1975). Clinicians' judgments of mental health: Specimen case descriptions and forms for the Health–Sickness Rating Scale. *Bulletin of the Menninger Clinic, 35,* 448–480.

Luborsky, L. (1976). Helping alliances in psychotherapy: The groundwork for a study of their relationship to its outcome. In J. Claghorn (Ed.), *Successful psychotherapy* (pp. 92–116). New York: Brunner/Mazel.

Luborsky, L. (1977a). Curative factors in psychoanalytic and psychodynamic psychotherapies. In J. P. Brady, J. Mendels, M. T. Orne, & W. Rieger (Eds.), *Psychiatry: Areas of promise and advancement* (pp. 187–203). New York: Spectrum.

Luborsky, L. (1977b). Measuring a pervasive psychic structure in psychotherapy: The Core Conflictual Relationship Theme. In N. Freedman & S. Grand (Eds.), *Communicative structures and psychic structures* (pp. 367–395). New York: Plenum Press.

Luborsky, L. (1978a). *A measure of self-understanding based on self-interpretation of one's own relationship anecdotes.* Unpublished manuscript.

Luborsky, L. (1978b). *The Relationship Anecdotes Paradigm (RAP) interview: A TAT-like method using actual narratives.* Unpublished manuscript.

Luborsky, L. (1980). *A free self-analysis: The therapist's own narratives analyzed by the CCRT.* Unpublished manuscript.

Luborsky, L. (1984). *Principles of psychoanalytic psychotherapy: A manual for supportive–expressive treatment.* New York: Basic Books.

Luborsky, L. (1986a). Evidence to lessen Professor Grunbaum's concern about Freud's clinical inference methods. [Review and commentary on the book *The foundations of psychoanalysis: A philosophical critique*]. *Behavioral and Brain Sciences, 9,* 247–249.

Luborsky, L. (1986b). *A set of standard categories for the CCRT, Edition 1.* Unpublished manuscript.

Luborsky, L. (1987). *A method of inferring unconscious conflicts: An extension beyond the CCRT.* Unpublished manuscript.

Luborsky, L. (1988a). A comparison of three transference-related measures applied to the same specimen hour. In H. Dahl, H. Kächele, & H. Thomae (Eds.), *Psychoanalytic process research strategies.* New York: Springer-Verlag.

Luborsky, L. (1988b). Recurrent momentary forgetting: Its content and context. In M. Horowitz (Ed.), *Psychodynamics and cognition* (pp. 223–251). Chicago: University of Chicago Press.

Luborsky, L. (1988c). Take a moment to really look at the little lawful world of momentary forgetting: A reply to Spence. In M. Horowitz (Ed.), *Psychodynamics and cognition* (pp. 265–268). Chicago: University of Chicago Press.

Luborsky, L. (1990a). A guide to the CCRT method. In L. Luborsky & P. Crits-Christoph (Eds.), *Understanding transference: The CCRT method* (pp. 15–36). New York: Basic Books.

Luborsky, L. (1990b). The Relationship Anecdotes Paradigms (RAP) interview as a versatile source of narratives. In L. Luborsky & P. Crits-Christoph (Eds.), *Understanding transference: The CCRT method* (pp. 102–116). New York: Basic Books.

Luborsky, L. (1990c). Theory and technique in dynamic psychotherapy: Curative factors and training therapists to maximize them. *Psychotherapy and Psychosomatics, 53,* 50–57.

Luborsky, L. (1996). *The Symptom–Context method: Symptoms as opportunities in psychotherapy.* Washington, DC: American Psychological Association.

Luborsky, L. (1997). *A CCRT-based personality theory of the inner and the interpersonal world.* Unpublished manuscript, University of Pennsylvania Medical School, Philadelphia.

Luborsky, L. (in press). The Core Conflictual Relationship Theme (CCRT): A basic case formulation method. In T. D. Eells (Ed.), *Handbook of psychotherapy case formulations.* New York: Guilford Press.

Luborsky, L., & Auerbach, A. H. (1969). The Symptom–Context Method: Quantitative studies of symptom formation in psychotherapy. *Journal of the American Psychoanalytic Association, 17,* 68–99.

Luborsky, L., & Bachrach, H. (1974). Factors influencing clinicians' judgments of ental health. Eighteen experiences with the Health–Sickness Rating Scale. *Archives of General Psychiatry, 31,* 292–299.

Luborsky, L., Barber, J. P., & Diguer, L. (1992). The meanings of the narratives told during psychotherapy: The fruits of a new operational unit. *Psychotherapy Research, 2,* 277–290.

Luborsky, L., Barber, J. P., & Schaffler, P. (1989). The assessment of the CCRT: Comparison of tailor-made with standard category rating scales on a specimen case. In J. C. Perry (Chair), *Progress in assessing psychodynamic functioning: A comparison of four methods on a single case.* Symposium conducted at the meeting of the Society for Psychotherapy Research, Toronto, Canada.

Luborsky, L., & Crits-Christoph, P. (1990). *Understanding transference: The CCRT method.* New York: Basic Books.

Luborsky, L., Crits-Christoph, P., & Alexander, K. (1990). Repressive style and relationship patterns: Three samples inspected. In J. Singer (Ed.), *Repression and dissociation: Implications for personality theory, psychopathology and health.* Chicago: University of Chicago Press.

Luborsky, L., Crits-Christoph, P., Alexander, L., Margolis, M., & Cohen, M. (1983). Two helping alliance methods for predicting outcomes of psychotherapy: A counting signs versus a global rating method. *Journal of Nervous and Mental Disease, 17,* 480–492.

Luborsky, L., Crits-Christoph, P., Friedman, S., Mark, D., & Schaffler, P. (1991). Freud's transference template compared with the Core Conflictual Relationship Theme (CCRT): Illustrations by the two specimen cases. In M. Horowitz (Ed.), *Person schemas and maladaptive interpersonal behavior* (pp. 167–195). Chicago: University of Chicago Press.

Luborsky, L., Crits-Christoph, P., & Mellon, J. (1986). The advent of objective measures of the transference concept. *Journal of Consulting and Clinical Psychology, 54*, 39–47.

Luborsky, L., Crits-Christoph, P., Mintz, J., & Auerbach, A. (1988). *Who will benefit from psychotherapy? Predicting therapeutic outcomes.* New York: Basic Books.

Luborsky, L., Diguer, L., Barber, J., Cacciola, J., Moras, K., Schmidt, K., & De-Rubeis, R. (1996). Outcomes of short term dynamic psychotherapy for chronic versus non-chronic major depression. *Journal of Psychotherapy Research and Practice, 5*, 152–159.

Luborsky, L., Diguer, L., Luborsky, E., McLellan, A. T., Woody, G., & Alexander, L. (1993). Psychological health as a predictor of the outcomes of psychotherapy. *Journal of Consulting and Clinical Psychology* [Special section], *61*, 542–548.

Luborsky, L., Graff, H., Pulver, S. S., & Curtis, H. (1973). A clinical–quantitative examination of consensus on the concept of transference. *Archives of General Psychiatry, 29*, 69–75.

Luborsky, L., & Kächele, H. (1988). *Der Zentrale Beziehungskonflikt: Ein Arbeitsbuch* [The CCRT: A workbook]. Ulm, Germany: PSZ.

Luborsky, L., Kächele, H., & Dahlbender, R. (Eds.). (1997). *The CCRT Newsletter.* University of Pennsylvania.

Luborsky, L., Luborsky, E. B., Diguer, L., Schaffler, P., Schmidt, K., Dengler, D., Faude, J., Morris, M., Buchsbaum, H., & Emde, R. (1995). Extending the Core Conflictual Relationship into childhood. In G. Noam & K. Fisher (Eds.), *Development and vulnerability in close relationships.* Hillsdale, NJ: Erlbaum.

Luborsky, L., Mark, D., Hole, A. V., Popp, C., Goldsmith, B., & Cacciola, J. (1995). Supportive–expressive dynamic psychotherapy of depression: A time-limited version. In J. P. Barber & P. Crits-Christoph (Eds.), *Psychodynamic psychotherapies for psychiatric disorders* (Axis I) (pp. 13–42). New York: Basic Books.

Luborsky, L., Mellon, J., & Crits-Christoph, P. (1985a). *An aid to reliability studies of the CCRT: Preset scoring categories.* Unpublished manuscript, University of Pennsylvania.

Luborsky, L., Mellon, J., & Crits-Christoph, P. (1985b, July). *Stalking a social phobia armed with the CCRT and the symptom–context methods.* Paper presented at a conference sponsored by the John D. and Catherine T. MacArthur Foundation, Stanford, CA.

Luborsky, L., Mellon, J., van Ravenswaay, P., Childress, A., Cohen, K. D., Hole, A. V., Ming, S., Crits-Christoph, P., Levine, F. J., & Alexander, K. (1985). A verification of Freud's grandest clinical hypothesis: The transference. *Clinical Psychology Review, 5*, 231–246.

Luborsky, L., & Popp, C. (1989). *A method of inferring unconscious conflicts: An extension beyond the CCRT.* Unpublished manuscript.

Luborsky, L., Popp, C., & Barber, J. P. (1994). Common and special factors in different transference-related measures. *Psychotherapy Research, 4,* 277–286.

Luborsky, L., Popp, C., Barber, J. P., & Shapiro, D. (1994). Editor's introduction. *Psychotherapy Research, 4,* 151.

Luborsky, L., Popp, C., Luborsky, E., & Mark, D. (1994). The Core Conflictual Relationship Theme. *Psychotherapy Research, 4,* 172–183.

Luborsky, L., & Schimek, J. (1964). Psychoanalytic theories of therapeutic and developmental change: Implications for assessment. In P. Worchel & D. Byrne (Eds.), *Personality change* (pp. 73–99). New York: Wiley.

Luborsky, L., & Spence, D. (1978). Quantitative research on psychoanalytic therapy. In S. L. Garfield & A. E. Bergin (Eds.), *Handbook of psychotherapy and behavior change: An empirical analysis* (2nd ed., pp. 331–368). New York: Wiley.

Luborsky, L., Stuart, J., Friedman, S., Seligman, D. A., Pulver, S., & Woody, G. (1997). *The Penn collection of tape-recorded psychoanalyses as a research resource.* Unpublished manuscript.

Luborsky, L., van Ravenswaay, P., Ball, W., Steinman, D., Sprehn, G., & Bryan, C. (1993). Come centrare il trattamento in ambiente psichiatrico. Uso del metodo CCRT-FIT (Trattamento ospedaliero centrato) [How to focus psychiatric hospital treatment: Use of the CCRT-FIT method (Focused In-patient Treatment)]. In *Prospective Psicoanalitiche nel Lavoro Instituzionale, 11,* 9–16.

Mackenzie, R. (1989, May). *Comparing methods to assess patients for therapy.* Paper presented at the meeting of the American Psychiatric Association, San Francisco.

Main, M., & Goldwyn, R. (1984). Predicting rejection of her infant from mother's representation of her own experiences: Implications for the abused–abusing intergenerational cycle. *Child Abuse and Neglect, 8,* 203–217.

Main, M., & Goldwyn, R. (1985). *Adult attachment classification system.* Unpublished manuscript, University of California, Berkeley.

Main, M., Kaplan, N., & Cassidy, J. (1985). Security in infancy, childhood, and adulthood: A move to the level of representation. *Growing Points of Attachment Theory and Research: Monographs of the Society for Research in Child Development, 50*(1–2, Serial No. 209), 66–104.

Malan, D. (1963). *A study of brief psychotherapy.* Springfield, IL: Charles C Thomas.

Malan, D., Bacal, H., Heath, E. S., & Balfour, F. H. G. (1968). A study of psychodynamic changes in untreated neurotic patients. *British Journal of Psychiatry, 114,* 525–551.

Mann, J. (1973). *Time-limited psychotherapy.* Cambridge, MA: Harvard University Press.

Marmar, C., & Horowitz, M. J. (1988). Diagnosis and phase-oriented treatment of post-traumatic stress disorders. In J. Wilson (Ed.), *Human adaptation to extreme stress: From the Holocaust to Vietnam.* New York: Brunner/Mazel.

Maslow, A. H. (1970). *Motivation and personality.* New York: Harper & Row.

Maxim, P. (1986). *The Seattle Psychotherapy Language Analysis Schema*. Seattle: University of Washington Press.

Maxim, P., & Sprague, M. (1989). *Metacommunication of interactive sequences in therapy*. Seattle: University of Washington Press.

Maxim, P., Straus, M., & Rosenfarb, I. (1986). *The Seattle Psychotherapy Language Analysis Schema: Reliability and validity*. Unpublished manuscript.

Mayman, M. (1968). Early memories and character structure. *Journal of Projective Techniques, 32,* 303–316.

Mayman, M. (1978). Trauma, stimulus barrier, ego boundaries and self-preservation: Ego psychology in *Beyond the pleasure principle*. In S. Smith (Ed.), *The human mind revisited: Essays in honor of Karl A. Menninger* (pp. 141–158). Madison, CT: International Universities Press.

Mayman, M., & Faris, N. (1960). Early memories as expressions of relationship paradigms. *American Journal of Orthopsychiatry, 30,* 507–520.

McLaughlin, J. T. (1987). The play of transference: Some reflections on enactment in the psychoanalytic situation. *Journal of the American Psychoanalytic Association, 35,* 557–582.

McMullen, L., & Conway, J. B. (1997). Dominance and nurturance in the narratives told by clients in psychotherapy. *Psychotherapy Research, 7,* 83–98.

Meichenbaum, D., & Gilmore, J. B. (1984). The nature of unconscious processes: A cognitive–behavioral perspective. In K. Bowers & D. Meichenbaum (Eds.), *The unconscious reconsidered* (pp. 273–298). New York: Wiley.

Merritt, J. M., Stickgold, R., Pace-Schott, E., Williams, J., & Hobson, J. A. (1994). Emotion profiles in the dreams of men and women. *Consciousness and Cognition, 3,* 46–60.

Miller, J. B. (1970). Waking and dreaming conceptualization in depression. In J. Masserman (Ed.), *Depression: Science and psychoanalysis: Vol. 17. Depression: Theories and therapies*. New York: Grune & Stratton.

Miller, N., Luborsky, L., Barber, J. P., & Docherty, J. (Eds.). (1993). Psychodynamic treatment research: A handbook for clinical practice. New York: Basic Books.

Mintz, J. (1981). Measuring outcome in psychodynamic psychotherapy. *Archives of General Psychiatry, 38,* 503–506.

Mintz, J., Auerbach, A., Luborsky, L., & Johnson, M. (1973). Patients', therapists', and observers' views of psychotherapy: A "Rashomon" experience or a reasonable consensus? *British Journal of Medical Psychology, 46,* 83–89.

Mintz, J., & Kiesler, D. J. (1982). Individualized measures of psychotherapy outcome. In P. C. Kendall & J. N. Butcher (Ed.), *Handbook of research methods in clinical psychology* (pp. 491–534). New York: Wiley.

Mischel, W. (1968). *Personality and assessment*. New York: Wiley.

Mitchell, J. (1995). Coherence of the relationship theme: An extension of Luborsky's Core Conflictual Relationship Theme Method. *Psychoanalytic Psychology, 12,* 495–512.

Morgan, R., Luborsky, L., Crits-Christoph, P., Curtis, H., & Solomon, J. (1982).

Predicting the outcomes of psychotherapy by the Penn Helping Alliance Rating method. *Archives of General Psychiatry, 39,* 397–402.

Murphy, G. (1938). *Historical introduction to modern psychology.* New York: Harcourt Brace.

Murray, H. (1938). *Explorations in personality. A clinical and experimental study of fifty men of college age.* Oxford, England: Oxford University Press.

Nathans, S. (1988). *Plan Attainment: An individualized measure for assessing outcome in psychodynamic psychotherapy.* Unpublished doctoral dissertation, California School of Professional Psychology at Berkeley.

Nisbett, R. E., & Wilson, T. D. (1977). Telling more than we can know: Verbal reports on mental processes. *Psychological Review, 84,* 231–259.

Noam, G. (1991). Beyond Freud and Piaget: Biographical worlds—interpersonal self. In T. Wren (Ed.), *The moral domain* (pp. 360–399). Cambridge, MA: MIT Press.

Norville, R., Sampson, H., & Weiss, J. (1996). Accurate interpretations and brief psychotherapy outcome. *Psychotherapy Research, 6,* 16–29.

Nunberg, H. (1951). Transference and reality. *International Journal of Psychoanalysis, 32,* 1–9.

O'Malley, S., Suh, C., & Strupp, H. (1983). The Vanderbilt Psychotherapy Process Scale: A report on the scale development and a process–outcome study. *Journal of Consulting and Clinical Psychology, 51,* 581–586.

Orlinsky, D., Grawe, K., & Parks, B. (1994). Process and outcome in psychotherapy—Noch ein mal. In A. Bergin & J. S. Garfield (Eds.), *Handbook of psychotherapy and behavior change* (4th ed., pp. 270–378). New York: Wiley.

Orlinsky, D., & Howard, K. (1978). The relation of process to outcome in psychotherapy. In S. Garfield & A. Bergin (Eds.), *Handbook of psychotherapy and behavior change: An empirical analysis* (2nd ed., pp. 283–329). New York: Wiley.

Orlinsky, D., & Howard, K. (1986). Process and outcome in psychotherapy. In S. Garfield & A. Bergin (Eds.), *Handbook of psychotherapy and behavior change: An empirical analysis* (3rd ed., pp. 311–381). New York: Wiley.

Perry, J. C. (1993). Assessing psychodynamic patterns using the Idiographic Conflict Formulation (ICF) Method. In N. Miller, L. Luborsky, & J. Docherty (Eds.), *Dynamic psychotherapy research: A handbook for clinical practice.* New York: Basic Books.

Perry, J. C. (1994). Assessing psychodynamic patterns using the Idiographic Conflict Formulation Method. *Psychotherapy Research, 4,* 239–252.

Perry, J. C., Augusto, F., & Cooper, S. H. (1989). Assessing psychodynamic conflicts: I. Reliability of the Idiographic Conflict Formulation Method. *Psychiatry, 52,* 289–301.

Perry, J. C., & Cooper, S. H. (1989). An empirical study of defense mechanisms: I. Clinical interview and life vignette ratings. *Archives of General Psychiatry, 46,* 444–452.

Perry, J. C., Luborsky, L., Silberschatz, G., & Popp, C. (1989). An examination of three methods of psychodynamic formulation based on the same videotaped interview. *Psychiatry, 52,* 302–323.

Persons, J. (1989). *Cognitive therapy in practice: A case formulation approach.* New York: Norton.

Peterson, C., Bettes, B., & Seligman, M. E. (1985). Depressive symptoms and spontaneous casual attributions: Content analysis. *Behavior Therapy and Research, 23,* 379–382.

Peterson, C., Luborsky, L., & Seligman, M. E. (1983). Attributions and depressive mood shifts: A case study using the symptom–context method. *Journal of Abnormal Psychology, 92,* 96–103.

Peterson, C., & Seligman, M. E. (1984). *Content analysis of verbatim explanations: The CAVE technique for assessing explanatory style.* Unpublished manuscript.

Pfeffer, A. (1963). The meaning of the analyst after analyses: A contribution to the theory of therapeutic results. *Journal of the American Psychoanalytic Association, 11,* 229–244.

Piotrowski, C., & Keller, J. (1984). Psychodiagnostic testing in APA approved clinical psychology programs. *Professional Psychology: Research and Practice, 15,* 450–456.

Piper, W. E., Azim, H. F., Joyce, A. S., & McCallum, M. (1991). Transference interpretations, therapeutic alliance, and outcome in short-term individual psychotherapy. *Archives of General Psychiatry, 4,* 946–953.

Popp, C., Diguer, L., Luborsky, L., Faude, J., Johnson, S., Morris, M., Schafer, N., Schaffler, P., & Schmidt, K. A. (1996). Repetitive relationship themes in waking narratives and dreams. *Journal of Consulting and Clinical Psychology, 64,* 1073–1078.

Popp, C., Luborsky, L., & Crits-Christoph, P. (1990). The parallel of the CCRT from therapy narratives with the CCRT from dreams. In L. Luborsky & P. Crits-Christoph (Eds.), *Understanding transference: The CCRT method* (pp. 37–50). New York: Basic Books.

Pulver, S. E. (1987). The manifest dream in psychoanalysis: A clarification. *Journal of the American Psychoanalytic Association, 35,* 99–118.

Rapaport, D. (1951). *Organization and pathology of thought.* New York: Columbia University Press.

Rapaport, D. (1960). The structure of psychoanalytic theory: A systemizing attempt. *Psychological Issues* [Monograph No. 6].

Rapaport, D., & Gill, M. (1967). The points of view and assumptions of metapsychology. In D. Rapaport (Ed.), *Collected papers* (pp. 795–811). New York: Basic Books.

Rapaport, D., Gill, M., & Schafer, R. (1968). *Diagnostic psychological testing.* Madison, CT: International Universities Press.

Raskin, N. J. (1949). An analysis of six parallel studies of the therapeutic process. *Journal of Consulting Psychology, 13,* 206–221.

Rawn, M. (1958). An experimental study of transference and resistance phenomena in psychoanalytically-oriented psychotherapy. *Journal of Clinical Psychology, 14,* 418.

Rawn, M. (1981). A note on unwitting replication: Quantitative studies of transference and resistance twenty years apart. *Journal of Clinical Psychology, 37,* 782.

Reiser, M. (1984). *Mind, brain, body: Toward a convergence of psychoanalysis and neurobiology.* New York: Basic Books.

Reiser, M. (1986, November). *The durable core of Freud's empirical science.* The 38th A. A. Brill lecture, The New York Psychoanalytic Society.

Rhode, A. B., Geller, J. D., & Farber, B. A. (1992). Dreams about the therapist: Mood, interactions, and themes. *Psychotherapy, 29,* 536–544.

Rice, L., & Greenberg, L. (Eds.). (1984). *Patterns of change.* New York: Guilford Press.

Rosenbaum, M., Friedlander, J., & Kaplan, S. (1956). Evaluation of results of psychotherapy. *Psychosomatic Medicine, 18,* 113–132.

Rosenberg, S. E., Horowitz, L. M., Hanks, S., Hartley, D., Lebenson, H., Schulman, T., & Skuja, A. (1984). The consensual psychodynamic formulation: Part II. Application to case of Ms. Smithfield. *Psychotherapy Research, 4,* 234–238.

Rosenberg, S. E., Silberschatz, G., Curtis, J., Sampson, H., & Weiss, J. (1986). A method for establishing reliability of statements from psychodynamic case formulations. *American Journal of Psychiatry, 143,* 1454–1456.

Ryle, A. (1990). *Cognitive–analytic active participation and change: A new integration in brief psychotherapy.* Chichester, England: Wiley.

Ryle, A. (1991). Object relations theory and activity theory: A proposed link by way of the procedural sequence model. *British Journal of Medical Psychology, 64,* 307–316.

Sachs, J. S. (1983). Negative factors in brief psychotherapy: An empirical assessment. *Journal of Consulting and Clinical Psychology, 51,* 557–564.

Schacht, T. B., & Binder, J. (1982). *Focusing: A manual for identifying a circumscribed area of work for time-limited dynamic psychotherapy (TLDP).* Unpublished manuscript, Vanderbilt University.

Schacht, T. B., Binder, J., & Strupp, H. (1984). The dynamic focus. In H. Strupp & J. Binder (Eds.), *Psychotherapy in a new key: A guide to time limited dynamic psychotherapy* (pp. 65–109). New York: Basic Books.

Schafer, R. (1983). Narration in the psychoanalytic dialogue. *Critical Inquiry, 12,* 29–53.

Schaffer, N. (1982). Multidimensional measures of therapist behavior as predictors of outcome. *Psychological Bulletin, 92,* 670–681.

Schaffer, N. (1983). Methodological issues of measuring the skillfulness of therapeutic techniques. *Psychotherapy: Theory, Research, and Practice, 20,* 486–493.

Schlesinger, H. J. (1974). Problems of doing research on the therapeutic process in psychoanalysis. *Journal of the American Psychoanalytic Association, 22,* 3–13.

Schlessinger, N., & Robbins, F. (1975). The psychoanalytic process: Recurrent patterns of conflict and changes in ego. *Journal of the American Psychoanalytic Association, 23,* 761–782.

Seitz, P. (1966). The consensus problem in psychoanalytic research. In L. Gottschalk & A. Auerbach (Eds.), *Methods of research in psychotherapy* (pp. 209–225). New York: Appleton-Century-Crofts.

Seligman, M. (1975). *Helplessness: On depression, development and death.* San Francisco: Freedman.

Seligman, M. (1980). A learned helplessness point of view. In L. Rhem (Ed.), *Behavior therapy for depression* (pp. 123–142). New York: Academic Press.

Seligman, M. (1991). *Learned optimism.* New York: Pocket Books.

Seligman, M., Kamaen, L., & Nolen-Hoeksema, S. (1988). Explanatory style across the life span: Achievement and health. In E. Hetherington, R. Lerner, & M. Perlmutter (Eds.), *Child development in life-span perspective* (pp. 91–114). Hillsdale, NJ: Erlbaum.

Seligman, M., Peterson, C., Kaslow, N., Tannenbaum, R., Alloy, L., & Abramson, L. (1984). Attributional style and depressive symptoms among children. *Journal of Abnormal Psychology, 93,* 235–238.

Shultz, L. H., Hauser, S. T., & Allen, J. P. (1990). *Autonomy and relatedness development in early adult close peer relationships.* Paper presented at the Fifth Biennial International Conference on Personal Relationships, Oxford, England.

Sifneos, P. (1979). *Short term dynamic psychotherapy: Evaluation and technique.* New York: Plenum Press.

Silberschatz, G. (1986). Testing pathogenic beliefs. In J. Weiss, H. Sampson, & the Mount Zion Psychotherapy Research Group (Eds.), *The psychoanalytic process: Theory, clinical observations, and empirical research* (pp. 256–266). New York: Guilford Press.

Silberschatz, G., Curtis, J. T., Fretter, P. B., & Kelly, T. (1988). Testing hypotheses of psychotherapeutic change processes. In H. Dahl, H. Kächele, & H. Thomae (Eds.), *Psychoanalytic process research strategies* (pp. 129–145). Berlin: Springer-Verlag.

Silberschatz, G., Curtis, J. T., & Nathans, S. (1989). Using the patient's plan to assess progress in psychotherapy. *Psychotherapy, 26,* 40–46.

Silberschatz, G., Fretter, P., & Curtis, J. (1986). How do interpretations influence the process of psychotherapy? *Journal of Consulting and Clinical Psychology, 54,* 646–652.

Singer, B., & Luborsky, L. (1977). Countertransference: The status of clinical vs. quantitative research. In A. Gurman & A. Razin (Eds.), *The therapist's handbook for effective psychotherapy: An empirical assessment* (pp. 431–448). New York: Pergamon Press.

Singer, J. (1985). Transference and the human condition: A cognitive–affective perspective. *Psychoanalytic Psychology, 2,* 189–219.

Singer, J., & Salovey, P. (1991). Organized knowledge structures and personality: Person schemas, self-schemas, prototypes and scripts. In M. Horowitz (Ed.), *Person schemas and maladaptive interpersonal patterns.* Chicago: University of Chicago Press.

Spence, D. (1983a). Narrative persuasion. *Psychoanalysis and Contemporary Thought, 6,* 457–481.

Spence, D. (1983b). *Narrative truth and historical truth.* New York: Norton.

Spitz, R. (1956). Transference, the analytic setting and its prototype. *International Journal of Psychoanalysis, 37,* 380–385.

SPSS/PC & Advanced Statistics [Computer software]. (1986). Chicago, IL: SPSS Inc.

Sroufe, L. A. (1983). Infant–caregiver attachment and patterns of adaptation in pre-school: The roots of maladaptation and competence. In M. Perlmutter (Ed.), *Minnesota Symposium on Child Psychology* (Vol. 16, pp. 41–81). Hillsdale, NJ: Erlbaum.

Sroufe, L. A., & Fleeson, J. (1986). Attachment and the construction of relationships. In W. Hartug & Z. Rubin (Eds.), *Relationships and development* (pp. 51–71). Cambridge, England: Cambridge University Press.

Sroufe, L. A., & Waters, E. (1977). Attachment as an organizational construct. *Child Development, 48,* 1184–1199.

Stein, K., & Beall, L. (1971). Externalizing–internalizing symptoms and psychotherapeutic outcome. *Psychotherapy: Therapy, Research and Practice, 8,* 269–272.

Stern, D. (1985). *The interpersonal world of the infant.* New York: Basic Books.

Stern, D. (1989). The representations of relational patterns: Development considerations. In A. Sameroff & R. Emde (Eds.), *Relationship disturbances in early childhood* (pp. 52–69). New York: Basic Books.

Stickgold, R., Pace-Schott, E., & Hobson, J. A. (1994). A new paradigm for dream research: Mentation reports following spontaneous arousal from REM and NREM sleep recorded in a home setting. *Consciousness and Cognition, 3,* 16–29.

Strupp, H. (1973). *Psychotherapy: Clinical, research, and theoretical issues.* Northvale, NJ: Jason Aronson.

Strupp, H., & Binder, J. (1984). *Psychotherapy in a new key: A guide to time-limited dynamic psychotherapy.* New York: Basic Books.

Strupp, H., Chassan, J., & Ewing, J. (1966). Toward the longitudinal study of the psychotherapeutic process. In L. Gottschalk & A. Auerbach (Eds.), *Methods of research in psychotherapy* (pp. 361–400). New York: Appleton-Century-Crofts.

Subotnick, L. (1966a). Transference in child therapy: A third replication. *Psychological Record, 16,* 265–277.

Subotnick, L. (1966b). Transference in client-centered play therapy. *Psychology, 3,* 2–17.

Sulloway, F. J. (1996). *Born to rebel: Birth order, family dynamics, and creative lies.* New York: Pantheon Books.

Teller, V., & Dahl, H. (1981). The framework for a model of psychoanalytic inference. *Proceedings of the Seventh International Joint Conference on Artificial Intelligence, 1,* 394–400.

Teller, V., & Dahl, H. (1986). The microstructure of free association. *Journal of the American Psychoanalytic Association, 34,* 763–798.

Thorne, A. (1989). Conditional patterns, transference, and the coherence of personality across time. In D. Buss & N. Cantor (Eds.), *Personality psychology: Recent trends and emerging directions* (pp. 150–159). New York: Springer-Verlag.

Thorne, A. (1995a). Developmental truths in memories of childhood and adolescence. *Journal of Personality, 63,* 139–163.

Thorne, A. (1995b). Juxtaposed scripts, traits, and the dynamics of personality. *Journal of Personality, 63,* 593–616.

Thorne, A., & Michaelieu, Q. (1996). Situating adolescent gender and self-esteem with personal memories. *Child Development, 67,* 1374–1390.

Tomkins, S. (1947). *The Thematic Apperception Test: The theory and technique of interpretation.* New York: Grune & Stratton.

Tomkins, S. (1979). Script theory: Differential magnification of affects. In H. E. Howe, Jr., & R. A. Diensbier (Eds.), *Nebraska Symposium on Motivation* (Vol. 26, pp. 201–236). Lincoln: University of Nebraska Press.

Tomkins, S. (1987). Script theory. In V. Aronoff, A. A. Rabin, & R. Zucker (Eds.), *The emergence of personality* (pp. 147–216). New York: Springer-Verlag.

Toolan, M. (1989). *Narrative: A critical linguistic introduction.* London: Routledge & Kegan Paul.

Tronick, E. (1982). *Social interchange in infancy.* Baltimore: University Park Press.

Vaillant, G. (1977). *Adaptation to life.* Boston: Little, Brown.

van Ravenswaay, P., Luborsky, L., & Childress, A. (1983, July). *Consistency of the transference in versus out of psychotherapy.* Paper presented at the meeting of the Society for Psychotherapy Research, Sheffield, England.

Wachtel, P. (1993). *Therapeutic communication: Principles and effective practice.* New York: Guilford Press.

Waelder, R. (1936). The principle of multiple function: Observations on overdetermination. *Psychoanalytic Quarterly, 5,* 45–62.

Waldinger, R. (1997a). *Continuities and discontinuities in relationship themes from adolescence to young adulthood.* Manuscript in preparation.

Waldinger, R. (1997b). *Relationship narratives in 5-year-olds: A comparison of abused and neglected children with normal children.* Manuscript in preparation.

Wallerstein, R. (1986). *Forty-two lives in treatment: A study of psychoanalysis and psychotherapy.* New York: Guilford Press.

Wallerstein, R., Robbins, L., Sargent, H., & Luborsky, L. (1956). The psycho-therapy research project of the Menninger Foundation: Rationale, method and sample use. *Bulletin of the Menninger Clinic, 20*, 221–280.

Weinberger, D. (1990). The construct validity of the repressive copying style. In J. L. Singer (Ed.), *Repression and dissociation*. Chicago: University of Chicago Press.

Weiss, D. S., DeWitt, K. N., Kaltreider, N. B., & Horowitz, M. J. (1985). Proposed method for measuring change beyond symptoms. *Archives of General Psychiatry, 42*, 703–708.

Weiss, J. (1986). Theory and clinical observations. In J. Weiss, H. Sampson, & the Mount Zion Psychotherapy Research Group (Eds.), *The psychoanalytic process: Theory, clinical observations, and empirical research* (pp. 3–138). New York: Guilford Press.

Weiss, J., Sampson, H., Caston, J., & Silberschatz, G. (Eds.). (1977). *Research on the psychoanalytic process*. San Francisco: Psychotherapy Research Group, Department of Psychiatry, Mount Zion Hospital and Medical Center.

Weiss, J., Sampson, H., & the Mount Zion Psychotherapy Research Group. (1986). *The psychoanalytic process: Theory, clinical observations, and empirical research*. New York: Guilford Press.

White, R. (1952). *Lives in progress*. Hinsdale, IL: Dryden Press.

Wilson, A., Passik, S., Morral, A., Turner, A., & Kuras, M. (1994). *An epigenetic-TAT approach to the assessment of modes of organization (EPI-TAT)*. Manuscript in preparation.

Winget, C., & Kramer, M. (1979). *Dimensions of dreams*. Gainesville: University of Florida Press.

Witkin, H. A. (1949). Sex differences in perceptions. *Transactions of the New York Academy of Sciences, 12*, 22–26.

Wolpert, L., & Richards, A. (1988). *A passion for science*. Oxford, England: Oxford University Press.

Zander, B., Strack, M., Cierpka, M., Reich, G., Steats, H., assisted by Biskey, J., Homburg, H., Krannich, S., Ratzke, K., & Seide, L. (1995). Coder agreement using the German edition of Luborsky's CCRT method in videotaped or transcribed RAP interviews. *Psychotherapy Research, 5*, 231–236.

Zolik, E. S., & Hollon, T. W. (1960). Factors characteristic of patients responsive to brief psychotherapy [Abstract]. *American Psychologist, 15*, 387.

INDEX

Interpretations (*continued*)
    treatment outcome, 204
    wish plus response from other as
        best predictor of outcome, 205–
        206
    congruence with CCRT, 207–208

Judgments, guided, 124

Malan outcome rating, 152
Mann's 12-session psychotherapy, 283
Mastery, 261–262
    need to repeat in service of gaining,
        339–340
    see also Conflicts, measurement of mas-
        tery
Mastery Scale, 263–264, 268–269
Mother–infant exchange, 234
Murray, Henry, central relationship pat-
        tern, 6–7

Narratives
    about relationship events versus behav-
        ioral enactments, 331
    CCRT
        comparison with dreams, 101–104
        reasons for relying on as basis for,
            333–336
        therapy and RAP, 330
    characteristics, 334
    common types of components, 191–
        192
    doll family story method, 236–238
    interpretability, 335–336
    number and completeness, 136
    pervasiveness across, 159–160
    redundancy across, 127–128
    revelations about modes of thought,
        335
    session versus relationship anecdote
        paradigm, 104
    told by young children, 235
    truth value, 334–335
    waking, parallel with dreams, 175–196
        case studies
            Mr. Crane, 184
            Ms. Apfel, 177–181
            Ms. Bauman, 182–183

selection of dreams, narratives, and
    judges, 176–177
tailor-made and standard categories,
    177
validation, 187–196
    component similarity, 191, 193
    components in dreams and narra-
        tives, 191–192
    method, 187–190
    negativity of responses, 194–195
    reliability, 190–191
see also Psychotherapy, narratives told
    during; Relationship Anecdotes
    Paradigm
Negative responses, 30–31, 55–63,
    319–320
    changes in course of psychotherapy,
        59–61
    children at ages 3 and 5, 247–250
    dreams and narratives, 194–195
    judging as, 126
    narratives told during psychotherapy,
        145–146
    proportion in children, adult patients,
        and normal controls, 58–59
    relationship to psychotherapy out-
        comes, 61–62
    scoring, 56–58

Object relations researchers, central rela-
    tionship patterns, 8–9
Others, see Responses from
Outcome assessment, 152–153

Paired-comparisons method, 34
Parental relationships, central relation-
    ship pattern origins, 311–312,
    337
Patient
    main communication in session as
        focus for interpretations, 10
    perspective, focus on, 131
Patient's Experience of the Relationship
    with the Therapist, 293–294
Personality researchers, central relation-
    ship pattern, 6–7
Personal scripts, 299–300
Persons, main other, in narratives, 137–
    138

ABOUT THE AUTHORS

There is one main theme in Lester Luborsky's research over the past five decades: the translation of clinically useful concepts, now 36 of them, into clinically useful clinical–quantitative measures. His favorites include the Health–Sickness Rating Scale, the Core Conflictual Relationship Theme, the Helping Alliance, and the symptom onset state, including helplessness and hopelessness. After receiving a PhD at Duke University in 1945, he has been working at the University of Pennsylvania for the past 38 years, having turned out eight books, with six of those in the past dozen years, along with 370 articles and chapters.

Paul Crits-Christoph, PhD, is Associate Professor of Psychology in Psychiatry, School of Medicine, University of Pennsylvania, where he is also Director of the Center for Psychotherapy Research. He is coeditor, with Jacques P. Barber, Phd, of the *Handbook of Short-Term Dynamic Psychotherapy* (1991) and *Dynamic Therapies for Psychiatric Disorders* (1995), both published by Basic Books. In addition, he has published over 100 articles and chapters.